Hibernate 3

for Beginners

Hibernate 3

for Beginners

Sharanam Shah
Vaishali Shah

SHROFF PUBLISHERS & DISTRIBUTORS PVT. LTD.
Mumbai *Bangalore* *Chennai* *Kolkata* *New Delhi*

Hibernate 3 For Beginners
by Sharanam Shah and Vaishali Shah

Series Editor: Ivan Bayross

First Edition: April 2009

Fourth Print: January 2012

ISBN 13: 978-81-8404-705-9

Published by **Shroff Publishers & Distributors Pvt. Ltd.** C-103, T.T.C. Industrial Area, M.I.D.C., Pawane, Navi Mumbai - 400 705. Tel.: (91-22) 4158 4158 Fax: (91-22) 4158 4141 E-mail: spdorders@shroffpublishers.com Printed at Decora Book Prints Pvt. Ltd., Mumbai.

Foreword

Welcome to Hibernate 3!

Thank you for picking up this book.

This book is dedicated to our family. Thank you for your patience, support and love.

About This Book

Object-oriented programming has become the dominant type of programming over the last few years and the Java programming language seems to have been driving it.

Even though Java provides an object oriented view of business entities in an application, the data underlying these entities is heavily relational in nature. There is a huge difference between the tabular representation of data in a relational system and the networks of objects in an object-oriented Java application.

This difference has led to the so-called Object/Relational paradigm **mismatch**.

An **O**bject/**R**elational **M**apping tool is the **solution** to this **mismatch**. Implementing an object-relational mapping [O/R mapping] is a general need for a lot of projects in the software development.

Hibernate [an open source project] is an ORM tool and is considered the best solution to this mismatch. Since its release, Hibernate has quickly become one of the leading and widely used ORM technologies.

This book teaches Hibernate 3 from the ground up with an aim to get the reader up to speed with Hibernate as quickly as possible. It follows the learning by doing pattern with a lot of ready-to-use examples. This pattern has proven to be the best approach for beginners.

The examples are well described and easy to understand, yet sophisticated enough to demonstrate Hibernate in a real-world context.

Getting started and following along with the examples is easier as all the examples in this book are built and demonstrated using an **I**ntegrated **D**evelopment **E**nvironment called **NetBeans**.

This book demonstrates a complete application building lifecycle by building and following a sample application, chapter-by-chapter, starting from the basics to advanced using the technology and processes covered in this book.

After reading this book, you will have an in-depth and **practical** understanding of Hibernate 3 and how to use it in the applications.

Who Is This Book For?

The book you're holding is written for Java developers who already understand how to build server-side Java applications. The book assumes the reader with general familiarity with Web development, Java [with some Java EE experience], SQL and JDBC.

This book would appeal to those developers who want a hands-on practical book demonstrating examples for almost every topic in this book.

What You'll Learn?

- Building a web application:
  - Using Hibernate 3
  - Using Java Persistence API with Hibernate 3
  - Using Struts 2 with Hibernate 3
- Using the NetBeans IDE to develop Hibernate based applications
- Porting an application developed using Hibernate to another database [MySQL to Oracle]
- Reverse Engineering POJOs and Mapping Documents from Database Tables
- Pagination using Hibernate 3
- Connection Pooling using:
  - An Application Server [Glassfish] via JNDI
  - Hibernate's built-in mechanism [C3P0]

Roadmap

The organization of this book aims to walk you through Hibernate 3 in a sequence of increasing complexity.

We start with a couple of preliminary chapters enclosed in a section called **Introduction** that introduce the technological and fundamental context of Persistence and Object/Relational Mapping. This section also introduces Hibernate 3 with a high-level overview of the architecture and the components.

After this introduction, we quickly get started with writing the first application using Hibernate 3. It walks you through the complete process of creating and running the application using the NetBeans IDE. It also discusses how Hibernate is integrated into an application.

This section also shows building the same example by reverse engineering the code spec from the database tables using Hibernate Plugins for the NetBeans IDE.

We then set off into a series of chapters [held within Understanding Configuration And Mapping] that cover the fundamentals of Hibernate, including configuration, the mapping elements and the new Java 5 Annotation feature.

Section 4 of this book, details the native API of Hibernate 3 along with the Session objects in detail, explaining the various methods that it provides. The section also discusses the use of transactions.

The most useful topic this section covers is Connection Pooling. This topic explains what is connection pooling and demonstrates how to implement it using Hibernate's built-in mechanism called C3P0 as well as an application server such as Glassfish.

Section V describes how Hibernate can be used to make sophisticated queries against the underlying relational database using the built-in Hibernate Query Language [HQL]. It also details the Criteria API, which is a programmatic analog of the query language. The most interesting topic of this section is **Pagination** which demonstrates creating a Web application with pagination support. This section ends with a topic called Filters [an innovative new approach to handling data with visibility rules], which demonstrates implementing them in a Web application.

All the learning done so far is strongly reinforced using a small project in section 6. This section demonstrates a step-by-step guide to developing a Web application using JSP, Servlets, Ajax, MySQL with Hibernate using Hibernate's native API.

This section then moves towards re-developing the same application using Java Persistence API [JPA] instead of Hibernate's native API. This re-development exercise helps the reader understand the practical differences between the two APIs.

This section also demonstrates integrating the same application with an application development framework called Struts 2.

Finally this section shows the magic of porting the same application from MySQL to the Oracle database.

This book's accompanying CD-ROM holds:

Downloaded executables of the following:

- Java Development Kit [JDK] 6 Update 11
- MySQL Community Server 6.0.7
- Oracle Database 10g eXpress Edition
- NetBeans IDE 6.5
- Library Files for:
    - Struts 2.1.6
    - Hibernate Core 3.3.1.GA
    - Hibernate Annotations 3.4.0.GA
    - Hibernate EntityManager 3.4.0.GA
    - Display Tags
- JDBC drivers for:
    - MySQL Connector/J 5.1.7
    - Oracle JDBC Driver [ojdbc14.jar]

Source Code for the examples:

This book's accompanying CDROM provides source code for all the examples demonstrated in this book.

Each example's source code is placed under the appropriate chapter number to make it distinguishable. These examples can be directly opened and executed using the NetBeans IDE.

Acknowledgments

Writing this book has been one of the most challenging endeavors we've taken on and it would not have been possible without the help and support from several people.

Our sincere thanks go to:

- Our publisher Mr. Aziz Shroff for bringing up the X-Team concept that has brought enormous changes in our lives
- Ms. Stuti Shah who is in charge of quality control. Who personally took care that everything in the manuscript was rigidly bound to the specifications of our quality manual. You've done a really fine job
- Our family for their patience, support and love
- Mr. Sriram Kumar for his huge contribution in the Application Development With Hibernate section of this book
- Mr. Manoj Kumar Mohanty who provided appropriate directions whilst coding
- The many programmers who read this book. We welcome both your brickbats and bouquets
- All those who helped through their comments, feedback and suggestions

If you have any questions, comments or just feel like communicating, please contact us at **enquiries@sharanamshah.com**.

We hope that you will enjoy reading this book as much as we enjoyed writing it.

For additional information on this book visit:

- http://www.sharanamshah.com
- http://www.vaishalishahonline.com

Sharanam & Vaishali Shah

Table Of Contents

SECTION IV: WORKING WITH HIBERNATE

SECTION VI: APPLICATION DEVELOPMENT WITH HIBERNATE

SECTION I: INTRODUCTION

Persistence And Object/Relational Mapping

It would be an ideal world, indeed, if there was no need to worry about bugs or power failures.

The following are a few obvious facts:

- The attention span of a computer is only as long as its cord is connected to a power supply
- The precious data is within the confines of electronic memory

If the application does not preserve data when it was powered off, the application is of little or rather no practical use.

Hence, it is required to make the precious data live longer than the application. This is where Persistence comes in.

What Is Persistence

Persistence is one of the fundamental concepts of application development. It allows DATA to outlive the execution of an application that created it. It is one of the most vital piece of an application without which all the data is simply lost.

Often when choosing the persistence storage medium the following fundamental qualifiers are considered:

- The length of time data must be persisted
- The volume of data

For example, an HTTP session can be considered when the life of a piece of data is limited to the user's session. However, persistence over several sessions or several users requires a larger data store.

Large amounts of data should not be stored in an HTTP session, instead a database should be considered.

The type of database that is chosen also plays an important influence on the architecture and design.

Persistence In Java

Persistence in Java usually means storing data in a relational database using SQL.

In Java, persistence is accomplished by storing data in a **R**elational **D**atabase **M**anagement **S**ystem [RDBMS]. SQL is used to get data in and out of the relational database.

Java **D**ata**B**ase **C**onnectivity [JDBC] - The Java API is used to connect to the RDBMS and fire SQL statements.

Object Persistence

Object Persistence deals with persistence in object oriented programs such as Java. It means determining how objects and their relationships are persisted in a relational database.

Object persistence is about:

- Mapping object state

- Determining how an object's state [data stored in member variables of an object] is stored in database table columns
- Dealing with the fact that object state types may not align with relational database types
- Mapping object relationships
- Determining how associations between objects are stored as relational database keys or in relational database intersection tables

Most of the development is carried out in an object oriented manner using languages such as Smalltalk, C++ and Java.

Object Oriented Programming is based on **Objects** that represent the business model [the real world]. Objects are easily traversed through relationship graphs using inheritance, associations.

Why Object Oriented Models

Object Oriented Models are a choice because of the following:

- Business logic can be implemented in Java as opposed to stored procedures
- Design patterns and sophisticated object oriented concepts such as inheritance and polymorphism can be used
- Provides code reusability and maintainability

In most of these applications, **storing** and **retrieving** information usually involves some kind of interaction with a **relational database**.

Why Relational Database

A relational database is a choice because of the following:

- It is a proven data persistence technology
- Provides flexible and robust approach to data management
- It is the De-facto standard in software development

HINT

A Relational database is not considered good for business modeling.

Getting the data and associations from objects into relational table structure and vice versa requires a lot of tedious programming due to the difference between the two.

```
public class Books
{
    private int BookNo;
    private String Name;
    private int Cost;
    private String ISBN;
    private String Author;
    private String Publisher;
}
```

Books	
PK	BookNo
	Name
	Cost
	ISBN
	Author
	Publisher

This difference is called **The Impedance Mismatch**.

Object/Relational Mapping

The Impedance Mismatch

In most of the applications, **storing** and **retrieving** information usually involves some kind of interaction with a relational database.

This kind of interaction has a fundamental issue. This issue arises as the design of relational data and object-oriented instances share a very different relationship structure within their respective environments.

Relational databases are structured in a **tabular** manner and the object oriented instances are structured in a **hierarchical** manner.

This means that in this object oriented world, data is represented as **OBJECTS** [often called a **DOMAIN** model]. However, the storage medium is based on a **RELATIONAL** paradigm.

Hence, there exists an inevitable **mismatch**, the so called Object/Relational **impedance mismatch** which creates a **vacuum** between the Object Oriented Model of a well designed application [the **DOMAIN** model] and the relational model in a database schema.

This vacuum is surprisingly wide.

How To Map One To The Other

The most native approach that is usually taken is a simple mapping between each class and the database table. This approach requires writing a lot of code spec that maps one to the other. This code spec is often complex, tedious and costly to develop.

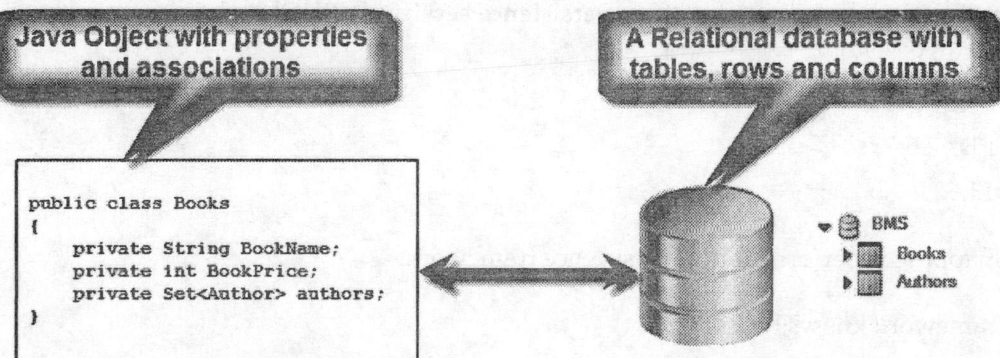

The Solution To The Impedance Mismatch

This **impedance mismatch** has led to the development of several different object persistence technologies attempting to bridge the gap between the relational world and the object oriented world.

Hence the solution is:

Use an Object Relational Mapping Tool.

An **Object Relational Mapping** Tool provides a simple API for **storing** and **retrieving** Java objects directly to and from the relational database.

Object/Relational Mapping [ORM] is a technique that allows an application written in an object oriented language to deal with the information [it manipulates] as objects, rather than using database specific concepts such as **ROWS, COLUMNS** and **TABLES** which is facilitated by a software called **Object/Relational Mapper**.

An **Object/Relational Mapper** is a piece of software that is used to **transform:**

- An **OBJECT** view of the data

  INTO

- A **RELATIONAL** view

Object/Relational Mapper also offers **persistence services** [CRUD] such as:

- CREATE
- READ
- UPDATE
- DELETE

O/R mapping is performed by a persistence framework.

This framework knows how to:

- **Query** the database to retrieve objects
- **Persist** those objects back to their representation in the database's tables and columns

All this is known with the help of Mappings. Mappings are defined in **metadata**, typically XML files.

HINT

ORM is not specific to Java. However, it has become particularly popular among Java developers.

ORM has several benefits. In particular:

- Eliminates writing SQL to load and persist object state, leaving the developer free to concentrate on the business logic
- Enables creating an appropriate DOMAIN model, after which, the developer only needs to think in terms of OBJECTS, rather than TABLES, ROWS and COLUMNS
- Reduces dependence on database specific SQL and thus provides Portability across databases
- Reduces more than 30% of the amount of Java code spec that needs to be written by adopting an ORM

All this amounts to a huge productivity gain.

WARNING

Do not misunderstand ORM, by assuming, that it allows the developers remain ignorant of SQL or the database's locking mechanism. This is a big risk!

ORM is a tool that makes doing what is desired easier. It **does not** free the developers from the need of understanding what it is, that they desire, doing.

Why Object Relational Mapping

An ORM provides the following advantages:

Better System Architecture

Most of the times all the application functionality and the database access code spec is held together. This brings in some severe disadvantages.

It becomes really difficult to reuse code spec. Hence code repetitions occur at several different places. Changing anything becomes quite difficult, as each and every place that holds the repetitive code spec needs to be located and changed accordingly.

If the application functionality [business logic] and the database access code spec [persistence mechanism] is separated, applying changes become very easy. Changes can be made to one part without influencing the other parts.

Reduce Coding Time

Most of the time the database access code spec is simple inserts, updates or deletes. These are SQL statements which sometimes are quite tedious to code.

ORM tool helps here, by generating them on the fly and thereby saves a lot of time.

Caching And Transactions

Most ORM tools such as Hibernate come with features such as Caching and Transactions.

These features, if chosen to hand code are not so easy to implement. And it definitely does not make sense to develop them when they already exist.

Hibernate As The ORM Of Choice

There are several good ORM tools available today. While in the past it was common and even justifiable for having an in-house ORM frameworks developed for individual applications which is an expensive undertaking and the results are never as good as generic commercial or open source solutions.

Today, there are several good generic solutions in this space and it is best to choose one of them.

- Hibernate
- Enterprise JavaBeans Entity Beans
- Java Data Objects
- Castor
- TopLink
- Spring DAO

And many more...

Hibernate [an open source object/relational mapping tool] seems to be one of the most popular Object/Relational mapper. It is considered highly portable, provides good mapping flexibility and good performance.

A Quick Overview

Hibernate was developed by Gavin King in 2001 with an aim to relieve the developers from 95% of common data persistence related programming tasks.

Hibernate makes use of persistent objects commonly known as **POJO [Plain Old Java Object]** along with **XML** mapping documents for persisting objects to the database layer.

It acts as a **layer** between the application and the database by taking care of loading and saving of objects.

HINT

POJO refers to a simple Java object that does not serve any other special role or implement any special interfaces of any of the Java frameworks such as EJB, JDBC, DAO and so on.

Hibernate helps the developers to develop persistent classes and persistent logic without bothering about how to handle the data.

Hibernate takes care of the mapping:

- From Java classes to database tables

AND

- From Java data types to SQL data types

The objects [POJO classes] to be persisted are defined in a mapping document, which serves to describe the persistent fields and associations of the persistent object.

The mapping documents are compiled when the application starts. These documents provide the framework with the necessary information about a class.

It also provides data query and retrieval facilities and significantly reduces the development time that would have been otherwise spent with manual data handling in SQL and JDBC.

All that needs to be done is:

- Write a simple POJO
- Create an XML mapping file that describes relationship between the database and the class attributes
- Call a few Hibernate APIs to load/store the persistent objects

Hibernate thus makes it far easier to build robust, high-performance database applications with Java.

That's enough for a quick overview. Let's move on to the next chapter that introduces Hibernate and its underlying architecture.

<u>This book focuses on Hibernate 3.x.</u>

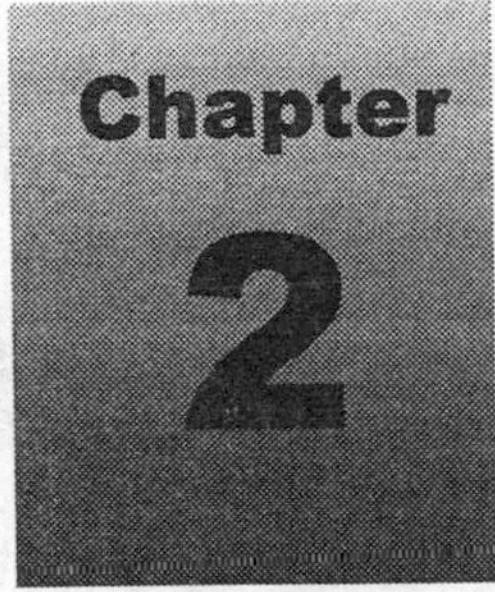

SECTION I: INTRODUCTION

Introduction To Hibernate

Usually when dealing with applications, one probably imagines that an application has some specific functions [business logic] and all that it has to do is process and then finally save data in a database.

When thinking in terms of Java as the programming language of choice, the business logic of an application works with OBJECTS of different CLASS types. However, when dealing with the storage medium, it's important to note that the tables of a database are not OBJECTS which becomes an issue.

<u>This is where Hibernate comes in!</u>

Hibernate provides a solution to map database tables to a Java class.

It does this by:

- Copying the data available in the database tables to a Java class
- Saving OBJECTS to the database tables

  In this process the object is transformed to one or more tables.

Saving data to a storage medium is called **persistence**.

Copying of tables to objects and vice versa is called **Object/Relational Mapping**.

What Is Hibernate

Hibernate is the latest Open Source persistence technology. It is available as a free open source [distributed under the GNU Lesser General Public License] Object/Relational Mapping [ORM] library for the Java programming language. It provides a framework for mapping an object oriented DOMAIN model to a traditional Relational Database.

Hibernate was developed by a team of Java software developers around the world led by Gavin King, JBoss Inc. [now part of Red Hat].

Hibernate has become the de-facto ORM [Object/Relational Mapping] framework for most of the organizations today.

Hibernate was developed with a goal to relieve the developers from 95% of common data persistence related programming tasks by:

- Making the developer feel as if the database contains plain Java objects, without having them worry about how to get them out of [or back into] database tables
- Allowing the developers to focus on the objects and features of the application, without having to worry about how to store them or find them later

Its primary feature is mapping from:

- Java Classes → Database Tables
- Java Data Types → SQL Data Types

In addition to this, Hibernate also allows querying and retrieving data. It generates all the necessary SQL calls to achieve this and thereby, relieves the developers from manual result set handling and object conversion.

Hibernate provides transparent persistence that enables the applications [using Hibernate as the ORM] to switch to any database [supported by Hibernate].

To use Hibernate:

- Java bean classes [POJOs] that represents the table in the database are created
- The instance variables of the class are mapped to the columns in the database table

Why Hibernate

Because of the following reasons:

- Hibernate is Free under LGPL i.e. Hibernate can be used to develop/package and distribute the applications for free
- It eliminates the need for repetitive SQL
- It allows working with classes and objects instead of queries and result sets which makes the approach more Object Oriented and less Procedural
- Handles all **C**reate, **R**ead, **U**pdate, **D**elete [CRUD] operations
- Brings in portability across databases
- Supports IDEs such as Eclipse, NetBeans by providing a suite of plug-ins
- Reduces the development time by supporting inheritance, polymorphism, composition and the Java Collection framework
- Supports the multiple primary key generation including built-in support for identity [Auto increment] columns, sequences, UUID algorithm and HI/LO algorithm. Hibernate also includes support for application assigned identifiers and composite keys
- **H**ibernate's **D**ual **L**ayer **C**ache **A**rchitecture [HDCLCA] delivers thread safeness, non-blocking data access, session level cache, optional second-level cache and optional query cache. Hibernate also works well when other applications have simultaneous access to the database
- Supports connection pooling
- Supports wide range of database such as:
  - Oracle
  - DB2
  - Sybase
  - MS SQL Server
  - PostgreSQL
  - MySQL
  - HypersonicSQL
  - Mckoi SQL
  - SAP DB
  - Interbase
  - Pointbase
  - Progress

- FrontBase
- Ingres
- Informix
- Firebird
- TimesTen
- InterSystems Cache'
- Apache Derby
- HP NonStop SQL/MX
- MS Access
- Corel Paradox
- Xbase

Hibernate, Database And The Application

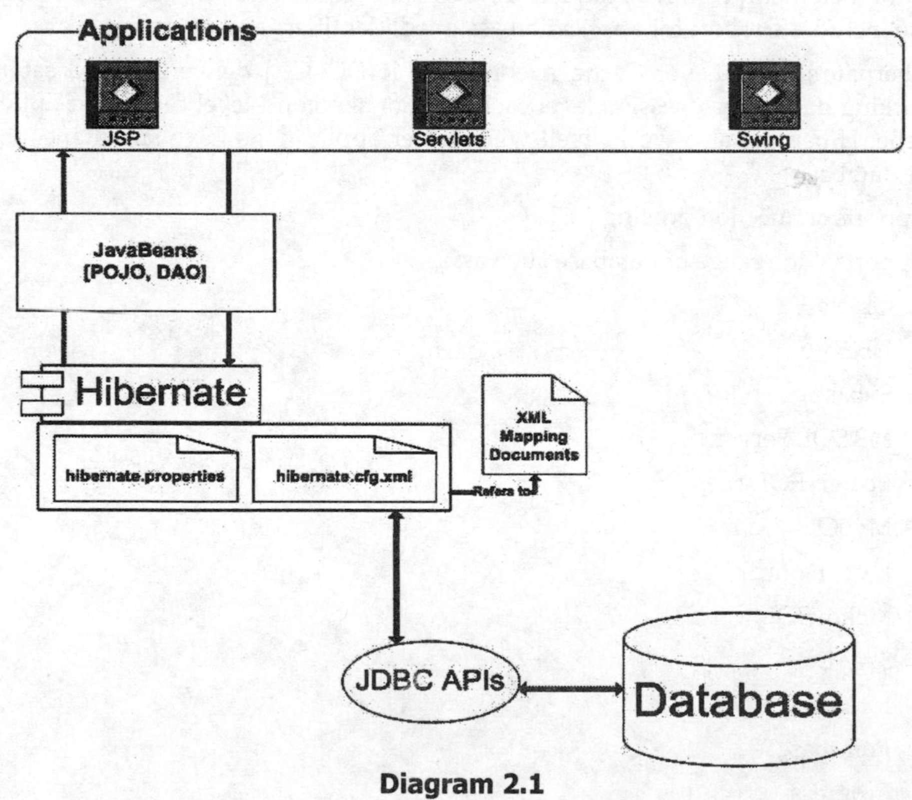

Diagram 2.1

Diagram 2.1 depicts the following:

Hibernate uses the **database** and **configuration data** to provide persistence services [and **Persistent Objects**] to the application.

The configuration data may be defined as:

- hibernate.properties

OR

- hibernate.cfg.xml

The configuration holds references to:

- Mapping Documents/Files
- The Database Dialect

The instance variables of these classes are mapped with the columns of the tables in the database in the Mapping Documents.

POJOs are Java classes that represent the tables in the database. Data Access Object [DAO] is the design pattern that can be used [if required] to deal with database operations.

Hibernate then allows performing the SELECT, INSERT, UPDATE and DELETE operations on the database tables by automatically creating the required SQL queries and firing them using the JDBC APIs.

Components Of Hibernate

Hibernate is made up of the following three components:

Connection Management

Hibernate's Connection management service provides efficient management of the database connections. Database connection is the most expensive portion of an application that allows interacting with the database.

Transaction Management

Transaction management service provides the ability to execute more than one database statements at a time.

Object Relational Mapping

Object relational mapping is a technique of mapping the data representation from an object model to a relational data model. This part of Hibernate is used to SELECT, INSERT, UPDATE and DELETE records from the underlying database tables.

Usually a populated object of a POJO is passed to **Session.save()** method. Hibernate reads the state of the variables of that object and executes the necessary SQL query.

Architecture Of Hibernate

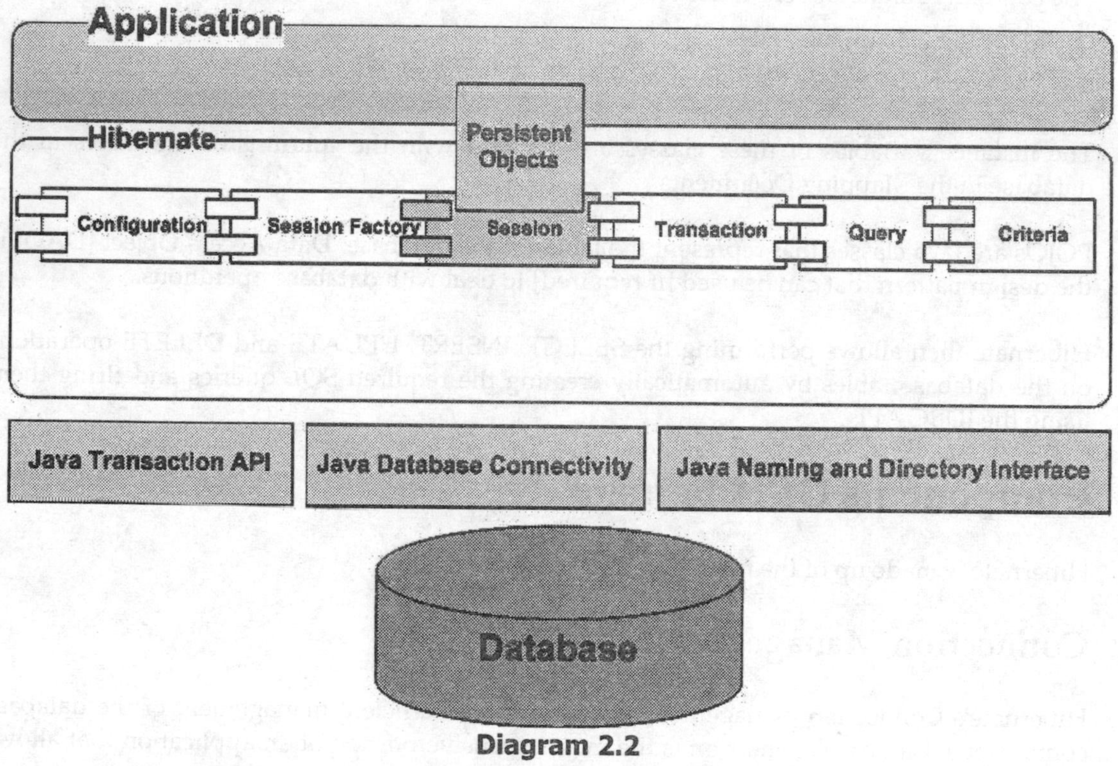

Diagram 2.2

Configuration Object

The Configuration object represents a configuration or properties file for Hibernate. It is usually created once during application initialization.

The Configuration object reads the properties [hibernate.properties/hibernate.cfg.xml] to establish a database connection. Typically, a Configuration object is spawned to create a SessionFactory.

Session Factory

The SessionFactory is created with the help of a Configuration object during the application start up. It serves as a factory for spawning Session objects when required.

Typically, it is created once [one SessionFactory object per database] and kept alive for later use.

However, for applications that require interacting with multiple databases, multiple SessionFactory objects [each with a separate Configuration object].

Session

Session objects are lightweight and inexpensive to create. They provide the main interface to perform actual database operations.

All the POJOs i.e. persistent objects are saved and retrieved with the help of a Session object.

Typically, session objects are created as needed and destroyed when not required.

Transaction

A Transaction represents a unit of work with the database.

Any kind of modifications initiated via the session object are placed with in a transaction. A Session object helps creating a Transaction object.

Transaction objects are typically used for a short time and are closed by either committing or rejecting.

Query

Persistent objects are retrieved using a Query object.

Query objects allow using SQL or **H**ibernate **Q**uery **L**anguage [HQL] queries to retrieve the actual data from the database and create objects.

Criteria

Persistent objects can also be retrieved using a Criteria object.

Criteria uses an object/method based means of constructing and executing a request to retrieve objects.

How Hibernate Works

An **XML mapping document** is created, which informs Hibernate about:

- The classes needed to store the data
- How the classes are related to the tables and columns in the database

The mapping document is compiled, when the application starts up. It provides the Hibernate framework with all the necessary information.

During the runtime, Hibernate reads the XML mapping document and dynamically builds Java classes to manage the translation between the database and the Java objects.

A SessionFactory is created from the compiled collection of mapping documents. The SessionFactory provides the mechanism for managing persistent classes and the Session interface.

The Session class provides the interface between the persistent data store and the application. The Session interface wraps a JDBC connection, which can be user managed or controlled by Hibernate and is only intended to be used by a single application thread, then closed and discarded.

All the database interaction is done via a simple, intuitive API that Hibernate provides. This API allows performing queries against the objects represented by the database. This API informs Hibernate:

- To save the changes whenever the objects are changed
- To store the objects in the database whenever new objects are created

This chapter introduced Hibernate along with its underlying architecture and its components. It also glossed over how hibernate works.

Let's move forward and jump right in. The next chapter deals with installing, building an application and integrating Hibernate with that application.

SECTION II: GETTING STARTED

Writing The First Application

Hibernate when compared to other Java persistence solutions, is quite easy. In fact, it is considered the de-facto ORM library for most of the organizations today. Any project that requires database interaction have started looking at Hibernate than considering the traditional approach i.e. JDBC. This, therefore, saves a huge amount of time revolving around unnecessary chores.

However, to make this more convincible, let's look at a practical implementation and work on it.

This is the only compelling reason why this chapter has been introduced. This chapter aims at convincing the readers/developers about how easy it is, to begin using Hibernate.

This chapter does not cover the basics or a detailed explanation of Hibernate configurations or API. Those topics will be covered in the chapters that follow. This Chapter leads through the building of a small example called **GuestBook** that uses Hibernate.

To get the first Hibernate application to work, the following needs to be setup:

- Database
- Mapping files
- Configuration
- Plain old Java objects [POJOs]

Once all this is in place, the application logic needs to be written which uses the Hibernate session to actually do something.

Application Requirement Specifications

The application [example] to be built is called **GuestBook**. This application should be capable of accepting and displaying visitor's comments.

To achieve this, it should provide a user interface that accepts visitor's name and message/comments.

Diagram 3.1: GuestBook data entry form

After such information is captured and stored, other visitors to the application should be able to view all the available comments as shown in diagram 3.2.

This user interface displays the visitor's name along with the message and the date when the message was keyed in. It should also provide a link to sign the GuestBook which when clicked should display the GuestBook data entry form as shown in diagram 3.1.

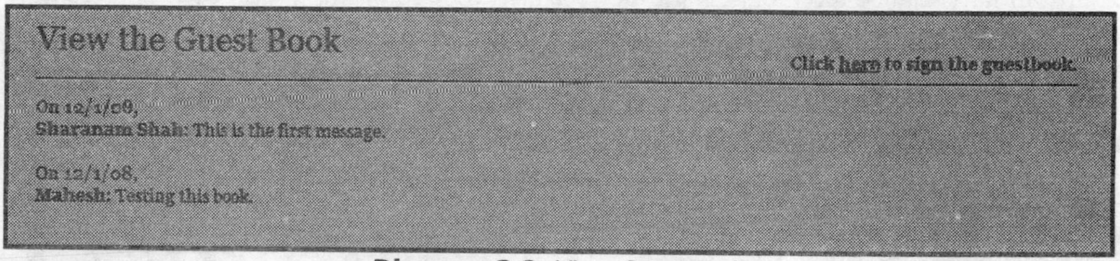

View the Guest Book

Click here to sign the guestbook.

On 12/1/08,
Sharanam Shah: This is the first message.

On 12/1/08,
Mahesh: Testing this book.

Diagram 3.2: View GuestBook

Where Does Hibernate Fit

Hibernate can be invoked from a Java application either directly or via another framework such as Struts or Spring and so on.

Hibernate's API makes it easy for these frameworks to support Hibernate in one way or another.

Frameworks such as Spring / Struts provide excellent Hibernate integration including generic support for persistence objects, a generic set of persistence exceptions and transaction management.

Section V: Application Development With Hibernate explains how Hibernate can be configured and integrated with such frameworks.

Hibernate can also be invoked from:

- A Swing application
- A Servlet
- A Portlet
- A JSP
- Any other kind of Java application that has access to a database

Typically, Hibernate is used to create a Data Access Layer for an application.

The most typical workflow would be:

- Define the configuration details. These details are then represented by a Configuration object
- Create a **SessionFactory** object from the Configuration object

- Instantiate the Session object through which the application accesses Hibernate's representation of the database

From this application's [GuestBook] point of view, Hibernate will be used as follows:

- The user invokes the application
- The "Sign the Guest Book" data entry form is served to allow capturing the visitor's name and comments

- The user keys in the details and clicks **Submit**

After such information is captured and the form is submitted, the server-side script in this case a JSP [GuestBookView.jsp] takes charge.

This script invokes Hibernate as follows:

- Creates a **SessionFactory** object from the Configuration object
- Instantiate the **Session** object
- Uses the **save()** method of the instantiated Session object to save the captured data to the configured database
- Uses the **createQuery()** method of the instantiated Session object to query the configured database and fetch all the entries to display them

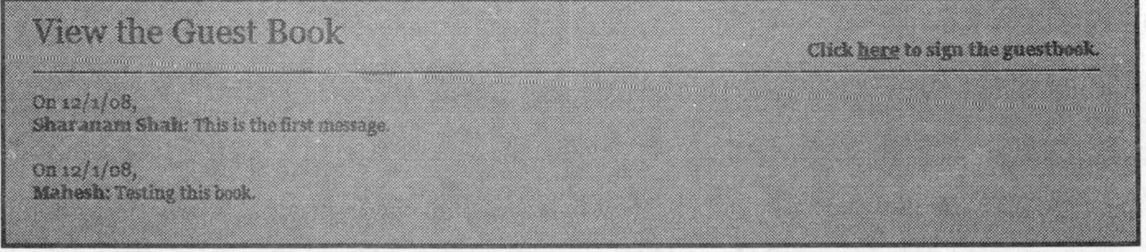

This user interface displays the visitor's name along with the message and the date when the message was keyed in.

Let's begin!

Software Requirements

From the application development perspective, the following software will be required on the development machine:

- Java Development Kit
- NetBeans IDE [The development IDE]
- MySQL Community Server [The database server]
- Hibernate 3 [The ORM tool]

Downloading Hibernate

Hibernate can be downloaded from:
http://www.hibernate.org/Download/DownloadOverview

From the download page that appears, choose to download the current latest release of **Hibernate Core**. At the time of writing this book the latest version that was available for download is **3.3.1.GA** [available in the Book's accompanying CDROM].

REMINDER

The above mentioned software setups are available in this book's accompanying CDROM.

Library Files

To integrate Hibernate with a Java application, a few Java libraries [.JAR] are required:

- **JDBC driver:** This will be specific to a relational database to be used. In this case MySQL is used as the database of choice, hence, the database specific JDBC driver file will be **MySQL Connector/J 5.1.7** [can be downloaded from http://www.mysql.com also available in the Book's accompanying CDROM]

HINT

Hibernate does not include any database specific JDBC drivers. These must be obtained separately. Typically, the database provider offers them, as a separate downloads or bundled with the database installation.

- **Hibernate Library Files**

  These include:

  - From the **hibernate-distribution-3.3.1.GA** directory
    - hibernate3.jar
  - From the **hibernate-distribution-3.3.1.GA → lib → required** directory
    - antlr-2.7.6.jar
    - jta-1.1.jar
    - javassist-3.4.GA.jar
    - commons-collections-3.1.jar
    - dom4j-1.6.1.jar
  - From the **hibernate-distribution-3.3.1.GA → lib → bytecode → cglib** directory
    - hibernate-cglib-repack-2.1_3.jar
  - From the **hibernate-annotations-3.4.0.GA → lib** directory
    - slf4j-api.jar
    - slf4j-log4j12.jar
  - From the **hibernate-annotations-3.4.0.GA → lib → test** directory
    - log4j.jar

These files are available in the lib directory of the Hibernate Core and Hibernate Annotations download.

REMINDER

The Hibernate Core lib directory holds several optional library files. These libraries provide connection pools, additional caching functionality and the JCA API. The purpose of each library is detailed in the README file, which also states which libraries are optional and which are required.

The Application Development Approach

This application will be built using **JSP**.

The **data entry form** that captures the data will be called GuestBookEntry.jsp and the page that will fetch and display the entries will be called GuestBookView.jsp.

The **captured data** will be stored in a **table** called **GuestBook** under the **MySQL** database server.

In the Java application, the **POJO** that will represent the GuestBook database table will be called myApp.Guestbook.java.

Just to make this simple, the application development will be carried out/demonstrated using a development IDE called NetBeans IDE 6.5. Ensure that this IDE [available in the Book's accompanying CDROM] is installed on the development machine prior proceeding further.

Refer to *Appendix A: Installing The NetBeans IDE* for the installation steps.

The following are the steps that will help build this application.

1. Create the database schema
2. Create the Web Application using the NetBeans IDE
3. Add the Java libraries [Hibernate and JDBC driver] to the application
4. Create a POJO to represent the table in the database schema
5. Create a Hibernate [XML] configuration file that points to the database server [MySQL]
6. Create a Hibernate [XML] mapping files for the POJO that maps the JavaBean properties to the columns in the table
7. Add the Hibernate mapping file as a reference to the Hibernate configuration file
8. Create JSPs
    a. Create a Hibernate **Configuration object** that references the XML configuration file
    b. Build a Hibernate **SessionFactory** object from the Configuration object
    c. Finally, retrieve Hibernate **Session objects** from the SessionFactory and write the data access logic for the application to allow the operations CREATE and RETRIEVE

Creating Database And Tables In MySQL

Since MySQL is the database server of choice, ensure that the MySQL database engine [available in the Book's accompanying CDROM] is installed on the development machine prior proceeding further. This can also be downloaded from the website http://www.mysql.com/download.

Login to the MySQL database using a valid username and password. The pre-created default user called **root** can also be used.

Create the database named GuestBook:

```
CREATE DATABASE GuestBook;
```

Switch to the database GuestBook:

```
USE GuestBook;
```

Create the table named GuestBook:

```
CREATE TABLE GuestBook(
  VisitorNo Int PRIMARY KEY AUTO_INCREMENT,
  VisitorName varchar(50),
  Message varchar(100),
  MessageDate varchar(40));
```

Creating A Web Application

Since NetBeans is the IDE of choice throughout this book. Use it to create a new Web Application Project called **GuestBook**.

Run the NetBeans IDE and create a new **Web Application** project, as shown in diagram 3.3.1.

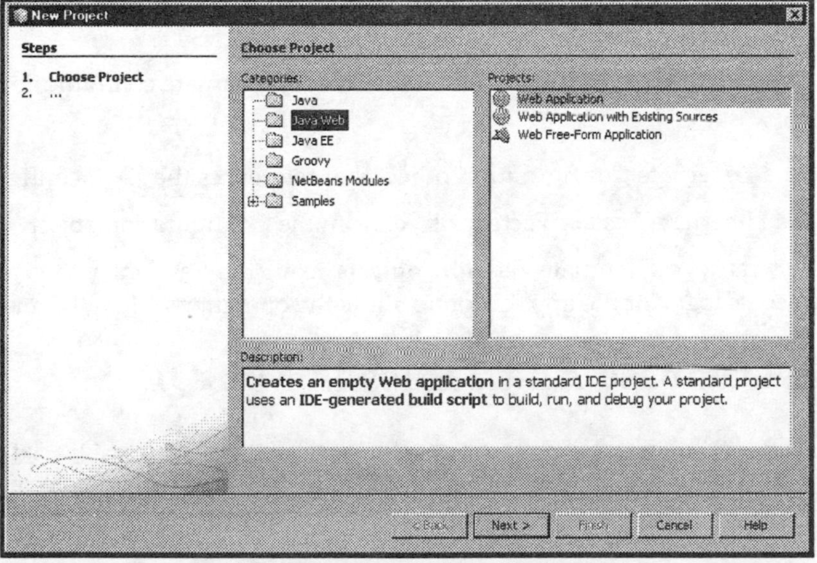

Diagram 3.3.1: New Project

Click [Next >]. Name this Web application as **GuestBook** as shown in diagram 3.3.2.

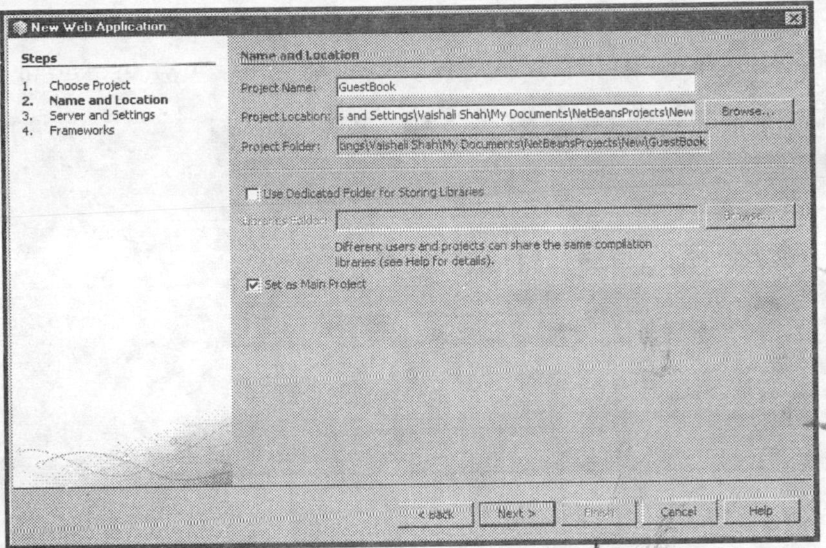

Diagram 3.3.2: Name and Location

Click [Next >]. Choose the desired Web server, the Java EE version and the context path as shown in diagram 3.3.3.

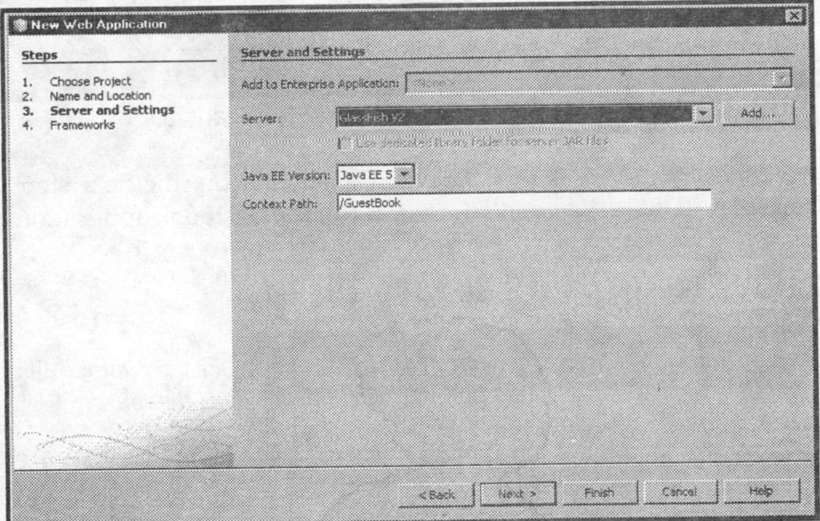

Diagram 3.3.3: Server and Settings

Click Next >. Do not choose a framework, in the Frameworks dialog box.

Click Finish.

The GuestBook application is created in the NetBeans IDE as shown in diagram 3.3.4.

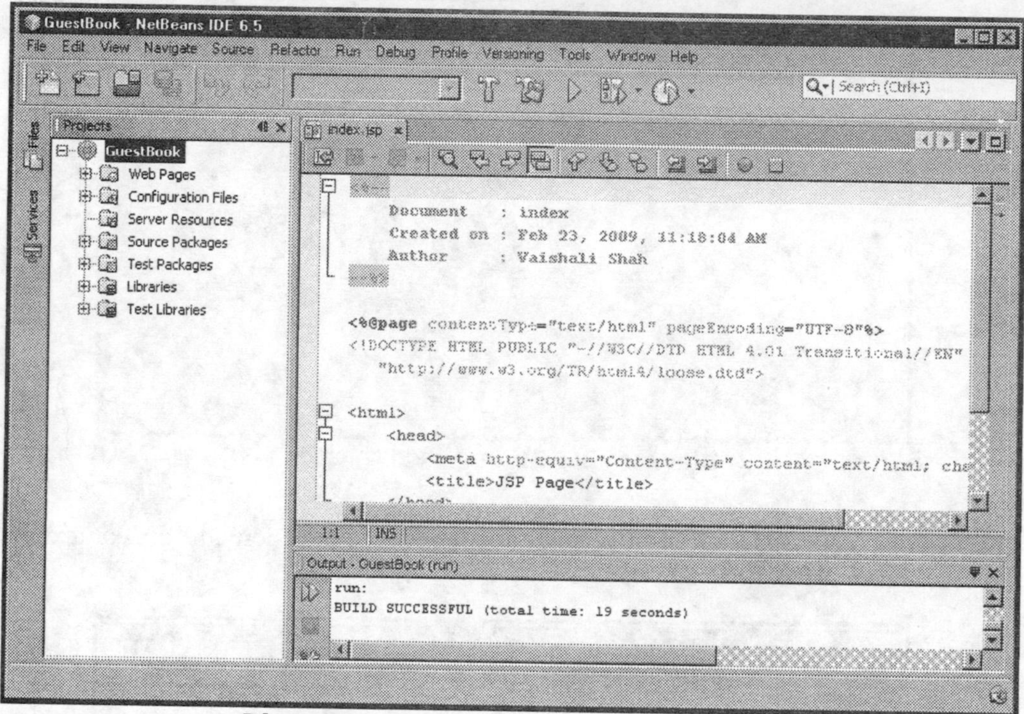

Diagram 3.3.4: GuestBook in NetBeans IDE

Once the NetBeans IDE brings up the GuestBook application, the next step is to add the required library files [JDBC driver and Hibernate] to the GuestBook application.

Adding The Required Library Files

It's a good practice to manually create a dedicated ***lib*** *folder with all the required library files in the project folder and then using NetBeans add libraries from this folder as the source.*

To do so,

Create a directory called **lib** under <Drive>:**NetBeansProjects**\GuestBook. [**NetBeansProjects** is the folder where NetBeans places the projects created]

Hibernate Library Files

Copy the following library files to the lib directory:

- From the **hibernate-distribution-3.3.1.GA** directory
  - hibernate3.jar
- From the **hibernate-distribution-3.3.1.GA → lib → required** directory
  - antlr-2.7.6.jar
  - jta-1.1.jar
  - javassist-3.4.GA.jar
  - commons-collections-3.1.jar
  - dom4j-1.6.1.jar
- From the **hibernate-distribution-3.3.1.GA → lib → bytecode → cglib** directory
  - hibernate-cglib-repack-2.1_3.jar
- From the **hibernate-annotations-3.4.0.GA → lib** directory
  - slf4j-api.jar
  - slf4j-log4j12.jar
- From the **hibernate-annotations-3.4.0.GA → lib → test** directory
  - log4j.jar

Now add these libraries in the NetBeans. Expand the Web application project structure in the **Project** pane, if not already expanded. Right-click on the **Libraries** folder, select the **Add JAR/Folder...** menu item as shown in diagram 3.4.1.

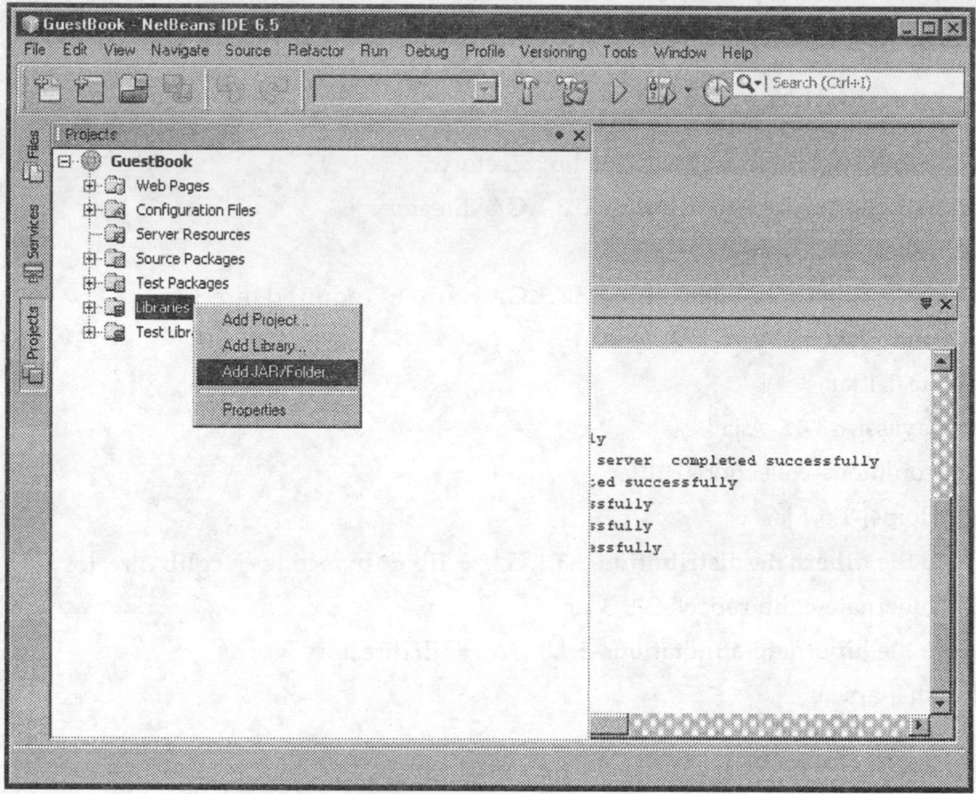

Diagram 3.4.1: Add Jar/Folder

Clicking the **Add JAR/Folder...** option displays the **Add JAR/Folder** dialog box to choose the JAR files.

Browse to the **lib** directory [in this case it will be project's directory\lib] and select all the **JAR** files to add to the project.

Hold down the **Ctrl** key to select multiple JAR files.

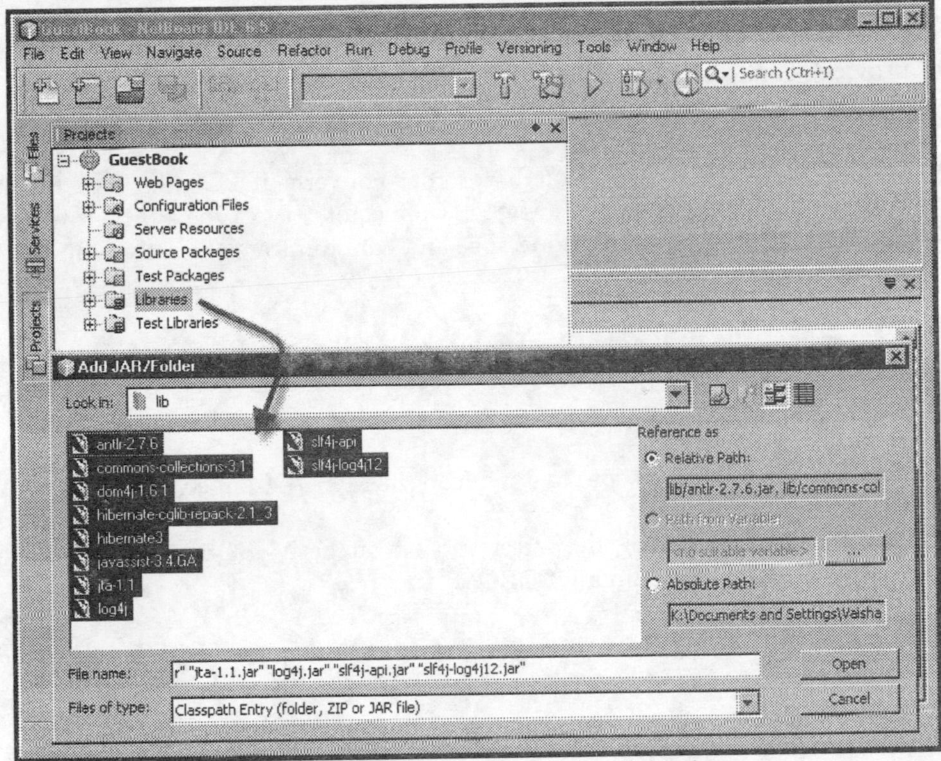

Diagram 3.4.2: Add Jar/Folder dialog box

After adding the **required JAR files**, the **Libraries** directory now appears as shown in diagram 3.4.3:

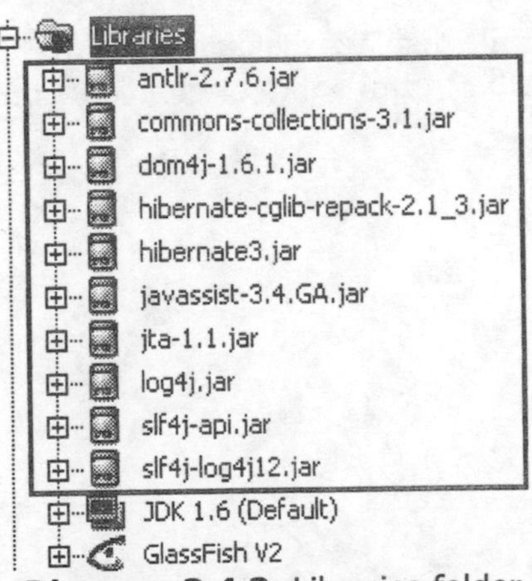

Diagram 3.4.3: Libraries folder

JDBC Driver For MySQL

MySQL provides connectivity to client applications developed in the Java EE 5 via a JDBC driver named **MySQL Connector/J**.

MySQL Connector/J is a native Java driver that converts JDBC calls into the network protocol used by the MySQL database. MySQL Connector/J is a Type 4 driver, which means that MySQL Connector is pure Java code spec and communicates directly with the MySQL server using the MySQL protocol.

MySQL Connector/J allows the developers working with Java EE 5, to build applications, which interact with MySQL and connect all corporate data even in a heterogeneous environment.

Visit the site http://www.mysql.com to download the MySQL Connector/J JDBC Driver.

At the time of writing this book the latest version of the **MySQL Connector/J** was **5.1.7** [available in this Book's accompanying CDROM].

After it is downloaded, using any unzip utility such as Winzip unzip the contents of the zip file.

Copy the **mysql-connector-java-X.X.X-bin.jar** library file to the **lib** directory created earlier under <Drive>:\NetBeansProjects\GuestBook to store the JDBC library file.

Using NetBeans IDE add this library file to the project. Right-click on the **Libraries** directory, click the **Add JAR/Folder...** menu item.

Clicking the **Add JAR/Folder** file displays the dialog box to choose the JAR files as shown in diagram 3.4.4. Browse to the **lib** directory and select **mysql-connector-java-X.X.X-bin.jar** JAR file to add to the project.

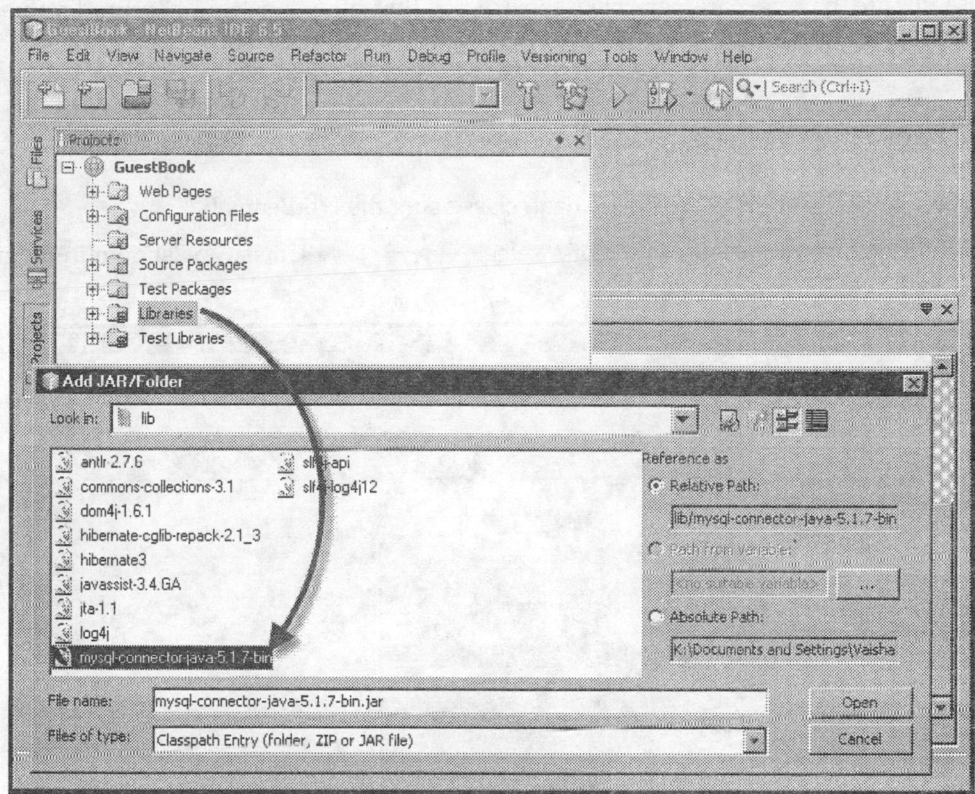

Diagram 3.4.4: Add Jar/Folder dialog box

This adds the JDBC driver file [mysql-connector JAR file] to the project.

Now, let's move to the application development area.

Creating A JavaBean Class

To hold the captured data in a structured manner, a bean class is required. This class should expose the following properties:

Property Name	To Store
visitorNo	The Primary Key value
visitorName	Visitor's Name
message	Message that the visitor enters
messageDate	The date/time on which the message was entered

The class should have a parameterized constructor that allows setting captured values to these properties.

The primary purpose of having such a class is to hold individual guestbook entry as and when they are captured.

The following are the steps to create the Bean class using the NetBeans IDE:

1. Right click **Sources Package** directory, select **New → Java Class...** as shown in diagram 3.5.1

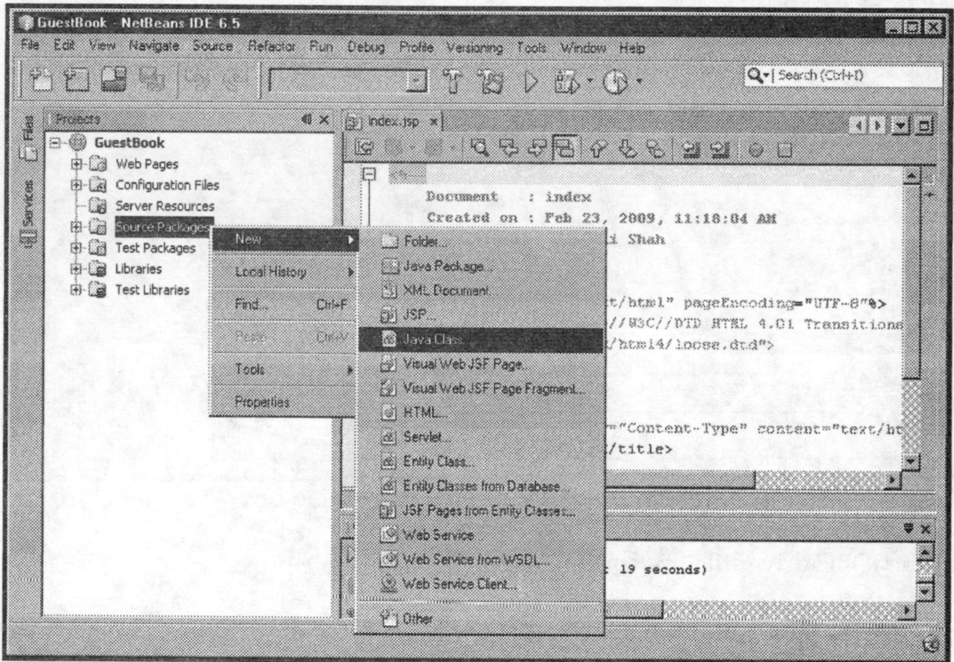

Diagram 3.5.1: Creating Java Bean Class

2. Enter **Guestbook** in the Class Name textbox and enter **myApp** in the Package textbox as shown in diagram 3.5.2

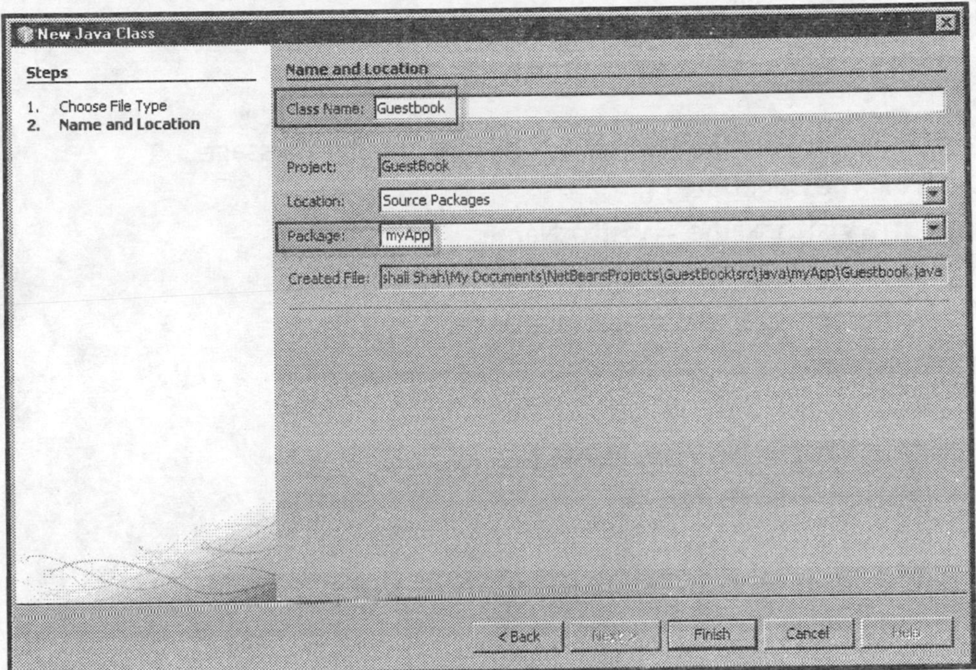

Diagram 3.5.2: Naming the Java class file

3. Click **Finish**

This creates the bean class named Guestbook.java under the package called **myApp**.

Guestbook.java [Code Spec]

Edit the **Guestbook.java** file with the following contents.

```
package myApp;

public class Guestbook implements java.io.Serializable {
    private Integer visitorNo;
    private String visitorName;
    private String message;
    private String messageDate;

    public Guestbook() {
```

```
    }

    public Guestbook(String visitorName, String message,
    String messageDate) {
        this.visitorName = visitorName;
        this.message = message;
        this.messageDate = messageDate;
    }

    public Integer getVisitorNo() {
        return this.visitorNo;
    }
    public void setVisitorNo(Integer visitorNo) {
        this.visitorNo = visitorNo;
    }

    public String getVisitorName() {
        return this.visitorName;
    }
    public void setVisitorName(String visitorName) {
        this.visitorName = visitorName;
    }

    public String getMessage() {
        return this.message;
    }
    public void setMessage(String message) {
        this.message = message;
    }

    public String getMessageDate() {
        return this.messageDate;
```

```
    }
    public void setMessageDate(String messageDate) {
        this.messageDate = messageDate;
    }
}
```

Explanation:

A package named **myApp** is declared. This creates a directory named **myApp** under the <Web Application>\build\web\WEB-INF\classes\ and the **Guestbook.class** file is placed in the myApp directory when deployed.

The Guestbook class is a simple bean class that holds individual visitor entries.

It holds four attributes.

- visitorNo: The identifier attribute
- visitorName: The name of the visitor
- message: The message text
- messageDate: The date on which the message was captured

The identifier attribute [visitorNo] allows the application to access the database identity [Primary Key] of a persistent object.

The identifier chosen is of type **integer**, but this is not a compulsion. Hibernate allows virtually anything for the identifier type.

The Primary Key will be automatically generated by MySQL [**AUTO_INCREMENT**]:

```
CREATE TABLE GuestBook(
  VisitorNo Int PRIMARY KEY AUTO_INCREMENT,
  VisitorName varchar(50),
  Message varchar(100),
  MessageDate varchar(40));
```

All these attributes of the **Guestbook** class have JavaBean style property **accessor methods**.

The class also has a constructor with no parameters and a parameterized constructor.

Creating Hibernate Configuration File

Hibernate uses the **hibernate.cfg.xml** file to create the connection and setup the required environment. This file is used to provide the information which is necessary for making database connections.

The **hibernate.cfg.xml** configuration file defines information such as:

- The database connection
- Resource mappings

To do so, right-click the **Source Packages** folder. Select **New → Other...** as shown in diagram 3.6.1.

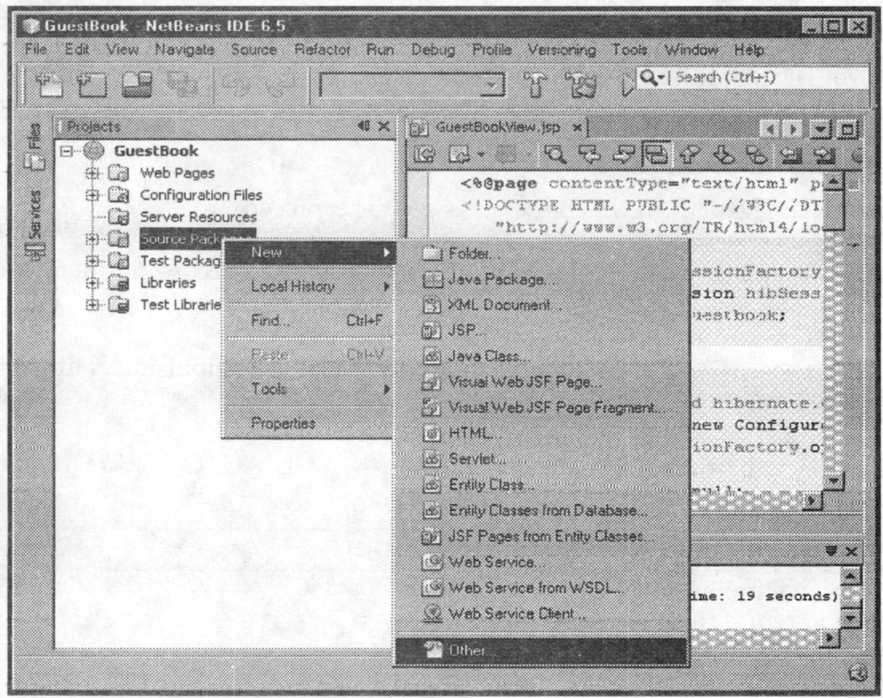

Diagram 3.6.1: Creating hibernate.cfg.xml file

New File dialog appears. Select **XML** from the **Categories** list and select **XML Document** from the **File Types** as shown in diagram 3.6.2.

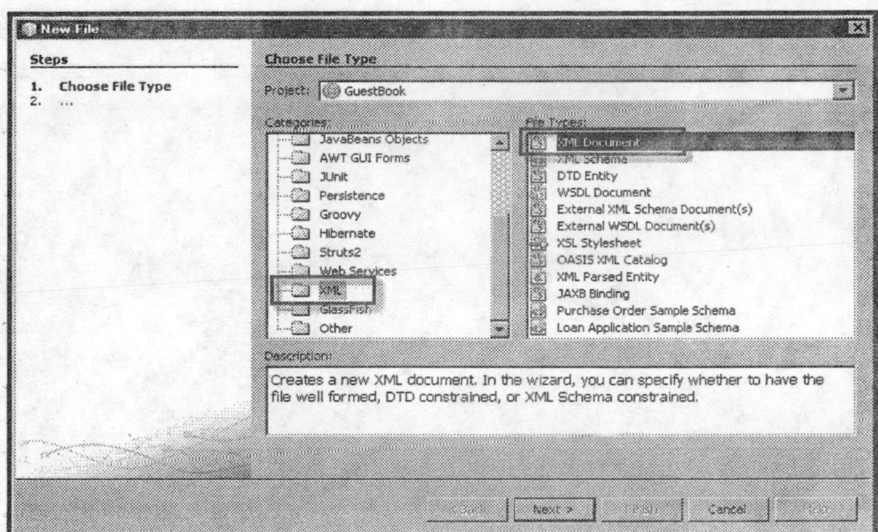

Diagram 3.6.2: Selecting XML file type

Click Next >. Enter **hibernate.cfg** as the file name as shown in diagram 3.6.3.

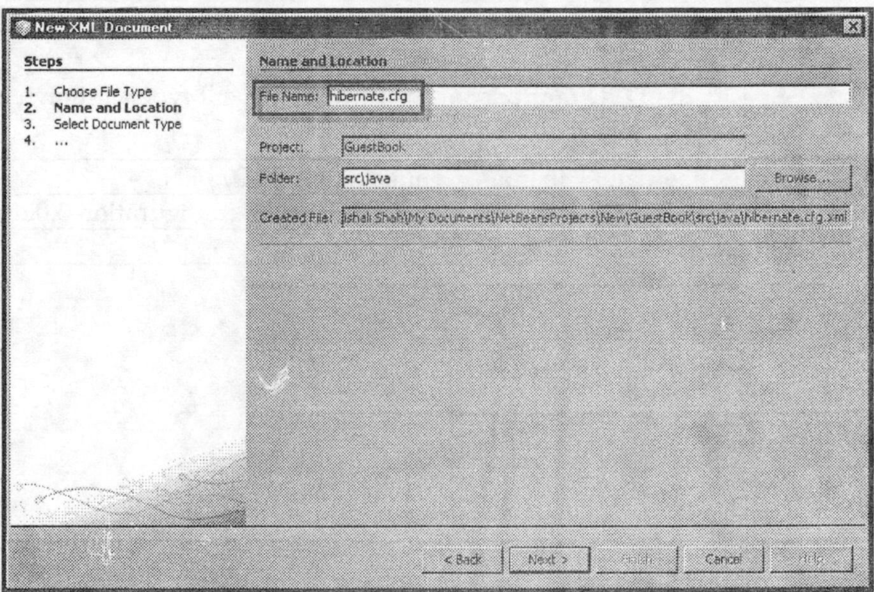

Diagram 3.6.3: Naming the XML file type

Click Next >. Select the option **DTD-Constrained Document** as shown in diagram 3.6.4.

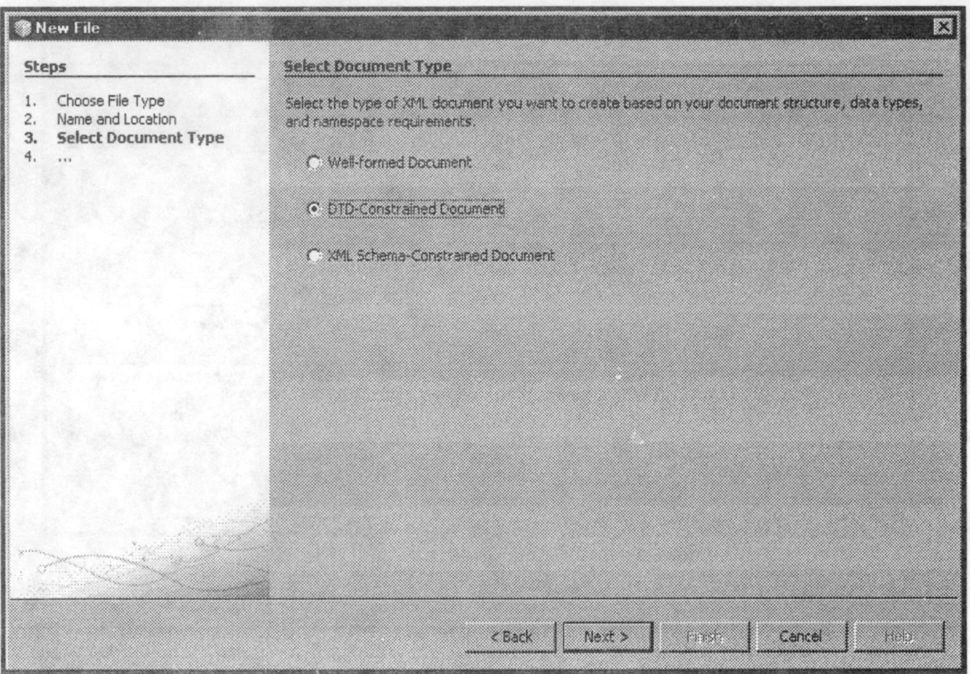

Diagram 3.6.4: Selecting the document type

Click **Next >**. Specify the **DTD Options** for the XML document type as shown in diagram 3.6.5. Populate the following fields:

DTD Public ID	-//Hibernate/Hibernate Configuration DTD//EN
DTD System ID	http://hibernate.sourceforge.net/hibernate-configuration-3.0.dtd
Document Root	hibernate-configuration

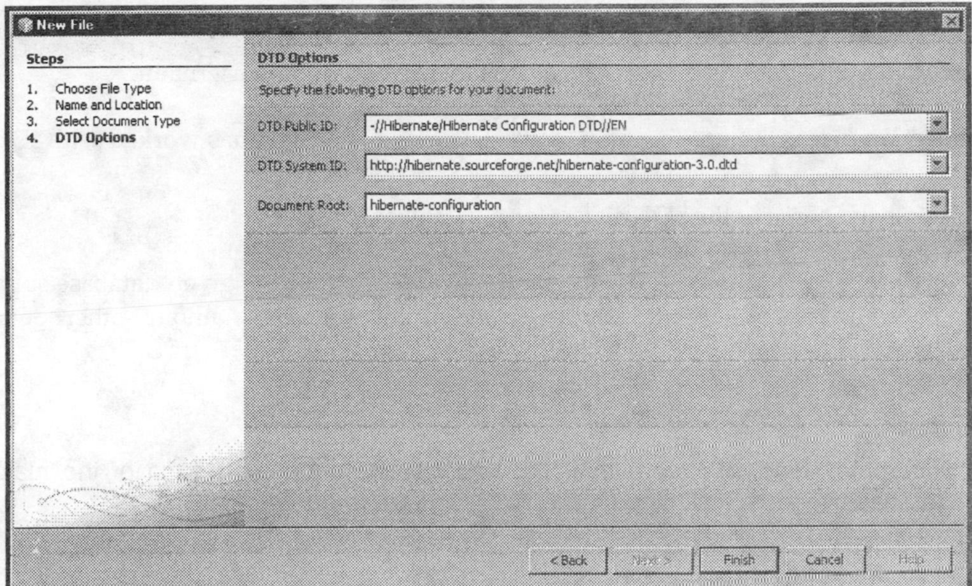

Diagram 3.6.5: Specifying the DTD options for XML document type

Click 

.

The **hibernate.cfg.xml** file should hold the following code spec:

```
<?xml version="1.0" encoding="UTF-8"?>
<!DOCTYPE hibernate-configuration PUBLIC '-//Hibernate/Hibernate Configuration DTD//EN'
'http://hibernate.sourceforge.net/hibernate-configuration-3.0.dtd'>
<hibernate-configuration>
   <session-factory>
      <property name="connection.driver_class">com.mysql.jdbc.Driver</property>
      <property name="connection.url">jdbc:mysql://localhost:3306/GuestBook</property>
      <property name="connection.username">root</property>
      <property name="connection.password">12345678</property>
      <property name="dialect">org.hibernate.dialect.MySQLDialect</property>
   </session-factory>
</hibernate-configuration>
```

Explanation:

The configuration file requires the following properties:

- **connection.driver_class:** Is the JDBC connection class for the specific database
- **connection.url:** Is the full JDBC URL to the database

- **connection.username:** Is the username used to connect to the database
- **connection.password:** Is the password used to authenticate the username

The connection properties are common to any Java developer who has worked with JDBC in the past.

- **dialect:** Is the name of the SQL dialect for the database

The **dialect** property informs the Hibernate framework whether the given database supports identity columns, altering relational tables and unique indexes, among other database specific details.

HINT

Hibernate ships with more than 20 SQL dialects supporting each of the major database vendors including Oracle, DB2, MySQL and PostgreSQL.

Creating Hibernate Mapping File

Mapping definitions [also called mapping documents] are used to provide Hibernate with information to persist objects to a relational database. The mapping files also provide support features such as creating the database schema from a collection of mapping files.

In Hibernate, mapping a bean to a relational database is done by creating a mapping file in XML.

In this application, a Guestbook.hbm.xml file will be created that holds mappings between the database, table and column names to the properties in the **Guestbook** bean [created earlier].

This provides a one-to-one correspondence between a bean to be mapped and the Hibernate configuration file.

The naming convention for mapping files is to use the name of the persistent class with the **.hbm.xml** extension. In the Guestbook application, the persistent class is named Guestbook. The mapping file for the Guestbook class is thus named Guestbook.hbm.xml.

To do so, right-click the **myApp** directory. Select **New → Other...** as shown in diagram 3.7.1.

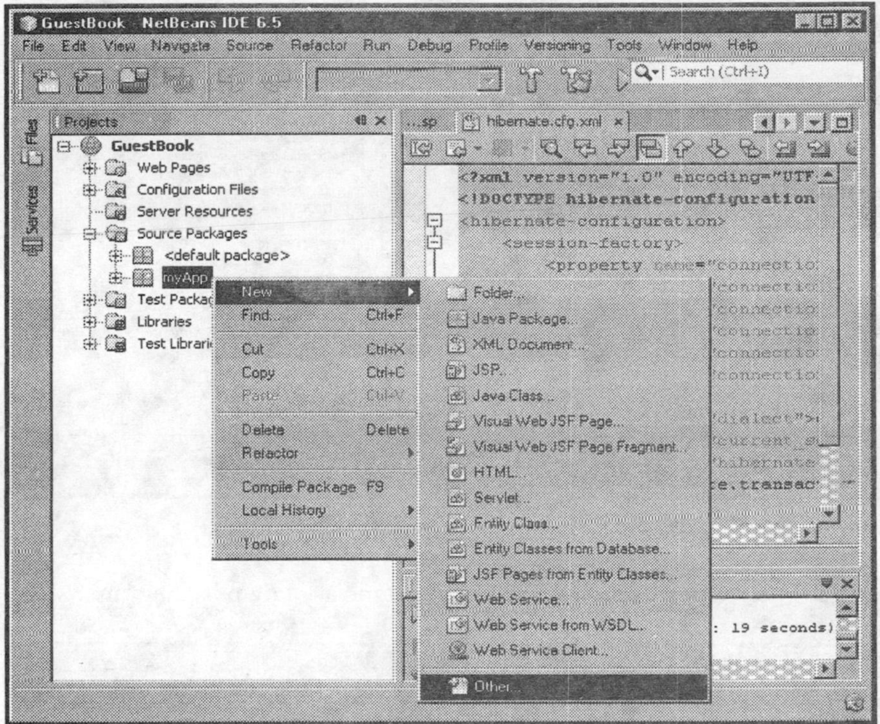

Diagram 3.7.1: Creating GuestBook.hbm.xml file

New File dialog appears. Select **XML** from the **Categories** list and select **XML Document** from the **File Types** as shown in diagram 3.7.2.

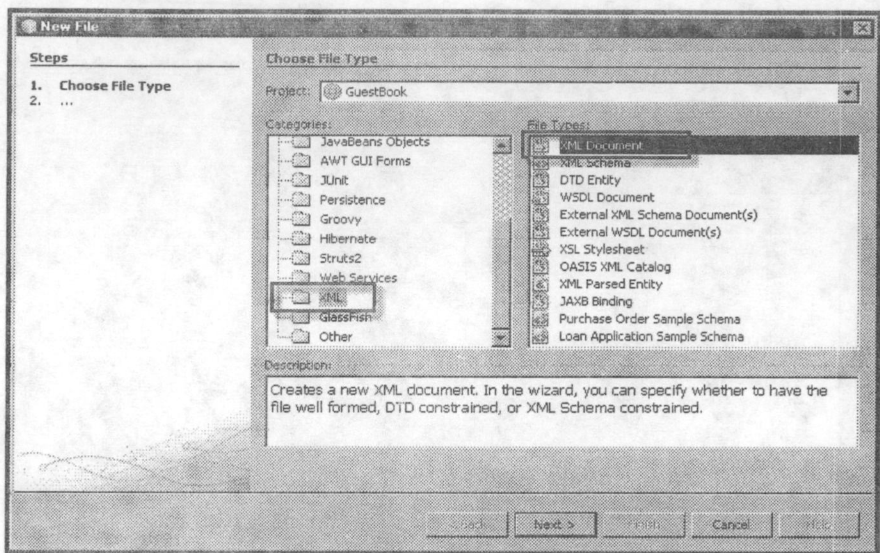

Diagram 3.7.2: Selecting XML file type

Click Next >. Enter **Guestbook.hbm** as the file name as shown in diagram 3.7.3.

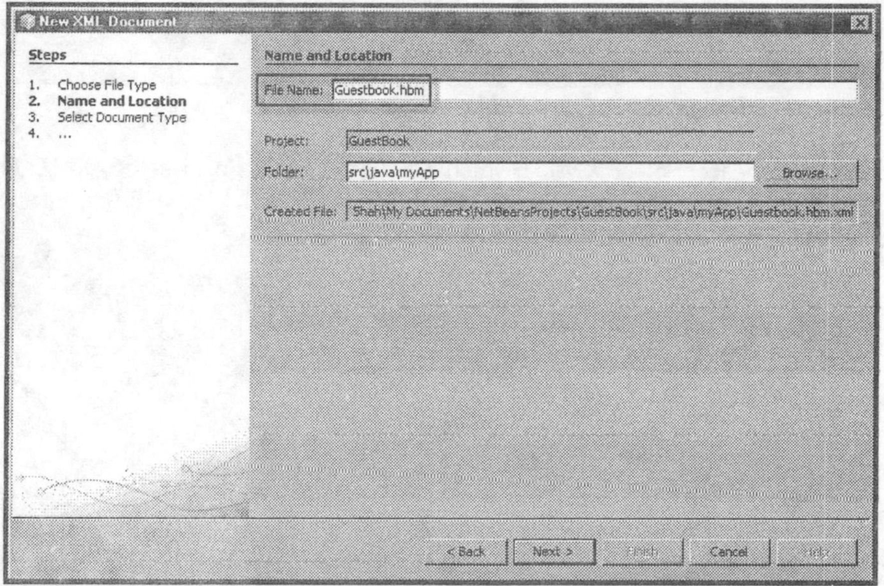

Diagram 3.7.3: Naming the XML file type

Click Next >. Select the option **DTD-Constrained Document** as shown in diagram 3.7.4.

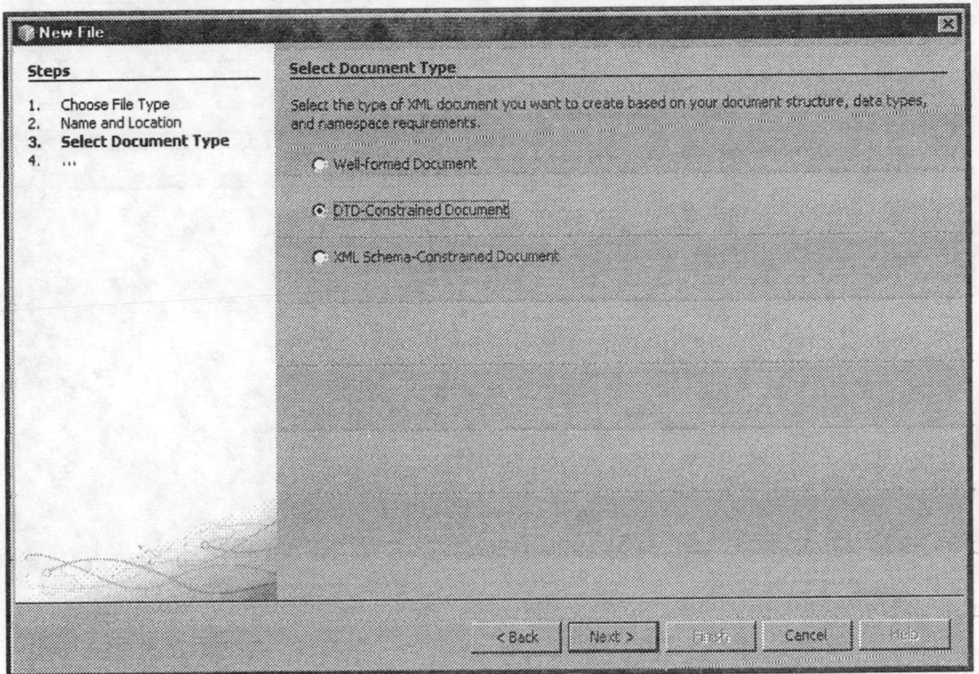

Diagram 3.7.4: Selecting the document type

Click Next >. Specify the **DTD Options** for the XML document type as shown in diagram 3.7.5. Populate the following fields:

DTD Public ID	-//Hibernate/Hibernate Mapping DTD 3.0//EN
DTD System ID	http://hibernate.sourceforge.net/hibernate-mapping-3.0.dtd
Document Root	hibernate-mapping

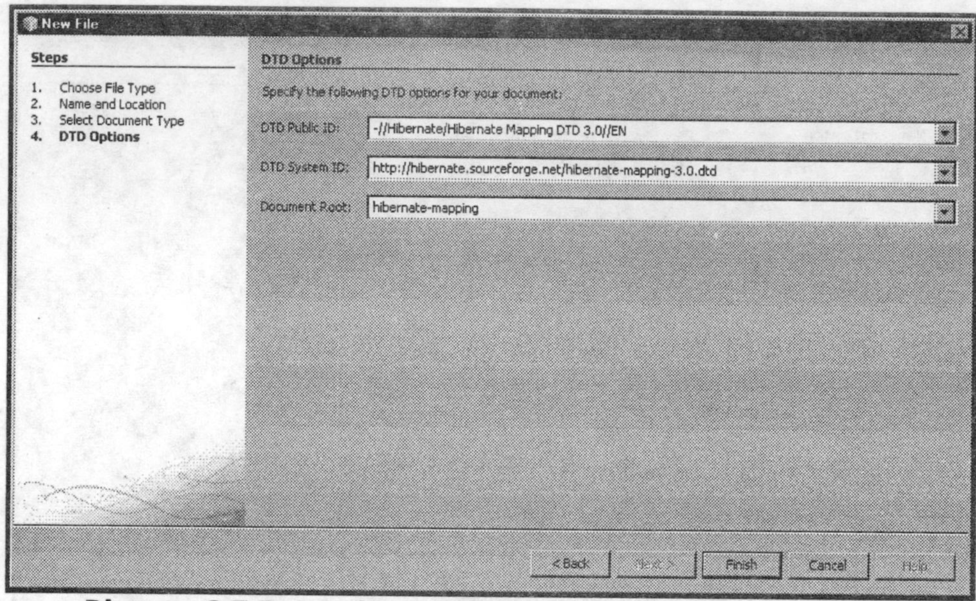

Diagram 3.7.5: Specifying the DTD options for XML document type

Click 
.

The **Guestbook.hbm.xml** file should hold the following code spec:

```
<?xml version="1.0"?>
<!DOCTYPE hibernate-mapping PUBLIC "-//Hibernate/Hibernate Mapping DTD 3.0//EN"
"http://hibernate.sourceforge.net/hibernate-mapping-3.0.dtd">
<hibernate-mapping>
   <class name="myApp.Guestbook" table="guestbook" catalog="guestbook">
      <id name="visitorNo" type="java.lang.Integer">
         <column name="VisitorNo" />
         <generator class="identity" />
      </id>
      <property name="visitorName" type="string">
         <column name="VisitorName" length="50" />
      </property>
      <property name="message" type="string">
         <column name="Message" length="100" />
      </property>
      <property name="messageDate" type="string">
         <column name="MessageDate" length="40" />
```

```
        </property>
    </class>
</hibernate-mapping>
```

Explanation:

This mapping document informs the following to the Hibernate:

- The **Guestbook** class is to be persisted to the **guestbook** table
- The identifier property **visitorNo** maps to a column named **VisitorNo**
    - The Primary Key value will be generated by MySQL [generator class="native"]
- The text properties **visitorNo, visitorName, message, messageDate** map to columns **VisitorNo, VisitorName, Message, MessageDate** respectively

Adding A Mapping Resource

Before a session factory is created, Hibernate must be informed about the mapping files that define how the Java classes relate to the database tables.

Now that the mapping file is available, the same can be informed to the Hibernate framework. This can be done by adding a <mapping> tag to the **hibernate.cfg.xml** file [created earlier].

Edit the **hibernate.cfg.xml** file to hold a mapping resource as shown below:

```
<?xml version="1.0" encoding="UTF-8"?>
<!DOCTYPE hibernate-configuration PUBLIC '-//Hibernate/Hibernate Configuration DTD//EN'
'http://hibernate.sourceforge.net/hibernate-configuration-3.0.dtd'>
<hibernate-configuration>
    <session-factory>
        <property name="connection.driver_class">com.mysql.jdbc.Driver</property>
        <property name="connection.url">jdbc:mysql://localhost:3306/GuestBook</property>
        <property name="connection.username">root</property>
        <property name="connection.password">12345678</property>
        <property name="dialect">org.hibernate.dialect.MySQLDialect</property>
        <mapping resource="myApp/Guestbook.hbm.xml"/>          Add this
    </session-factory>
</hibernate-configuration>
```

Explanation:

Hibernate also needs to know the location and names of the mapping files describing the persistent classes. The mapping element provides the name of each mapping file as well as its location relative to the application classpath. Mapping file **Guestbook.hbm.xml** is included in the configuration file.

Creating JSPs

Before creating the JSP, let's create a directory to hold JSP.

The following are the steps to create the directory:

1. Right click **Web Pages** directory, select **New → Folder...** as shown in diagram 3.8.1

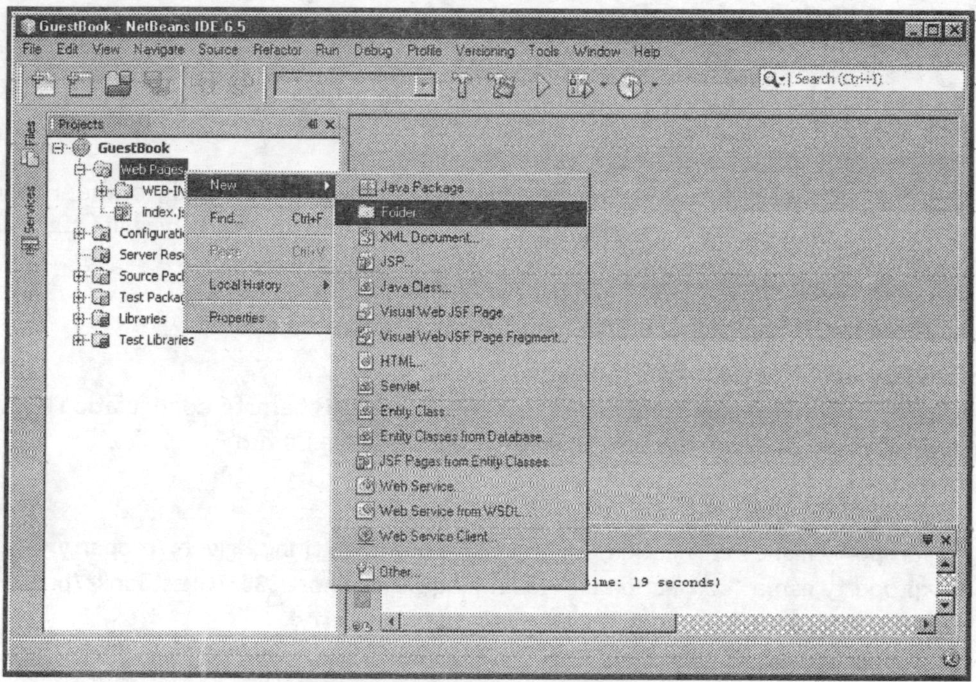

Diagram 3.8.1: Creating Folder

2. Enter the name **JSP** in the **Folder Name** textbox as shown in diagram 3.8.2

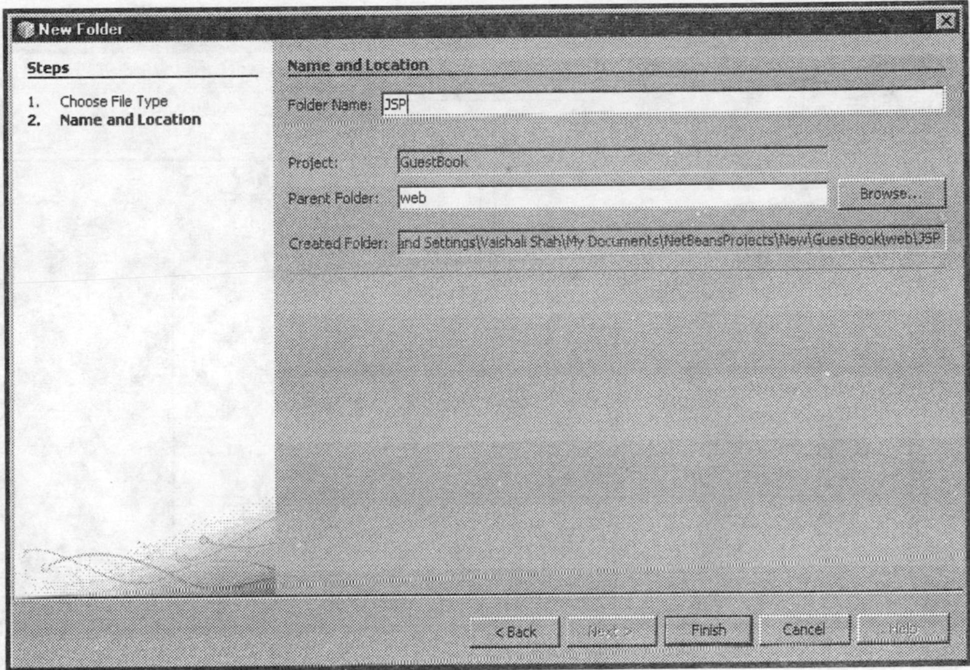

Diagram 3.8.2: Naming the folder

3. Click **Finish**

This creates the directory named **JSP** under **Web Pages**.

The following are the steps to create the JSP file:

1. Right click **JSP** directory, select **New → JSP...** as shown in diagram 3.8.3

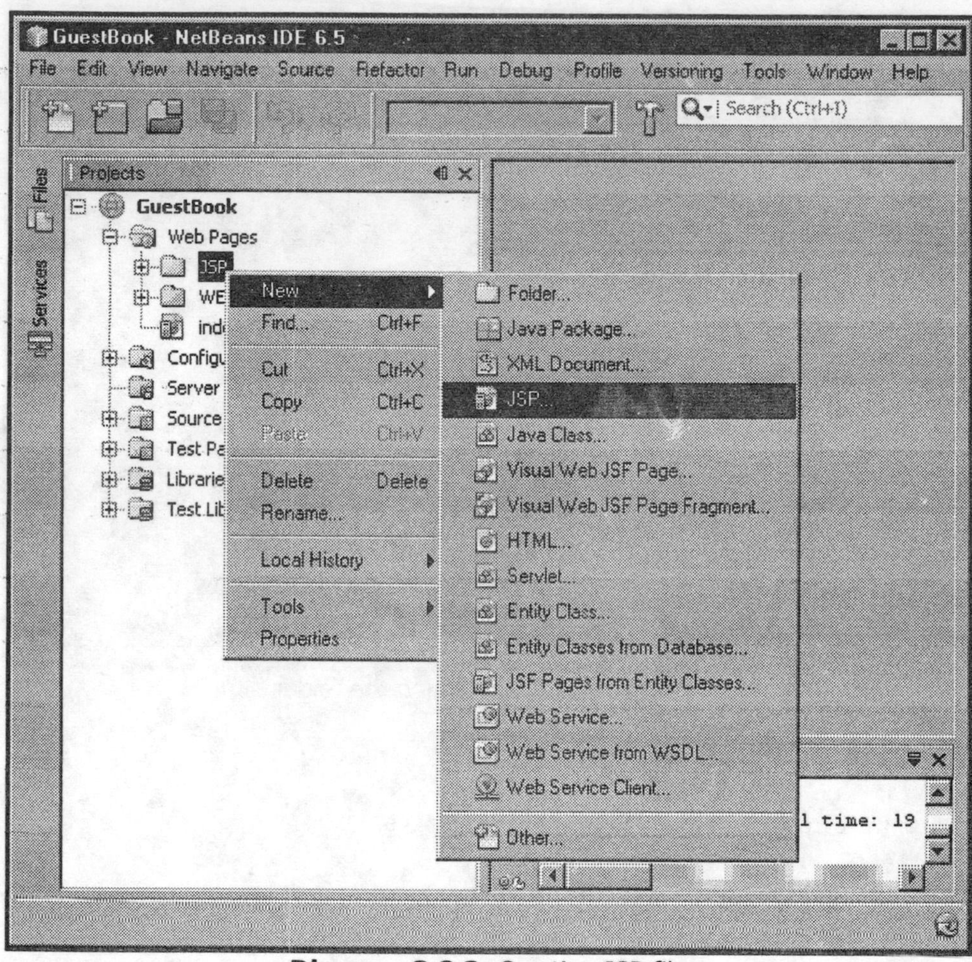

Diagram 3.8.3: Creating JSP file

2. Enter the name **GuestBookEntry** in the **JSP File Name** textbox as shown in diagram 3.8.4

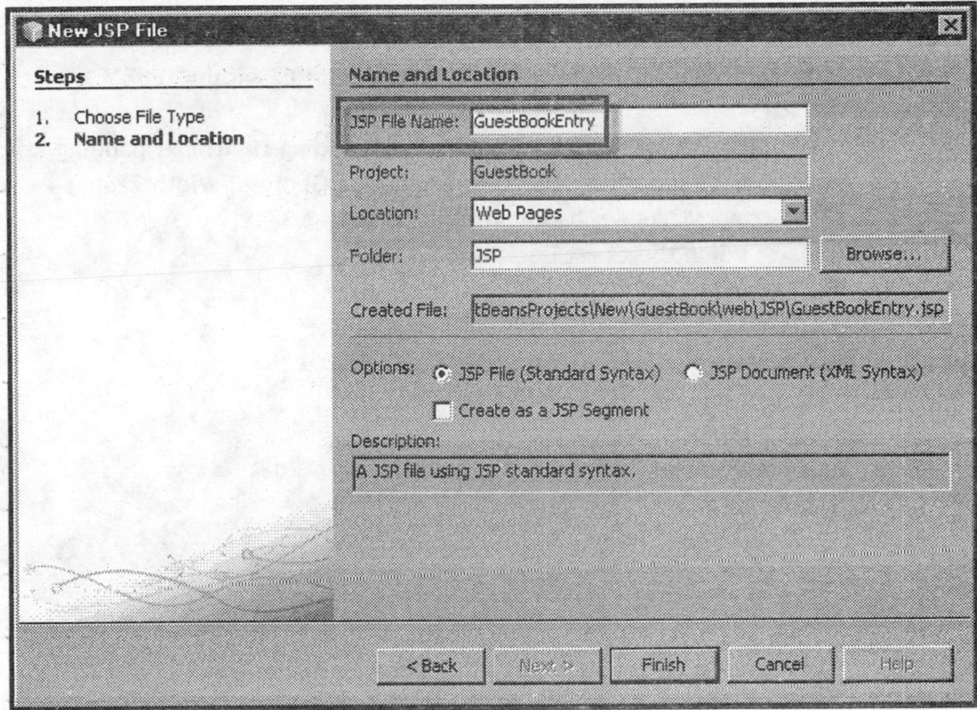

Diagram 3.8.4: Naming the JSP file

3. Click **Finish**

This creates the JSP named GuestBookEntry.jsp under the JSP directory created earlier.

GuestBookEntry.jsp [Code Spec]

Edit the **GuestBookEntry.jsp** file with the following contents.

```
<%@ page language="java" contentType="text/html; charset=ISO-8859-1"
pageEncoding="ISO-8859-1"%>
<!DOCTYPE html PUBLIC "-//W3C//DTD HTML 4.01 Transitional//EN"
"http://www.w3.org/TR/html4/loose.dtd">
<html>
  <head>
    <meta http-equiv="Content-Type" content="text/html;charset=ISO-8859-1">
    <title>Guest Book</title>
  </head>
  <body bgcolor="pink">
    <table border="0" cellpadding="0" cellspacing="0" align="center" width="760">
```

```
<tr>
    <td>
        <table border="0" cellpadding="0" cellspacing="0" width="100%">
            <tr>
                <td valign="top" align="left" style="padding-right:0px; padding-left:0px;
                padding-bottom:0px; font:24px/30px Georgia; width:228px;
                color:#786e4e; padding-top:0px; height:37px;">
                    Sign the Guest Book
                </td>
            </tr>
        </table>
    </td>
</tr>
<tr align="left" valign="top">
    <td height="20">
        <hr />
    </td>
</tr>
<tr>
    <td>
        <form action="<%=request.getContextPath()%>/JSP/GuestBookView.jsp"
        method="post">
            <table border="0" cellpadding="0" cellspacing="2">
                <tr>
                    <td align="right">
                        <font style="font-size:15px; font-family:Arial,Times,serif;
                        font-weight:bold;">Visitor Name:</font>
                    </td>
                    <td>
                        <input name="guest" maxlength="25" size="50" />
                    </td>
                </tr>
                <tr>
                    <td align="right">
                        <font style="font-size:15px; font-family:Arial,Times,serif;
                        font-weight:bold;">Message:</font>
                    </td>
                    <td>
                        <textarea rows="5" cols="40" name="message"></textarea>
                    </td>
```

```
                    </tr>
                    <tr>
                        <td colspan="2" align="right">
                            <input type="submit" name="btnSubmit" value="Submit" />
                        </td>
                    </tr>
                </table>
            </form>
        </td>
    </tr>
  </table>
 </body>
</html>
```

Explanation:

This is the data entry form that allows capturing the visitor's name and comments and submits the data to another server-side script called GuestBookView.jsp for further processing.

GuestBookView.jsp [Code Spec]

Using NetBeans create one more JSP called GuestBookView.jsp using the same steps as shown earlier.

Edit the **GuestBookView.jsp** file with the following contents.

```
<%@page contentType="text/html" pageEncoding="UTF-8"
import="org.hibernate.SessionFactory, org.hibernate.cfg.Configuration,
org.hibernate.Session, org.hibernate.Transaction, java.util.List, java.util.Iterator,
myApp.Guestbook" %>
<!DOCTYPE HTML PUBLIC "-//W3C//DTD HTML 4.01 Transitional//EN"
  "http://www.w3.org/TR/html4/loose.dtd">
<%!
  SessionFactory sessionFactory;
  org.hibernate.Session hibSession;
  List<Guestbook> guestbook;
%>

<%
  sessionFactory = new Configuration().configure().buildSessionFactory();
  hibSession = sessionFactory.openSession();
```

```
    Transaction tx = null;

    String submit = request.getParameter("btnSubmit");
    if(submit != null && ("Submit").equals(submit)) {
        Guestbook gb = new Guestbook();
        try {
            tx = hibSession.beginTransaction();

            String guest = request.getParameter("guest");
            String message = request.getParameter("message");
            String messageDate = new java.util.Date().toString();
            gb.setVisitorName(guest);
            gb.setMessage(message);
            gb.setMessageDate(messageDate);

            hibSession.save(gb);
            tx.commit();
        }
        catch (RuntimeException e) {
            if(tx != null) tx.rollback();
            throw e;
        }
        response.sendRedirect("GuestBookView.jsp");
    }

    try {
        hibSession.beginTransaction();
        guestbook = hibSession.createQuery("from Guestbook").list();
    }
    catch (RuntimeException e) {
        throw e;
    }

    hibSession.close();
%>
<html>
    <head>
        <meta http-equiv="Content-Type" content="text/html;charset=ISO-8859-1">
        <title>Guest Book</title>
    </head>
```

```
<body bgcolor="pink">
    <table border="0" cellpadding="0" cellspacing="0" align="center" width="760">
        <tr>
            <td>
                <table border="0" cellpadding="0" cellspacing="0" width="100%">
                    <tr>
                        <td width="60%" valign="top" align="left" style="padding-right:0px;
                        padding-left:0px; padding-bottom:0px; font:24px/30px Georgia;
                        width:228px; color:#786e4e; padding-top:0px; height:37px;">
                            View the Guest Book
                        </td>
                        <td valign="bottom" align="right" style="font:12px/16px Georgia, serif;
                        color:#786e4e;">
                            <b>Click <a
                            href="<%=request.getContextPath()%>/JSP/GuestBookEntry.jsp">
                            here</a> to sign the guestbook.</b>
                        </td>
                    </tr>
                </table>
            </td>
        </tr>
        <tr align="left" valign="top">
            <td height="20">
                <hr />
            </td>
        </tr>
        <tr>
            <td>
                <table border="0" cellpadding="0" cellspacing="0" align="center" width="100%">
                <%
                    Iterator iterator = guestbook.iterator();
                    while (iterator.hasNext()) {
                        Guestbook objGb = (Guestbook) iterator.next();
                %>
                    <tr>
                        <td style="font:12px/16px Georgia; color:#786e4e;">
                            On <%=objGb.getMessageDate()%>,<br />
                            <b><%=objGb.getVisitorName()%>:</b>
                            <%=objGb.getMessage()%>
                            <br /><br />
```

```
                    </td>
                </tr>
            <%
                }
            %>
            </table>
        </td>
    </tr>
  </table>
 </body>
</html>
```

Explanation:

This is a server-side script that saves the captured data, fetches all the available entries and displays them.

Imports

```
<%@page contentType="text/html" pageEncoding="UTF-8"
import="org.hibernate.SessionFactory, org.hibernate.cfg.Configuration,
org.hibernate.Session, org.hibernate.Transaction, java.util.List, java.util.Iterator,
myApp.Guestbook" %>
```

To allow all this, the following interfaces/classes are imported:

- org.hibernate.SessionFactory: Allows creating sessions. The SessionFactory caches generate SQL statements and other mapping metadata that Hibernate uses at runtime
- org.hibernate.cfg.Configuration: Is used to configure and bootstrap Hibernate. It is meant only as a initialization-time object. The application uses a Configuration instance to specify the location of mapping documents and Hibernate-specific properties and then create the SessionFactory
- org.hibernate.Session: Is the main runtime interface between a Java application and Hibernate. This is the central API class abstracting the notion of a persistence service. The main function of the Session is to offer create, read and delete operations for instances of mapped entity classes
- org.hibernate.Transaction: Is a package, which abstracts the underlying transaction mechanism [JTA or JDBC] and provides strategies for obtaining application server TransactionManagers
- java.util.List: Is an ordered collection. The user of this interface has precise control over where in the list each element is inserted. The user can access elements by their integer index [position in the list] and search for elements in the list

- java.util.Iterator: Is used to sequence over a collection of objects. Iterator allows the caller to remove elements from the underlying collection during the iteration with well-defined semantics

Variable Declaration

The following variables are declared:

```
<%!
    SessionFactory sessionFactory;
    org.hibernate.Session hibSession;
    List<Guestbook> guestbook;
%>
```

- To represent the connections to the database, variable named **sessionFactory** is declared
- To create an instance of Session, variable named **hibSession** is declared
- A list of type **Guestbook** is created. This will hold the entries for view purposes

Application Logic

Creating A Configuration Instance And Building A Session Factory

```
sessionFactory = new Configuration().configure().buildSessionFactory();
```

An instance of the Configuration interface is created. Using it's **configure()** method, the session factory is built. This step indicates Hibernate to load the **hibernate.cfg.xml** file.

HINT

The default name of the configuration file is **hibernate.cfg.xml**. If this is changed, the new file name needs to be passed explicitly as an argument to the **configure()** method.

The configure() method returns an instance of Configuration, which can be used to obtain a Hibernate SessionFactory instance by calling the **buildSessionFactory()** method.

The **buildSessionFactory()** method decides about various SQL statements that must be used to access the data and creates the **SessionFactory** object, which is stored in the private variable declared earlier.

Obtaining A Session Object

After obtaining the SessionFactory, Hibernate org.hibernate.Session objects can be retrieved.

```
hibSession = sessionFactory.openSession();
```

The **openSession()** method of the SesisonFactory interface creates an instance of Session. This instance represents the primary interface to the Hibernate framework

HINT

All the persistence operations are performed using Session objects.

A typical application will usually have:

- A single **Configuration** object, which will only be used in initialization
- One **SessionFactory** object that will exist throughout the life cycle of the application

The application will typically ask this SessionFactory object for a Session, retrieve an object, make the desired property changes and then persist it, all within one session. Finally, the application will close the Session object

Instantiating A Transaction

```
Transaction tx = null;
```

An empty instance of **Transaction** is created

Instantiating The JavaBean class [POJO]

```
Guestbook gb = new Guestbook();
```

An object of the GuestBook **JavaBean** class is created

Persisting Data

To insert the captured data:

```
tx = hibSession.beginTransaction();
```

- An instance of the Transaction class is created by invoking the **beginTransaction()** method of the Session interface

```
String guest = request.getParameter("guest");
String message = request.getParameter("message");
```

- The data captured is stored in variables via the getParameter() method

```
String messageDate = new java.util.Date().toString();
```

- The current date is set when the visitor entered data in the Guest Book

```
gb.setVisitorName(guest);
gb.setMessage(message);
gb.setMessageDate(messageDate);
```

- The variable values are then set in the Guestbook list via the setter methods of the JavaBean class

```
hibSession.save(gb);
```

- The session interface then saves the Guestbook list by invoking the **save()** method. The save() method of the session object allows saving the information to the database table. When an object is passed to the **save()** method, Hibernate reads the state of the variables of that object and executes the required SQL query
- Hibernate would automatically create and fire the INSERT query:

```
INSERT INTO GuestBook (VisitorName, Message, MessageDate)
  VALUES (visitorName, message, messageDate);
```

```
tx.commit();
```

- Finally, the transaction is committed

```
catch (RuntimeException e) {
    if(tx != null) tx.rollback();
    throw e;
}
```

- In case of errors, if any, it is determined if the transaction object is empty. If not, then the transaction is rolled backed

Retrieving Data

To view the data captured via the GuestBookView.jsp file:

```
hibSession.beginTransaction();
```

- An instance of the Transaction class is created by invoking the **beginTransaction()** method of the Session interface

```
guestbook = hibSession.createQuery("from Guestbook").list();
```

- Using **createQuery()** method of the Session object the persistent objects are retrieved. HQL statements are object-oriented, meaning that the query on object properties instead of database table and column names. The createQuery() method returns a collection of all **GuestBook** instances
- Hibernate would automatically create and fire the SELECT query:

```
SELECT * FROM GuestBook;
```

```
    catch (RuntimeException e) {
        throw e;
    }
```

- In case of errors, if any, is trap in the catch block

```
    hibSession.close();
```

- It is a good practice to close the Session when all the work for a transaction is completed

Displaying Retrieved Data

The displaying of the records fetched is handled by:

```
                <%
                    Iterator iterator = guestbook.iterator();
                    while (iterator.hasNext()) {
                        Guestbook objGb = (Guestbook) iterator.next();
                %>
                    <tr>
                        <td style="font:12px/16px Georgia; color:#786e4e;">
                            On <%=objGb.getMessageDate()%>,<br />
                            <b><%=objGb.getVisitorName()%>:</b>
                            <%=objGb.getMessage()%>
                            <br /><br />
                        </td>
                    </tr>
                <%
                    }
                %>
```

Here, an iterator is used to traverse through the List object called guestbook. This list object was populated earlier by:

```
guestbook = hibSession.createQuery("from Guestbook").list();
```

Using <TABLE>, <TR> and <TD> the elements of the List object are placed.

Editing The web.xml File

In NetBeans, by default, the web.xml file uses the index.jsp file as the welcome file i.e. whenever the application is run the web.xml file will display the index.jsp file.

This file needs to be edited to invoke the application's data entry form [GuestBookEntry.jsp] every time it's invoked.

Edit the web.xml file with following contents:

```
<?xml version="1.0" encoding="UTF-8"?>
<web-app version="2.5" xmlns="http://java.sun.com/xml/ns/javaee" xmlns:xsi="http://www.w3.org/2001/XMLSchema-instance" xsi:schemaLocation="http://java.sun.com/xml/ns/javaee http://java.sun.com/xml/ns/javaee/web-app_2_5.xsd">
    <session-config>
        <session-timeout>
            30
        </session-timeout>
    </session-config>
    <welcome-file-list>
        <welcome-file>index.jsp</welcome-file>
        <welcome-file>JSP/GuestBookEntry.jsp</welcome-file>
    </welcome-file-list>
</web-app>
```

Replace this with this

Running The GuestBook Application

Now that the application is ready, let's run this application [source code available on this Book's accompanying CDROM].

Begin by **building** the project, using the NetBeans IDE.

To do so, right click the **GuestBook project** and select the **Build** menu item as shown in diagram 3.9.1.

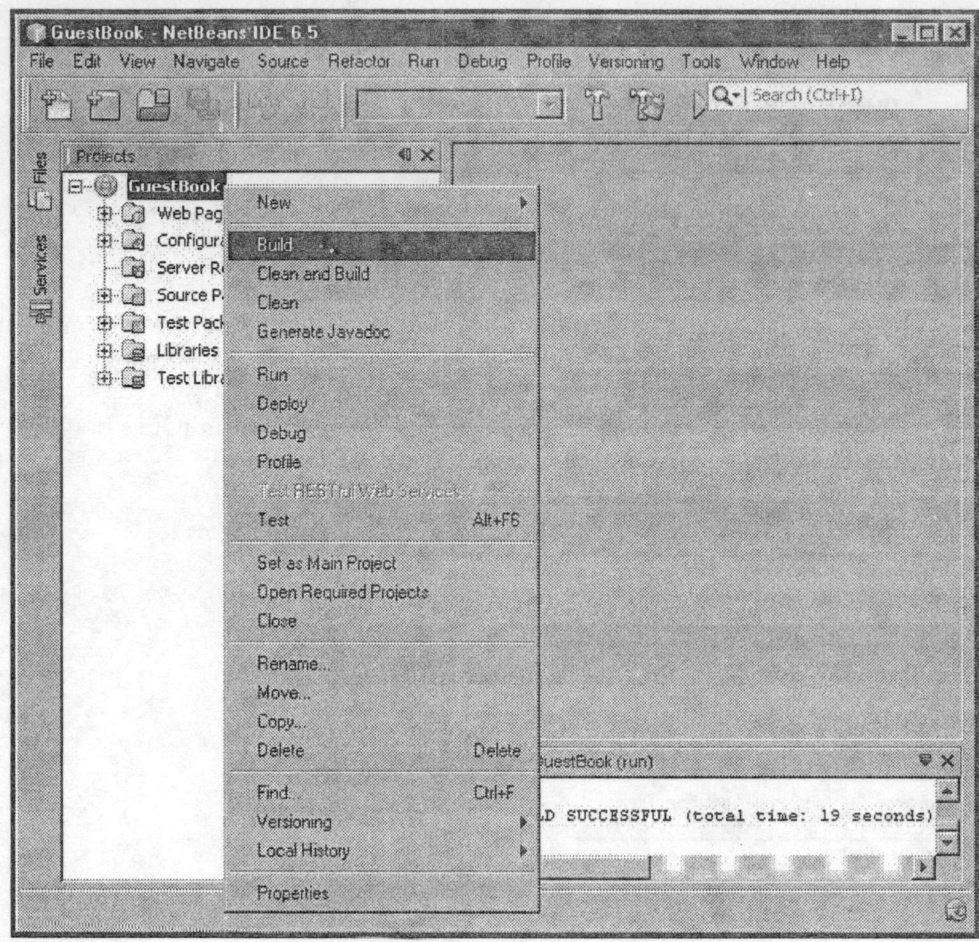

Diagram 3.9.1: Building the project

Then run the application by right clicking the **GuestBook project** and selecting the **Run** menu item as shown in diagram 3.9.2.

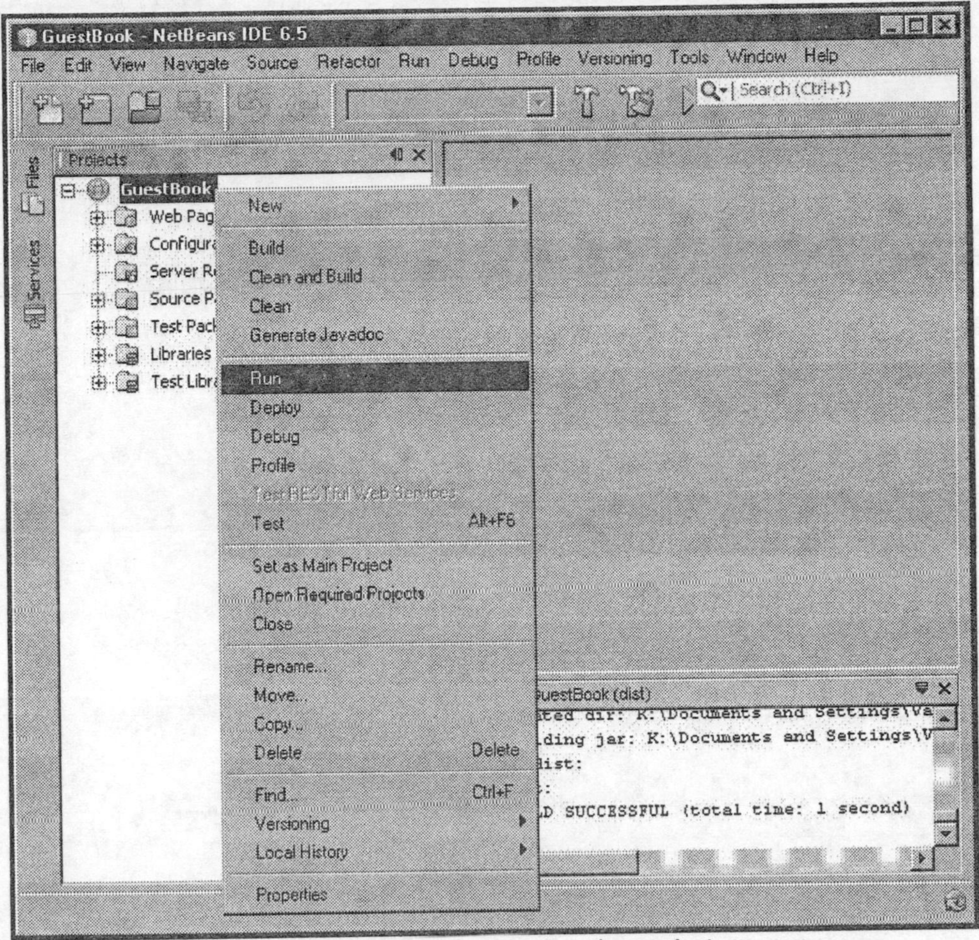

Diagram 3.9.2: Running the project

The GuestBookEntry.jsp page is served in the Web browser as shown in diagram 3.9.3.

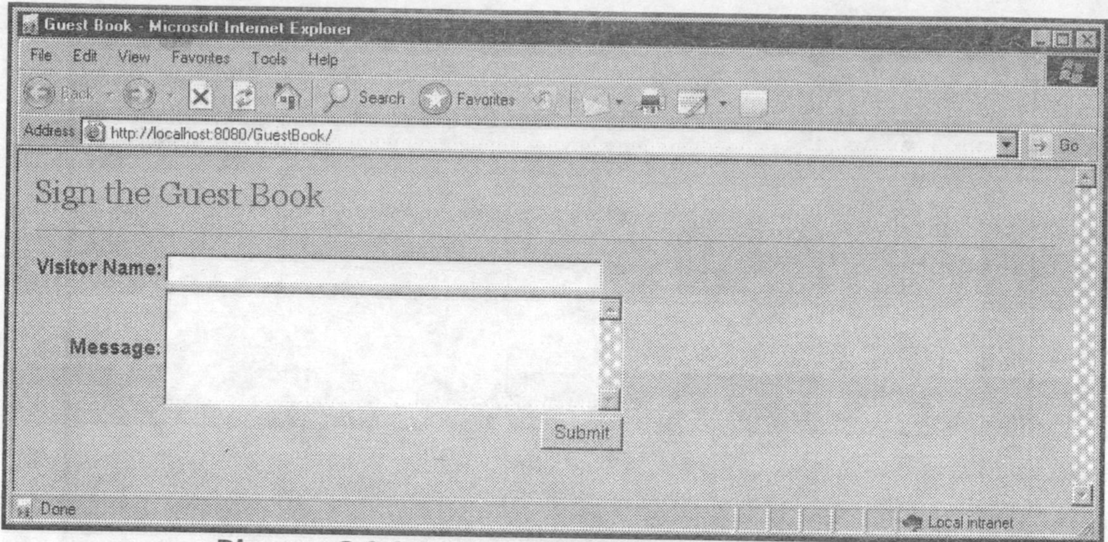

Diagram 3.9.3: The application run in the Web browser

Enter the name and the comments in the Name and Message fields as shown in diagram 3.9.4.

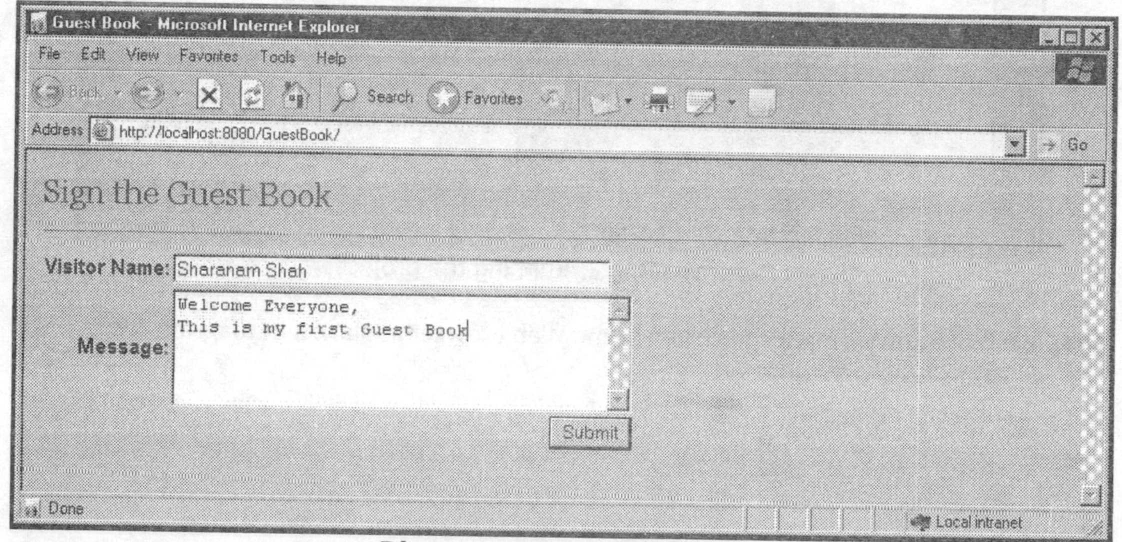

Diagram 3.9.4: Entering data

Click Submit. This displays the already existing messages [entered by others who visited the site before] along with the newly added message.

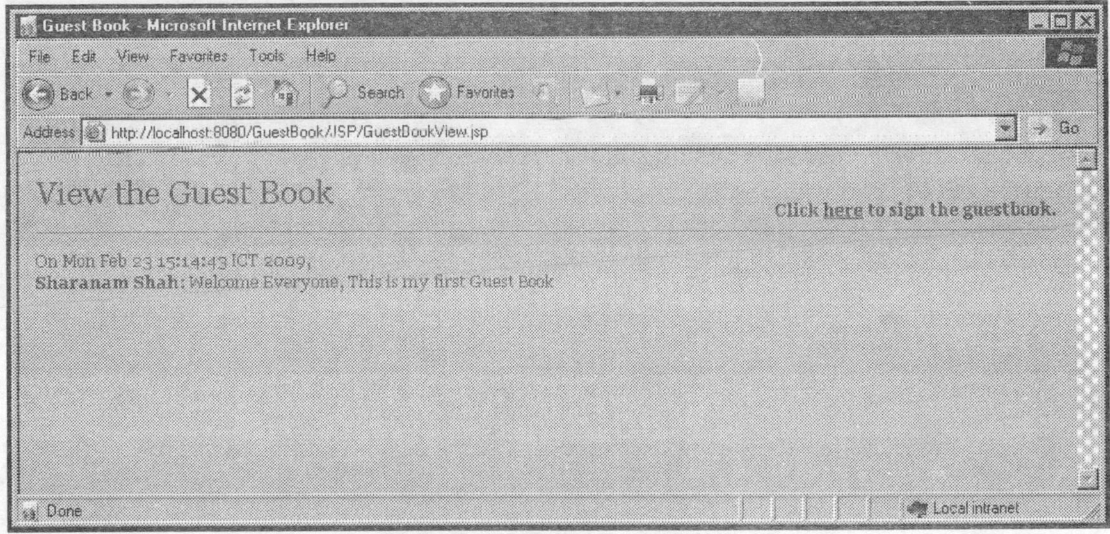

Diagram 3.9.5: Viewing data

When the GuestBookView.jsp page appears, the data entered by the user is stored in the MySQL database table named GuestBook that was created earlier.

To ensure that this was done successfully, open MySQL command line utility and query the table to view the following output:

```
+-----------+---------------+----------------------------------------------+------------------------------+
| VisitorNo | VisitorName   | Message                                      | MessageDate                  |
+-----------+---------------+----------------------------------------------+------------------------------+
|         1 | Sharanam Shah | Welcome Everyone, This is my first Guest Book | Mon Feb 23 15:14:43 ICT 2009 |
+-----------+---------------+----------------------------------------------+------------------------------+
1 row in set (0.00 sec)
```

Click **here** link available on the top right corner of the page to go back to the Guest Book data entry form.

This chapter dealt with building a web application and integrating Hibernate into that application that exemplifies the core Hibernate concepts discussed in the first two chapters.

The next chapter demonstrates building the same application using Hibernate plugins [reverse engineering from database tables] available in the NetBeans IDE. This approach helps reduce a lot of manual code spec.

The Book CDROM holds the complete application source code built using the NetBeans IDE for the following application:

- GuestBook_Chap03

This can be directly used by making appropriate changes [username/password] to the configuration file.

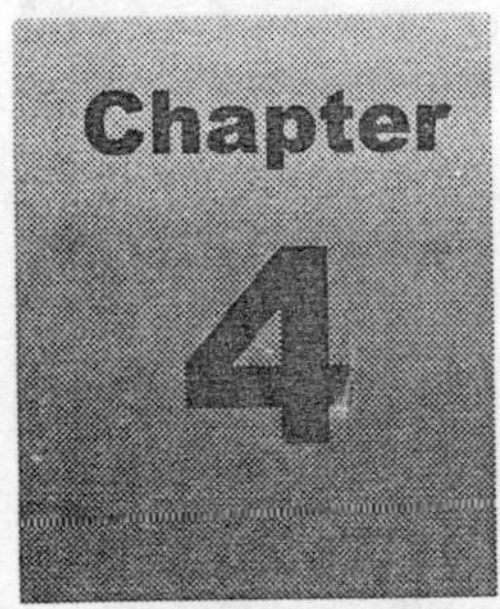

SECTION II: GETTING STARTED

Using Hibernate Tools/Plugins With NetBeans

NetBeans 6.5 ships with Hibernate plug-in [libraries and generators], making it easier than ever to get started with Hibernate.

This plug-in is a set of tools that help the developers to quickly generate the configuration file and database objects from existing database schema. This plug-in can be used to edit hibernate configuration file in the GUI mode. It also highlights the syntax in the editor.

The following list enumerates the hibernate support in the NetBeans IDE 6.5:

- Wizard based creation of hibernate configuration file
- Wizard based creation of hibernate mapping file
- Reverse engineering support
- Support for creating POJO classes
- Code generation for hibernate utility class
- Code completion in hibernate mapping file and configuration file
- HQL Editor

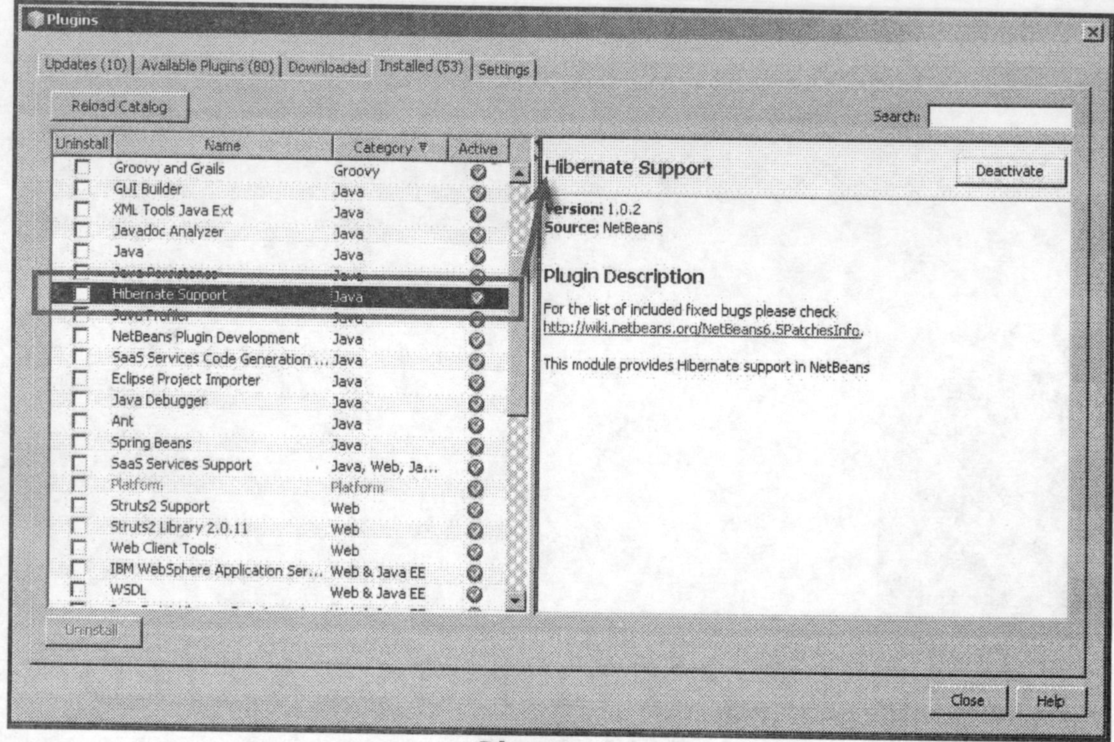

Diagram 4.1

Diagram 4.1 show the Plugins window of the NetBeans IDE [Tools → Plugins] depicting the Hibernate Support plug-in.

Building The GuestBook Application

Let's build the same application created earlier using the Hibernate support plug-in in the NetBeans IDE 6.5.

Preparing The Database

Log in to the MySQL database server using the root user and the appropriate password.

Creating The GuestBook Database

```
CREATE DATABASE GuestBook;

USE GuestBook;
```

Creating The GuestBook Table

```
CREATE TABLE GuestBook(
  VisitorNo Int PRIMARY KEY AUTO_INCREMENT,
  VisitorName varchar(50),
  Message varchar(100),
  MessageDate varchar(40));
```

Creating A Web Application

Open the NetBeans IDE and create a new Web application [File → New Project → Java Web → Web Application] called **GuestBook**.

Choose the desired server, keep the defaults for the Java EE version and the context path as shown in diagram 4.2.1.

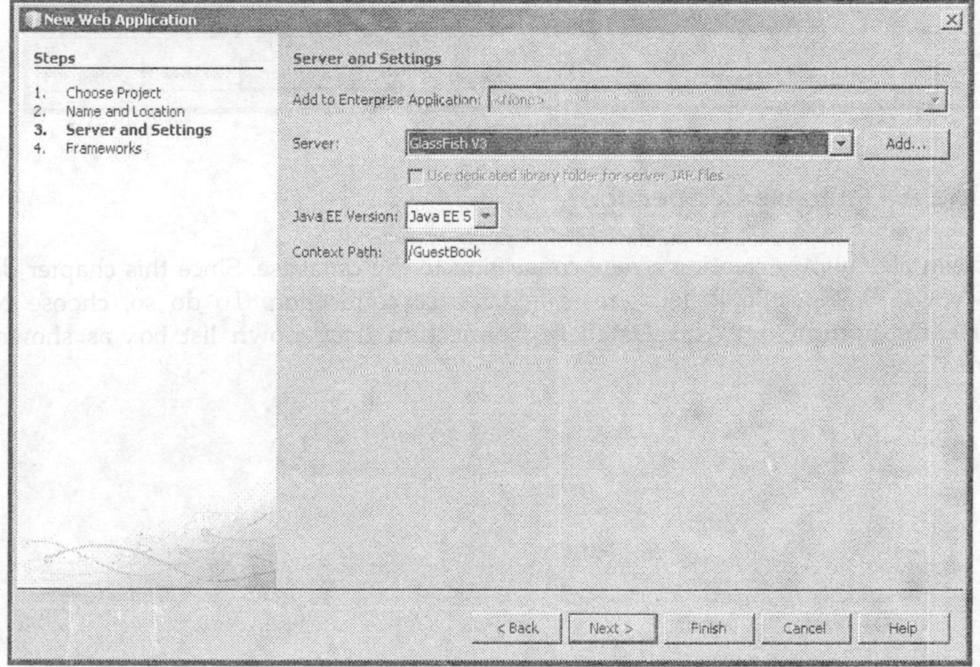

Diagram 4.2.1

Click Next >. This prompts to choose a framework. Choose **Hibernate 3.2.5** as the framework as shown in diagram 4.2.2.

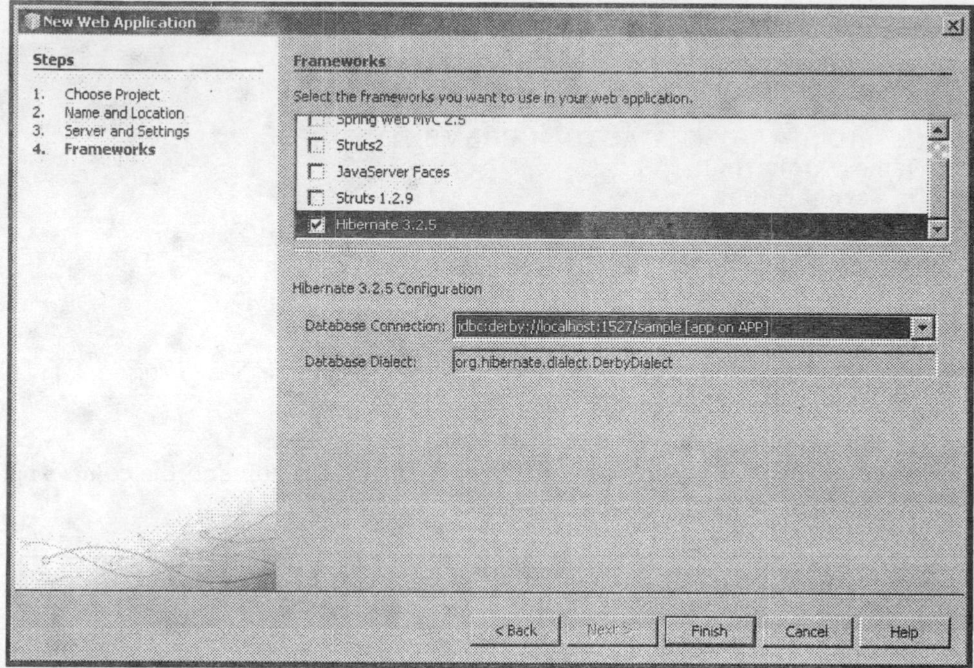

Diagram 4.2.2

Creating A Database Connection

This screen also allows creating a new connection to the database. Since this chapter deals with MySQL → GuestBook, let's create a database connection. To do so, choose **New Database Connection** from the **Database Connection** drop down list box as shown in diagram 4.2.3.

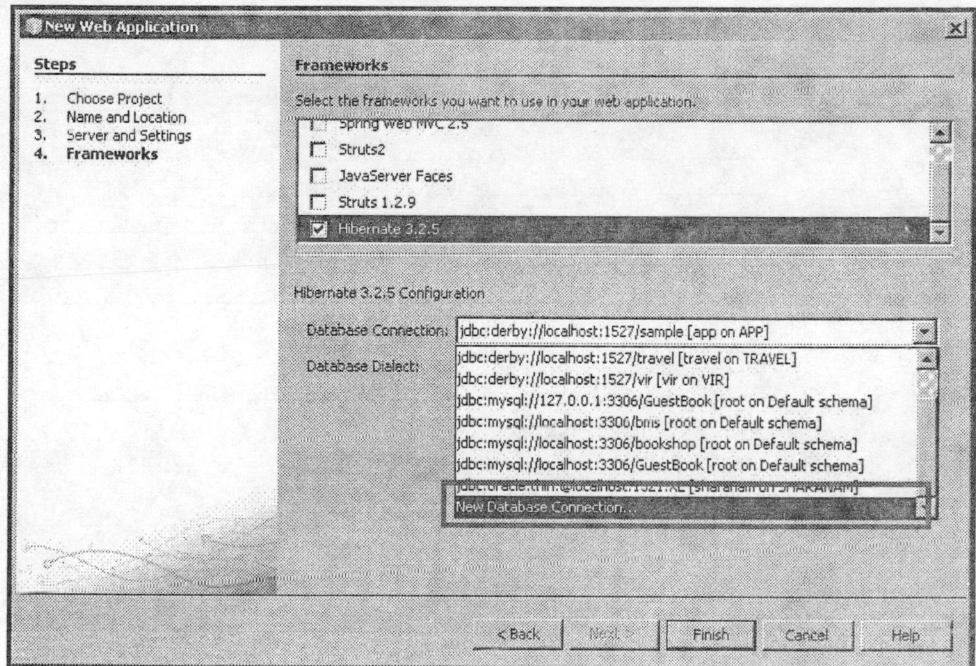

Diagram 4.2.3

This brings up the **New Database Connection** dialog box. Key in the following details as shown in diagram 4.2.4:

- **Name:** MySQL (Connector/J driver)
- **Host:** localhost
- **Port:** 3306
- **Database:** GuestBook
- **User Name:** root
- **Password:** <the_actual_password>

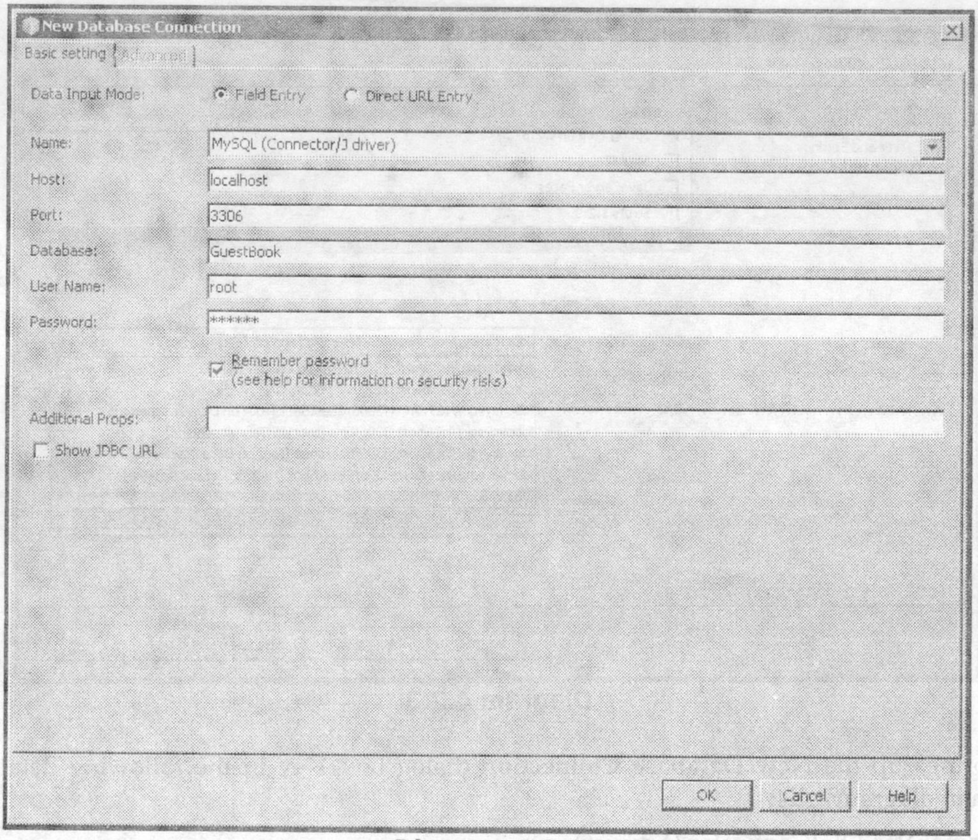

Diagram 4.2.4

Click [OK] when done. The new connection is added to the list of already existing connections as shown in diagram 4.2.5.

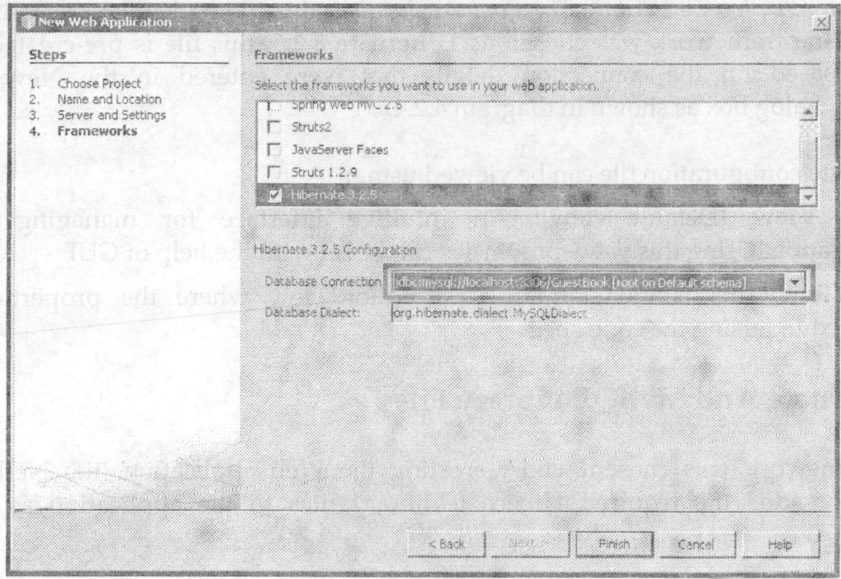

Diagram 4.2.5

Click Finish when done. This brings up the Web application in NetBeans IDE with the Hibernate Configuration file [hibernate.cfg.xml], pre-created and pre-populated as shown in diagram 4.2.6.

The Hibernate Configuration File

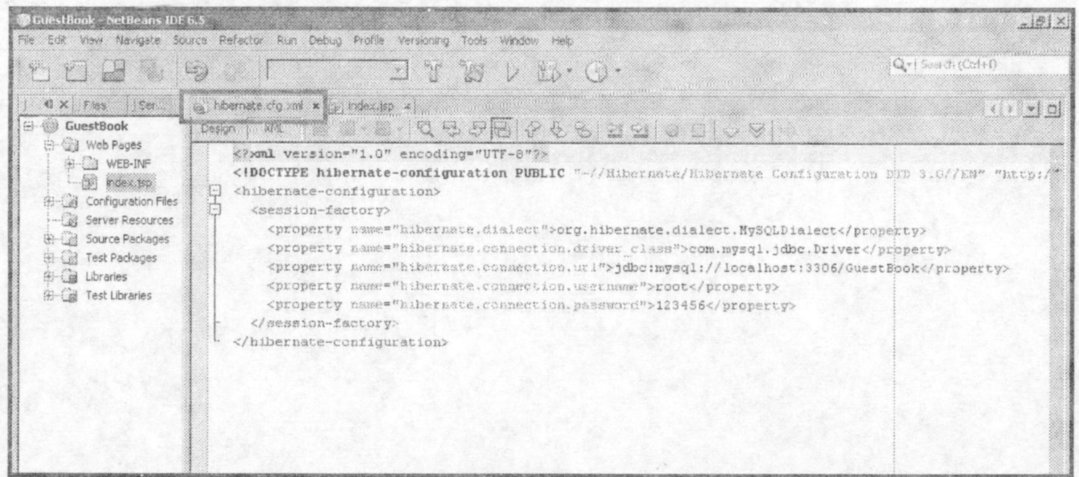

Diagram 4.2.6

In the earlier *Chapter 03: Writing The First Application*, this file had to be created manually. Here, since the framework was chosen as **Hibernate 3.2.5**, this file is pre-created and pre-populated based on the connection details that were entered in the **New Database Connection** dialog box as shown in diagram 4.2.4.

The Hibernate configuration file can be viewed using:

- **Design View** [Default view]: An intuitive interface for managing Hibernate configuration. Using this view, properties can be set with the help of GUI
- **XML View:** This is the standard text editor view where the properties can be added/edited using the code spec

The Hibernate And MySQL Library Files

Since a framework was chosen whilst creating the Web application, the NetBeans IDE automatically adds the required Hibernate library files to the application as shown in diagram 4.2.7.

In addition to the library files required for Hibernate, the wizard also adds the appropriate JDBC driver file to the Web application. In this case the database server of choice being MySQL, the MySQL JDBC driver is added as well as shown in diagram 4.2.7.

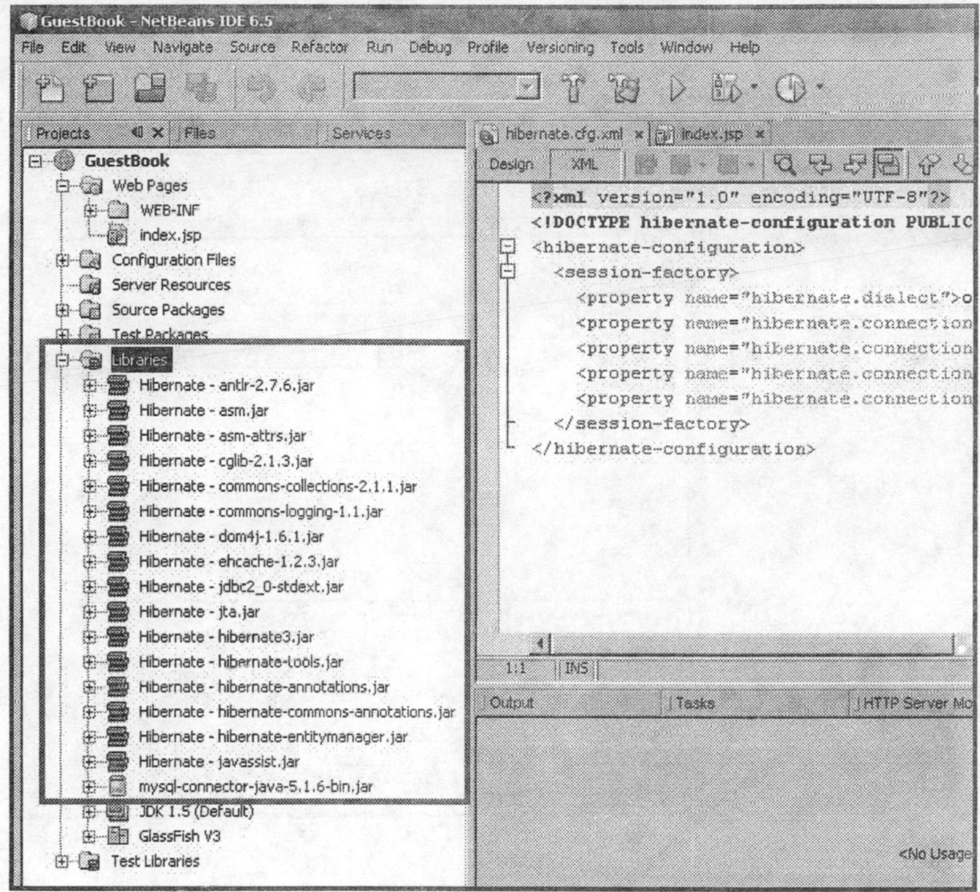

Diagram 4.2.7

Generating POJOs And Mapping Documents [Reverse Engineering]

The GuestBook database has a table called GuestBook. It is required to create a corresponding **Java class** [POJO] with fields corresponding to the columns available in the GuestBook table as well a **Hibernate Mapping document**.

POJOs, are the entity classes. With the support of the Hibernate plug-in in NetBeans, these POJO will now be automatically created.

To do so, right click on the project [GuestBook] under the **Projects** tab and select **New → Other**.

This brings up the **New file** dialog box.

Choose **Hibernate** under the **Categories** list and **Hibernate Mapping Files and POJOs from Database** under the **File Types** list as shown in diagram 4.2.8.

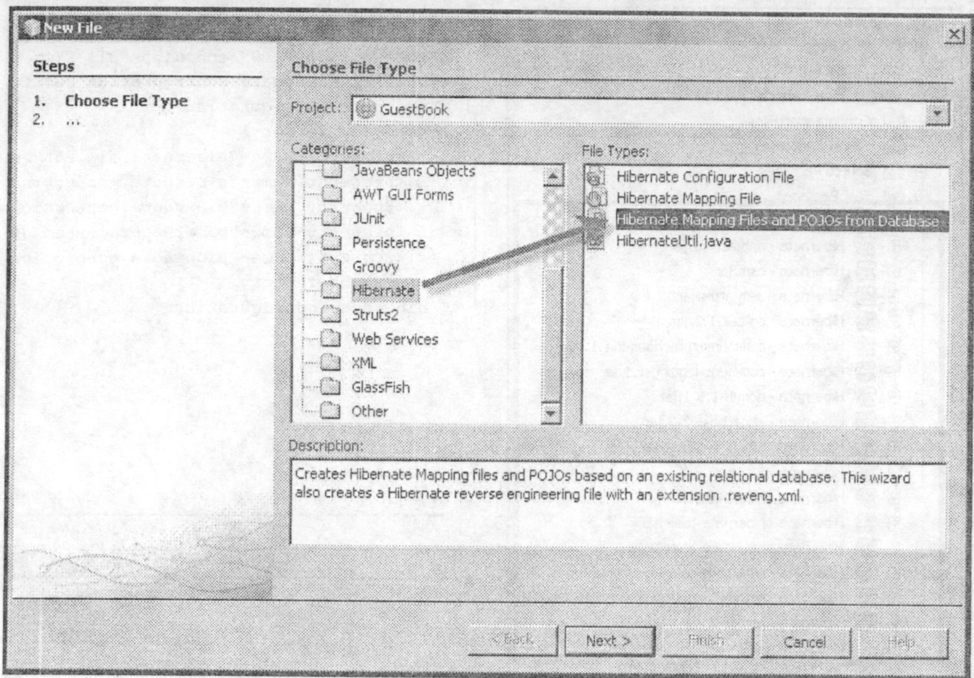

Diagram 4.2.8

Click Next >. This shows the **New Hibernate Mapping Files and POJOs from Database** dialog box as shown in diagram 4.2.9.

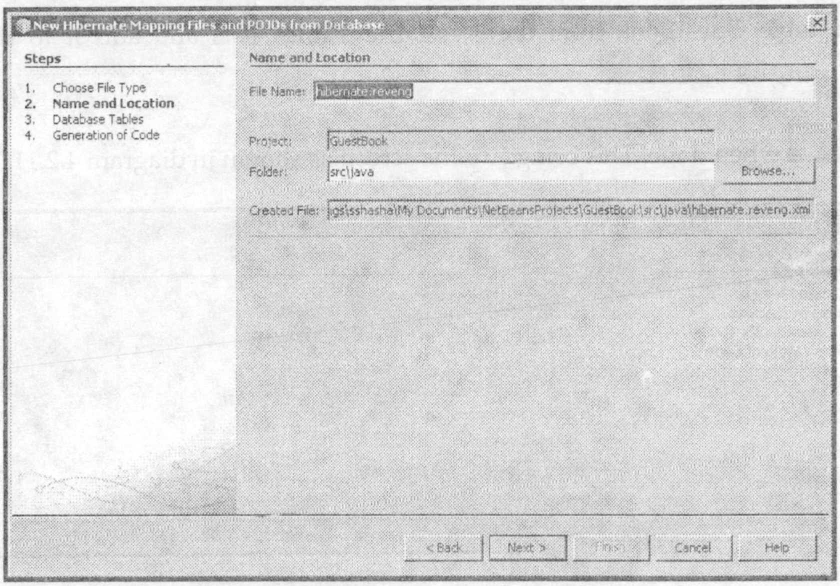

Diagram 4.2.9

Keep the defaults and click Next >. This brings up the screen as shown in diagram 4.2.10.

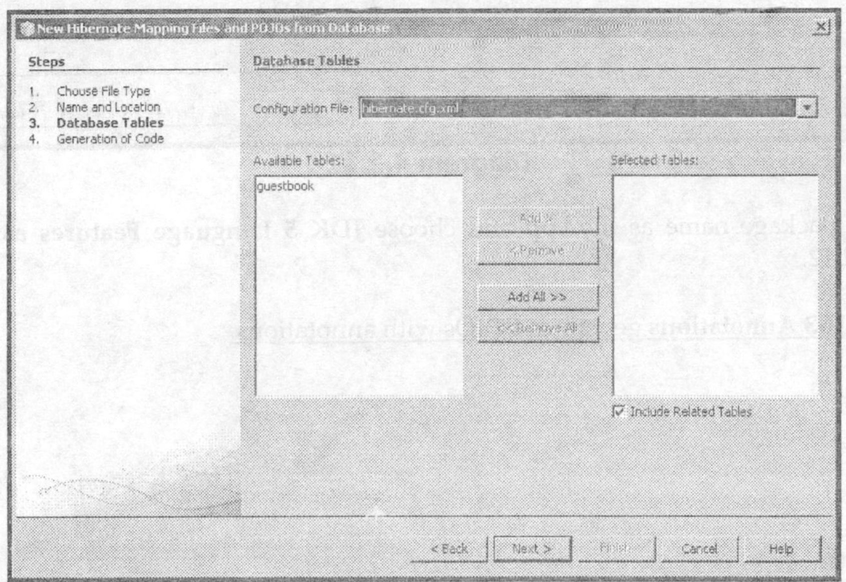

Diagram 4.2.10

Choose the table GuestBook from the **Available Tables** lists and add it to the **Selected Tables** list using [Add >].

Click [Next >] when done. This brings up the screen as shown in diagram 4.2.11.

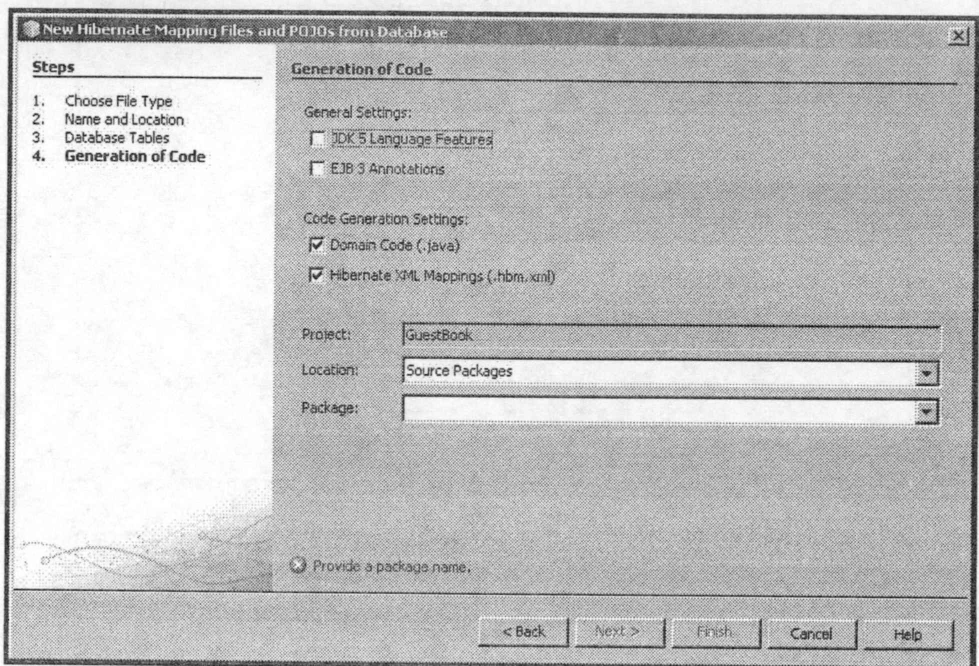

Diagram 4.2.11

Key in the package name as **myApp** and choose **JDK 5 Language Features** as shown in diagram 4.2.12.

<u>Choosing **EJB3 Annotations** generates POJOs with annotations.</u>

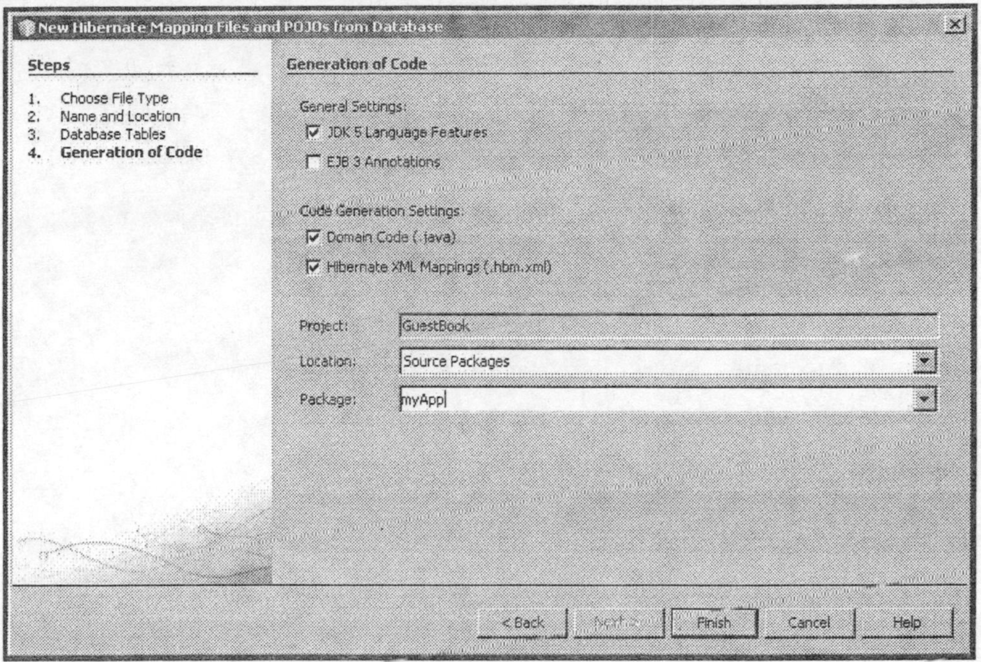

Diagram 4.2.12

Click Finish when done. This begins the file creation process and the progress is indicated using a progress bar.

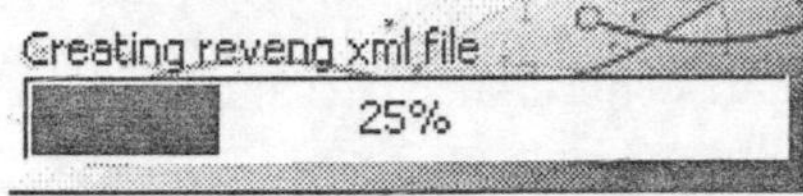

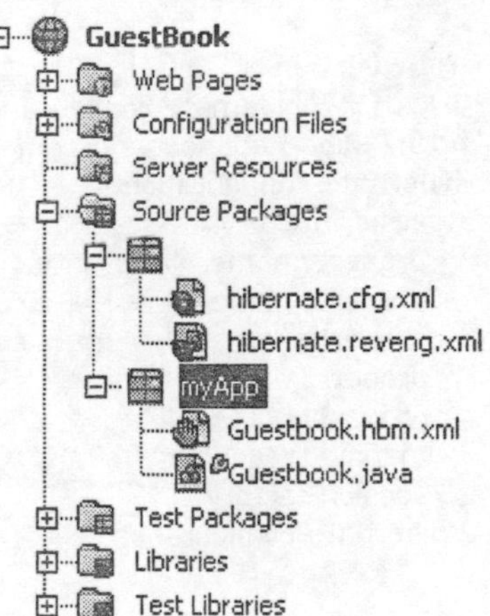

This creates the following files:

- hibernate.reveng.xml: Placed under src/java

  This file simply holds the details of the reverse engineering performed. <u>This file can be deleted</u>

- Guestbook.hbm.xml: Placed under the package that the user selected

  <u>This is the Hibernate Mapping document</u>

- Guestbook.java: Placed under the package that the user selected in the fourth pane

  <u>This is the POJO</u>

The Mapping Document [Guestbook.hbm.xml]

```
<?xml version="1.0"?>
<!DOCTYPE hibernate-mapping PUBLIC "-//Hibernate/Hibernate Mapping DTD 3.0//EN"
"http://hibernate.sourceforge.net/hibernate-mapping-3.0.dtd">
<!-- Generated Feb 27, 2009 9:53:48 AM by Hibernate Tools 3.2.1.GA -->
<hibernate-mapping>
  <class name="myApp.Guestbook" table="guestbook" catalog="guestbook">
    <id name="visitorNo" type="java.lang.Integer">
      <column name="VisitorNo" />
      <generator class="identity" />
    </id>
    <property name="visitorName" type="string">
      <column name="VisitorName" length="50" />
    </property>
    <property name="message" type="string">
      <column name="Message" length="100" />
    </property>
    <property name="messageDate" type="string">
      <column name="MessageDate" length="40" />
    </property>
  </class>
</hibernate-mapping>
```

Since a mapping file is created using the wizard, the wizard automatically adds the mapping reference to the Hibernate configuration file [hibernate.cfg.xml].

The Modified Hibernate Configuration File [hibernate.cfg.xml]

```
<?xml version="1.0" encoding="UTF-8"?>
<!DOCTYPE hibernate-configuration PUBLIC "-//Hibernate/Hibernate Configuration DTD 3.0//EN"
"http://hibernate.sourceforge.net/hibernate-configuration-3.0.dtd">
<hibernate-configuration>
  <session-factory>
    <property name="hibernate.dialect">org.hibernate.dialect.MySQLDialect</property>
    <property name="hibernate.connection.driver_class">com.mysql.jdbc.Driver</property>
    <property name="hibernate.connection.url">jdbc:mysql://localhost:3306/GuestBook</property>
    <property name="hibernate.connection.username">root</property>
    <property name="hibernate.connection.password">123456</property>
    <mapping resource="myApp/Guestbook.hbm.xml"/>
  </session-factory>
</hibernate-configuration>
```

The POJO [Guestbook.java]

```
package myApp;
// Generated Feb 27, 2009 9:53:40 AM by Hibernate Tools 3.2.1.GA
/**
 * Guestbook generated by hbm2java
 */
public class Guestbook  implements java.io.Serializable {
     private Integer visitorNo;
     private String visitorName;
     private String message;
     private String messageDate;

    public Guestbook() {
    }

    public Guestbook(String visitorName, String message, String messageDate) {
       this.visitorName = visitorName;
       this.message = message;
       this.messageDate = messageDate;
    }

    public Integer getVisitorNo() {
        return this.visitorNo;
    }

    public void setVisitorNo(Integer visitorNo) {
        this.visitorNo = visitorNo;
    }
    public String getVisitorName() {
        return this.visitorName;
    }

    public void setVisitorName(String visitorName) {
        this.visitorName = visitorName;
    }
    public String getMessage() {
        return this.message;
    }

    public void setMessage(String message) {
        this.message = message;
    }
    public String getMessageDate() {
        return this.messageDate;
    }

    public void setMessageDate(String messageDate) {
        this.messageDate = messageDate;
    }
}
```

Reverse Engineering

Column Name	Datatype	NOT NULL	AUTO INC
VisitorNo	INTEGER	✔	✔
VisitorName	VARCHAR(50)		
Message	VARCHAR(100)		
MessageDate	VARCHAR(40)		

Adding Web Pages [JSP]

Before creating the JSP, let's create a directory to hold JSP.

The following are the steps to create the directory:

1. Right click **Web Pages** directory, select **New → Folder...** as shown in diagram 4.2.13

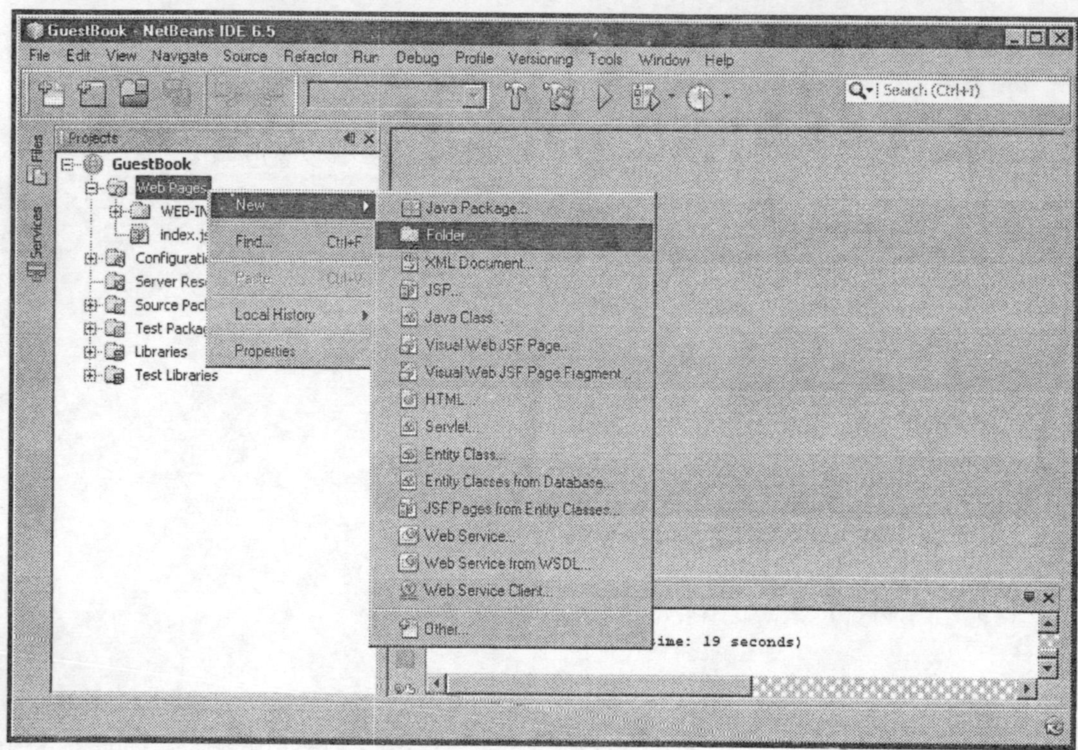

Diagram 4.2.13: Creating Folder

2. Enter the name **JSP** in the **Folder Name** textbox as shown in diagram 4.2.14

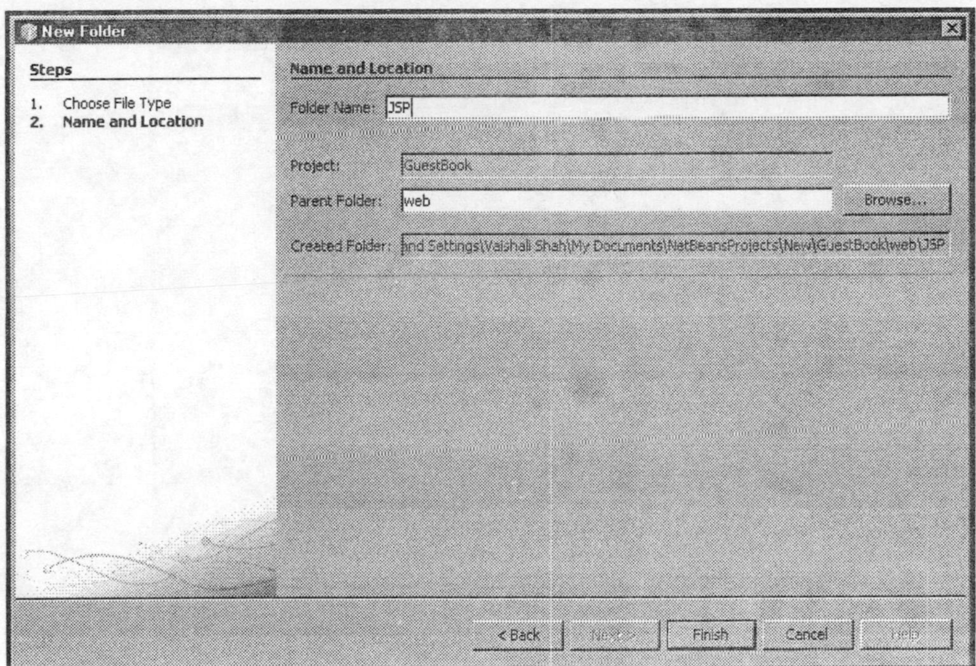

Diagram 4.2.14: Naming the folder

3. Click **Finish**

This creates the directory named **JSP** under **Web Pages**.

The following are the steps to create the JSP file:

1. Right click **JSP** directory, select **New → JSP...** as shown in diagram 4.2.15

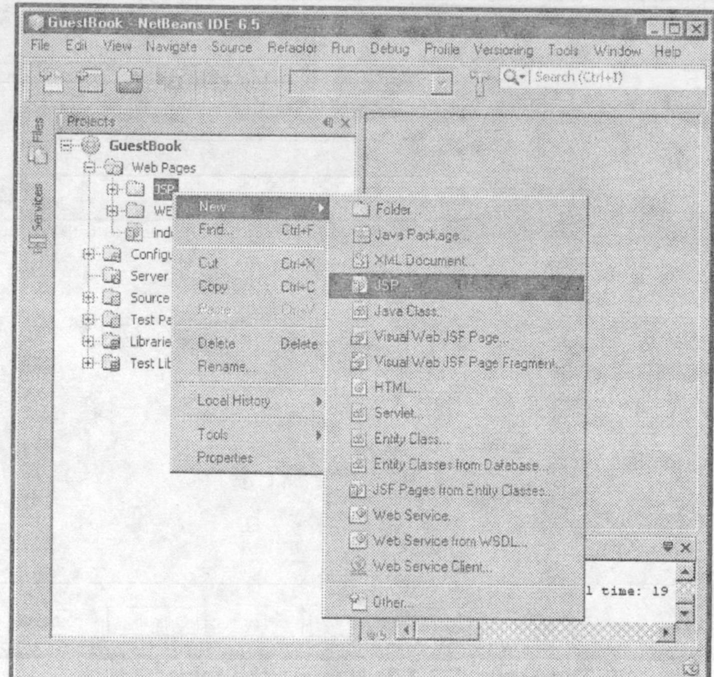

Diagram 4.2.15: Creating JSP file

2. Enter the name **GuestBookEntry** in the **JSP File Name** textbox as shown in diagram 4.2.16

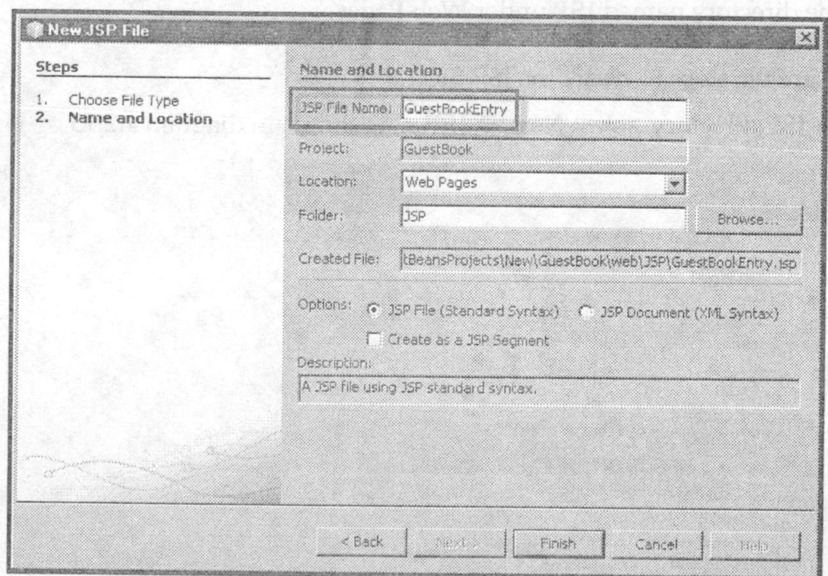

Diagram 4.2.16: Naming the JSP file

3. Click **Finish**

This creates the JSP named GuestBookEntry.jsp under the JSP directory created earlier.

GuestBookEntry.jsp [Code Spec]

Edit the **GuestBookEntry.jsp** file with the following contents.

```
<%@ page language="java" contentType="text/html; charset=ISO-8859-1"
pageEncoding="ISO-8859-1"%>
<!DOCTYPE html PUBLIC "-//W3C//DTD HTML 4.01 Transitional//EN"
"http://www.w3.org/TR/html4/loose.dtd">
<html>
   <head>
      <meta http-equiv="Content-Type" content="text/html;charset=ISO-8859-1">
      <title>Guest Book</title>
   </head>
   <body bgcolor="pink">
      <table border="0" cellpadding="0" cellspacing="0" align="center" width="760">
         <tr>
            <td>
               <table border="0" cellpadding="0" cellspacing="0" width="100%">
                  <tr>
                     <td valign="top" align="left" style="padding-right:0px; padding-left:0px;
                     padding-bottom:0px; font:24px/30px Georgia; width:228px;
                     color:#786e4e; padding-top:0px; height:37px;">
                        Sign the Guest Book
                     </td>
                  </tr>
               </table>
            </td>
         </tr>
         <tr align="left" valign="top">
            <td height="20">
               <hr />
            </td>
         </tr>
         <tr>
            <td>
```

```
            <form action="<%=request.getContextPath()%>/JSP/GuestBookView.jsp"
            method="post">
                <table border="0" cellpadding="0" cellspacing="2">
                    <tr>
                        <td align="right">
                            <font style="font-size:15px; font-family:Arial,Times,serif;
                            font-weight:bold;">Visitor Name:</font>
                        </td>
                        <td>
                            <input name="guest" maxlength="25" size="50" />
                        </td>
                    </tr>
                    <tr>
                        <td align="right">
                            <font style="font-size:15px; font-family:Arial,Times,serif;
                            font-weight:bold;">Message:</font>
                        </td>
                        <td>
                            <textarea rows="5" cols="40" name="message"></textarea>
                        </td>
                    </tr>
                    <tr>
                        <td colspan="2" align="right">
                            <input type="submit" name="btnSubmit" value="Submit" />
                        </td>
                    </tr>
                </table>
            </form>
        </td>
    </tr>
  </table>
 </body>
</html>
```

GuestBookView.jsp [Code Spec]

Using NetBeans create one more JSP called GuestBookView.jsp using the same steps as shown earlier.

Edit the **GuestBookView.jsp** file with the following contents.

```
<%@page contentType="text/html" pageEncoding="UTF-8"
import="org.hibernate.SessionFactory, org.hibernate.cfg.Configuration,
org.hibernate.Session, org.hibernate.Transaction, java.util.List, java.util.Iterator,
myApp.Guestbook" %>
<!DOCTYPE HTML PUBLIC "-//W3C//DTD HTML 4.01 Transitional//EN"
  "http://www.w3.org/TR/html4/loose.dtd">
<%!
   SessionFactory sessionFactory;
   org.hibernate.Session hibSession;
   List<Guestbook> guestbook;
%>

<%
   sessionFactory = new Configuration().configure().buildSessionFactory();
   hibSession = sessionFactory.openSession();
   Transaction tx = null;

   String submit = request.getParameter("btnSubmit");
   if(submit != null && ("Submit").equals(submit)) {
      Guestbook gb = new Guestbook();
      try {
         tx = hibSession.beginTransaction();

         String guest = request.getParameter("guest");
         String message = request.getParameter("message");
         String messageDate = new java.util.Date().toString();
         gb.setVisitorName(guest);
         gb.setMessage(message);
         gb.setMessageDate(messageDate);

         hibSession.save(gb);
         tx.commit();
      }
      catch (RuntimeException e) {
         if(tx != null) tx.rollback();
         throw e;
      }
      response.sendRedirect("GuestBookView.jsp");
   }
```

```

  try {
      hibSession.beginTransaction();
      guestbook = hibSession.createQuery("from Guestbook").list();
  }
  catch (RuntimeException e) {
      throw e;
  }

  hibSession.close();
%>
<html>
  <head>
      <meta http-equiv="Content-Type" content="text/html;charset=ISO-8859-1">
      <title>Guest Book</title>
  </head>
  <body bgcolor="pink">
      <table border="0" cellpadding="0" cellspacing="0" align="center" width="760">
          <tr>
              <td>
                  <table border="0" cellpadding="0" cellspacing="0" width="100%">
                      <tr>
                          <td width="60%" valign="top" align="left" style="padding-right:0px; padding-left:0px; padding-bottom:0px; font:24px/30px Georgia; width:228px; color:#786e4e; padding-top:0px; height:37px;">
                              View the Guest Book
                          </td>
                          <td valign="bottom" align="right" style="font:12px/16px Georgia, serif; color:#786e4e;">
                              <b>Click <a href="<%=request.getContextPath()%>/JSP/GuestBookEntry.jsp">here</a> to sign the guestbook.</b>
                          </td>
                      </tr>
                  </table>
              </td>
          </tr>
          <tr align="left" valign="top">
              <td height="20">
                  <hr />
```

```
            </td>
        </tr>
        <tr>
            <td>
                <table border="0" cellpadding="0" cellspacing="0" align="center" width="100%">
                <%
                    Iterator iterator = guestbook.iterator();
                    while (iterator.hasNext()) {
                        Guestbook objGb = (Guestbook) iterator.next();
                %>
                    <tr>
                        <td style="font:12px/16px Georgia; color:#786e4e;">
                            On <%=objGb.getMessageDate()%>,<br />
                            <b><%=objGb.getVisitorName()%>:</b>
                            <%=objGb.getMessage()%>
                            <br /><br />
                        </td>
                    </tr>
                <%
                    }
                %>
                </table>
            </td>
        </tr>
    </table>
  </body>
</html>
```

Editing web.xml

In NetBeans, by default, the web.xml file takes the index.jsp file as the welcome file i.e. whenever the application is run the web.xml file will display the index.jsp file.

This file needs to be edited to invoke the application's data entry form [GuestBookEntry.jsp] every time it's invoked.

Edit the web.xml file with following contents:

```
<?xml version="1.0" encoding="UTF-8"?>
<web-app version="2.5" xmlns="http://java.sun.com/xml/ns/javaee" xmlns:xsi="http://www.w3.org/2001/XMLSchema-instance"
xsi:schemaLocation="http://java.sun.com/xml/ns/javaee http://java.sun.com/xml/ns/javaee/web-app_2_5.xsd">
    <session-config>
        <session-timeout>
            30
        </session-timeout>
    </session-config>
    <welcome-file-list>
        <welcome-file>index.jsp</welcome-file>
        <welcome-file>JSP/GuestBookEntry.jsp</welcome-file>
    </welcome-file-list>
</web-app>
```

Replace this with this

Running The Web Application

Now that the application is ready, run this application as shown in the earlier chapter [source code available on this Book's accompanying CDROM] to see it working.

The HQL Editor

The queries written in Hibernate are called **H**ibernate **Q**uery **L**anguage. NetBeans IDE provides an HQL editor to test run queries written using HQL.

The HQL Editor can be typically used to construct the HQL queries and sub-queries before using it in the application.

To invoke the HQL editor, right click the Hibernate configuration file [hibernate.cfg.xml] and choose **Run HQL Query**.

This brings up the HQL editor as shown in diagram 4.3.1.

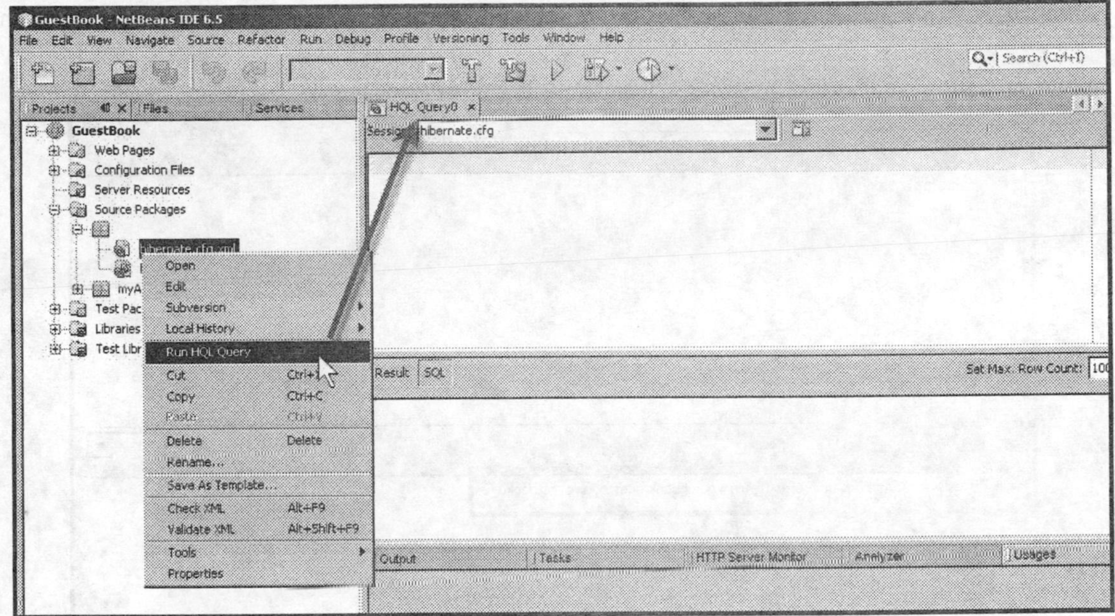

Diagram 4.3.1

Key in the query written using HQL earlier in the GuestBookView.jsp file and click as shown in diagram 4.3.2.

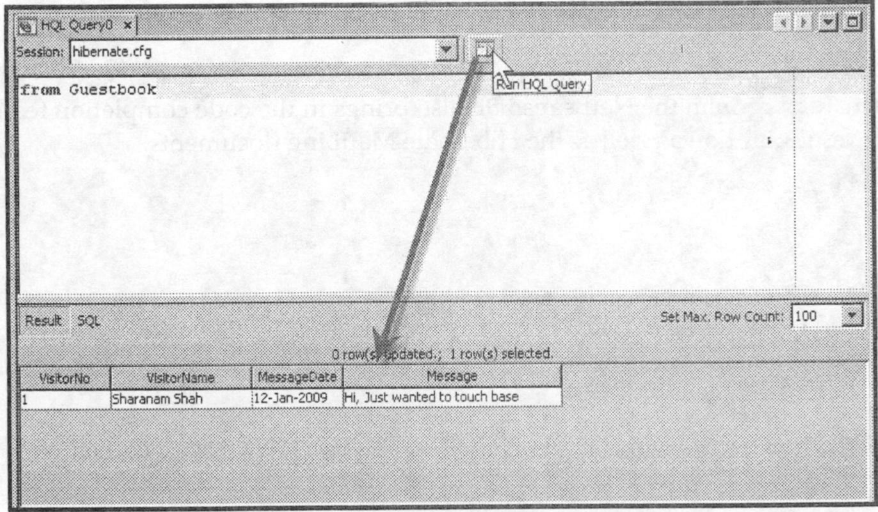

Diagram 4.3.2

Click **SQL** to view the actual SQL query that Hibernate generates and fires as shown in diagram 4.3.3.

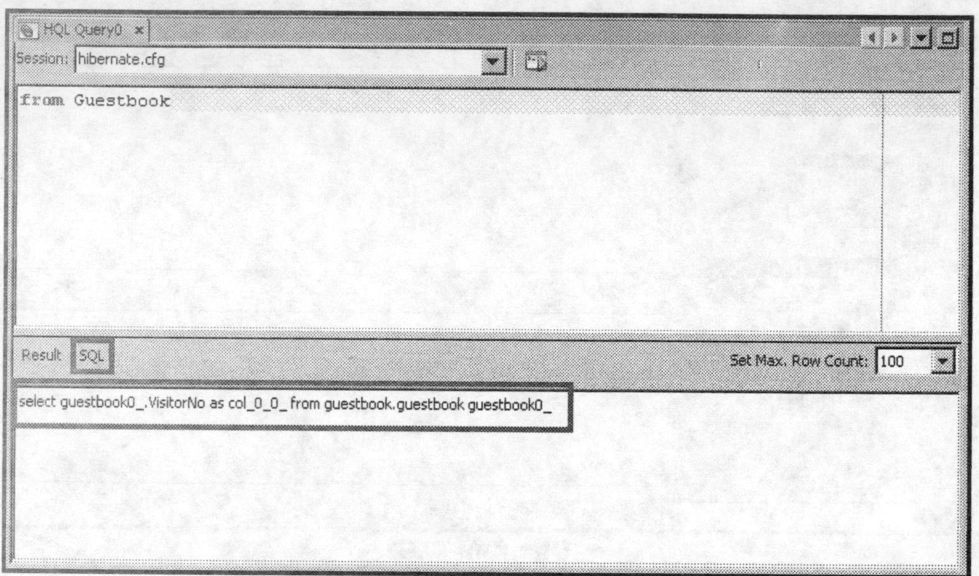

Diagram 4.3.3

HQL will be covered in detail later.

Code Completion

The Hibernate plug-in in the NetBeans IDE also brings in the code completion feature for the Hibernate Configuration as well as the Hibernate Mapping documents.

The Hibernate Configuration File

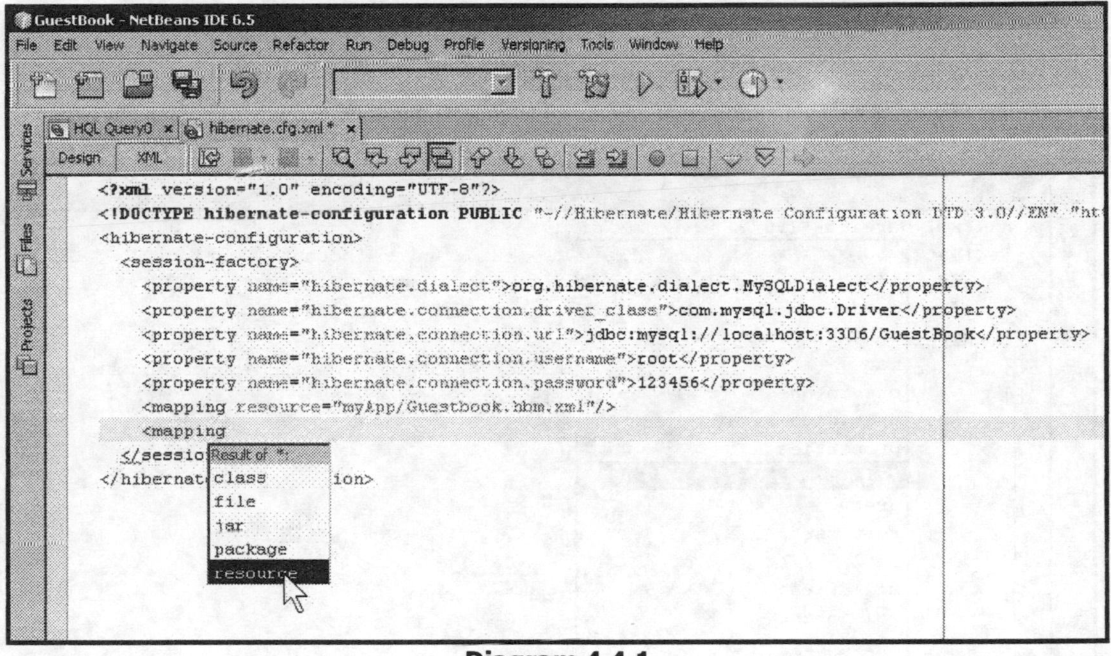

Diagram 4.4.1

The Hibernate Mapping Document

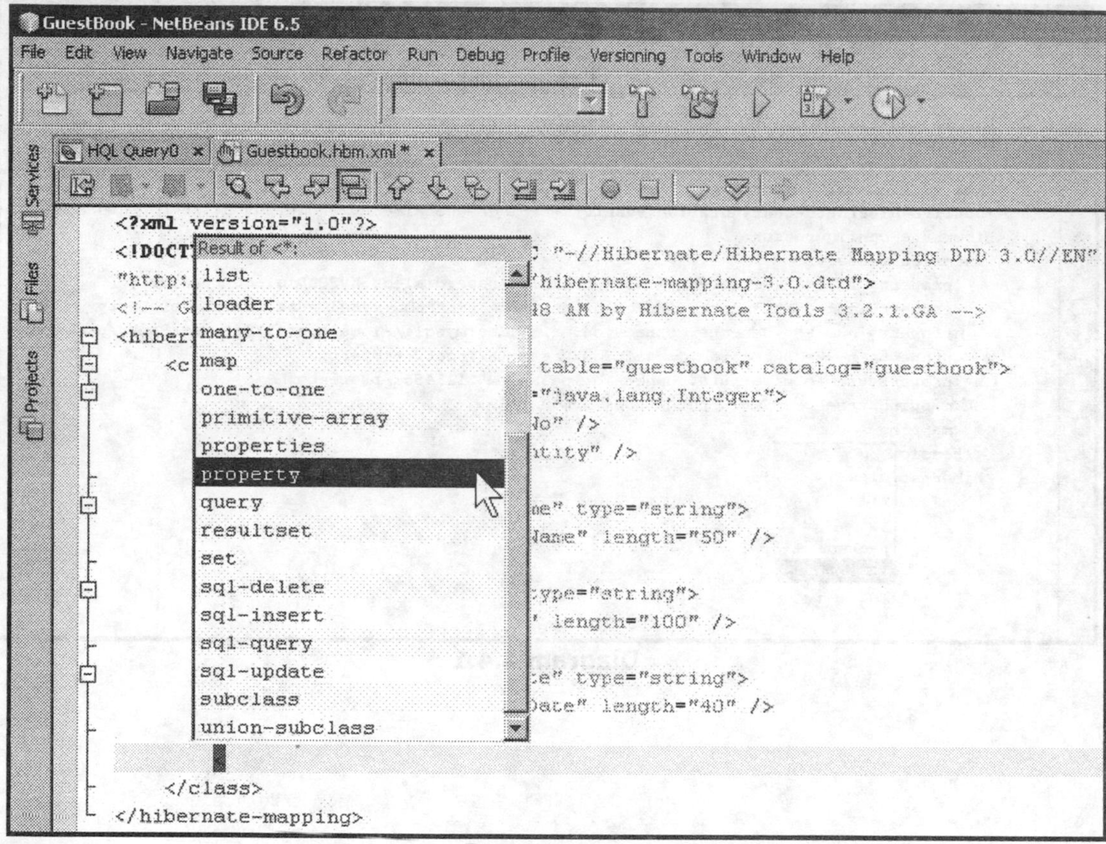

Diagram 4.4.2

Hibernate Annotations Support

Whilst creating the POJO and the Mapping Document, if the user chooses Domain Code [.java] with EJB 3 annotations and without Hibernate XML Mapping [.hbm] as shown in diagram 4.5.1, the wizard generates POJOs with annotations and the configuration file is automatically updated with POJOs.

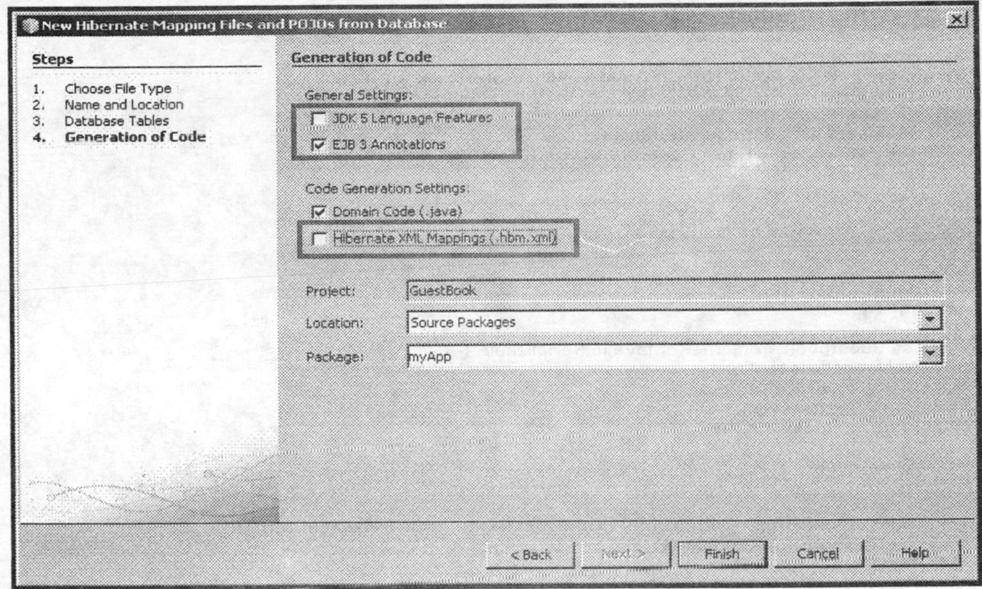

Diagram 4.5.1

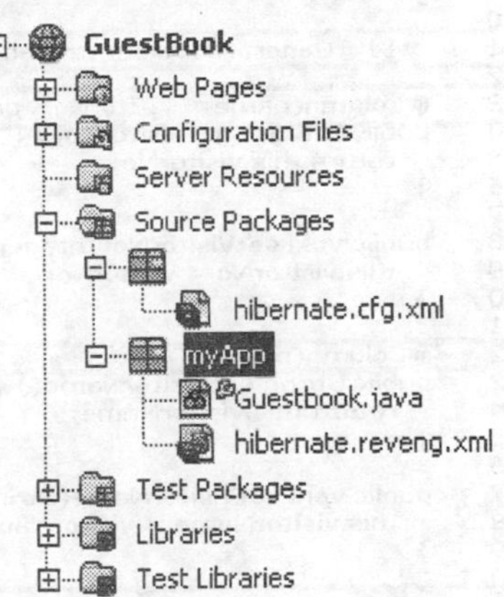

This creates two files:

- hibernate.reveng.xml: Placed under src/java

  This fie simply holds the details of the reverse engineering performed. <u>This file can be deleted</u>

- Guestbook.java: Placed under the package that the user selected in the fourth pane

  <u>This is the POJO</u>

The POJO With Annotations [Guestbook.java]

```
package myApp;
// Generated Feb 27, 2009 10:58:10 AM by Hibernate Tools 3.2.1.GA
import javax.persistence.Column;
import javax.persistence.Entity;
import javax.persistence.GeneratedValue;
import static javax.persistence.GenerationType.IDENTITY;
import javax.persistence.Id;
import javax.persistence.Table;
/**
 * Guestbook generated by hbm2java
 */
@Entity
@Table(name="guestbook"
   ,catalog="guestbook"
)
public class Guestbook  implements java.io.Serializable {
     private Integer visitorNo;
     private String visitorName;
     private String message;
     private String messageDate;

    public Guestbook() {
    }

    public Guestbook(String visitorName, String message, String messageDate) {
       this.visitorName = visitorName;
       this.message = message;
       this.messageDate = messageDate;
    }

     @Id @GeneratedValue(strategy=IDENTITY)

    @Column(name="VisitorNo", unique=true, nullable=false)
    public Integer getVisitorNo() {
       return this.visitorNo;
    }

    public void setVisitorNo(Integer visitorNo) {
       this.visitorNo = visitorNo;
    }

    @Column(name="VisitorName", length=50)
    public String getVisitorName() {
       return this.visitorName;
    }

    public void setVisitorName(String visitorName) {
       this.visitorName = visitorName;
    }

    @Column(name="Message", length=100)
    public String getMessage() {
       return this.message;
    }

    public void setMessage(String message) {
       this.message = message;
    }

    @Column(name="MessageDate", length=40)
    public String getMessageDate() {
       return this.messageDate;
    }

    public void setMessageDate(String messageDate) {
       this.messageDate = messageDate;
    }
}
```

The Updated Hibernate Configuration File [hibernate.cfg.xml]

```
<?xml version="1.0" encoding="UTF-8"?>
<!DOCTYPE hibernate-configuration PUBLIC "-//Hibernate/Hibernate Configuration DTD 3.0//EN"
"http://hibernate.sourceforge.net/hibernate-configuration-3.0.dtd">
<hibernate-configuration>
  <session-factory>
    <property name="hibernate.dialect">org.hibernate.dialect.MySQLDialect</property>
    <property name="hibernate.connection.driver_class">com.mysql.jdbc.Driver</property>
    <property name="hibernate.connection.url">jdbc:mysql://localhost:3306/GuestBook</property>
    <property name="hibernate.connection.username">root</property>
    <property name="hibernate.connection.password">123456</property>
    <mapping class="myApp.Guestbook"/>
  </session-factory>
</hibernate-configuration>
```

Annotations will be covered in detail later.

Re-factoring Support

The Hibernate mapping files are usually referenced by the Hibernate configuration files using the mapping elements:

```
<mapping resource="myApp/Guestbook.hbm.xml"/>
```

If a mapping file is renamed or moved into a different package, the referred mapping entries in the configuration files are changed accordingly.

Try renaming the Mapping file as shown in diagram 4.6.1 and 4.6.2.

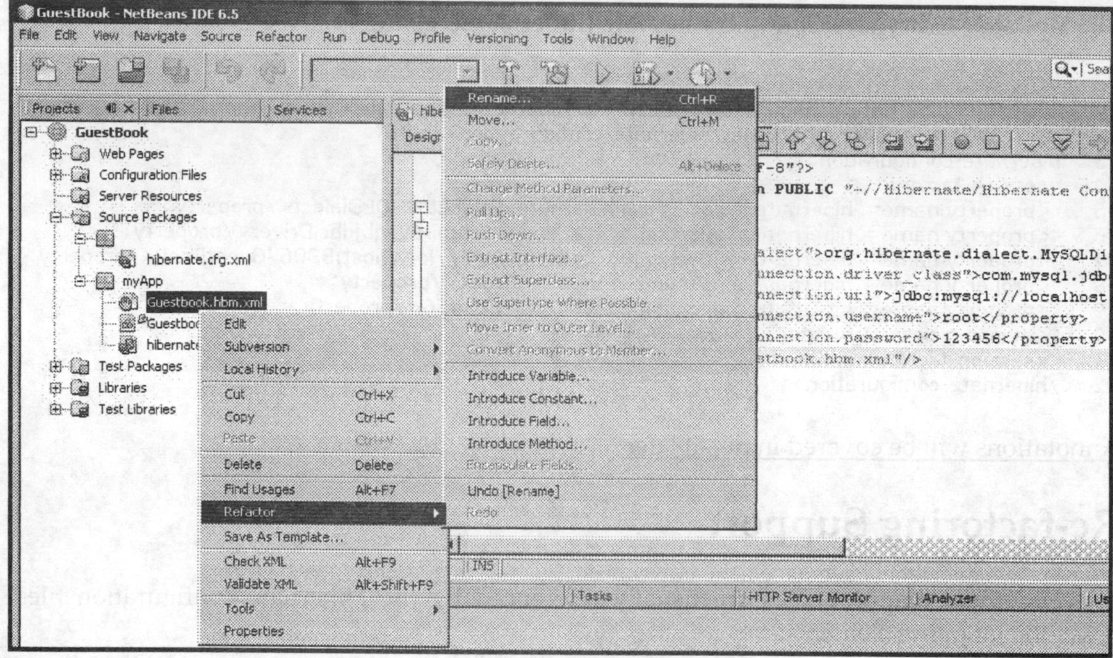

Diagram 4.6.1

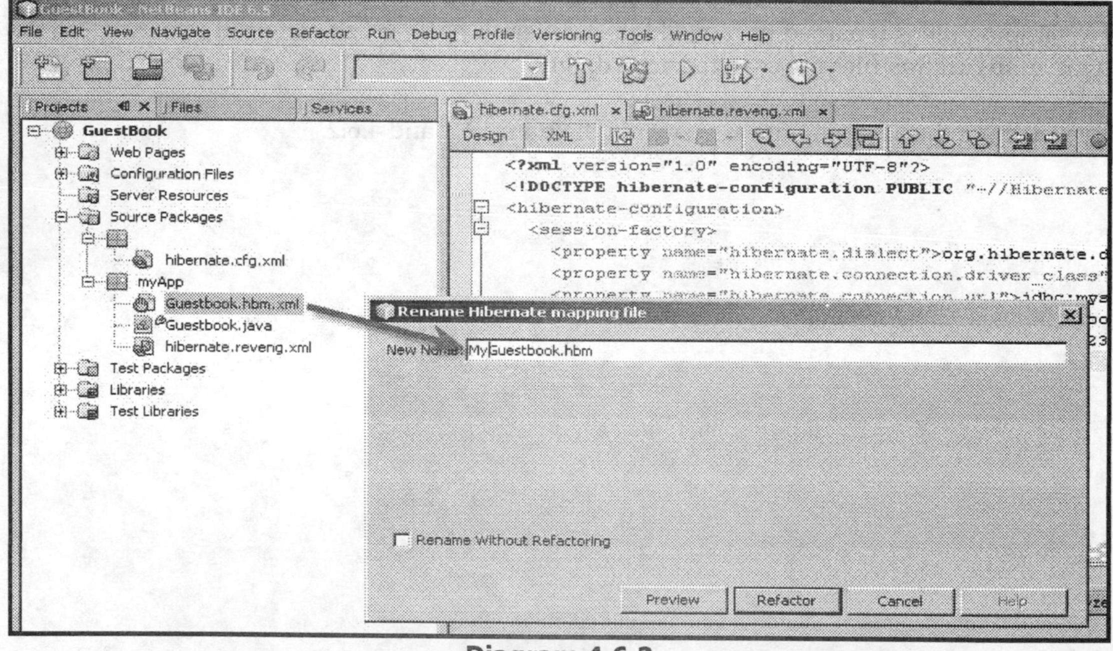

Diagram 4.6.2

Click Refactor.

Notice that the Hibernate configuration file is automatically updated.

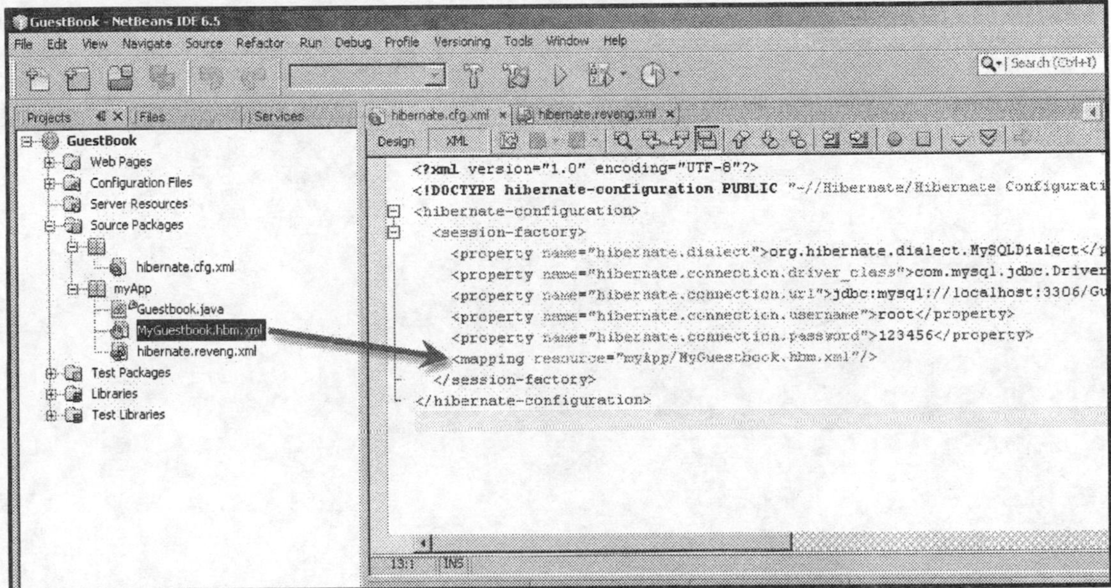

Diagram 4.6.3

The Book CDROM holds the complete application source code built using the NetBeans IDE for the following applications:

- GuestBook_Chap04_Mapping
- GuestBook_Chap04_Annotations

These can be directly used by making appropriate changes [username/password] to the configuration file.

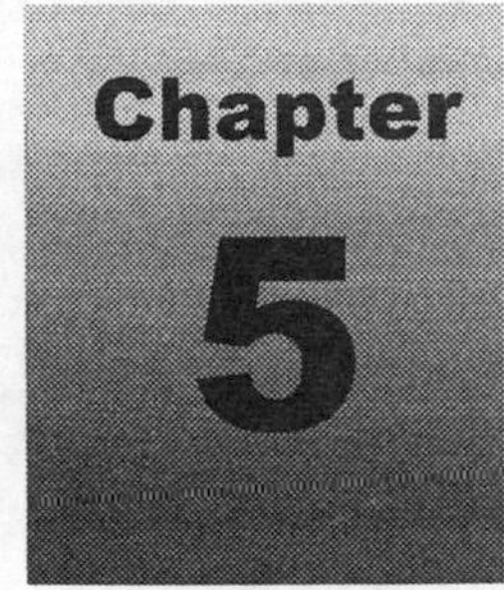

SECTION III: UNDERSTANDING CONFIGURATION AND MAPPING

Configuring Hibernate

Hibernate can be configured to run in almost any Java application and development environment.

Now that a Hibernate application is up and running, it's well worth understanding all the Hibernate configuration parameters and the steps involved in configuring it.

Kinds Of Configurations

Hibernate provides the following kinds of configuration:

- A standard Java .properties file - **hibernate.properties**
- An XML formatted file - **hibernate.cfg.xml**
- Configuring programmatically i.e. in a **.java** file

All the above kinds of configuration perform the same function i.e. configuring the Hibernate service.

Hibernate looks for the configuration file in the class path. If it fails to find one, Hibernate complains about the same using an error message.

HINT

XML formatted file is the recommended option, as it allows specifying the location of the mapping files.

If the standard Java .properties file is used, then the mapping file location needs to be programmatically supplied to Hibernate via the Configuration class.

Configuring Using The hibernate.cfg.xml File

Hibernate offers XML based configuration capabilities. To use them, create an XML configuration file called hibernate.cfg.xml.

This file needs to be placed in the root of the application's class path.

The XML configuration file must confirm to the Hibernate 3 Configuration DTD, which is available from http://hibernate.sourceforge.net/hibernate-configuration-3.0.dtd.

A sample XML based configuration file:

```
<?xml version="1.0" encoding="UTF-8"?>
<!DOCTYPE hibernate-configuration PUBLIC '-//Hibernate/Hibernate Configuration DTD//EN'
'http://hibernate.sourceforge.net/hibernate-configuration-3.0.dtd'>
<hibernate-configuration>
   <session-factory>
      <property name="connection.driver_class">com.mysql.jdbc.Driver</property>
      <property name="connection.url">jdbc:mysql://localhost:3306/GuestBook</property>
      <property name="connection.username">root</property>
      <property name="connection.password">12345678</property>
      <property name="dialect">org.hibernate.dialect.MySQLDialect</property>
      <mapping resource="myApp/GuestBook.hbm.xml"/>
   </session-factory>
</hibernate-configuration>
```

Explanation:

The document type declaration is used by the XML parser to validate this document against the Hibernate configuration DTD.

REMINDER

This DTD is not the same DTD as the one that is used for Hibernate XML mapping files.

HINT

When the XML configuration file is used, there is no need to use the [**hibernate.**] prefix for properties. For example, in the above code spec,

The dialect property is simply called **dialect**
And
Not **hibernate.dialect**

The outer-most element is the hibernate-configuration element which forms the root element for specifying the configuration information.

The next inner element is the session-factory element which corresponds to the SessionFactory class.

The properties within the session-factory element are represented in Hibernate Configuration file using the <property> element.

The configuration file begins with the database connection settings:

```
<property name="connection.driver_class">com.mysql.jdbc.Driver</property>
<property name="connection.url">jdbc:mysql://localhost:3306/GuestBook</property>
<property name="connection.username">root</property>
<property name="connection.password">12345678</property>
```

Here, Hibernate needs to be informed about the following:

- Which database JDBC driver to use
- Which URL to use to connect to the database
- The username and the password

A Dialect is set to inform Hibernate which SQL variation it has to generate to talk to the database:

```
<property name="dialect">org.hibernate.dialect.MySQLDialect</property>
```

Hibernate comes with several dialects [explained later].

Hibernate needs to be informed about the mapping documents to refer to:

```
<mapping resource="myApp/GuestBook.hbm.xml"/>
```

The mapping files that are needed for the application can be defined and referenced in the Hibernate configuration file using the <mapping> element.

After the XML configuration file is ready and available in the root directory of the classpath, the **configure()** method has to be invoked using the application's Configuration object.

In the application:

```
Configuration cfg = new Configuration().configure();
```

This spawns a Configuration object by calling new **Configuration().configure()**. This method scans the classpath for the presence of hibernate.cfg.xml file.

If it finds one, it loads the configuration file called **hibernate.cfg.xml** from the application's classpath.

The default name for the Hibernate Configuration file is **hibernate.cfg.xml**.

If the configuration file was provided a different file name, the same needs to be passed as an argument to the configure() method:

```
File cgfFile = new File("mySQLcfg.xml");
Configuration cfg = new Configuration().configure(cfgFile);
```

In the application:

```
SessionFactory sessionFactory = configuration.buildSessionFactory();
```

This populates the **SessionFactory** object with the set of property values. These are fetched from the **<session-factory>** element of the XML configuration file.

The same configuration information that is available in the **XML based** Hibernate configuration file can be provided in a **Properties based** Hibernate configuration file.

Configuring Using The hibernate.properties File

Hibernate configuration can also be specified using a properties file called **hibernate.properties**.

This file has to be placed in the root directory of the application's class path.

A sample **hibernate.properties** file:

```
hibernate.connection.driver_class=com.mysql.jdbc.Driver
hibernate.connection.url=jdbc:mysql://localhost:3306/GuestBook
hibernate.connection.username=root
hibernate.connection.password=12345678
hibernate.dialect=org.hibernate.dialect.MySQLDialect
```

REMINDER

If there exist both the kinds of configuration files i.e. hibernate.properties as well as hibernate.cfg.xml in the classpath, the settings of the XML configuration file overrides the settings used in the properties.

This can be useful when it is required to have some base settings in properties and the same needs to be overridden for each deployment with an XML configuration file.

Configuring Programmatically

Configuration can also be done programmatically instead of using the .properties file and/or the XML file.

In programmatic configuration, the details such as JDBC connection details and resource mapping details are supplied in the program using the Configuration API.

An instance of **org.hibernate.cfg.Configuration** is used to achieve programmatic configuration. This instance represents an entire set of mappings of an application's Java types to an SQL database.

org.hibernate.cfg.Configuration is used to build an immutable **org.hibernate.SessionFactory**.

Creating An Instance Of Configuration

Create an instance of **org.hibernate.cfg.Configuration** with the following code spec:

```
Configuration cfg = new Configuration();
```

Specifying The Mapping Documents And The Associated POJOs

Adding Mapping Documents

If the XML mapping documents are in the class path then use the following code spec to add them:

```
cfg.addResource("Authors.hbm.xml");
cfg.addResource("Books.hbm.xml");
```

addResource() method reads the mappings from an application resource. addResource() method will try to load the resource first from the thread context class loader and then from the class loader that loaded Hibernate.

Adding The POJO Class

The other alternative is to have Hibernate load the XML mapping document based on the persistent class:

```
cfg.addClass(bean.Authors.class);
cfg.addClass(bean.Books.class);
```

addclass() method reads the mapping from an application resource using a convention.

In the above code spec, Hibernate loads the following XML mapping document:

- /bean/Authors.hbm.xml
- /bean/Books.hbm.xml

Based on the following persistent classes:

- /bean/Authors.class
- /bean/Books.class

This alternative has the advantage of eliminating hard coded filenames in the source code.

The org.hibernate.cfg.Configuration also allows specifying configuration properties.

Setting The Properties

The following code spec sets the configuration details i.e. specifies the configuration properties:

```
cfg.setProperty("hibernate.connection.driver_class", "com.mysql.jdbc.Driver");
cfg.setProperty("hibernate.connection.url", "jdbc:mysql://localhost:3306/GuestBook");
```

```
cfg.setProperty("hibernate.connection.username", "root");
cfg.setProperty("hibernate.connection.password", "12345678");
cfg.setProperty("hibernate.dialect", "org.hibernate.dialect.MySQLDialect");
```

HINT

The org.hibernate.cfg.Configuration is intended as a startup time object. It is discarded once a SessionFactory is created.

Obtaining A SessionFactory

When all the mappings have been parsed by the org.hibernate.cfg.Configuration, the application must obtain a factory for org.hibernate.Session instance. The factory obtained is intended to be shared by all application threads.

The following code spec obtains a SessionFactory:

```
SessionFactory sessions = cfg.buildSessionFactory();
```

buildSessionFactory() method instantiate a new SessionFactory, using the properties and mappings in this configuration.

REMINDER

The SessionFactory is immutable, so changes made to the Configuration after building the SessionFactory will not affect it.

HINT

Hibernate allows an application to instantiate more than one SessionFactory. This is useful, if more than one database is used.

Understanding The Configuration Properties

There are a number of properties that control the behaviour of Hibernate at runtime. All are optional and have reasonable default values.

The following are the configuration properties:

Configuration Properties

- **hibernate.session_factory_name:** The SessionFactory is automatically bound to this name in JNDI after it has been created

- **hibernate.max_fetch_depth:** Determines how deep Hibernate should go to fetch the results of an outer join. If this property is set to 0 [zero], then Hibernate disables the default outer join fetching. It is recommended to use values between 0 to 3
- **hibernate.default_batch_fetch_size:** Sets the default size for Hibernate batch fetching the associations. It is recommended to use values 4, 8, 16
- **hibernate.default_entity_mode:** Sets a default mode for entity representation for all sessions opened from this SessionFactory. It accepts values dynamic-map, dom4j or pojo
- **hibernate.order_updates:** Orders SQL UPDATE statements by the primary key value of the items being updated. It accepts values true or false

REMINDER

This property will result in fewer transaction deadlocks in highly concurrent systems.

- **hibernate.generate_statistics:** Determines whether statistics are collected for performance tuning. It accepts values true or false
- **hibernate.use_identifier_rollback:** Determines whether Hibernate uses identifier rollback. If this property is set to true, then the generated identifier property is reset to default values when objects are deleted. It accepts values true or false
- **hibernate.use_sql_comments:** Generates SQL with comments. If this property is set to true, then Hibernate generates comments inside the SQL, for easier debugging. By default, the value of this property is false
- **hibernate.dialect:** The class name of an SQL dialect to be used. The SQL dialect allows Hibernate to generate SQL statements optimized for a particular database. The dialect varies by database
- **hibernate.show_sql:** Writes all SQL statements to the console. It accepts values true or false
- **hibernate.format_sql:** Pretty print the SQL statements in a console and the log. It accepts values true or false
- **hibernate.default_catalog:** The default database catalog name, which Hibernate uses to generate SQL for unqualified table names
- **hibernate.default_schema:** The default database owner name [schema / tablespace], which Hibernate uses to generate SQL for unqualified table names

Connection Properties

- **hibernate.connection.provider_class:** The class name that implements Hibernate's ConnectionProvider interface

- **hibernate.connection.isolation:** The transaction isolation level for the JDBC connection. It is recommended to use values 1, 2, 4 or 8

WARNING

Most databases do not support all isolation levels.

- **hibernate.connection.autocommit:** Allows autocommit mode to be used for the JDBC connection. It is not usually recommended. It accepts values true or false
- **hibernate.connection.<JDBCPropertyName>:** Passes any JDBC property to the JDBC connection [The code spec DriverManager.getConnection() represents the JDBC connection]. For example, hibernate.connection.debuglevel=info would pass a JDBC property called debuglevel
- **hibernate.connection.datasource:** The Datasource name for a container managed data source
- **hibernate.connection.driver_class:** The JDBC driver class
- **hibernate.connection.password:** The database password
- **hibernate.connection.pool_size:** Limits the number of connections waiting in the Hibernate database connection pool
- **hibernate.connection.url:** The JDBC URL to the database instance
- **hibernate.connection.username:** The database username
- **hibernate.connection.release_mode:** Specify when Hibernate should release JDBC connections. By default, a JDBC connection is held until the session is explicitly closed or disconnected. For an application server JTA datasource, use **after_statement** value to aggressively release connections after every JDBC call. For a non-JTA connection, it often makes sense to release the connection at the end of each transaction by using **after_transaction** value. **auto** value will choose after_statement for the JTA and CMT transaction strategies and after_transaction for the JDBC transaction strategy

JDBC Properties

- **hibernate.jdbc.batch_size:** The maximum batch size for updates. It is recommended to use values between 5 to 30
- **hibernate.jdbc.batch_versioned_data:** Determines whether Hibernate batches versioned data, which depends on the JDBC driver properly implementing row counts for batch updates. Hibernate uses the row count to determine whether the update is successful. It accepts values true or false

If the JDBC driver returns correct row counts from the executeBatch() method, then set this property to true. Hibernate then uses the batched DML for automatically versioned data. It is usually safe to turn this option on.

- **hibernate.jdbc.factory_class:** The class name of a custom implementation of the org.hibernate.jdbc.Batcher interface for controlling JDBC prepared statements
- **hibernate.jdbc.fetch_size:** Determines how many rows the JDBC connection should try to buffer with every fetch. This is a balance between memory and minimizing database network traffic
- **hibernate.jdbc.use_get_generated_keys:** Determines Hibernate's behavior with respect to generated keys. If this property is set to true and if the database driver supports the JDBC 3.0 generated keys API, then the Hibernate retrieves the generated keys from the statement after it executes an SQL query. It accepts values true or false. By default, it tries to determine the driver capabilities using connection metadata
- **hibernate.jdbc.use_scrollable_resultset:** Determines whether Hibernate should use JDBC scrollable result sets for a user-provided JDBC connection. This property is only necessary when using user supplied JDBC connections, Hibernate uses connection metadata otherwise. It accepts values true or false
- **hibernate.jdbc.use_streams_for_binary:** Determines whether binary data is read or written over JDBC as streams. It is a System-level property. It accepts values true or false

JNDI Properties

- **hibernate.jndi.class:** The InitialContext class for JNDI
- **hibernate.jndi.<JNDIPropertyName>:** Passes any JNDI property to the JNDI InitialContext
- **hibernate.jndi.url:** Provides the URL for JNDI

Cache Properties

- **hibernate.cache.provider_class:** Specifies the class that implements the CacheProvider interface
- **hibernate.cache.query_cache_factory:** Specifies the class that implements the QueryCacheFactory interface for retrieving QueryCache objects
- **hibernate.cache.region_prefix:** The prefix to be used for the name of the cache
- **hibernate.cache.use_minimal_puts:** Optimizes second-level cache operation to minimize writes at the cost of more frequent reads. It accepts values true or false

HINT

hibernate.cache.use_minimal_puts property is most useful for clustered caches. In Hibernate 3, hibernate.cache.use_minimal_puts property is enabled by default for clustered cache implementations.

- **hibernate.cache.use_query_cache:** Specifies whether to use the query cache
- **hibernate.cache.use_second_level_cache:** Determines whether to use the Hibernate second level cache. It accepts values true or false. By default, this property is enabled for classes, which specify a <cache> mapping
- **hibernate.cache.use_structured_entries:** Stores data in the second level cache in a more human-friendly format. It accepts values true or false

Transaction Properties

- **hibernate.transaction.auto_close_session:** Automatically closes the session after a transaction. It accepts values true or false. Built-in and automatic session context management is preferred
- **hibernate.transaction.factory_class:** Specifies the class that implements the TransactionFactory interface
- **hibernate.transaction.flush_before_completion:** Automatically flushes the session before completion of a transaction. It accepts values true or false. Built-in and automatic session context management is preferred
- **hibernate.transaction.manager_lookup_class:** Specifies the class that implements the TransactionManagerLookup interface. This property is required when JVM level caching is enable or when using hilo in a JTA environment
- **jta.UserTransaction:** The JNDI name for the UserTransaction object

Miscellaneous Properties

- **hibernate.cglib.use_reflection_optimizer:** Instead of using slower standard Java reflection, uses the CGLib code generation library to optimize access to business object properties. The application may be slower at startup if this is enabled, but with faster runtime performance. It is System-level property. This property cannot be set in the hibernate.cfg.xml file
- **hibernate.hbm2ddl.auto:** Automatically creates, updates or drops the database schema on startup and shut down. It accepts values validate, create, create-drop or update

WARNING

Be careful with **create-drop** value, as the database schema will be dropped when the SessionFactory is closed explicitly.

- **hibernate.query.factory_class:** Specifies an HQL query factory class name
- **hibernate.query.substitutions:** Any possible SQL token substitutions that Hibernate should use. Tokens might be function or literal names. For example, hqlfunction=SQLFUNC
- **hibernate.current_session_context_class:** Supplies a custom strategy for the scoping of the current session. It accepts values jta, thread, managed or a custom class
- **hibernate.sql_exception_converter:** Specifies which SQLExceptionConverter to use to convert SQLExceptions into JDBCExceptions
- **hibernate.wrap_result_sets:** Turns on JDBC result set wrapping with column names
- **hibernate.xml.output_stylesheet:** Specifies an XSLT style sheet for Hibernate's XML data binder. This property requires the JAR file named xalan.jar
- **hibernate.proxool:** Prefix for the Proxool database connection pool
- **hibernate.proxool.existing_pool:** Configures Proxool with an existing pool
- **hibernate.proxool.pool_alias:** The alias to be used for any of the configured Proxool pools previously mentioned
- **hibernate.proxool.properties:** Path to a Proxool properties file
- **hibernate.proxool.xml:** Path to a Proxool XML configuration file
- **hibernate.c3p0.acquire_increment:** After the connection pool is completely utilized, determines how many new connections are added to the pool
- **hibernate.c3p0.idle_test_period:** Determines how long to wait before a connection is validated
- **hibernate.c3p0.max_size:** The maximum size of the connection pool for C3PO
- **hibernate.c3p0.min_size:** The minimum size of the connection pool for C3PO
- **hibernate.c3p0.max_statements:** The upper limit for the SQL statement cache for C3PO
- **hibernate.c3p0.timeout:** The timeout for C3PO [in seconds]

Dialects

JDBC abstracts away many of the underlying connection details for each relational database, yet every relational database supports a different set of features and uses a slightly different version of SQL. Among the features that differ between relational databases are the syntax for marking identity columns, column data types, available SQL functions, foreign key constraint syntax, limits, GUID support and support for cascade deletes.

Hibernate abstracts away all of these changes into **dialect classes**. Each supported database has its own dialect. When Hibernate constructs an SQL query, it obtains appropriate syntax information for the current database from the dialect. Hibernate 3 comes with over 20 different dialects. All of these standard dialects are supplied within the org.hibernate.dialect package.

The following table displays the database supported by Hibernate along with their dialect class names used by Hibernate:

Database Name	Dialect Class Name
DB2 OS390	org.hibernate.dialect.DB2390Dialect
DB2 AS/400	org.hibernate.dialect.DB2400Dialect
DB2	org.hibernate.dialect.DB2Dialect
Derby	org.hibernate.dialect.DerbyDialect
Firebird	org.hibernate.dialect.FirebirdDialect
FrontBase	org.hibernate.dialect.FrontbaseDialect
HSQLDB	org.hibernate.dialect.HSQLDialect
Informix	org.hibernate.dialect.InformixDialect
Ingres	org.hibernate.dialect.IngresDialect
InterBase	org.hibernate.dialect.InterbaseDialect
JDataStore	org.hibernate.dialect.JDataStoreDialect
Mimer SQL	org.hibernate.dialect.MimerSQLDialect
Mckoi	org.hibernate.dialect.MckoiDialect
MySQL	org.hibernate.dialect.MySQLDialect
MySQL with InnoDB tables	org.hibernate.dialect.MySQLInnoDBDialect
MySQL with MyISAM tables	org.hibernate.dialect.MySQLMyISAMDialect
Oracle 9i/10g	org.hibernate.dialect.Oracle9Dialect
Oracle9i [DataDirect drivers]	org.hibernate.dialect.DataDirectOracle9Dialect
Oracle [Any Version]	org.hibernate.dialect.OracleDialect
PointBase	org.hibernate.dialect.PointbaseDialect
PostgreSQL	org.hibernate.dialect.PostgreSQLDialect
Progress	org.hibernate.dialect.ProgressDialect

Database Name	Dialect Class Name
RDMS for Unisys OS2200	org.hibernate.dialect.RDMSOS2200Dialect
SAP DB	org.hibernate.dialect.SAPDBDialect
SQL Server	org.hibernate.dialect.SQLServerDialect
Sybase	org.hibernate.dialect.SybaseDialect
Sybase 11	org.hibernate.dialect.Sybase11Dialect
Sybase Anywhere	org.hibernate.dialect.SybaseAnywhereDialect
Times Ten 5.1	org.hibernate.dialect.TimesTenDialect
Microsoft SQL Server	org.hibernate.dialect.SQLServerDialect
HypersonicSQL	org.hibernate.dialect.HSQLDialect

Guest Book Application

Example

Now that the fundamentals of how to configure Hibernate are in place, let's learn how to configure the GuestBook application in all the three different ways:

- XML based configuration file
- Configuration using a Properties File
- Programmatic configuration

The following information needs to be populated as a part of configuration.

Database	MySQL
Username	root
Password	12345678
Dialect	MySQLDialect
Mapping File	myApp/GuestBook.hbm.xml

To create the GuestBook application from scratch, refer to *Chapter 03: Writing The First Application*. The following examples only depict the steps involved in adding the configuration.

Using An XML Based Configuration File

Right-click the **Source Packages** folder. Select **New → Other...** as shown in diagram 5.1.1.

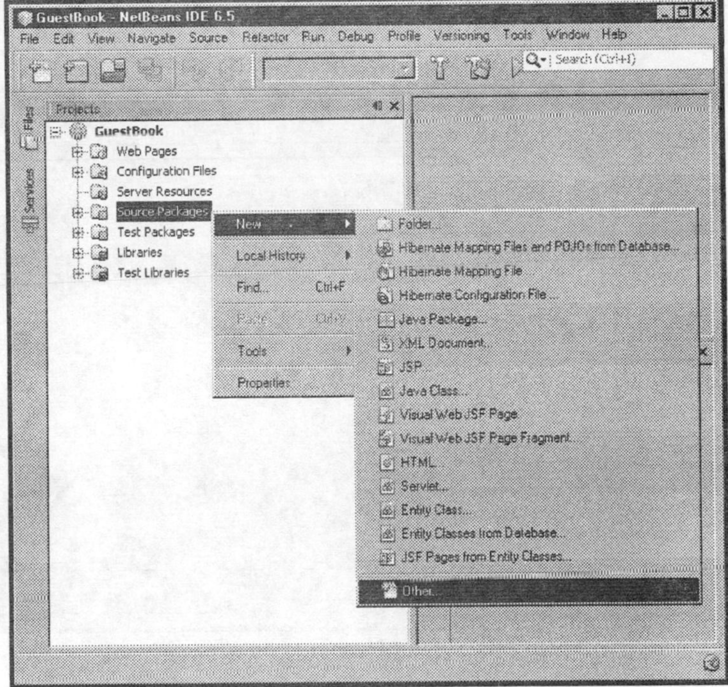

Diagram 5.1.1: Creating hibernate.cfg.xml file

New File dialog appears. Select **XML** from the **Categories** list and select **XML Document** from the **File Types** as shown in diagram 5.1.2.

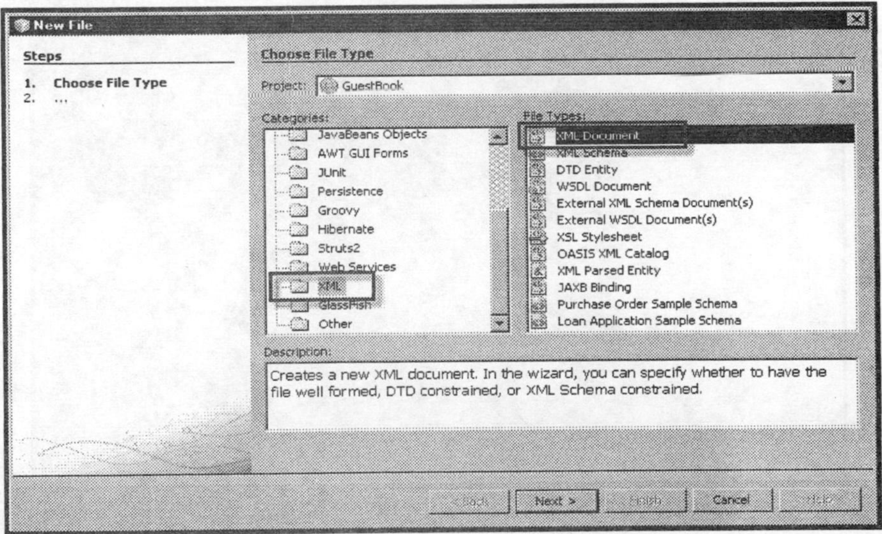

Diagram 5.1.2: Selecting XML file type

Click Next >. Enter **hibernate.cfg** as the file name as shown in diagram 5.1.3.

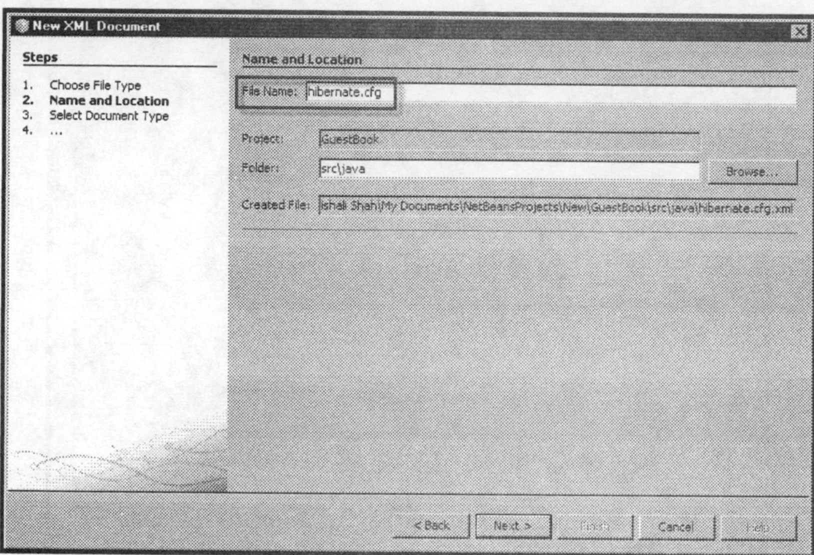

Diagram 5.1.3: Naming the XML file

Click Next >. Select the option **DTD-Constrained Document** as shown in diagram 5.1.4.

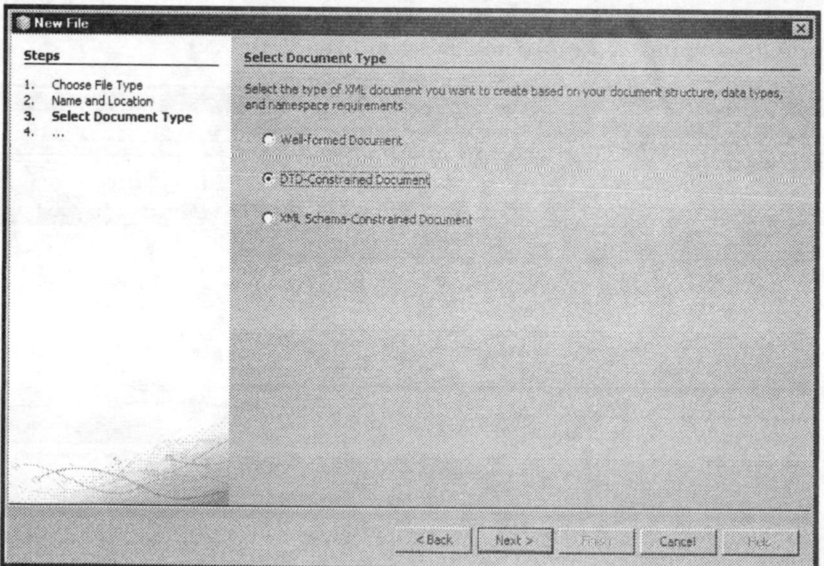

Diagram 5.1.4: Selecting the document type

Click Next >. Specify the **DTD Options** for the XML document type as shown in diagram 5.1.5. Populate the following fields:

DTD Public ID	-//Hibernate/Hibernate Configuration DTD//EN
DTD System ID	http://hibernate.sourceforge.net/hibernate-configuration-3.0.dtd
Document Root	hibernate-configuration

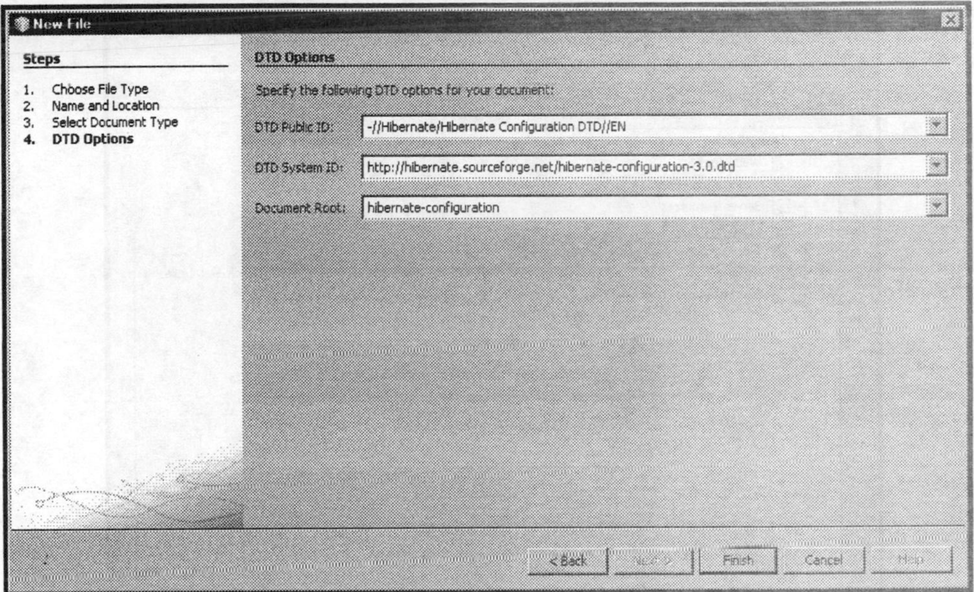

Diagram 5.1.5: Specifying the DTD options for XML document type

Click .

The hibernate.cfg.xml file should hold the following contents:

```
<?xml version="1.0" encoding="UTF-8"?>
<!DOCTYPE hibernate-configuration PUBLIC "-//Hibernate/Hibernate Configuration DTD 3.0//EN"
"http://hibernate.sourceforge.net/hibernate-configuration-3.0.dtd">
<hibernate-configuration>
  <session-factory>
    <property name="hibernate.dialect">org.hibernate.dialect.MySQLDialect</property>
    <property name="hibernate.connection.driver_class">com.mysql.jdbc.Driver</property>
    <property name="hibernate.connection.url">jdbc:mysql://localhost:3306/GuestBook</property>
    <property name="hibernate.connection.username">root</property>
    <property name="hibernate.connection.password">12345678</property>
    <mapping resource="myApp/Guestbook.hbm.xml"/>
```

```
  </session-factory>
</hibernate-configuration>
```

Configuration Using A Properties File

Right-click the **Source Packages** folder. Select **New → Other...** as shown in diagram 5.2.1.

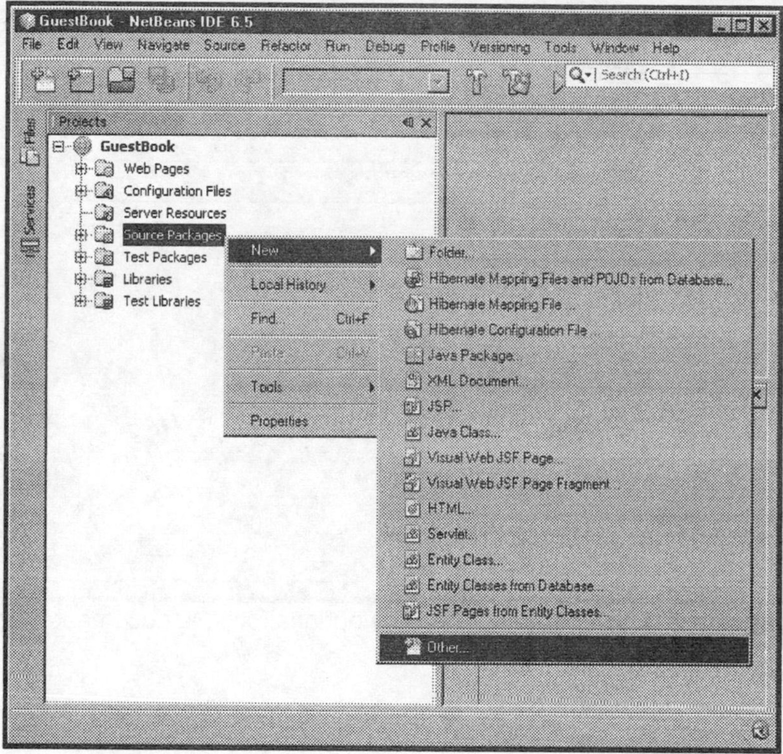

Diagram 5.2.1: Creating hibernate.cfg.xml file

New File dialog appears. Select **Other** from the **Categories** list and select **Properties File** from the **File Types** as shown in diagram 5.2.2.

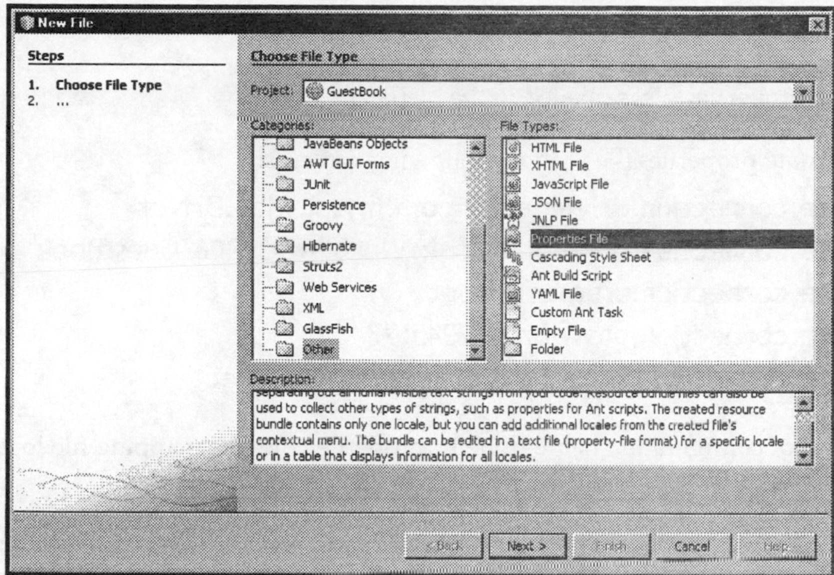

Diagram 5.2.2: Selecting Properties File file type

Click **Next >**. The **New Properties File** window appears as shown in diagram 5.2.3. Enter the file name as **hibernate**.

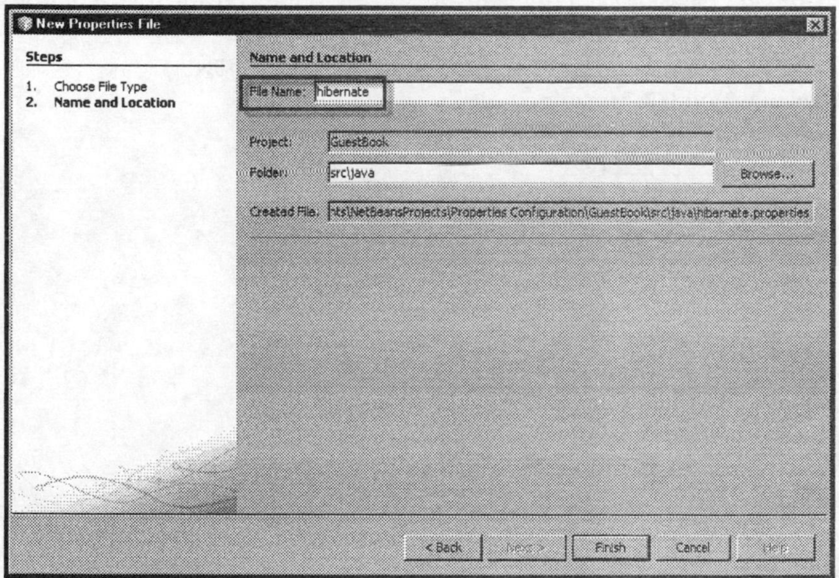

Diagram 5.2.3: The New Hibernate Configuration File window

Click Finish.

The hibernate.properties file is opened in the NetBeans IDE.

Edit the hibernate.properties file with the following contents:

```
hibernate.connection.driver_class=com.mysql.jdbc.Driver
hibernate.connection.url=jdbc:mysql://localhost:3306/GuestBook
hibernate.connection.username=root
hibernate.connection.password=12345678
hibernate.dialect=org.hibernate.dialect.MySQLDialect
```

Since, the kind of configuration being done is .properties file, the mapping file location needs to be programmatically supplied to Hibernate via the Configuration class.

In the GuestBook application the Configuration code spec is written in the GuestBookView.jsp file. Hence, this file needs to be edited to now include the mapping file location.

Edit the GuestBookView.jsp as shown below:

```
<%@page contentType="text/html" pageEncoding="UTF-8" import="org.hibernate.SessionFactory, org.hibernate.cfg.Configuration, org.hibernate.Session, org.hibernate.Transaction, java.util.List, java.util.Iterator, myApp.Guestbook" %>
<!DOCTYPE HTML PUBLIC "-//W3C//DTD HTML 4.01 Transitional//EN"
  "http://www.w3.org/TR/html4/loose.dtd">
<%!
   SessionFactory sessionFactory;
   org.hibernate.Session hibSession;
   List<Guestbook> guestbook;
%>

<%
   Configuration cfg = new Configuration();
   cfg.addClass(myApp.Guestbook.class);
   sessionFactory = cfg.buildSessionFactory();
   hibSession = sessionFactory.openSession();
   Transaction tx = null;
```

<u>Only the section that needs change is shown, the rest remains the same.</u>

Programmatic Configuration

In programmatic configuration additional files such as hibernate.cfg.xml or hibernate.properties are not required.

All the configuration details are placed in the Configuration class.

In the GuestBook application, the Configuration code spec is written in the GuestBookView.jsp file. Hence, this file needs to be edited to now include the configuration details.

Edit the GuestBookView.jsp as shown below:

```
<%@page contentType="text/html" pageEncoding="UTF-8" import="org.hibernate.SessionFactory,
org.hibernate.cfg.Configuration, org.hibernate.Session, org.hibernate.Transaction, java.util.List,
java.util.Iterator, myApp.Guestbook" %>
<!DOCTYPE HTML PUBLIC "-//W3C//DTD HTML 4.01 Transitional//EN"
  "http://www.w3.org/TR/html4/loose.dtd">
<%!
   SessionFactory sessionFactory;
   org.hibernate.Session hibSession;
   List<Guestbook> guestbook;
%>

<%
   Configuration cfg = new Configuration();
   cfg.addClass(myApp.Guestbook.class);
   cfg.setProperty("hibernate.dialect", "org.hibernate.dialect.MySQLDialect");
   cfg.setProperty("hibernate.connection.driver_class", "com.mysql.jdbc.Driver");
   cfg.setProperty("hibernate.connection.url", "jdbc:mysql://localhost:3306/GuestBook");
   cfg.setProperty("hibernate.connection.username", "root");
   cfg.setProperty("hibernate.connection.password", "123456");

   sessionFactory = cfg.buildSessionFactory();
   hibSession = sessionFactory.openSession();
   Transaction tx = null;
```

Only the section that needs change is shown, the rest remains the same.

The Book CDROM holds the complete application source code built using the NetBeans IDE for the following applications:

- GuestBook_Chap05_XML
- GuestBook_Chap05_Properties
- GuestBook_Chap05_Programmatic

These can be directly used by making appropriate changes [username/password] to the configuration file.

SECTION III: UNDERSTANDING CONFIGURATION AND MAPPING

Getting Started With Mapping

Hibernate allows the developers to consider as if the database stores Java objects, which practically is not true. A database stores data in form of tables, rows and columns.

This is a fundamental difference between an object-oriented association and a relational database association.

Diagram 6.1 depicts the fundamental difference.

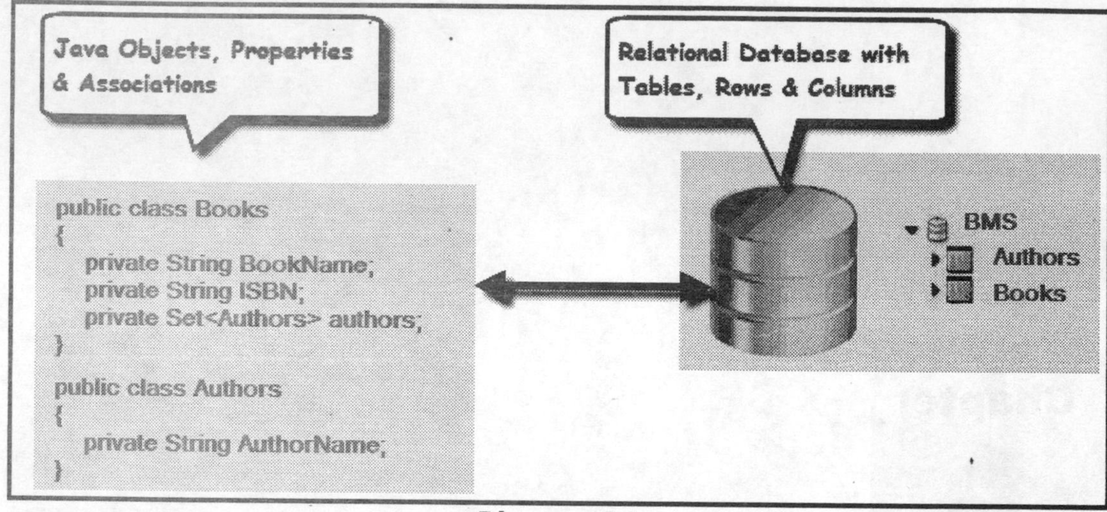

Diagram 6.1

Unfortunately, there is no simple way to correlate the data stored in a database with the data represented by Java objects.

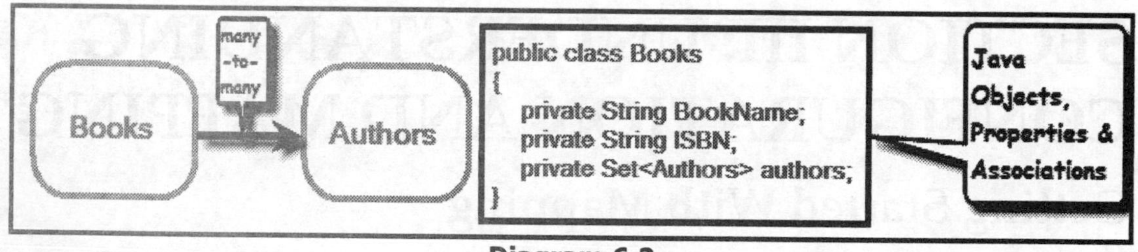

Diagram 6.2

Books object contains a **Set** property referring to the **Authors** objects. This way, it's quite possible to determine the associated Authors object using a Books object. However, the reverse is not possible i.e. it will not be possible to determine the associated Books object using an Authors object.

To represent the same kind of scenario in a relational database, the following questions need to be answered:

- How is a unique book identified?
- Can an author write multiple books?
- Can a book be written by multiple authors?
- Should the relationship be represented in the Books table?
- Should the relationship be represented in the Authors table?

❑ Should the relationship be represented in a completely new table?

Assuming the **answers** to the above questions as following:

❑ How is a unique book identified?

Answer: BookNo

❑ Can an author write multiple books?

Answer: Yes

❑ Can a book be written by multiple authors?

Answer: Yes

❑ Should the relationship be represented in the Books table?

Answer: No

❑ Should the relationship be represented in the Authors table?

Answer: No

❑ Should the relationship be represented in a completely new table?

Answer: Yes

The database representation will be as shown in diagram 6.3.

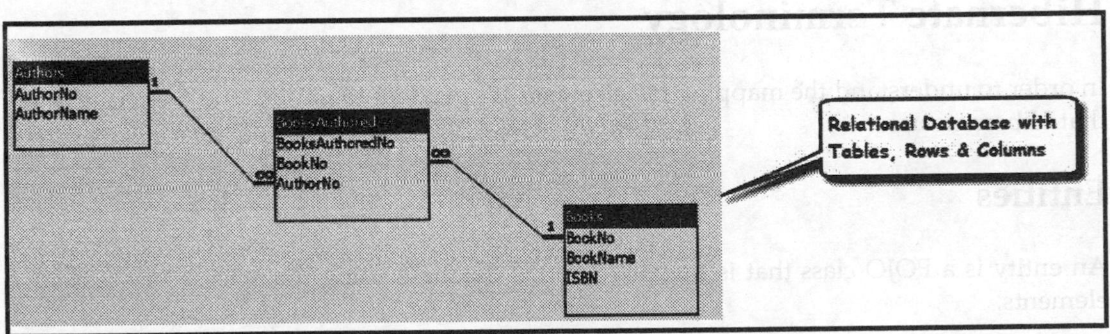

Diagram 6.3

Even though the context between the relational database and the Java objects look similar, the type of association is different.

Referring to a record in the BooksAuthored table, it's possible to determine:

❑ The Authors who have written a particular Book

❑ The Books which have been written by a particular Author

This relationship is established by a **Foreign Key** constraint.

Given the differences between the two worlds, it is necessary to manually intervene to determine how the Java classes should be represented in database tables.

This is where the Hibernate's Object/Relational Mappings [mapping documents] comes in. These mapping documents inform Hibernate about how to load and store objects of the persistent class.

Object/Relational Mappings are usually defined using XML documents. The mapping language is Java-centric i.e. mappings are constructed around persistent class declarations, not table declarations.

At present, Hibernate supports two standard ways to express the mappings:

- **XML Mapping Documents**

  This is the most mature approach and gives the best way to control Hibernate

- **Annotations**

  Hibernate also supports the Annotations feature introduced in Java 5. This technique allows using a special syntax to include metadata directly in the application's source code

Hibernate Terminology

In order to understand the mapping file elements, it's prudent to understand the terminology that Hibernate uses.

Entities

An entity is a POJO class that is mapped into the database using the <class> or <subclass> elements.

An entity has its own life cycle i.e. it may exist independently of any other entity.

Diagram 6.4 depicts a sample entity.

```
package bms;
import java.util.HashSet;
import java.util.Set;

public class Authors  implements java.io.Serializable {
     private int authorNo;
     private String authorName;
     private Set<Booksauthored> booksauthoreds = new HashSet<Booksauthored>(0);

     public Authors() {
     }

     public Authors(int authorNo) {
        this.authorNo = authorNo;
     }
     public Authors(int authorNo, String authorName, Set<Booksauthored> booksauthoreds) {
        this.authorNo = authorNo;
        this.authorName = authorName;
        this.booksauthoreds = booksauthoreds;
     }

     public int getAuthorNo() {
        return this.authorNo;
     }

     public void setAuthorNo(int authorNo) {
        this.authorNo = authorNo;
     }
     public String getAuthorName() {
        return this.authorName;
     }

     public void setAuthorName(String authorName) {
        this.authorName = authorName;
     }
     public Set<Booksauthored> getBooksauthoreds() {
        return this.booksauthoreds;
     }

     public void setBooksauthoreds(Set<Booksauthored> booksauthoreds) {
        this.booksauthoreds = booksauthoreds;
     }
}
```

Diagram 6.4

Values

The data types supported by the database, the collections and optionally some user-defined types are considered as Values.

The lifespan of a value is bounded by the lifespan of the owning entity.

The following table displays the Hibernate values for corresponding Java data types and database data types:

Java Data Type	Database Data Type	Hibernate Data Type
Integer, int, long short	integer, number, int	integer, long short
char	char	character
java.math.BigDecimal	NUMERIC, NUMBER	big_decimal
float, double	float, double	float, double
java.lang.Boolean, boolean	boolean, int	boolean
java.lang.string	varchar, varchar2	string
Very long strings	CLOB, TEXT	text
java.util.Date	DATE, TIME, TIMSTAMP	date, time, timestamp
java.util.Calendar	TIMESTAMP, DATE	calendar, calendar_date
java.util.Locale	varchar, varchar2	locale
java.util.TimeZone	varchar, varchar2	timezone
java.util.Currency	varchar, varchar2	Currency
java.sql.Clob	CLOB	clob
java.sql.Blob	BLOB	blob
Java object	binary field	serializable
byte array	binary field	binary field
java.lang.Class	varchar, varchar2	class

Components

A component is placed somewhere between entities and values.

A component is a class whose representation is simple and its instances have a strong one-to-one relationship with instances of another class.

```
public class Books
{
    private String BookName;
    private String ISBN;
    private Authors author;
}
```

```
public class Authors
{
    private String AuthorName;
    private String Address;
    private String ContactNo;
}
```

Diagram 6.5

A component is mapped as a column in the same table that represents most of the attributes of the owning class.

Here [as show in diagram 6.5], the **Authors** class is a component mapped as a column named **author** that represents most of the attributes of the owning class.

Mapping Document

For an object to be persisted to a database, Hibernate needs a mapping document for all of the objects that are to be persisted.

Hibernate traditionally uses an XML document to track the mapping between Java classes and relational database tables. A mapping file can map a single class or multiple classes to the database.

The mapping document must be saved with the **.hbm.xml** extension. This kind of extension informs Hibernate that this is a mapping file. This file must be located in the same directory as the **.java** file [POJO class] it is related to.

A mapping document is made up of several elements.

The following is a sample mapping document:

```
<?xml version="1.0"?>
<!DOCTYPE hibernate-mapping PUBLIC "-//Hibernate/Hibernate Mapping DTD 3.0//EN"
"http://hibernate.sourceforge.net/hibernate-mapping-3.0.dtd">
<hibernate-mapping>
   <class name="bms.Authors" table="authors" catalog="bms">
      <id name="authorNo" type="int">
         <column name="AuthorNo" />
         <generator class="assigned" />
      </id>
      <property name="authorName" type="string">
         <column name="AuthorName" length="50" />
      </property>
      <set name="booksauthoreds" inverse="true">
         <key>
            <column name="AuthorNo" />
         </key>
         <one-to-many class="bms.Booksauthored" />
      </set>
   </class>
</hibernate-mapping>
```

Elements Of Mapping Document

The following are the elements of the XML mapping document:

DOCTYPE

All mapping XML documents should refer to hibernate-mapping-3.0.dtd using the DOCTYPE element. This is required for enforcing syntactic validation of the XML.

Syntax:

```
<!DOCTYPE hibernate-mapping PUBLIC
"-//Hibernate/Hibernate Mapping DTD 3.0//EN"
"http://hibernate.sourceforge.net/hibernate-mapping-3.0.dtd">
```

<hibernate-mapping> Element

Mappings are declared inside a <hibernate-mapping> element.

<hibernate-mapping> element is the root element of the mapping document. This root element can include multiple class mappings.

Being the top-level element, its attributes are usually used to define default behaviors and settings to apply to its child elements.

Syntax:

```
<hibernate-mapping schema="<SchemaName>" catalog="<CatalogName>"
  default-cascade="<all | none | save-update | delete>"
  default-access="<field | property | ClassName>"
  default-lazy="<true | false>" auto-import="<true | false>"
  package="<PackageName>" />
```

The schema Attribute

The schema attribute is used to specify the name of the database schema against which queries should apply and is optional. If this attribute holds a value then that value is appended to the table name.

```
<hibernate-mapping schema="bms">
   <class table="Books"></class>
</hibernate-mapping>
```

Here, the fully qualified name [after appending the value] is **bms.**Books.

The catalog Attribute

The catalog attribute is used to specify the name of the database catalog against which the queries should apply and is optional.

HINT

The schema and catalog attributes specify that tables referred to in the mapping belong to the named schema and/or catalog. If specified, then the table names will be qualified by the given schema and catalog names. If not specified, then the table names will be unqualified.

The default-cascade Attribute

The default-cascade attribute specifies what cascade style should be assumed for properties and collections, which do not specify a cascade attribute and is optional.

This attribute value indicates how the actions that are performed on a parent will be cascaded to a child.

The possible attribute values are:

- all
- none
- save-update
- delete

By default, the cascade style is none.

The default-access Attribute

The default-access attribute, informs Hibernate, the strategy to be used to access the properties and is optional.

If this attribute is set to **property**, then **get** and **set** methods are used to access the data.

If this attribute is set to **field**, then the data is accessed directly.

Alternatively, this attribute can also be set to a class name of a PropertyAccessor implementation which defines any other access mechanism.

By default, the value of this attribute is property.

The default-lazy Attribute

The default-lazy attribute, if set to true, specifies the unspecified lazy attributes of class and collection mappings and is optional.

This attribute brings in some performance benefits. By default, the value of this attribute is true.

HINT

There are times when all the information is not necessary to be loaded, when classes are loaded into the memory from the database. Hibernate allows a flexible approach, known as **Lazy Loading**, where in certain relationships can be marked as being lazy and they will not be loaded from the disk until they are actually required.

The auto-import Attribute

The auto-import attribute specifies whether to use unqualified class names in the query language and is optional.

This is set to false, only if, the class name is **ambiguous**. If it is set to false, Hibernate does not allow specifying un-qualified class

By default, the value of this attribute is true.

The package Attribute

The package attribute specifies a package prefix to assume for unqualified class names in the mapping document and is optional.

It becomes tedious to specify a package name every time a class is named in the mapping documents.

```
<hibernate-mapping>
   <class name="com.bms.Books" table="Books">
      . . .
   </class>
</hibernate-mapping>
```

The package name need not be repeated whenever a class is named in an association, subclass or component mapping. For this, the package name can be specified using the package attribute.

```
<hibernate-mapping package="com.bms">
  <class name="Books" table="Books">
    . . .
  </class>
</hibernate-mapping>
```

After a package name is specified, all unqualified class names that appear in this mapping document will be prefixed with the declared package name.

<class> Element

Since the mapping file documents the relationship between a Java class and a database table, a class that this mapping document references needs to be specified. This is done using the <class> element.

<class> element maps the domain object [Java class] with corresponding entity [table] in the database.

HINT

It is a good practice to map only a single persistent class in one mapping document and name it after the persistent class name.

For example, for the persistent class named **Books.**java, name the mapping document as **Books.**hbm.xml.

Syntax:

```
<class name="<ClassName>" table="<TableName>" rowid="<ROWID>"
  discriminator-value="<is null | is not null>" node="<XML Element>"
  mutable="<true | false>" schema="<Owner>" catalog="<Catalog>"
  proxy="<ProxyInterface>" dynamic-update="<true | false>"
  dynamic-insert="<true | false>" check="<SQL CHECK Condition>"
  select-before-update="<true | false>" batch-size="<BatchSize>"
  polymorphism="<implicit | explicit>" lazy="<true | false>"
  where="<SQL WHERE Condition>" persister="<PersisterClass>"
  optimistic-lock="<none | version | dirty | all>"
  entity-name="<EntityName>" subselect="<SQL Expression>"
  abstract="<true | false>"/>
```

The name Attribute

The name attribute specifies the fully qualified class name of the persistent class and is optional.

A fully qualified class named needs to be specified, if the package name is not specified in the **<hibernate-mapping>**.

If this attribute is not specified, Hibernate assumes that the mapping is for a non-POJO entity.

The table Attribute

The table attribute is the name of the database table to be used when persisting the Java Object and is optional.

If this attribute is not specified, then the unqualified class name is used.

The rowid Attribute

The rowid attribute specifies whether the rowid should be used and is optional. By default, the value of this attribute is **false**.

HINT

If Oracle is used as the database of choice, Hibernate can use the rowid for fast updates, if this option is set.

A ROWID is an implementation detail and represents the physical location of a stored tuple.

The discriminator-value Attribute

The discriminator-value attribute is a value that distinguishes individual sub classes used for polymorphic behaviour and is optional.

The node Attribute

The node attribute specifies the name of the XML element or attribute, which should be used by the XML relational persistence features and is optional.

The mutable Attribute

The mutable attribute specifies that instances of the class are mutable and is optional. By default, the value of this attribute is true.

If this attribute is set to **false**, the object becomes read-only. If it is set to **true**, the object can be updated/deleted.

The schema Attribute

The schema attribute, if specified, overrides the schema name specified in the root i.e. <hibernate-mapping> element and is optional.

Example

```
<hibernate-mapping>
   <class name="bms.Books" table="books" schema="bms">
      . . .
   </class>
</hibernate-mapping>
```

It can even be declared for the whole document.

Example

```
<hibernate-mapping default-schema="bms">
   . . .
</hibernate-mapping>
```

The catalog Attribute

The catalog attribute, if specified, overrides the catalog name specified in the root i.e. <hibernate-mapping> element and is optional.

The proxy Attribute

The proxy attribute specifies a class or an interface [usually the class name that is used in the name attribute] to use as proxies for lazy initialization and is optional. By default, Hibernate uses runtime generated proxies.

Lazy initialization enables Hibernate to stub out the data in an object.

The dynamic-update Attribute

The dynamic-update attribute specifies whether all columns should appear in the UPDATE SQL statement and is optional. By default, the value of this attribute is false.

If this attribute is set to true, then an UPDATE SQL statement is generated at runtime and only those columns whose values have changed appear in the UPDATE SQL statement.

Example

```
<class name="bms.Books" dynamic-update="true"
    . . .
</class>
```

The check Attribute

The check attribute is an SQL expression used to generate a multi-row check constraint for automatic schema generation and is optional.

The check attribute defines a row-level check constraint, effectively adding this as an SQL CHECK(. . .) clause during table generation.

The dynamic-insert Attribute

The dynamic-insert attribute specifies whether all columns should appear in the INSERT SQL statement and is optional. By default, the value of this attribute is false.

If this attribute is set to true, then an INSERT SQL statement is generated at runtime and only those columns whose values are not null appear in the INSERT SQL statement.

HINT

On very wide tables, the dynamic-insert attribute may improve performance, but since INSERT SQL statements are **cached**, the dynamic-insert can easily produce a performance hit.

Example

```
<class name="bms.Books" dynamic-insert="true"
   . . .
</class>
```

The batch-size Attribute

The batch-size attribute specifies the number of items that can be batched together when retrieving instances of the class by identifier and is optional. By default, the value of this attribute is 1.

The select-before-update Attribute

The select-before-update attribute specifies whether Hibernate should perform a SELECT to determine if an UPDATE is needed and is optional. By default, the value of this attribute is false.

If this attribute is set to true, then Hibernate issues an SELECT SQL statement to check whether an UPDATE SQL statement is actually required.

HINT

The select-before-update attribute is less efficient, it can prevent database triggers from being invoked unnecessarily.

The polymorphism Attribute

The polymorphism attribute determines how polymorphism is to be used and is optional. By default, the value of this attribute is implicit, which returns:

- Instances of the class, if super class or implemented interfaces are named in the query
- Sub classes, if the class itself is named in the query

The lazy Attribute

The lazy attribute is used to **disable** or **enable** the lazy fetching against the enclosing mapping's default and is optional.

The where Attribute

The where attribute specifies a global WHERE condition to be used when retrieving objects of this class from the database table and is optional.

The persister Attribute

The persister attribute specifies a custom ClassPersister object to be used when persisting the entity and is optional.

The optimistic-lock Attribute

The optimistic-lock attribute determines the optimistic locking strategy and is optional. By default, the value of this attribute is version.

The entity-name Attribute

The entity-name attribute specifies the entity name to be used in place of class name and is optional.

HINT

Hibernate 3 allows a class to be mapped multiple times to different tables, potentially and allows entity mappings that are represented by Maps or XML at the Java level. In this case, provide an explicit arbitrary name for the entity.

The subselect Attribute

The subselect attribute maps an immutable and read-only [because the SQL defined cannot be reversed] entity to database subselect and is optional. By default, the value of this attribute is false.

The abstract Attribute

The abstract attribute specifies whether the class being mapped is abstract and is optional. By default, the value of this attribute is false.

<property> Element

A typical property mapping defines

- A JavaBeans property name
- A database column name

- The name of a Hibernate type

The property element allows mapping a JavaBean property to a database table column.

Syntax:

```
<property name="<PropertyName>" column="<ColumnName>"
  type="<TypeName>" update="<true | false>"
  insert="<true | false>" formula="<SQL expression>"
  access="<field | property | ClassName>" lazy="<true | false>"
  unique="<true | false>" not-null="<true | false>"
  optimistic-lock="<true | false>" index="<IndexName>"
  length="<ColumnLength>" node="<XML Element>"
  precision="<Precision>" scale="<Scale>" unique-key="<UniqueKey>"/>
```

Example

```
<property name="FirstName" column="FirstName" type="string"/>
```

The type name can be omitted.

Example

```
<property name="FirstName" column="FirstName" />
```

This means if FirstName is a property of Java type [java.lang.String], Hibernate automatically uses the Hibernate type string by default.

Hibernate uses reflection to determine the Java type of the property.

Example

```
<property name="FirstName" />
```

Even the column name can be omitted, if the column name is the same as the property name, ignoring case.

Example

```
<property name="FirstName" type="string">
   <column name="FirstName"/>
</property>
```

The column can also be defined using a <column> element instead of the column attribute.

The <column> element provides more flexibility. It has more optional attributes and may appear more than once.

The name Attribute

The name attribute is the name of the property, with an initial lowercase letter.

The column Attribute

The column attribute is the name of the database table column where this attribute should be saved and is optional.

If this attribute is not specified, then Hibernate uses the value given in the name attribute.

This can also be specified by the nested <column> element(s).

By default, Hibernate does not quote table and column names in the generated SQL. If a table or column name is quoted using with backticks [`], Hibernate will always quote this identifier in the generated SQL statements.

Example

```
<property name="FirstName" column="`FirstName`"/>
```

The type Attribute

The type attribute is a name, which indicates the Hibernate data type and is optional.

The type name could be:

- The name of a Hibernate data type [example: integer, string, character, date, timestamp, float, binary, serializable, object, blob]
- The name of a Java class with a default data type [example: int, float, char, java.lang.String, java.util.Date, java.lang.Integer, java.sql.Clob]
- The name of a serializable Java class
- The class name of a custom type [example: com.illflow.type.MyCustomType]

The update Attribute

The update attribute specifies whether the column should be included in the SQL UPDATE statement and is optional.

Example

```
<property name="IPAddress" column="IPAddress" update="false" />
```

This property will never be written to the database when a record is being **updated**, however, will only be written on **inserts**.

By default, the value of this attribute is true.

The insert Attribute

The insert attribute specifies whether the column should be included in the SQL INSERT statement and is optional.

Example

```
<property name="IPAddress" column="IPAddress" insert="false" />
```

This property will never be written to the database when a record is being **inserted**, however, will only be written on **updates**.

By default, the value of this attribute is true.

REMINDER

If the update or insert attribute is set to false, then it allows a pure derived property whose value is initialized from some other property that maps to the same column(s) or by a trigger or other application.

Example

```
<property name="Username" column="Username" insert="false" update="false" />
```

This property will never be written to the database on either **inserts** or **updates**. This makes the Username property immutable which means it can be read from the database but not modified in any way.

The formula Attribute

The formula attribute is an SQL query that defines the value for a computed property and is optional.

REMINDER

Computed property is the one that is calculated dynamically, rather than represented in a column.

HINT

Computed properties do not have a column mapping of their own.

This attribute is a powerful feature, which is a derived property. The properties are by definition read-only, the property value is computed at load time.

Example

```
<property name="Total" formula="Total - DiscountRate * TOTAL" type="big_decimal"/>
```

Here, a property called Total is mapped without having a database table column for it.

REMINDER

A formula is evaluated every time the entity is retrieved from the database.

Such a property will:

- Never have a column attribute / element
- Never appear in an SQL INSERT or UPDATE
- Appear only in SQL SELECT

A formula may refer to table columns, invoke SQL functions and include SQL sub-selects.

Example

```
<property name="NumberOfBooks" formula="(SELECT COUNT(ISBN) FROM Books)" type="big_decimal"/>
```

Here, a derived property called **NumberOfBooks** is mapped using a SELECT to calculate the number of books.

The access Attribute

The access attribute, informs Hibernate, the strategy to be used to access the properties and is optional.

Example

```
<property name="FirstName" column="FirstName" access="property" />
```

If this attribute is set to **property**, then **get** and **set** methods are used to access the data.

Example

```
<property name="FirstName" column="FirstName" access="field" />
```

If this attribute is set to **field**, then the data is accessed directly.

Alternatively, this attribute can also be set to a class name of a PropertyAccessor implementation which defines any other access mechanism.

By default, the value of this attribute is property.

HINT

It is advisable to provide access to properties only via accessor methods. This brings in an additional level of abstraction between the Java DOMAIN model and the data model.

The lazy Attribute

The lazy attribute specifies whether this property should be fetched lazily when the instance variable is first accessed and is optional. By default, the value of this attribute is false.

The unique Attribute

The unique attribute specifies whether duplicate values are permitted for the column and is optional. By default, the value of this attribute is false.

This attribute enables the DDL generation of a UNIQUE constraint for the column.

The not-null Attribute

The not-null attribute specifies whether the column is permitted to contain NULL values and is optional. By default, the value of this attribute is false.

HINT

Detection of illegal null values is useful for providing sensible exceptions in the development phase.

This attribute enables the DDL generation of a NOT NULL / NULL constraint for the column.

The optimistic-lock Attribute

The optimistic-lock attribute determines whether the optimistic locking should be used when the attribute has been updated and is optional. By default, the value of this attribute is true.

The index Attribute

The index attribute is the name of an index to be maintained for the column and is optional.

The node Attribute

The node attribute specifies the name of the XML element or attribute, which should be used by the XML relational persistence features and is optional.

The length Attribute

The length attribute is the column length to be used and is optional.

The precision Attribute

The precision attribute allows the precision [the number of digits to the left of the decimal point] to be specified for the numeric data and is optional.

The scale Attribute

The scale attribute allows the scale [the number of digits to the right of the decimal point] to be specified for the numeric data and is optional.

The unique-key Attribute

The unique-key attribute groups the columns together by its value and is optional.

<component> Element

<component> element is used to map classes that will be represented as extra columns within a table describing some other class.

A component is a contained object that is persisted as a value type, not an entity reference. The term component refers to the object-oriented notion of composition and not to architecture-level components.

Syntax:

```
<component name="<PropertyName>" class="<ClassName>"
  update="<true | false>" insert="<true | false>"
  access="<field | property | ClassName>" lazy="<true | false>"
  unique="<true | false>" optimistic-lock="<true | false>"
  node="<XML Element>" />
```

The name Attribute

The name attribute is the name of the component to be persisted.

The class Attribute

The class attribute is the class that the parent class incorporates by composition.

The update Attribute

The update attribute specifies whether changes to this attribute in instances of the class should result in the column associated with this attribute being included in SQL UPDATE statements and is optional. By default, the value of this attribute is true.

The insert Attribute

The insert attribute specifies whether creation of an instance of the class should result in the column associated with this attribute being included in SQL INSERT statements and is optional. By default, the value of this attribute is true.

The access Attribute

The access attribute, informs Hibernate, the strategy to be used to access the properties and is optional.

If this attribute is set to **property**, then **get** and **set** methods are used to access the data.

If this attribute is set to **field**, then the data is accessed directly.

Alternatively, this attribute can also be set to a class name of a PropertyAccessor implementation which defines any other access mechanism.

By default, the value of this attribute is property.

The lazy Attribute

The lazy attribute specifies whether this property should be fetched lazily when the instance variable is first accessed and is optional. By default, the value of this attribute is false.

The unique Attribute

The unique attribute specifies whether the values that represent the component must be unique within the table and is optional. By default, the value of this attribute is false.

The optimistic-lock Attribute

The optimistic-lock attribute determines whether the optimistic locking should be used when the attribute has been updated and is optional. By default, the value of this attribute is true.

The node Attribute

The node attribute specifies the name of the XML element or attribute, which should be used by the XML relational persistence features and is optional.

<discriminator> Element

The discriminator element allows indicating, the column name in a table, that can be used to distinguish one class from another, in the hierarchy, when retrieving such classes from the database.

This element is often required for polymorphic persistence using the table-per-class-hierarchy mapping strategy where a generic base type is created with one or more specialized subclasses.

In a table-per-class-hierarchy mapping strategy, all the classes in the hierarchy are stored in a single table.

For example,
A table called Vehicles stores all kinds of vehicles and its details.

The Base class is the Vehicles class with **Cars** and **Bikes** as its subclasses.

In this situation, there exists a single table and multiple classes [One Base class and Two Subclasses].

For a single table to work properly, a column is used to distinguish one class from another in the hierarchy. This kind of distinction is possible using the <discriminator> element which helps identify the column in the table. This discriminator column contains marker values that inform the persistence layer what subclass to instantiate for a particular row.

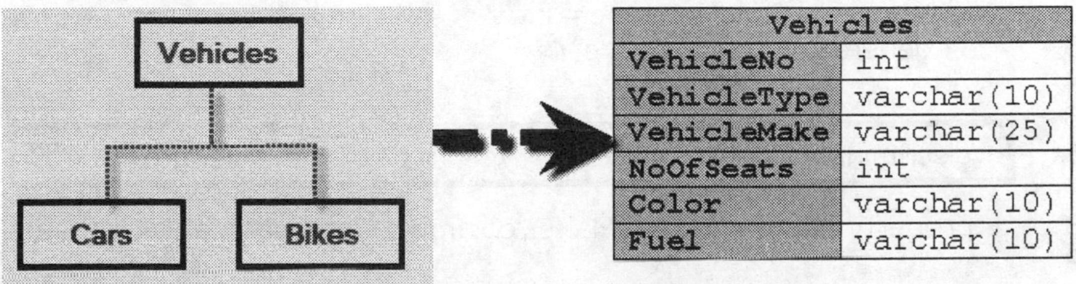

Vehicles	
VehicleNo	int
VehicleType	varchar(10)
VehicleMake	varchar(25)
NoOfSeats	int
Color	varchar(10)
Fuel	varchar(10)

One table contains the fields for all the objects in the hierarchy.

Suppose the properties of these classes are:

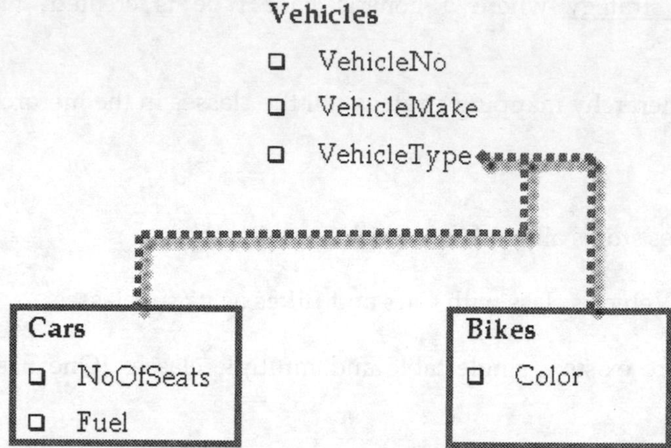

From this, it's clear that **VehicleType** is the discriminator column. Based on which, the mapping file will be:

```
<class name="Vehicles" table="Vehicles">
    <id name="VehicleNo" type="int">
        <generator class="native"/>
    </id>

    <discriminator column="VehicleType" type="string" length="10"/>

    <property name="VehicleMake" column="VehicleMake"/>

    <subclass name="Cars" discriminator-value="Car">
        <property name="NoOfSeats" column="NoOfSeats"/>
        <property name="Fuel" column="Fuel"/>
    </subclass>

    <subclass name="Bikes" discriminator-value="Bike">
        <property name="Color" column="Color"/>
    </subclass>
</class>
```

Here, the discriminator element informs Hibernate to look in the event_type column toı a string describing the class type.

Syntax:

```
<discriminator column="<ColumnName>" type="<DataType>"
  force="<true | false>" insert="<true | false>"
  formula="<SQL Expression>"/>
```

The column Attribute

The column attribute specifies the name of the column in the table to use as the discriminator column and is optional.

By default, this attribute takes the value of class.

The type Attribute

The type attribute specifies the type of discriminator column and is optional.

By default, the value of this attribute is string.

Following are the valid data types:

- string
- character
- integer
- byte
- short
- Boolean
- yes/no
- true/false

The force Attribute

The force attribute determines whether Hibernate uses discriminator values when retrieving all instances of a root class and is optional.

By default, the value of this attribute is false.

HINT

The force attribute is useful only if the table contains rows with extra discriminator values that are not mapped to a persistent class. This will not usually be the case.

The insert Attribute

The insert attribute informs Hibernate to not to include the column in an SQL INSERT statement and is optional.

By default, the value of this attribute is true.

If this attribute is set to false, then the discriminator column is also the part of a mapped composite identifier.

The formula Attribute

The formula attribute is an arbitrary SQL expression that is executed when a type has to be evaluated and is optional.

This attribute allows content-based discrimination.

This chapter provided an overview of the kinds of mapping. It also covered the following elements:

- hibernate-mapping
- class
- property
- component
- discriminator

There are several other elements. To make the learning simpler, these elements are divided logically and placed in the chapters that follow:

- The Database Identity
- Associations
- Collections
- Concurrency Control Using Versioning

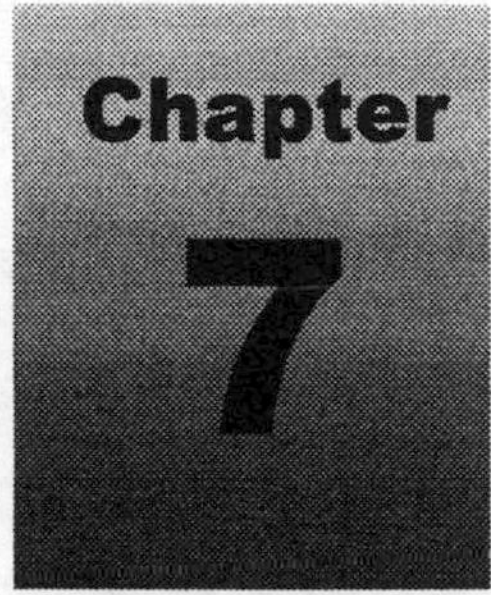

SECTION III: UNDERSTANDING CONFIGURATION AND MAPPING

The Database Identity

This chapter discusses database identity and how Hibernate manages identity.

<id> Element

When mapping a Java class to a database table, an ID [The Primary Key column of the database table] is required. Mapped classes must declare the **Primary Key** column of the database table. The <id> element allows specifying information about the ID column.

<id> element defines the mapping from that property to the primary key column as shown in diagram 7.1.

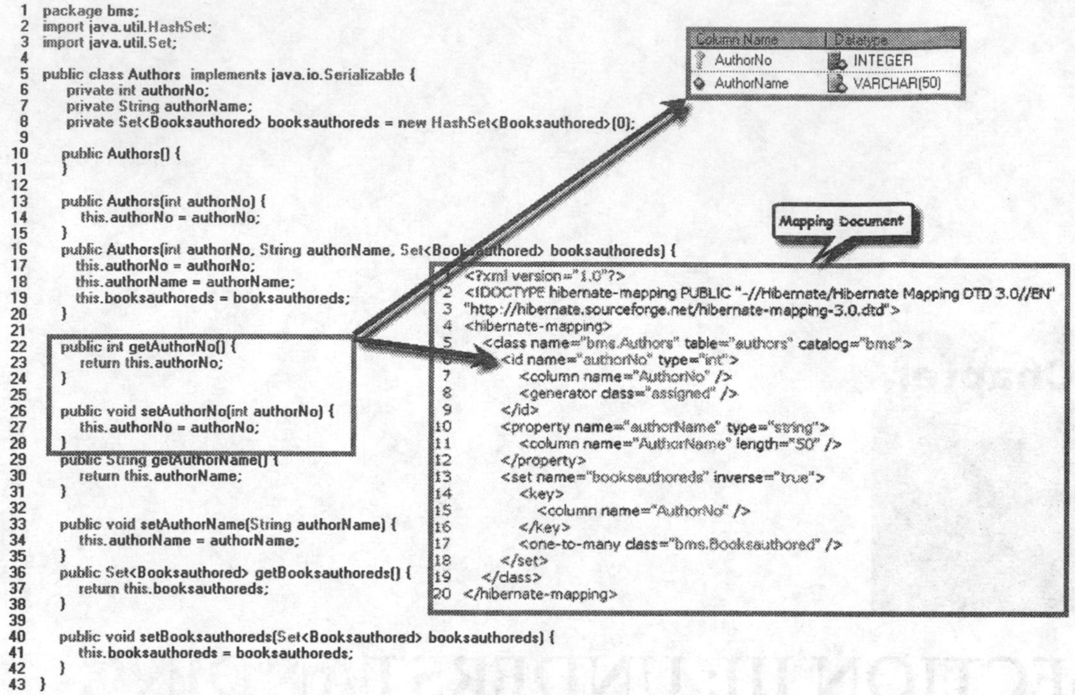

```java
package bms;
import java.util.HashSet;
import java.util.Set;

public class Authors  implements java.io.Serializable {
     private int authorNo;
     private String authorName;
     private Set<Booksauthored> booksauthoreds = new HashSet<Booksauthored>(0);

    public Authors() {
    }

    public Authors(int authorNo) {
       this.authorNo = authorNo;
    }
    public Authors(int authorNo, String authorName, Set<Booksauthored> booksauthoreds) {
       this.authorNo = authorNo;
       this.authorName = authorName;
       this.booksauthoreds = booksauthoreds;
    }

    public int getAuthorNo() {
        return this.authorNo;
    }

    public void setAuthorNo(int authorNo) {
        this.authorNo = authorNo;
    }
    public String getAuthorName() {
        return this.authorName;
    }

    public void setAuthorName(String authorName) {
        this.authorName = authorName;
    }
    public Set<Booksauthored> getBooksauthoreds() {
        return this.booksauthoreds;
    }

    public void setBooksauthoreds(Set<Booksauthored> booksauthoreds) {
        this.booksauthoreds = booksauthoreds;
    }
}
```

Column Name	Datatype
AuthorNo	INTEGER
AuthorName	VARCHAR(50)

Mapping Document

```xml
<?xml version="1.0"?>
<!DOCTYPE hibernate-mapping PUBLIC "-//Hibernate/Hibernate Mapping DTD 3.0//EN"
"http://hibernate.sourceforge.net/hibernate-mapping-3.0.dtd">
<hibernate-mapping>
  <class name="bms.Authors" table="authors" catalog="bms">
    <id name="authorNo" type="int">
       <column name="AuthorNo" />
       <generator class="assigned" />
    </id>
    <property name="authorName" type="string">
       <column name="AuthorName" length="50" />
    </property>
    <set name="booksauthoreds" inverse="true">
       <key>
          <column name="AuthorNo" />
       </key>
       <one-to-many class="bms.Booksauthored" />
    </set>
  </class>
</hibernate-mapping>
```

Diagram 7.1

The Authors class defines an identifier property called **AuthorNo**.

```java
public int getAuthorNo() {
    return this.authorNo;
}

public void setAuthorNo(int authorNo) {
    this.authorNo = authorNo;
}
```

The property type depends on the **Primary Key** type of the **Authors** table and the Hibernate mapping type.

Column Name	Datatype
AuthorNo	INTEGER
AuthorName	VARCHAR(50)

The identifier property is mapped to the primary key column AuthorNo of the Authors table. This information is made available to Hibernate using the **<id>** element in the mapping document.

```
<id name="authorNo" type="int">
   <column name="AuthorNo" />
   <generator class="assigned" />
</id>
```

The Hibernate type for this property is **INT**, which maps to an INT column type in most databases. The generator class chosen is **assigned**.

Using database identifiers in Hibernate is quite easy. However, the only important step is choosing a good key generation strategy [i.e. generator class].

Syntax:

```
<id name="<PropertyName>" type="<TypeName>" column="<ColumnName>"
    unsaved-value="<null | any | none | undefined | id_value>"
    access="<field | property | ClassName>" node="<XML Element>"
    length="<ColumnLength>">
  <generator class="<GeneratorClass>"/>
</id>
```

The name Attribute

The name attribute specifies the name of the attribute in the class representing this primary key and is optional.

If this attribute is not specified, then Hibernate assumes that the class does not have an attribute directly representing the primary key.

The type Attribute

The type attribute is a name, which indicates the Hibernate data type and is optional.

If type is not specified, Hibernate uses reflection, to determine the type.

The column Attribute

The column attribute is the name of the primary key column and is optional.

If this attribute is not specified, then Hibernate uses the value given in the name attribute.

The unsaved-value Attribute

The unsaved-value attribute is the value that the attribute should take when an instance of the class has been created but not yet persisted to the database and is optional.

The access Attribute

The access attribute, informs Hibernate, the strategy to be used to access the properties and is optional.

If this attribute is set to **property**, then **get** and **set** methods are used to access the data.

If this attribute is set to **field**, then the data is accessed directly.

Alternatively, this attribute can also be set to a class name of a PropertyAccessor implementation which defines any other access mechanism.

By default, the value of this attribute is property.

The node Attribute

The node attribute specifies the name of the XML element or attribute, which should be used by the XML relational persistence features and is optional.

The length Attribute

The length attribute is the column length to be used and is optional.

<generator> Element

<generator> element is the child element of <id> element.

When inserting a new record/row in a database table for the instantiated Java Object, the ID column must be populated with a unique value in order to uniquely identify that persisted object. The <generator> element helps define how to generate a new primary key [unique value] for a new instance of the class.

<generator> element accepts a Java class name that will be used to generate unique identifiers for instances of the persistent class.

Syntax:

```
<id name="<PropertyName>" type="<TypeName>" column="<ColumnName>">
  <generator class="<GeneratorClass>">
     <param name="<ParameterName>"><ParameterValue></param>
  </generator>
</id>
```

To pass parameters to the class the <param> element can be used.

Example

```
<id name="id" type="long" column="CustomerNo">
  <generator class="hilo">
     <param name="table">hi_value</param>
     <param name="column">next_value</param>
     <param name="max_lo">10</param>
  </generator>
</id>
```

All generators implement a very simple interface called org.hibernate.id.IdentifierGenerator.

Hibernate provides a range of built-in default IdentifierGenerator implementations, which can be referenced by convenient short names:

The increment Class

The increment class generates the primary key value by adding 1 to the current highest primary key value.

Technically, this is achieved as follows:

- The generator fires an SQL SELECT query and retrieves the highest value of the primary key column
- The generator then increments the primary key column value by 1

This class generates identifiers of type **long**, **short** or **int**.

WARNING

The increment class works, only if, other processes are not permitted to update the table at the same time.

If multiple processes are running, then depending on the constraints enforced by the database, the result may be an error in the application(s) or data corruption.

It is **not advisable** using the increment class in a cluster.

The identity Class

The identity class supports the identity columns in databases such as DB2, MySQL, MS SQL Server, Sybase and HypersonicSQL. This class, therefore, is not a fully portable option.

Example

```
<id name="id" type="long" column="CustomerNo" unsaved-value="0">
   <generator class="identity" />
</id>
```

This class generates identifiers of type **long**, **short** or **int**.

The sequence Class

The sequence class uses a sequence in databases such as DB2, PostgreSQL, Oracle, SAP DB, McKoi or a generator in Interbase. This class, therefore, is not a fully portable option.

Example

```
<id name="id" type="long" column="CustomerNo">
   <generator class="sequence">
      <param name="sequence">CustomerNo_Sequence</param>
   </generator>
</id>
```

This class generates identifiers of type **long**, **short** or **int**.

The hilo Class

The hilo class uses a hi/lo algorithm to efficiently and portably maintain and generate identifiers that are unique to that database. It uses a database table and columns [by default columns named as **hibernate_unique_key** and **next_hi**] as a source of hi values to generate unique identifiers.

HINT

The hi/lo algorithm generates identifiers that are unique only for a particular database.

Example

```
<id name="id" type="long" column="CustomerNo">
    <generator class="hilo">
        <param name="table">hi_value</param>
        <param name="column">next_value</param>
        <param name="max_lo">10</param>
    </generator>
</id>
```

This class generates identifiers of type **long**, **short** or **int**.

The seqhilo Class

The seqhilo class uses a hi/lo algorithm to efficiently generate identifiers that are unique to that database using a sequence as the source. This class, therefore, is not a fully portable option.

Example

```
<id name="id" type="long" column="CustomerNo">
    <generator class="seqhilo">
        <param name="sequence">hi_value</param>
        <param name="max_lo">10</param>
    </generator>
</id>
```

This class generates identifiers of type **long, short** or **int**.

The uuid Class

The uuid class uses a 128-bit UUID algorithm to generate identifiers, unique within a network.

The uuid class attempts to portably generate a unique primary key value, which is composed of the following:

- The local IP address
- The startup time of Java Virtual Machine [accurate to ¼ of a second]
- The system time
- A counter value [unique within the JVM]

This class, however, cannot guarantee that a given key is unique, but it is a good enough for most clustering purposes.

The UUID is encoded as a string of **hexadecimal** digits of length 32.

The guid Class

The GUID class uses a database generated GUID string.

REMINDER

This option is not portable across databases [except MS SQL Server and MySQL] that do not have a GUID type. Hence, the quality of the uniqueness of this key may vary from vendor to vendor.

The native Class

The native class selects one of the following depending upon the capabilities of the underlying database:

- identity
- sequence
- hilo

HINT

This class is a good compromise option since it uses the innate features of the database and is portable to most platforms. This is particularly appropriate if the application's code spec is likely to be deployed to a number of database implementations with differing capabilities.

The assigned Class

The assigned class allows the application to assign an identifier to the object before invoking the **save()** method. The assigned class is invoked, by default, if no <generator> element is specified.

REMINDER

If this technique is used, the **saveOrUpdate()** method cannot be used on a transient entity. Instead, appropriate **save()** or **update()** method needs to be invoked explicitly.

The select Class

The select class retrieves a primary key assigned by a database trigger by selecting the row by some unique key and retrieving the primary key value.

The foreign Class

The foreign class uses the identifier of another associated object. This class is usually used in conjunction with a <one-to-one> primary key association.

The sequence-identity Class

The sequence-identity class is a specialized sequence generation strategy which utilizes a database sequence for the actual value generation, but combines this with JDBC3 getGeneratedKeys to actually return the generated identifier value as part of the INSERT statement execution.

HINT

This strategy is only known to be supported on Oracle 10g drivers targeted for JDK 1.4.

The SequenceStyleGenerator Class

The SequenceStyleGenerator class is available with Hibernate release 3.2.3 and above. This class is intended as a replacement for the **sequence** generator. It offers a better portability generator than native because native generally chooses between identity and sequence which have largely different semantics which can cause subtle issues in applications eyeing portability.

SequenceStyleGenerator achieves portability. It chooses between using a table or a sequence in the database to store its incrementing values depending on the capabilities of the dialect being used.

The difference between this and the native is that table-based and sequence-based storage have the same exact semantic, in fact, sequences are exactly what Hibernate tries to emmulate with its table-based generators.

This generator class has a number of configuration parameters:

sequence_name

This parameter accepts the name of the sequence [or table] to be used and is an optional parameter. It defaults to **hibernate_sequence** if un-specified.

initial_value

This parameter accepts the initial value to be retrieved from the sequence/table and is optional. It defaults to 1 if unspecified.

It is very similar to the clause **STARTS WITH** used when creating a sequence.

increment_size

This parameter accepts the value by which subsequent calls to the sequence/table should differ and is optional. It defaults to 1 if unspecified.

It is very similar to the clause **INCREMENT BY** used when creating a sequence.

force_table_use

This parameter accepts true to indicate forcing the use of a table as the backing structure even though the dialect might support sequence and is optional. It defaults to false if unspecified.

value_column

This parameter accepts the name of the table column which is used to hold the value and is optional. It defaults to **next_val** if unspecified.

This parameter is only relevant for table structures.

optimizer

This parameter holds the name of a pluggable optimizer and is optional and defaults to none.

This optimizer is useful, for identifier generators which store values in the database, in which case, it becomes inefficient to hit the database on each and every call to generate a new identifier value.

Instead, a bunch of them can be grouped in memory. This ensures that the database will only be hit when the in-memory value group has exhausted.

This parameter accepts:

none

This is the default value if no optimizer is specified. none indicates not to perform any optimizations which means hitting the database on each and every request.

hilo

This applies a hi/lo algorithm around the database retrieved values. The values from the database for this optimizer are expected to be sequential. The values retrieved from the database structure for this optimizer indicates the group number. The increment_size [the value from the database] is multiplied by that value in memory to define a group **hi value**.

pooled

Very similar to hilo, this optimizer attempts to minimize the number of hits to the database. Here, however, the starting value for the **next group** is stored in the database structure rather than a sequential value in combination with an in-memory grouping algorithm.

The TableGenerator Class

The TableGenerator class is available with Hibernate release 3.2.3 and above.

This class is intended as a replacement for the existing table generator. Essentially this generator defines a table capable of holding a number of different increment values simultaneously by using multiple distinctly keyed rows. This generator has a number of configuration parameters:

table_name

This parameter accepts the name of the table to be used and is optional. It defaults to **hibernate_sequences** if unspecified.

value_column_name

This parameter accepts the name of the column on the table which is used to hold the value and is optional. It defaults to **next_val** if unspecified.

segment_column_name

This parameter accepts the name of the column on the table which is used to hold the **segement key** and is optional. It defaults to **sequence_name**.

This is the value which distinctly identifies which increment value to use.

segment_value

This parameter accepts the **segment key** value for the segment from which the incremented values for this generator has to be pulled and is optional. It defaults to default.

segment_value_length

This parameter accepts the column size to create this segment key column and is optional. It defaults to 255.

initial_value

This parameter accepts the initial value to be retrieved from the table and is optional. It defaults to 1.

increment_size

This parameter accepts the value by which subsequent calls to the table should differ and is optional. It defaults to 1.

optimizer

Same as the one specified earlier for the SequenceStyleGenerator class.

<composite-id> Element

Composite Identifiers are primary key identifiers for classes that consist of more than one primary key column.

For a table with a composite key, the <composite-id> element allows mapping multiple properties of the class as identifier properties. It accepts <key-property> property mappings and <key-many-to-one> mappings as child elements as shown in diagram 7.2.

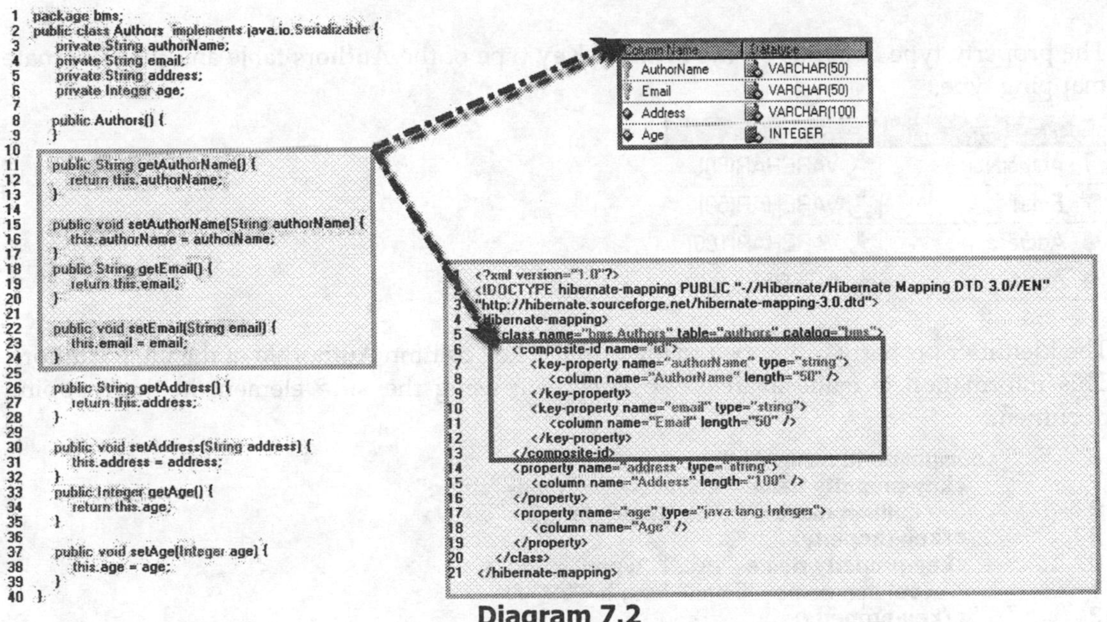

Diagram 7.2

The Authors class defines a composite key with two identifiers called **AuthorName** and **Email**.

```
    public String getAuthorName() {
        return this.authorName;
    }

    public void setAuthorName(String authorName) {
        this.authorName = authorName;
    }
    public String getEmail() {
        return this.email;
    }

    public void setEmail(String email) {
        this.email = email;
    }
```

The property type depends on the **Primary Key** type of the **Authors** table and the Hibernate mapping type.

Column Name	Datatype
AuthorName	VARCHAR(50)
Email	VARCHAR(50)
Address	VARCHAR(100)
Age	INTEGER

The identifier property is mapped to the primary key column AuthorNo of the table Authors. This information is made available to Hibernate using the <id> element in the mapping document.

```
    <composite-id name="id">
        <key-property name="authorName" type="string">
            <column name="AuthorName" length="50" />
        </key-property>
        <key-property name="email" type="string">
            <column name="Email" length="50" />
        </key-property>
    </composite-id>
```

Syntax:

```
<composite-id name="<PropertyName>" class="<ClassName>"
   unsaved-value="<any | none>" mapped="<true | false>"
   access="<field | property | ClassName>">
  <key-property name="<PropertyName>"/>
</composite-id>
```

The name Attribute

The name attribute is the name of the property of component type, which holds the composite identifier.

The class Attribute

The class attribute is the component class used as a composite identifier and is optional.

It defaults to the property type determined by reflection.

The unsaved-value Attribute

The unsaved-value attribute is the value that the attribute should take when an instance of the class has been created but not yet persisted to the database and is optional.

The mapped Attribute

The mapped attribute indicates that a mapped composite identifier is used and that the contained property mappings refer to both the entity class and the composite identifier class and is optional.

By default, the value of this attribute is false.

The access Attribute

The access attribute, informs Hibernate, the strategy to be used to access the properties and is optional.

If this attribute is set to **property**, then **get** and **set** methods are used to access the data.

If this attribute is set to **field**, then the data is accessed directly.

Alternatively, this attribute can also be set to a class name of a PropertyAccessor implementation which defines any other access mechanism.

By default, the value of this attribute is property.

Proceed to the chapters that follow for the remaining elements of the mapping document.

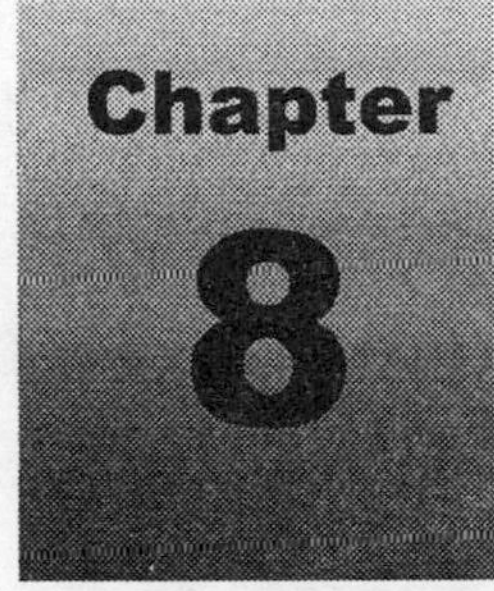

SECTION III: UNDERSTANDING CONFIGURATION AND MAPPING

Associations

Relationships between entities are represented by associations which form the core part of any ORM. So the prime task of an ORM is to create a mapping between the relationships and the associations. This mapping is known as an **association**.

To make it simpler, associations help represent relationships between classes.

A relationship between the objects can be expressed in the several ways based on the kind of relationship.

Kind Of Relationships

The following are the kind of relationships:

- ONE-TO-ONE
- ONE-TO-MANY
- MANY-TO-ONE

- MANY-TO-MANY

It is important to understand how to determine the kind of relationship between classes/objects.

ONE-TO-ONE

Let's take the following classes as an example to begin with.

Authors

- AuthorNo
- AuthorName
- AboutAuthor

ContactDetails

- AuthorNo
- Email
- MobileNumber

To determine the kind of relationship, it is best to begin by answering a few questions.

Now let's fire a few questions on these classes:

- Can an Author have multiple contact details?
- Can a contact detail be shared across multiple authors?

The following table helps determine the kind of relationship.

Answer 1	Answer 2	Relationship
No	No	ONE-TO-ONE
Yes	No	ONE-TO-MANY
No	Yes	MANY-TO-ONE
Yes	Yes	MANY-TO-MANY

Let's answer them:

- Can an Author have multiple contact details?

  No, An author will have only one contact details
- Can a contact detail be shared across multiple authors?

  No, every contact detail will map to exactly a single author

Based on the answers, it is clear that, an author can have exactly one contact detail and hence, the kind of relationship is **ONE-TO-ONE**.

From the database perspective, this relationship can be represented as shown in diagram 8.1.

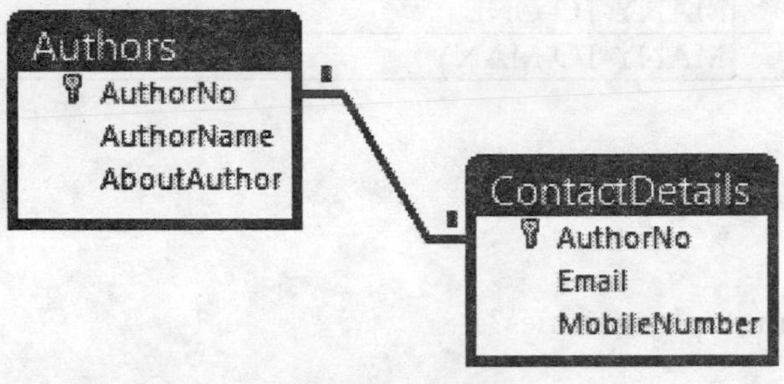

Diagram 8.1

ONE-TO-MANY / MANY-TO-ONE

Let's take the following classes as an example to begin with.

Countries

- CountryNo
- CountryName

States

- StateNo
- StateName
- CountryNo

To determine the kind of relationship, it is best to begin by answering a few questions.

Now let's fire a few questions on these classes:

- Can a country have multiple states?
- Can a state have multiple countries?

The following table helps determine the kind of relationship.

Answer 1	Answer 2	Relationship
No	No	ONE-TO-ONE
Yes	No	ONE-TO-MANY
No	Yes	MANY-TO-ONE
Yes	Yes	MANY-TO-MANY

Let's answer them:

- Can a country have multiple states?

  Yes

- Can a state have multiple countries?

  No

Based on the answers, it is clear that,

From the perspective of the Countries class:

- A country can have multiple states but the reverse is false and hence, the kind of relationship is ONE-TO-MANY

From the perspective of the States class:

- A state cannot have multiple countries but the reverse is true and hence, the kind of relationship is MANY-TO-ONE

From the database perspective, this relationship can be represented as shown in diagram 8.2.

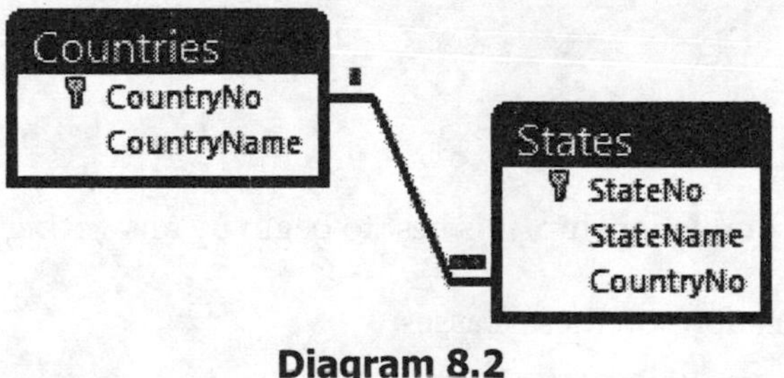

Diagram 8.2

MANY-TO-MANY

Let's take the following classes as an example to begin with.

Authors

- AuthorNo

- AuthorName
- AboutAuthor

Books

- BookNo
- BookName
- ISBN
- AboutBook
- Price

To determine the kind of relationship, it is best to begin by answering a few questions.

Now let's fire a few questions on these classes:

- Can an Author write multiple books?
- Can a book be written by multiple authors?

The following table helps determine the kind of relationship.

Answer 1	Answer 2	Relationship
No	No	ONE-TO-ONE
Yes	No	ONE-TO-MANY
No	Yes	MANY-TO-ONE
Yes	Yes	MANY-TO-MANY

Let's answer them:

- Can an Author write multiple books?

  Yes
- Can a book be written by multiple authors?

  Yes

Based on the answers, it is clear that an author can write multiple books and a book can be written by multiple authors and hence, the kind of relationship is **MANY-TO-MANY**.

From the database perspective, this relationship can be represented as shown in diagram 8.3.

Diagram 8.3

Now that the concepts of the kind of relationships are in place, let's explore the elements used to represent them.

<one-to-one> Element - Relationship Mapping

A one-to-one association to another persistent class is declared using <one-to-one> element.

Syntax:

```
<one-to-one name="<PropertyName>" class="<ClassName>"
  cascade="<CascadeStyle>" check="<SQL Expression>"
  constrained="<true | false>" fetch="<join | select>"
  embed-xml="<true | false>" foreign-key="<ForeignKeyName>"
  property-ref="<PropertyNameFromAssociatedClass>"
  access="<field | property | ClassName>" lazy="<true | false>"
  formula="<SQL Expression>" entity-name="<EntityName>"
  node="<XML Element>" outer-join="<true | false | auto>"/>
```

The name Attribute

The name attribute is the name of Java associated with the relationship.

The class Attribute

The class attribute is the name of the associated class and is optional.

It defaults to the property type determined by reflection.

The cascade Attribute

The cascade attribute specifies which operations should be cascaded from the parent object to the associated object and is optional.

The check Attribute

The check attribute is an SQL expression used to generate a multi-row check constraint for automatic schema generation and is optional.

The check attribute defines a row-level check constraint, effectively adding this as an SQL CHECK(. . .) clause during table generation.

The constrained Attribute

The constrained attribute specifies that a foreign key constraint on the primary key of the mapped table references the table of the associated class and is optional.

This option affects the order in which the save() and delete() methods are cascaded and determines whether the association may be proxied.

The fetch Attribute

The fetch attribute chooses between outer-join fetching or sequential select fetching and is optional. By default, the value of this attribute is select.

The embed-xml Attribute

The embed-xml attribute indicates whether the XML tree for the associated entity itself or only its identifier, will appear in the generated XML tree when using XML relational persistence and is optional.

The foreign-key Attribute

The foreign-key attribute is the name to assign to the foreign key enforcing the relationship and is optional.

The property-ref Attribute

The property-ref attribute is the name of a property of the associated class that is joined to the primary key of this class and is optional.

If this attribute is not specified, then the primary key of the associated class is used.

The access Attribute

The access attribute, informs Hibernate, the strategy to be used to access the properties and is optional.

If this attribute is set to **property**, then **get** and **set** methods are used to access the data.

If this attribute is set to **field**, then the data is accessed directly.

Alternatively, this attribute can also be set to a class name of a PropertyAccessor implementation which defines any other access mechanism.

By default, the value of this attribute is property.

The lazy Attribute

The lazy attribute overrides the entity-loading mode and is optional.

The formula Attribute

The formula attribute allows the value to which the associated class maps its foreign key to be overridden using an SQL formula and is optional.

Almost all one to one associations map to the primary key of the owning entity. In the rare case that this is not the case, one may specify some other column(s) or expression to join on using an SQL formula.

The entity-name Attribute

The entity-name attribute is the entity name of the associated class and is optional.

The node Attribute

The node attribute specifies the name of the XML element or attribute, which should be used by the XML relational persistence features and is optional.

The outer-join Attribute

The outer-join attribute specifies whether an outer join should be used and is optional.

Example

From the perspective of the Authors class [ONE-TO-ONE]:

```
<?xml version="1.0"?>
<!DOCTYPE hibernate-mapping PUBLIC "-//Hibernate/Hibernate Mapping DTD 3.0//EN"
"http://hibernate.sourceforge.net/hibernate-mapping-3.0.dtd">
<hibernate-mapping>
   <class name="myApp.Authors" table="authors" catalog="associations">
      <id name="authorNo" type="java.lang.Integer">
         <column name="AuthorNo" />
         <generator class="foreign">
            <param name="property">contactdetails</param>
         </generator>
      </id>
      <one-to-one name="contactdetails" class="myApp.Contactdetails" fetch="select"
      cascade="all"  />
      <property name="authorName" type="string">
         <column name="AuthorName" length="25" />
      </property>
      <property name="aboutAuthor" type="string">
         <column name="AboutAuthor" length="50" />
      </property>
   </class>
</hibernate-mapping>
```

From the perspective of the ContactDetails class:

```
<?xml version="1.0"?>
<!DOCTYPE hibernate-mapping PUBLIC "-//Hibernate/Hibernate Mapping DTD 3.0//EN"
```

```
"http://hibernate.sourceforge.net/hibernate-mapping-3.0.dtd">
<hibernate-mapping>
    <class name="myApp.Contactdetails" table="contactdetails" catalog="associations">
        <id name="authorNo" type="java.lang.Integer">
            <column name="AuthorNo" />
            <generator class="identity" />
        </id>
        <property name="email" type="string">
            <column name="Email" length="50" />
        </property>
        <property name="mobileNumber" type="java.lang.Integer">
            <column name="MobileNumber" />
        </property>
    </class>
</hibernate-mapping>
```

<many-to-one> Element - Relationship Mapping

<many-to-one> element represents the relationship in which multiple instances of one class can reference a single instance of another class.

The relational model is a <many-to-one> association i.e. a foreign key in one table is referencing the primary key column(s) of the target table.

Syntax:

```
<many-to-one name="<PropertyName>" column="<ColumnName>"
  class="<ClassName>" cascade="<CascadeStyle>" index="<IndexName>"
  fetch="<join | select>" update="<true | false>"
  insert="<true | false>" embed-xml="<true | false>"
  property-ref="<PropertyNameFromAssociatedClass>"
  access="<field | property | ClassName>" unique="<true | false>"
  not-null="<true | false>" optimistic-lock="<true | false>"
  lazy="<true | false>" entity-name="<EntityName>"
  formula="<SQL Expression>" foreign-key="<ForeignKeyName>"
  node="<XML Element>" not-found="<exception |ignore>"
  outer-join="<true | false | auto>" unique-key="<UniqueKey>" />
```

The name Attribute

The name attribute is the name of the Java associated with the relationship.

The column Attribute

The column attribute is the name of the foreign key column <u>and is optional</u>.

By default, this attribute takes the value of the name attribute.

This can also be specified by the nested <column> element(s).

The class Attribute

The class attribute is the name of the associated class <u>and is optional</u>.

It defaults to the property type determined by reflection.

The cascade Attribute

The cascade attribute specifies which operations should be cascaded from the parent object to the associated object <u>and is optional</u>.

The index Attribute

The index attribute is the name of an index to be applied to the foreign key column in the parent table representing the **many** side of the association <u>and is optional</u>.

The fetch Attribute

The fetch attribute chooses between outer-join fetching or sequential select fetching <u>and is optional</u>. By default, the value of this attribute is <u>select</u>.

The update Attribute

The update attribute specifies that the mapped columns should be included in the SQL UPDATE statement <u>and is optional</u>. By default, the value of this attribute is <u>true</u>.

The insert Attribute

The insert attribute specifies that the mapped columns should be included in the SQL INSERT statement <u>and is optional</u>. By default, the value of this attribute is <u>true</u>.

REMINDER

If the update or insert attribute is set to false, then it allows a pure derived property whose value is initialized from some other property that maps to the same column(s) or by a trigger or other application.

The embed-xml Attribute

The embed-xml attribute indicates whether the XML tree for the associated entity itself or only its identifier, will appear in the generated XML tree when using XML relational persistence and is optional.

The property-ref Attribute

The property-ref attribute is the name of a property of the associated class that is joined to the primary key of this class and is optional.

If this attribute is not specified, then the primary key of the associated class is used.

HINT

The property-ref attribute should be used only for mapping legacy data where a foreign key refers to a unique key of the associated table other than the primary key.

For example, suppose the Books class has a unique serial number, which is not the primary key:

```
<property name="SerialNo" unique="true" type="string" column="SerialNo"/>
```

Then the mapping for SerialNo would be:

```
<many-to-one name="Book" property-ref="SerialNo" column="SerialNo"/>
```

However, this is certainly not encouraged.

The access Attribute

The access attribute, informs Hibernate, the strategy to be used to access the properties and is optional.

If this attribute is set to **property**, then **get** and **set** methods are used to access the data.

If this attribute is set to **field**, then the data is accessed directly.

Alternatively, this attribute can also be set to a class name of a PropertyAccessor implementation which defines any other access mechanism.

By default, the value of this attribute is property.

The unique Attribute

The unique attribute specifies whether duplicate values are permitted for the column and is optional. By default, the value of this attribute is false.

This attribute enables the DDL generation of a UNIQUE constraint for the column.

HINT

Allow the unique attribute to be the target of the property-ref attribute as this makes the association multiplicity effectively one to one.

The not-null Attribute

The not-null attribute specifies whether the column is permitted to contain NULL values and is optional. By default, the value of this attribute is false.

This attribute enables the DDL generation of a NOT NULL / NULL constraint for the column.

The optimistic-lock Attribute

The optimistic-lock attribute determines whether the optimistic locking should be used when the attribute has been updated and is optional. By default, the value of this attribute is true.

The lazy Attribute

The lazy attribute specifies whether this property should be fetched lazily when the instance variable is first accessed and is optional. By default, the value of this attribute is false.

The entity-name Attribute

The entity-name attribute is the entity name of the associated class and is optional.

The formula Attribute

The formula attribute allows the value to which the associated class maps its foreign key to be overridden using an SQL formula and is optional.

The foreign-key Attribute

The foreign-key attribute is the name to assign to the foreign key enforcing the relationship and is optional.

The node Attribute

The node attribute specifies the name of the XML element or attribute, which should be used by the XML relational persistence features and is optional.

The not-found Attribute

The not-found attribute is the behavior to exhibit if the related entity does not exist i.e. either throw an exception or ignore the problem and is optional. By default, the value of this attribute is exception.

The outer-join Attribute

The outer-join attribute specifies whether an outer join should be used and is optional.

The unique-key Attribute

The unique-key attribute groups the columns together by its value and is optional.

Example

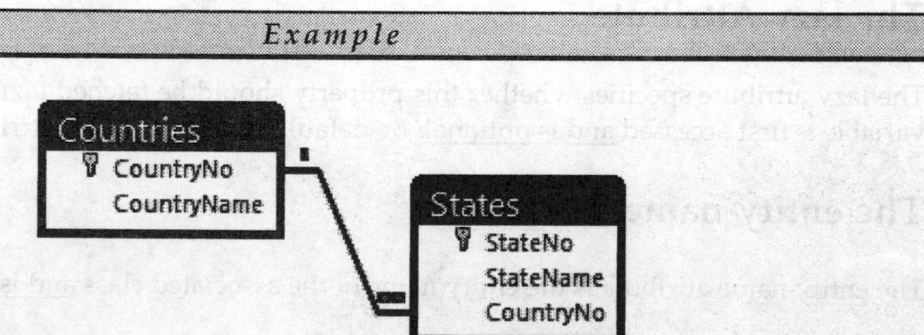

From the perspective of the States class [MANY-TO-ONE]:

```
<?xml version="1.0"?>
<!DOCTYPE hibernate-mapping PUBLIC "-//Hibernate/Hibernate Mapping
DTD 3.0//EN"
"http://hibernate.sourceforge.net/hibernate-mapping-3.0.dtd">
<hibernate-mapping>
    <class name="myApp.States" table="states" catalog="associations">
        <id name="stateNo" type="int">
            <column name="StateNo" />
            <generator class="assigned" />
        </id>
        <many-to-one name="countries" class="myApp.Countries"
        fetch="select">
            <column name="CountryNo" />
        </many-to-one>
        <property name="stateName" type="string">
            <column name="StateName" length="25" />
        </property>
    </class>
</hibernate-mapping>
```

From the perspective of the Countries class [ONE-TO-MANY]:

```
<?xml version="1.0"?>
<!DOCTYPE hibernate-mapping PUBLIC "-//Hibernate/Hibernate Mapping
DTD 3.0//EN"
"http://hibernate.sourceforge.net/hibernate-mapping-3.0.dtd">
<hibernate-mapping>
    <class name="myApp.Countries" table="countries"
    catalog="associations">
        <id name="countryNo" type="int">
            <column name="CountryNo" />
            <generator class="assigned" />
        </id>
        <property name="countryName" type="string">
            <column name="CountryName" length="25" />
        </property>
        <set name="stateses" inverse="true">
            <key>
```

```
            <column name="CountryNo" />
        </key>
        <one-to-many class="myApp.States" />
    </set>
  </class>
</hibernate-mapping>
```

<many-to-many> Element - Relationship Mapping

<many-to-many> element represents a collection.

Syntax:

```
<many-to-many column="<ColumnName>" class="<ClassName>"
  fetch="<join | select>" embed-xml="<true | false>"
  property-ref="<PropertyNameFromAssociatedClass>"
  unique="<true | false>" lazy="<true | false>"
  entity-name="<EntityName>" formula="<SQL Expression>"
  foreign-key="<ForeignKeyName>" node="<XML Element>"
  not-found="<exception |ignore>" outer-join="<true | false | auto>"
  where="<SQL WHERE clause>" order-by="<SQL ORDER BY clause>" />
```

The column Attribute

The column attribute is the name of the foreign key column and is optional.

This can also be specified by the nested <column> element(s).

The class Attribute

The class attribute is the name of the associated class and is optional.

It defaults to the property type determined by reflection.

The fetch Attribute

The fetch attribute chooses between outer-join fetching or sequential select fetching and is optional. By default, the value of this attribute is join.

REMINDER

This is a special case; for full eager fetching [in a single SELECT statement] of an entity and its many-to-many relationships to other entities, enable join fetching not only of the collection itself, but also with this attribute on the <many-to-many> nested element.

The embed-xml Attribute

The embed-xml attribute indicates whether the XML tree for the associated entity itself or only its identifier, will appear in the generated XML tree when using XML relational persistence and is optional.

The property-ref Attribute

The property-ref attribute is the name of a property of the associated class that is joined to the primary key of this class and is optional.

If this attribute is not specified, then the primary key of the associated class is used.

The unique Attribute

The unique attribute specifies whether duplicate values are permitted for the column and is optional. By default, the value of this attribute is false.

This attribute enables the DDL generation of a UNIQUE constraint for the column.

The lazy Attribute

The lazy attribute specifies whether this property should be fetched lazily when the instance variable is first accessed and is optional. By default, the value of this attribute is false.

The entity-name Attribute

The entity-name attribute is the entity name of the associated class and is optional.

The formula Attribute

The formula attribute allows the value to which the associated class maps its foreign key to be overridden using an SQL formula and is optional.

The foreign-key Attribute

The foreign-key attribute is the name to assign to the foreign key enforcing the relationship and is optional.

The node Attribute

The node attribute specifies the name of the XML element or attribute, which should be used by the XML relational persistence features and is optional.

The not-found Attribute

The not-found attribute is the behavior to exhibit if the related entity does not exist i.e. either throw an exception or ignore the problem and is optional. By default, the value of this attribute is exception.

The outer-join Attribute

The outer-join attribute specifies whether an outer join should be used and is optional.

The where Attribute

The where attribute specifies an SQL WHERE condition to be used when retrieving objects of this class from the database table and is optional.

The order-by Attribute

The order-by attribute specifies an SQL query's ORDER BY clause to constrain the results returned by an SQL query, which populates the set collection and is optional.

Example

From the perspective of the Authors class [MANY-TO-MANY]:

```
<?xml version="1.0"?>
<!DOCTYPE hibernate-mapping PUBLIC "-//Hibernate/Hibernate Mapping DTD 3.0//EN"
"http://hibernate.sourceforge.net/hibernate-mapping-3.0.dtd">
<hibernate-mapping>
    <class name="myApp.Authors" table="authors" catalog="associations">
        <id name="authorNo" type="int">
            <column name="AuthorNo" />
            <generator class="assigned" />
        </id>
        <property name="authorName" type="string">
            <column name="AuthorName" length="25" />
        </property>
        <property name="aboutAuthor" type="string">
            <column name="AboutAuthor" length="50" />
        </property>
        <set name="bookses" inverse="true" table="booksauthored">
            <key>
                <column name="AuthorNo" />
            </key>
            <many-to-many entity-name="myApp.Books">
                <column name="BookNo" />
            </many-to-many>
        </set>
    </class>
</hibernate-mapping>
```

From the perspective of the Books class [MANY-TO-MANY]:

```
<?xml version="1.0"?>
<!DOCTYPE hibernate-mapping PUBLIC "-//Hibernate/Hibernate Mapping DTD 3.0//EN"
"http://hibernate.sourceforge.net/hibernate-mapping-3.0.dtd">
<hibernate-mapping>
   <class name="myApp.Books" table="books" catalog="associations">
      <id name="bookNo" type="int">
         <column name="BookNo" />
         <generator class="assigned" />
      </id>
      <property name="bookName" type="string">
         <column name="BookName" length="25" />
      </property>
      <property name="isbn" type="string">
         <column name="ISBN" length="25" />
      </property>
      <property name="aboutBook" type="string">
         <column name="AboutBook" length="50" />
      </property>
      <property name="price" type="java.lang.Integer">
         <column name="Price" />
      </property>
      <set name="authorses" inverse="false" table="booksauthored">
         <key>
            <column name="BookNo" />
         </key>
         <many-to-many entity-name="myApp.Authors">
            <column name="AuthorNo" />
         </many-to-many>
      </set>
   </class>
</hibernate-mapping>
```

Refer to *Chapter 09: Collections* for an example that demonstrates associations.

SECTION III: UNDERSTANDING CONFIGURATION AND MAPPING

Collections

Now that working with individual objects and moving them into and out of a database is known, it's time to see how to work with groups and relationships between objects.

Any real world application would always deal with lists and groups. These lists and groups can be handled using a set of library classes [Collections utilities] provided by Java.

A collection in Java can be of type Map, Set, SortedMap, SortedSet, List, Collection, Array and so on. All of these can be persisted using Hibernate. Hibernate provides natural ways for mapping database relationships onto Collections.

Collections in Hibernate are elements that allow including an attribute in the class to represent a collection class.

For example, if the class holds an attribute of type Set, then, in Hibernate, a <bag> or a <set> element can be used to represent its relationship with the database table.

<set> Element

A set collection allows persisting collection attributes derived from the Set interface.

<set> element is a part of Collection Mapping.

It can only store unique objects i.e. no duplicate elements can be contained in a set. When the same element is added to a set for second time, it replaces the old one.

A set is unordered, by default, however, it can be sorted.

The corresponding type of <set> element in Java is java.util.Set.

Syntax:

```
<set name="<AttributeName>" schema="<SchemaName>"
  catalog="<CatalogName>" cascade="<CascadeStyle>"
  check="<SQL Expression>" table="<TableName>"
  where="<SQL WHERE clause>" embed-xml="<true | false>"
  batch-size="<BatchSize>" collection-type="<CollectionTypeName>"
  access="<field | property | ClassName>" fetch="<join | select>"
  sort="<unsorted | natural | ComparatorClass>"
  lazy="<true | false>" mutable="<true | false>"
  node="<XML Element>" optimistic-lock="<true | false>"
  persister="<ClassPersister>" outer-join="<true | false | auto>"
  subselect="<Subquery>" inverse="<true | false>"
  order-by="<SQL ORDER BY clause>"/>
```

Example

Let's assume the following tables:

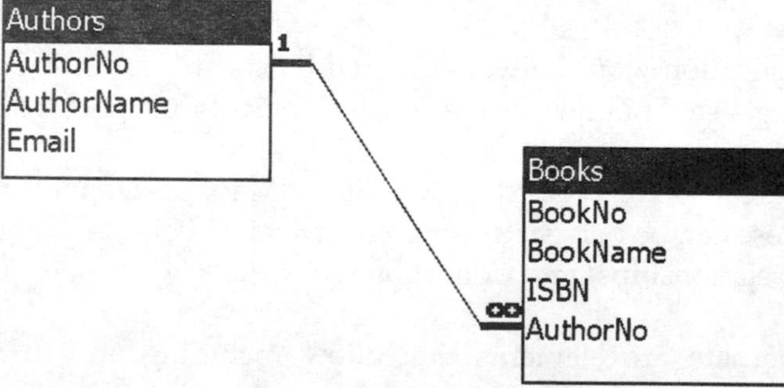

These tables indicate that an author can write multiple books.

This means, **Books** entities will have to be mapped [the **many** from the **one-to-many** association] into a **Set** property that belongs to an **Authors** entity

Based on this relationship, the POJO classes and the mapping documents would be:

From the Authors perspective:

```
package bms;

import java.util.HashSet;
import java.util.Set;

public class Authors  implements java.io.Serializable {

    private Integer authorNo;
    private String authorName;
    private String email;
    private String address;
    private Set<Books> bookses = new HashSet<Books>(0);

    public Authors() {
    }


    public Authors(String authorName, String email, String address) {
        this.authorName = authorName;
        this.email = email;
        this.address = address;
    }
    public Authors(String authorName, String email, String address, Set<Books> bookses) {
       this.authorName = authorName;
       this.email = email;
       this.address = address;
       this.bookses = bookses;
    }

    public Integer getAuthorNo() {
        return this.authorNo;
    }

    public void setAuthorNo(Integer authorNo) {
        this.authorNo = authorNo;
    }
    public String getAuthorName() {
        return this.authorName;
    }

    public void setAuthorName(String authorName) {
        this.authorName = authorName;
    }
    public String getEmail() {
        return this.email;
    }

    public void setEmail(String email) {
        this.email = email;
    }
    public String getAddress() {
        return this.address;
    }

    public void setAddress(String address) {
        this.address = address;
    }
    public Set<Books> getBookses() {
        return this.bookses;
    }

    public void setBookses(Set<Books> bookses) {
        this.bookses = bookses;
    }
}
```

Mapping Document

```
<?xml version="1.0"?>
<!DOCTYPE hibernate-mapping PUBLIC "-//Hibernate/Hibernate Mapping DTD 3.0//EN"
"http://hibernate.sourceforge.net/hibernate-mapping-3.0.dtd">
<hibernate-mapping>
    <class name="bms.Authors" table="authors" catalog="bms">
        <id name="authorNo" type="java.lang.Integer">
            <column name="AuthorNo" />
            <generator class="identity" />
        </id>
        <property name="authorName" type="string">
            <column name="AuthorName" length="45" not-null="true" />
        </property>
        <property name="email" type="string">
            <column name="Email" length="45" not-null="true" />
        </property>
        <property name="address" type="string">
            <column name="Address" length="45" not-null="true" />
        </property>
        <set name="bookses" inverse="true">
            <key>
                <column name="AuthorNo" not-null="true" />
            </key>
            <one-to-many class="bms.Books" />
        </set>
    </class>
</hibernate-mapping>
```

Collections are distinguished in the database by a foreign key of the entity that owns the collection. This foreign key is referred to as the collection key column [or columns] of the collection table. The collection key column is mapped using the <key> element [explained later].

```
<set name="bookses" inverse="true">
    <key>
        <column name="AuthorNo" not-null="true" />
    </key>
    <one-to-many class="bms.Books" />
</set>
```

From the Books perspective:

```
package bms;

public class Books implements java.io.Serializable {

    private Integer bookNo;
    private Authors authors;
    private String bookName;
    private String isbn;

    public Books() {
    }

    public Books(Authors authors) {
        this.authors = authors;
    }
    public Books(Authors authors, String bookName, String isbn) {
        this.authors = authors;
        this.bookName = bookName;
        this.isbn = isbn;
    }

    public Integer getBookNo() {
        return this.bookNo;
    }

    public void setBookNo(Integer bookNo) {
        this.bookNo = bookNo;
    }
    public Authors getAuthors() {
        return this.authors;
    }

    public void setAuthors(Authors authors) {
        this.authors = authors;
    }
    public String getBookName() {
        return this.bookName;
    }

    public void setBookName(String bookName) {
        this.bookName = bookName;
    }
    public String getIsbn() {
        return this.isbn;
    }

    public void setIsbn(String isbn) {
        this.isbn = isbn;
    }
}
```

```
<?xml version="1.0"?>
<!DOCTYPE hibernate-mapping PUBLIC "-//Hibernate/Hibernate Mapping DTD 3.0//EN"
"http://hibernate.sourceforge.net/hibernate-mapping-3.0.dtd">
<!-- Generated Feb 25, 2009 12:29:21 PM by Hibernate Tools 3.2.1.GA -->
<hibernate-mapping>
    <class name="bms.Books" table="books" catalog="bms">
        <id name="bookNo" type="java.lang.Integer">
            <column name="BookNo" />
            <generator class="identity" />
        </id>
        <many-to-one name="authors" class="bms.Authors" fetch="select">
            <column name="AuthorNo" not-null="true" />
        </many-to-one>
        <property name="bookName" type="string">
            <column name="BookName" />
        </property>
        <property name="isbn" type="string">
            <column name="ISBN" length="20" />
        </property>
    </class>
</hibernate-mapping>
```

<bag> Element

A <bag> element is an unordered collection, which can contain duplicate elements. This means, if a bag with some order of items is persisted, the same order cannot be expected when the collection is retrieved. The order in which the items are stored and retrieved from a bag is completely ignored.

The Java Collections framework does not define a Bag interface. However, Hibernate allows using a List in Java to simulate the bag behavior.

If the class represents data using a class derived from the List interface, but it is not desired to maintain an index column to keep track of the order of items, the bag collection can be used.

Syntax:

```
<bag name="<AttributeName>" schema="<SchemaName>"
  catalog="<CatalogName>" cascade="<CascadeStyle>"
  check="<SQL Expression>" table="<TableName>"
  where="<SQL WHERE clause>" embed-xml="<true | false>"
  batch-size="<BatchSize>" collection-type="<CollectionTypeName>"
  access="<field | property | ClassName>" fetch="<join | select>"
  lazy="<true | false>" mutable="<true | false>"
  node="<XML Element>" optimistic-lock="<true | false>"
  persister="<ClassPersister>" outer-join="<true | false | auto>"
  subselect="<Subquery>" inverse="<true | false>"
  order-by="<SQL ORDER BY clause>"/>
```

Example

Let's assume the following tables:

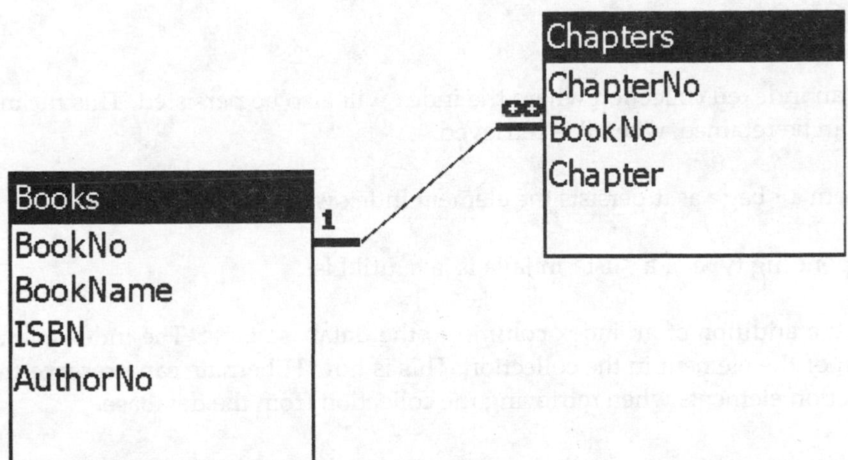

These tables indicate that a book can have multiple chapters.

Based on this relationship, the POJO classes and the mapping documents would be:

```java
package bms;

public class Books  implements java.io.Serializable {


    private Integer bookNo;
    private String bookName;
    private String isbn;
    private List chapters;

    public Books() {
    }

    public Books(Authors authors) {
        this.authors = authors;
    }

    public Integer getBookNo() {
        return this.bookNo;
    }

    public void setBookNo(Integer bookNo) {
        this.bookNo = bookNo;
    }

    public String getBookName() {
        return this.bookName;
    }

    public void setBookName(String bookName) {
        this.bookName = bookName;
    }
    public String getIsbn() {
        return this.isbn;
    }

    public void setIsbn(String isbn) {
        this.isbn = isbn;
    }

    public List getChapters() {
        return chapters;
    }

    public void setChapters(List chapters) {
        this.chapters = chapters;
    }
}
```

```xml
<?xml version="1.0"?>
<!DOCTYPE hibernate-mapping PUBLIC "-//Hibernate/Hibernate Mapping DTD 3.0//EN"
"http://hibernate.sourceforge.net/hibernate-mapping-3.0.dtd">
<hibernate-mapping>
    <class name="bms.Books" table="books" catalog="bms">
        <id name="bookNo" type="java.lang.Integer">
            <column name="BookNo" />
            <generator class="identity" />
        </id>
        <property name="bookName" type="string">
            <column name="BookName" />
        </property>
        <property name="isbn" type="string">
            <column name="ISBN" length="20" />
        </property>
        <bag name="Chapters" table="Chapters">
            <key column="BookNo" />
            <element column="Chapter" type="string" length="100" />
        </bag>
    </class>
</hibernate-mapping>
```

<list> Element

A <list> is an indexed collection where the index will also be persisted. This means the order of the list can be retained, when it is retrieved.

It differs from a <bag> as it persists the element index while a <bag> does not.

The corresponding type of a <list> in Java is java.util.List.

It requires the addition of an index column to the database table. The index column defines the position of the element in the collection. This is how Hibernate can preserve the ordering of the collection elements when retrieving the collection from the database.

Syntax:

```
<list name="<AttributeName>" schema="<SchemaName>"
  catalog="<CatalogName>" cascade="<CascadeStyle>"
  check="<SQL Expression>" table="<TableName>" lazy="<true | false>"
  where="<SQL WHERE clause>" embed-xml="<true | false>"
  batch-size="<BatchSize>" collection-type="<CollectionTypeName>"
  access="<field | property | ClassName>" inverse="<true | false>"
  fetch="<join | select>" outer-join="<true | false | auto>"
  mutable="<true | false>" node="<XML Element>"
  optimistic-lock="<true | false>" persister="<ClassPersister>"
  subselect="<Subquery>" />
```

Example

Let's assume the same tables with a minor change:

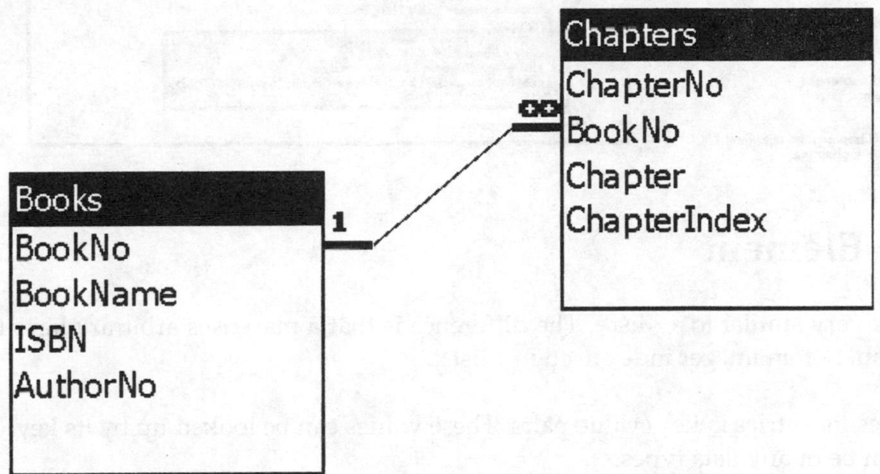

Based on this relationship, the POJO classes and the mapping documents would be:

```
package bms;

public class Books implements java.io.Serializable {


    private Integer bookNo;
    private String bookName;
    private String isbn;
    private List chapters;

    public Books() {
    }

    public Books(Authors authors) {
        this.authors = authors;
    }

    public Integer getBookNo() {
        return this.bookNo;
    }

    public void setBookNo(Integer bookNo) {
        this.bookNo = bookNo;
    }

    public String getBookName() {
        return this.bookName;
    }

    public void setBookName(String bookName) {
        this.bookName = bookName;
    }
    public String getIsbn() {
        return this.isbn;
    }

    public void setIsbn(String isbn) {
        this.isbn = isbn;
    }

    public List getChapters() {
        return chapters;
    }

    public void setChapters(List chapters) {
        this.chapters = chapters;
    }
}
```

```
<?xml version="1.0"?>
<!DOCTYPE hibernate-mapping PUBLIC "-//Hibernate/Hibernate Mapping DTD 3.0//EN"
"http://hibernate.sourceforge.net/hibernate-mapping-3.0.dtd">
<hibernate-mapping>
    <class name="bms.Books" table="books" catalog="bms">
        <id name="bookNo" type="java.lang.Integer">
            <column name="BookNo" />
            <generator class="identity" />
        </id>
        <property name="bookName" type="string">
            <column name="BookName" />
        </property>
        <property name="isbn" type="string">
            <column name="ISBN" length="20" />
        </property>
        <list name="Chapters" table="Chapters">
            <key column="BookNo" />
            <list-index column="ChapterIndex"/>
            <element column="Chapter" type="string" length="100" />
        </list>
    </class>
</hibernate-mapping>
```

<map> Element

A <map> is very similar to a <list>. The difference is that a map uses arbitrary keys to index the collection, not an integer index used in a list.

A map stores its entries in key/value pairs. These values can be looked up by its key. The key of a map can be of any data types.

The corresponding type of a <map> in Java is java.util.Map

Syntax:

```
<map name="<AttributeName>" schema="<SchemaName>"
  catalog="<CatalogName>" cascade="<CascadeStyle>"
  check="<SQL Expression>" table="<TableName>"
  where="<SQL WHERE clause>" embed-xml="<true | false>"
  batch-size="<BatchSize>" collection-type="<CollectionTypeName>"
  access="<field | property | ClassName>"
  sort="<unsorted | natural | ComparatorClass>"
```

```
fetch="<join | select>" lazy="<true | false>"
mutable="<true | false>" node="<XML Element>"
optimistic-lock="<true | false>" persister="<ClassPersister>"
outer-join="<true | false | auto>" subselect="<Subquery>"
inverse="<true | false>" order-by="<SQL ORDER BY clause>"/>
```

Example

Let's assume the same tables with a minor change:

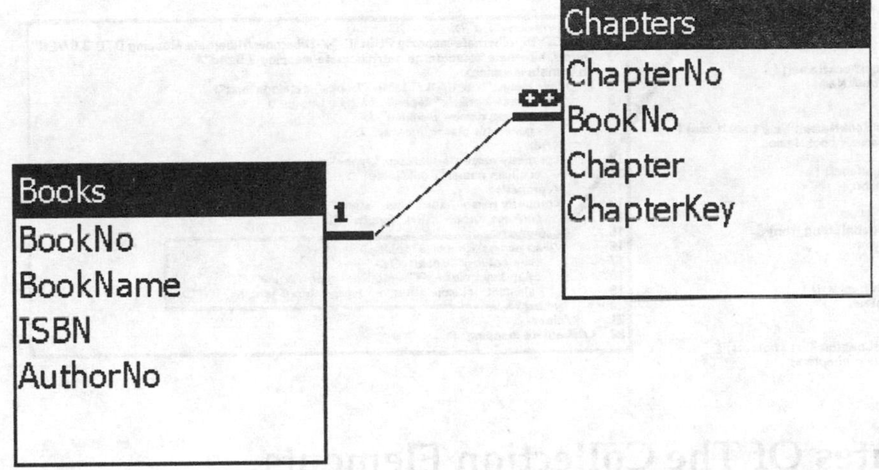

Based on this relationship, the POJO classes and the mapping documents would be:

```java
package bms;

public class Books  implements java.io.Serializable {


    private Integer bookNo;
    private String bookName;
    private String isbn;
    private List chapters;

    public Books() {
    }

    public Books(Authors authors) {
        this.authors = authors;
    }

    public Integer getBookNo() {
        return this.bookNo;
    }

    public void setBookNo(Integer bookNo) {
        this.bookNo = bookNo;
    }

    public String getBookName() {
        return this.bookName;
    }

    public void setBookName(String bookName) {
        this.bookName = bookName;
    }
    public String getIsbn() {
        return this.isbn;
    }

    public void setIsbn(String isbn) {
        this.isbn = isbn;
    }

    public List getChapters() {
        return chapters;
    }

    public void setChapters(List chapters) {
        this.chapters = chapters;
    }
}
```

```xml
<?xml version="1.0"?>
<!DOCTYPE hibernate-mapping PUBLIC "-//Hibernate/Hibernate Mapping DTD 3.0//EN"
"http://hibernate.sourceforge.net/hibernate-mapping-3.0.dtd">
<hibernate-mapping>
    <class name="bms.Books" table="books" catalog="bms">
        <id name="bookNo" type="java.lang.Integer">
            <column name="BookNo" />
            <generator class="identity" />
        </id>
        <property name="bookName" type="string">
            <column name="BookName" />
        </property>
        <property name="isbn" type="string">
            <column name="ISBN" length="20" />
        </property>
        <map name="Chapters" table="Chapters">
            <key column="BookNo" />
            <map-key column="ChapterKey" type="string" />
            <element column="Chapter" type="string" length="100" />
        </map>
    </class>
</hibernate-mapping>
```

Attributes Of The Collection Elements

The name Attribute

The name attribute is the name of the property, which should start with a lowercase.

The schema Attribute

The schema attribute is used to specify the name of the database schema and is optional.

The catalog Attribute

The catalog attribute is used to specify the name of the database catalog and is optional.

HINT

The schema and catalog attributes specify that tables referred to in the mapping belong to the named schema and/or catalog. If specified, then the table names will be qualified by the given schema and catalog names. If not specified, then the table names will be unqualified.

The cascade Attribute

The cascade attribute specifies which operations should be cascaded from the parent object to the associated object and is optional.

The check Attribute

The check attribute is an SQL expression used to generate a multi-row check constraint for automatic schema generation and is optional.

The check attribute defines a row-level check constraint, effectively adding this as an SQL CHECK(. . .) clause during table generation.

The table Attribute

The table attribute is the name of the database table where the collection needs to be saved and is optional.

The where Attribute

The where attribute specifies an SQL WHERE condition to be used when retrieving objects of this class from the database table and is optional.

The embed-xml Attribute

The embed-xml attribute indicates whether the XML tree for the associated entity itself or only its identifier, will appear in the generated XML tree when using XML relational persistence and is optional.

The batch-size Attribute

The batch-size attribute specifies the number of items that can be batched together when retrieving instances of the class by identifier and is optional. By default, the value of this attribute is 1.

The collection-type Attribute

The collection-type attribute is the name of the UserCollectionType class, which describes the collection type to be used in place of the defaults and is optional.

The access Attribute

The access attribute, informs Hibernate, the strategy to be used to access the properties and is optional.

If this attribute is set to **property**, then **get** and **set** methods are used to access the data.

If this attribute is set to **field**, then the data is accessed directly.

Alternatively, this attribute can also be set to a class name of a PropertyAccessor implementation which defines any other access mechanism.

By default, the value of this attribute is property.

The fetch Attribute

The fetch attribute chooses between outer-join fetching or sequential select fetching and is optional.

The sort Attribute

The sort attribute specifies the collection class sorting to be used and is optional.

The lazy Attribute

The lazy attribute is used to disable or enable the lazy fetching against the enclosing mapping's default and is optional.

The mutable Attribute

The mutable attribute specifies that instances of the class are mutable and is optional. By default, the value of this attribute is true.

If this attribute is set to **false**, the object becomes read-only. If it is set to **true**, the object can be updated/deleted.

This attribute allows Hibernate to make some performance optimizations when dealing with these classes.

The node Attribute

The node attribute specifies the name of the XML element or attribute, which should be used by the XML relational persistence features and is optional.

The optimistic-lock Attribute

The optimistic-lock attribute determines the optimistic locking strategy and is optional. By default, the value of this attribute is version.

The persister Attribute

The persister attribute specifies a custom ClassPersister object to be used when persisting the entity and is optional.

The outer-join Attribute

The outer-join attribute specifies whether an outer join should be used and is optional.

The subselect Attribute

The subselect attribute is an SQL query to enforce a sub-selection of the contents of the underlying table and is optional.

REMINDER

A class can only use subselect, if it is immutable and read-only, as an SQL query defined cannot be reversed.

Generally, the use of database view is preferable.

The inverse Attribute

The inverse attribute specifies that an entity is the opposite navigable end of a relationship expressed in another entity's mapping and is optional. By default, the value of this attribute is false.

The order-by Attribute

The order-by attribute specifies an SQL query's ORDER BY clause to constrain the results returned by an SQL query, which populates the set collection and is optional.

<key> Element

<key> element is a part of Collection Mapping.

<key> element defines the foreign key in the joined table, which references the primary key of the original table.

This element appears anywhere the parent mapping element defines a join to a new table.

Syntax:

```
<key column="<ColumnName>" on-delete="<noaction | cascade>"
  property-ref="<PropertyName>" not-null="<true | false>"
  update="<true | false>" unique="<true | false>"/>
```

The column Attribute

The column attribute is the name of the foreign key column.

This can also be specified by the nested <column> element(s).

The on-delete Attribute

The on-delete attribute specifies whether the foreign key constraint has database level cascade delete enabled and is optional. By default, the value of this attribute is noaction.

HINT

It is recommended that for systems where delete performance is important, all keys should be defined **on-delete="cascade"** and Hibernate will use a database-level ON CASCADE DELETE constraint, instead of many individual DELETE statements. Be aware that this feature bypasses Hibernate's usual optimistic locking strategy for versioned data.

The property-ref Attribute

The property-ref attribute is the name of a property of the associated class that is joined to the primary key of this class and is optional.

The not-null Attribute

The not-null attribute specifies whether the column is permitted to contain NULL values and is optional. By default, the value of this attribute is false.

This attribute enables the DDL generation of a NOT NULL / NULL constraint for the column.

The update Attribute

The update attribute specifies that the foreign key should never be updated and is optional. By default, the value of this attribute is true.

HINT

The **not-null** and **update** attributes are useful when mapping a unidirectional one-to-many association. If a unidirectional one-to-many is mapped to a non-nullable foreign key, then declare the key column using <key not-null="true">.

The unique Attribute

The unique attribute specifies that the foreign key should have a unique constraint and is optional. By default, the value of this attribute is false.

This attribute enables the DDL generation of a UNIQUE constraint for the column.

Author Details Using Associations [Mapping Documents]

Example

Now that the fundamentals of associations and collections are in place, let's learn how to use them practically.

Build a Web application using JSP, MySQL and Hibernate. This application will have a data entry form to capture the following:

- Author
  - Author Name
  - About Author
  - Contact Details [ONE-TO-ONE]
    - Email
    - Mobile Number
  - Book [ONE-TO-MANY]
    - Book Name
    - ISBN
    - About Book
    - Price

The relationship amongst the entities defined above is as follows:

- One author can have only single contact detail [One-To-One]
- One author can write multiple books [One-To-Many]

Based on these relationships the entity relationship diagram would be:

The data entry form as shown in diagram 9.1.1 should be capable of accepting 2 books and a single contact detail for an author.

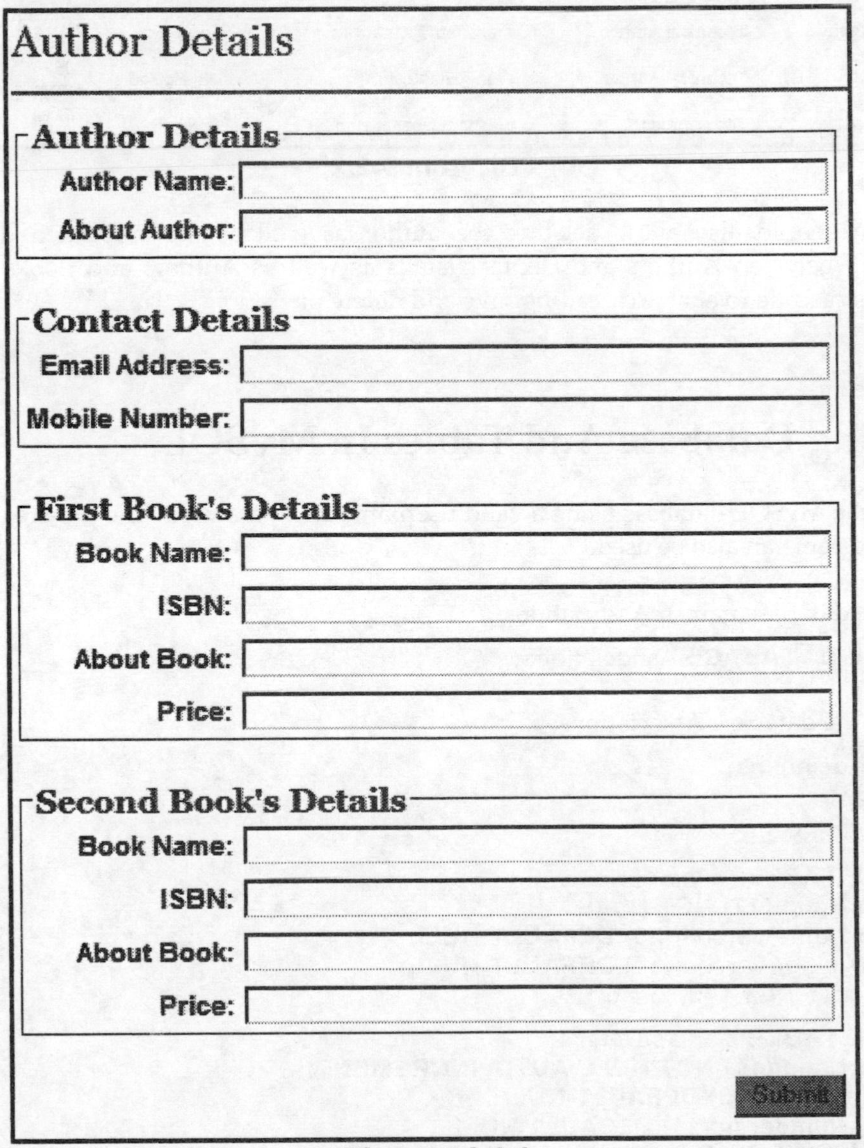

Author Details

Author Details

Author Name:

About Author:

Contact Details

Email Address:

Mobile Number:

First Book's Details

Book Name:

ISBN:

About Book:

Price:

Second Book's Details

Book Name:

ISBN:

About Book:

Price:

Submit

Diagram 9.1.1

After the data is captured and inserted using this data entry form, the same should be displayed as shown in diagram 9.1.2

View the Author Details

Click here to add an author.

Author Name	About Author	Email	Mobile	Books	
Sharanam Shah	Technical Author	sharanam@shah.com	1234567	Oracle MySQL	Delete
Vaishali Shah	Technical Author	shah@shah.com	98989898	JSP PHP	Delete
Prashant Bapat	Tech Author	prashant@bapat.com	878778	Java ASP	Delete

Diagram 9.1.2

This form should also allow deleting the author as well as the associated details. The association between Authors and ContactDetails as well as Authors and Books should be defined as cascade to enable cascading **save** and **delete** operations.

Let's begin.

Creating Database And Tables In MySQL

Login to the MySQL database using a valid username and password. The pre-created default user called **root** can also be used.

Create the database named Associations:

```
CREATE DATABASE Associations;
```

Switch to the database Associations:

```
USE Associations;
```

Create the following tables:

```
CREATE TABLE Authors(
   AuthorNo int(11) NOT NULL,
   AuthorName varchar(25) DEFAULT NULL,
   AboutAuthor varchar(50) DEFAULT NULL,
   PRIMARY KEY (AuthorNo));
CREATE TABLE ContactDetails(
   AuthorNo int(11) NOT NULL AUTO_INCREMENT,
   Email varchar(50) DEFAULT NULL,
   MobileNumber int(11) DEFAULT NULL,
   PRIMARY KEY (AuthorNo));
CREATE TABLE Books(
   BookNo int(11) NOT NULL AUTO_INCREMENT,
   BookName varchar(25) DEFAULT NULL,
   ISBN varchar(25) DEFAULT NULL,
   AboutBook varchar(50) DEFAULT NULL,
```

```
Price int(11) DEFAULT NULL,
AuthorNo int(11) DEFAULT NULL,
PRIMARY KEY (BookNo),
CONSTRAINT FK_books_1 FOREIGN KEY (AuthorNo)
    REFERENCES Authors(AuthorNo));
```

Creating A Web Application

Run the NetBeans IDE and create a new **Web Application** project named **Associations**. Refer to *Chapter 03: Writing The First Application* for the steps.

Once the NetBeans IDE brings up the **Associations** application, the next step is to add the required library files [JDBC driver and Hibernate] to the **Associations** application. Refer to *Chapter 03: Writing The First Application* for the steps.

Now, let's move to the application development area.

Creating A JavaBean Class

To hold the captured data in a structured manner, the following bean classes are required.

Contactdetails [Contactdetails.java]

This class should expose the following properties:

Property Name	To Store
authorNo	The Primary Key value [Will be automatically incremented by MySQL]
email	Email address
mobileNumber	The mobile number

The class should have a parameterized constructor that allows setting captured values to these properties.

Refer to *Chapter 03: Writing The First Application* for the steps.

Code Spec

Edit the **Contactdetails.java** file with the following contents.

```
package myApp;

public class Contactdetails implements java.io.Serializable {
```

```
    private Integer authorNo;
    private String email;
    private Integer mobileNumber;

    public Contactdetails() {
    }

    public Contactdetails(String email, Integer mobileNumber) {
       this.email = email;
       this.mobileNumber = mobileNumber;
    }

    public Integer getAuthorNo() {
        return authorNo;
    }
    public void setAuthorNo(Integer authorNo) {
        this.authorNo = authorNo;
    }

    public String getEmail() {
        return this.email;
    }
    public void setEmail(String email) {
        this.email = email;
    }

    public Integer getMobileNumber() {
        return this.mobileNumber;
    }
    public void setMobileNumber(Integer mobileNumber) {
        this.mobileNumber = mobileNumber;
    }
}
```

Books [Books.java]

This class should expose the following properties:

Property Name	To Store
bookNo	The Primary Key value [Will be automatically incremented by MySQL]
bookName	Book's Name
isbn	The ISBN
aboutBook	About the book
price	The cost
authors	The author details [An object of Authors class]

The class should have a parameterized constructor that allows setting captured values to these properties.

Refer to *Chapter 03: Writing The First Application* for the steps.

Code Spec

Edit the **Books.java** file with the following contents.

```
package myApp;

public class Books implements java.io.Serializable {
    private Integer bookNo;
    private Authors authors;
    private String bookName;
    private String isbn;
    private String aboutBook;
    private Integer price;

    public Books() {
    }

    public Books(Authors authors, String bookName,
    String isbn, String aboutBook, Integer price) {
```

```
        this.authors = authors;
        this.bookName = bookName;
        this.isbn = isbn;
        this.aboutBook = aboutBook;
        this.price = price;
    }

    public Integer getBookNo() {
        return this.bookNo;
    }
    public void setBookNo(Integer bookNo) {
        this.bookNo = bookNo;
    }

    public Authors getAuthors() {
        return this.authors;
    }
    public void setAuthors(Authors authors) {
        this.authors = authors;
    }

    public String getBookName() {
        return this.bookName;
    }
    public void setBookName(String bookName) {
        this.bookName = bookName;
    }

    public String getIsbn() {
        return this.isbn;
```

```
    }
    public void setIsbn(String isbn) {
        this.isbn = isbn;
    }

    public String getAboutBook() {
        return this.aboutBook;
    }
    public void setAboutBook(String aboutBook) {
        this.aboutBook = aboutBook;
    }

    public Integer getPrice() {
        return this.price;
    }
    public void setPrice(Integer price) {
        this.price = price;
    }
}
```

Authors [Authors.java]

This class should expose the following properties:

Property Name	To Store
authorNo	The Primary Key value [Will be picked up from the ContactDetails table]
authorName	Author's Name
aboutAuthor	About the author
contactdetails	The contact details [An object of the Contactdetails class]
bookses	The book's details [A collection object of the Books class]

The class should have a parameterized constructor that allows setting captured values to these properties.

Refer to *Chapter 03: Writing The First Application* for the steps.

Code Spec

Edit the **Authors.java** file with the following contents.

```
package myApp;

import java.util.HashSet;
import java.util.Set;

public class Authors implements java.io.Serializable {
    private Integer authorNo;
    private Contactdetails contactdetails;
    private String authorName;
    private String aboutAuthor;
    private Set<Books> bookses = new
    HashSet<Books>(0);

    public Authors() {
    }

    public Authors(Contactdetails contactdetails, String
    authorName, String aboutAuthor, Set<Books>
    bookses) {
       this.contactdetails = contactdetails;
       this.authorName = authorName;
       this.aboutAuthor = aboutAuthor;
       this.bookses = bookses;
    }

    public Integer getAuthorNo() {
        return this.authorNo;
```

```
    }
    public void setAuthorNo(Integer authorNo) {
        this.authorNo = authorNo;
    }

    public Contactdetails getContactdetails() {
        return this.contactdetails;
    }
    public void setContactdetails(Contactdetails
    contactdetails) {
        this.contactdetails = contactdetails;
    }

    public String getAuthorName() {
        return this.authorName;
    }
    public void setAuthorName(String authorName) {
        this.authorName = authorName;
    }

    public String getAboutAuthor() {
        return this.aboutAuthor;
    }
    public void setAboutAuthor(String aboutAuthor) {
        this.aboutAuthor = aboutAuthor;
    }

    public Set<Books> getBookses() {
        return this.bookses;
    }
```

```
    public void setBookses(Set<Books> bookses) {
        this.bookses = bookses;
    }
}
```

Creating Hibernate Mapping File

Refer to *Chapter 03: Writing The First Application* for the steps. In this application, there are three POJOs for which three Mapping documents are required.

Contactdetails [Contactdetails.hbm.xml]

The **Contactdetails.hbm.xml** file should hold the following code spec:

```
<?xml version="1.0"?>
<!DOCTYPE hibernate-mapping PUBLIC "-//Hibernate/Hibernate Mapping DTD 3.0//EN"
"http://hibernate.sourceforge.net/hibernate-mapping-3.0.dtd">
<hibernate-mapping>
    <class name="myApp.Contactdetails" table="contactdetails" catalog="associations">
        <id name="authorNo" type="java.lang.Integer">
            <column name="AuthorNo" />
            <generator class="identity" />
        </id>
        <property name="email" type="string">
            <column name="Email" length="50" />
        </property>
        <property name="mobileNumber" type="java.lang.Integer">
            <column name="MobileNumber" />
        </property>
    </class>
</hibernate-mapping>
```

Explanation:

This mapping document informs the following to the Hibernate:

- The **Contactdetails** class is to be persisted to the **ContactDetails** table
- The identifier property **authorNo** maps to a column named **AuthorNo**
    - The Primary Key value will be generated by MySQL [generator class="identity"]

- The text properties **email**, **mobileNumber** map to columns **Email**, **MobileNumber** respectively

Books [Books.hbm.xml]

The **Books.hbm.xml** file should hold the following code spec:

```
<?xml version="1.0"?>
<!DOCTYPE hibernate-mapping PUBLIC "-//Hibernate/Hibernate Mapping DTD 3.0//EN"
"http://hibernate.sourceforge.net/hibernate-mapping-3.0.dtd">
<hibernate-mapping>
   <class name="myApp.Books" table="books" catalog="associations">
      <id name="bookNo" type="java.lang.Integer">
         <column name="BookNo" />
         <generator class="identity" />
      </id>
      <many-to-one name="authors" class="myApp.Authors" fetch="select">
         <column name="AuthorNo" />
      </many-to-one>
      <property name="bookName" type="string">
         <column name="BookName" length="25" />
      </property>
      <property name="isbn" type="string">
         <column name="ISBN" length="25" />
      </property>
      <property name="aboutBook" type="string">
         <column name="AboutBook" length="50" />
      </property>
      <property name="price" type="java.lang.Integer">
         <column name="Price" />
      </property>
   </class>
</hibernate-mapping>
```

Explanation:

This mapping document informs the following to the Hibernate:

- The **Books** class is to be persisted to the **Books** table
- The identifier property **bookNo** maps to a column named **BookNo**
    - The Primary Key value will be generated by MySQL [generator class="identity"]
- This class is associated to the Authors class with the help <many-to-one> element using AuthorNo as the column

```
<many-to-one name="authors" class="myApp.Authors"
fetch="select">
   <column name="AuthorNo" />
</many-to-one>
```

- The text properties **bookName, isbn, aboutBook, price** map to columns **BookName,** **ISBN, AboutBook, Price** respectively

Authors [Authors.hbm.xml]

The **Authors.hbm.xml** file should hold the following code spec:

```
<?xml version="1.0"?>
<!DOCTYPE hibernate-mapping PUBLIC "-//Hibernate/Hibernate Mapping DTD 3.0//EN"
"http://hibernate.sourceforge.net/hibernate-mapping-3.0.dtd">
<hibernate-mapping>
   <class name="myApp.Authors" table="authors" catalog="associations">
      <id name="authorNo" type="java.lang.Integer">
         <column name="AuthorNo" />
         <generator class="foreign">
            <param name="property">contactdetails</param>
         </generator>
      </id>
      <one-to-one name="contactdetails" class="myApp.Contactdetails" fetch="select"
      cascade="all" />
      <property name="authorName" type="string">
         <column name="AuthorName" length="25" />
      </property>
      <property name="aboutAuthor" type="string">
         <column name="AboutAuthor" length="50" />
      </property>
```

```
    <set name="bookses" inverse="true" cascade="all">
        <key>
            <column name="AuthorNo" />
        </key>
        <one-to-many class="myApp.Books" />
    </set>
  </class>
</hibernate-mapping>
```

Explanation:

This mapping document informs the following to the Hibernate:

- The **Authors** class is to be persisted to the **Authors** table
- The identifier property **authorNo** maps to a column named **AuthorNo**
  - The Primary Key value will be automatically picked up from the foreign key in this case **ContactDetails.AuthorNo** using **generator class="foreign"**

```
<generator class="foreign">
    <param name="property">contactdetails</param>
</generator>
```

  contactdetails is passed as a parameter to the generator element to indicate the identifier of another associated object that should be used to obtain the identity value
- This class is associated to the Contactdetails class with the help <one-to-one> element

```
<one-to-one name="contactdetails" class="myApp.Contactdetails" fetch="select"
cascade="all"  />
```

  cascade="all" is used to cascade all the operations from the parent object [Authors] to the associated object [Contactdetails]
- This class is also associated to the Books class with the help <one-to-many> element using AuthorNo as the column

```
<set name="bookses" inverse="true" cascade="all">
    <key>
        <column name="AuthorNo" />
    </key>
    <one-to-many class="myApp.Books" />
</set>
```

  cascade="all" is used to cascade all the operations from the parent object [Authors] to the associated object [Books]

- The text properties **authorName**, **aboutAuthor** map to columns **AuthorName**, **AboutAuthor** respectively

Creating Hibernate Configuration File

Refer to *Chapter 03: Writing The First Application* for the steps.

The **hibernate.cfg.xml** file should hold the following code spec:

```
<?xml version="1.0" encoding="UTF-8"?>
<!DOCTYPE hibernate-configuration PUBLIC "-//Hibernate/Hibernate Configuration DTD 3.0//EN"
"http://hibernate.sourceforge.net/hibernate-configuration-3.0.dtd">
<hibernate-configuration>
 <session-factory>
   <property name="hibernate.dialect">org.hibernate.dialect.MySQLDialect</property>
   <property name="hibernate.connection.driver_class">com.mysql.jdbc.Driver</property>
   <property
   name="hibernate.connection.url">jdbc:mysql://localhost:3306/associations</property>
   <property name="hibernate.connection.username">root</property>
   <property name="hibernate.connection.password">123456</property>
   <mapping resource="myApp/Authors.hbm.xml"/>
   <mapping resource="myApp/Books.hbm.xml"/>
   <mapping resource="myApp/Contactdetails.hbm.xml"/>
 </session-factory>
</hibernate-configuration>
```

Creating JSPs

Refer to *Chapter 03: Writing The First Application* for the steps.

Create the following JSPs under a directory called **JSP**.

Entry.jsp [Code Spec]

Edit the **Entry.jsp** file with the following contents.

```
<%@ page language="java" contentType="text/html; charset=ISO-8859-1"
pageEncoding="ISO-8859-1"%>
<!DOCTYPE html PUBLIC "-//W3C//DTD HTML 4.01 Transitional//EN"
"http://www.w3.org/TR/html4/loose.dtd">
<html>
   <head>
      <meta http-equiv="Content-Type" content="text/html;charset=ISO-8859-1">
      <title>Author Details</title>
```

```
</head>
<body>
  <table border="0" cellpadding="0" cellspacing="0" align="center" width="760">
    <tr>
      <td>
        <table border="0" cellpadding="0" cellspacing="0" width="100%">
          <tr>
            <td valign="top" align="left" style="padding-right:0px;
            padding-left:0px; padding-bottom:0px; font:24px/30px Georgia;
            width:228px; color:#786e4e; padding-top:0px; height:37px;">
              Author Details
            </td>
          </tr>
        </table>
      </td>
    </tr>
    <tr align="left" valign="top">
      <td height="20">
        <hr />
      </td>
    </tr>
    <tr>
      <td>
        <form action="<%=request.getContextPath()%>/JSP/View.jsp"
        method="post">
          <table border="0" cellpadding="0" cellspacing="2">
            <tr>
              <td align="right">
                <fieldset>
                  <legend style="font-size:18px; font-weight:bold;
                  color:maroon; font-family:Georgia, serif;">Author
                  Details</legend>
                  <table border="0" cellspacing="3" cellpadding="0">
                    <tr>
                      <td align="right">
                        <font style="font-size:15px;
                        font-family:Arial,Times,serif;
                        font-weight:bold;">Author Name:</font>
```

```
                        </td>
                        <td>
                            <input name="txtAuthorName" maxlength="23"
                            size="50" />
                        </td>
                    </tr>
                    <tr>
                        <td align="right">
                            <font style="font-size:15px;
                            font-family:Arial,Times,serif;
                            font-weight:bold;">About Author:</font>
                        </td>
                        <td>
                            <input name="txtAboutAuthor" maxlength="48"
                            size="50" />
                        </td>
                    </tr>
                </table>
            </fieldset>
        </td>
    </tr>
    <tr>
        <td align="right">
            <br/>
            <fieldset>
                <legend style="font-size:18px; font-weight:bold;
                color:maroon; font-family:Georgia, serif;">Contact
                Details</legend>
                <table border="0" cellpadding="3" cellspacing="0">
                    <tr>
                        <td align="right">
                            <font style="font-size:15px;
                            font-family:Arial,Times,serif;
                            font-weight:bold;">Email Address:</font>
                        </td>
                        <td>
                            <input name="txtEmailAddress" maxlength="48"
                            size="50" />
```

```
                        </td>
                    </tr>
                    <tr>
                        <td align="right">
                            <font style="font-size:15px;
                            font-family:Arial,Times,serif;
                            font-weight:bold;">Mobile Number:</font>
                        </td>
                        <td>
                            <input name="txtMobileNumber" maxlength="10"
                            size="50" />
                        </td>
                    </tr>
                </table>
            </fieldset>
        </td>
    </tr>
    <tr>
        <td align="right">
            <br/>
            <fieldset>
                <legend style="font-size:18px; font-weight:bold;
                color:maroon; font-family:Georgia, serif;">First Book's
                Details</legend>
                <table border="0" cellpadding="3" cellspacing="0">
                    <tr>
                        <td align="right">
                            <font style="font-size:15px;
                            font-family:Arial,Times,serif;
                            font-weight:bold;">Book Name:</font>
                        </td>
                        <td>
                            <input name="txtBookName1" maxlength="23"
                            size="50" />
                        </td>
                    </tr>
                    <tr>
```

```
                    <td align="right">
                        <font style="font-size:15px;
                        font-family:Arial,Times,serif;
                        font-weight:bold;">ISBN:</font>
                    </td>
                    <td>
                        <input name="txtISBN1" maxlength="23"
                        size="50" />
                    </td>
                </tr>
                <tr>
                    <td align="right">
                        <font style="font-size:15px;
                        font-family:Arial,Times,serif;
                        font-weight:bold;">About Book:</font>
                    </td>
                    <td>
                        <input name="txtAboutBook1" maxlength="48"
                        size="50" />
                    </td>
                </tr>
                <tr>
                    <td align="right">
                        <font style="font-size:15px;
                        font-family:Arial,Times,serif;
                        font-weight:bold;">Price:</font>
                    </td>
                    <td>
                        <input name="txtPrice1" maxlength="10" size="50"
                        />
                    </td>
                </tr>
            </table>
        </fieldset>
    </td>
</tr>
<tr>
    <td align="right">
```

```
        <br/>
        <fieldset>
            <legend style="font-size:18px; font-weight:bold;
            color:maroon; font-family:Georgia, serif;">Second Book's
            Details</legend>
            <table border="0" cellpadding="3" cellspacing="0">
                <tr>
                    <td align="right">
                        <font style="font-size:15px;
                        font-family:Arial,Times,serif;
                        font-weight:bold;">Book Name:</font>
                    </td>
                    <td>
                        <input name="txtBookName2" maxlength="23"
                        size="50" />
                    </td>
                </tr>
                <tr>
                    <td align="right">
                        <font style="font-size:15px;
                        font-family:Arial,Times,serif;
                        font-weight:bold;">ISBN:</font>
                    </td>
                    <td>
                        <input name="txtISBN2" maxlength="23" size="50"
                        />
                    </td>
                </tr>
                <tr>
                    <td align="right">
                        <font style="font-size:15px;
                        font-family:Arial,Times,serif;
                        font-weight:bold;">About Book:</font>
                    </td>
                    <td>
                        <input name="txtAboutBook2" maxlength="48"
                        size="50" />
                    </td>
```

```
                        </tr>
                        <tr>
                            <td align="right">
                                <font style="font-size:15px;
                                font-family:Arial,Times,serif;
                                font-weight:bold;">Price:</font>
                            </td>
                            <td>
                                <input name="txtPrice2" maxlength="10" size="50"
                                />
                            </td>
                        </tr>
                    </table>
                </fieldset>
            </td>
        </tr>
        <tr>
            <td align="right">
                <br/>
                <input type="submit" name="btnSubmit" value="Submit" />
            </td>
        </tr>
    </table>
</form>
</td>
</tr>
</table>
</body>
</html>
```

Explanation:

This is the data entry form that allows capturing the author details along with the associated contact and books details and submits the data to another server-side script called View.jsp for further processing.

View.jsp [Code Spec]

Using NetBeans create one more JSP called View.jsp using the same steps as shown earlier.

Edit the **View.jsp** file with the following contents.

```
<%@page contentType="text/html" pageEncoding="UTF-8"
import="org.hibernate.SessionFactory, org.hibernate.cfg.Configuration,
org.hibernate.Session, org.hibernate.Transaction, java.util.*, myApp.*" %>
<!DOCTYPE HTML PUBLIC "-//W3C//DTD HTML 4.01 Transitional//EN"
  "http://www.w3.org/TR/html4/loose.dtd">
<%!
   SessionFactory sessionFactory;
   org.hibernate.Session hibSession;
   List<Authors> authors;
%>

<%
   sessionFactory = new Configuration().configure().buildSessionFactory();
   hibSession = sessionFactory.openSession();
   Transaction tx = null;

   try {
      hibSession.beginTransaction();
      authors = hibSession.createQuery("from Authors").list();
   }
   catch (RuntimeException e) {
      throw e;
   }

   String submit = request.getParameter("btnSubmit");
   if(submit != null && ("Submit").equals(submit)) {
      Authors objAuthors = new Authors();
      objAuthors.setAuthorName(request.getParameter("txtAuthorName"));
      objAuthors.setAboutAuthor(request.getParameter("txtAboutAuthor"));

      Contactdetails objContactdetails = new
      Contactdetails(request.getParameter("txtEmailAddress"),
      Integer.parseInt(request.getParameter("txtMobileNumber")));
      objAuthors.setContactdetails(objContactdetails);

```

```
        Books objBooks1 = new Books(objAuthors,
        request.getParameter("txtBookName1"), request.getParameter("txtISBN1"),
        request.getParameter("txtAboutBook1"),
        Integer.parseInt(request.getParameter("txtPrice1")));
        Books objBooks2 = new Books(objAuthors,
        request.getParameter("txtBookName2"), request.getParameter("txtISBN2"),
        request.getParameter("txtAboutBook2"),
        Integer.parseInt(request.getParameter("txtPrice2")));
        objAuthors.getBookses().add(objBooks1);
        objAuthors.getBookses().add(objBooks2);

        tx = hibSession.beginTransaction();
        hibSession.save(objAuthors);
        tx.commit();
        response.sendRedirect("View.jsp");
    }

    String authorno = request.getParameter("AuthorNo");
    if(authorno != null) {
        Authors objAuthor = new Authors();
        objAuthor = (Authors) hibSession.load(Authors.class, Integer.parseInt(authorno));
        tx = hibSession.beginTransaction();
        hibSession.delete(objAuthor);
        tx.commit();
        response.sendRedirect("View.jsp");
    }

%>
<html>
    <head>
        <meta http-equiv="Content-Type" content="text/html;charset=ISO-8859-1">
        <title>Author Details - View</title>
    </head>
    <body>
        <table border="0" cellpadding="0" cellspacing="0" align="center" width="760">
            <tr>
                <td>
                    <table border="0" cellpadding="0" cellspacing="0" width="100%">
```

```
            <tr>
                <td width="60%" valign="top" align="left" style="padding-right:0px;
                padding-left:0px; padding-bottom:0px; font:24px/30px Georgia;
                width:228px; color:#786e4e; padding-top:0px; height:37px;">
                    View the Author Details
                </td>
                <td valign="bottom" align="right" style="font:12px/16px Georgia,
                serif; color:#786e4e;">
                    <b>Click <a
                    href="<%=request.getContextPath()%>/JSP/Entry.jsp"> here</a>
                    to add an author.</b>
                </td>
            </tr>
        </table>
    </td>
</tr>
<tr align="left" valign="top">
    <td height="20">
        <hr />
    </td>
</tr>
<tr>
    <td>
        <table border="0" cellpadding="0" cellspacing="0" align="center"
        width="100%">
            <tr>
                <td style="font:12px/16px Georgia;font-weight:bolder;
                color:red;">
                    Author Name
                </td>
                <td style="font:12px/16px Georgia;font-weight:bolder;
                color:red;">
                    About Author
                </td>
                <td style="font:12px/16px Georgia;font-weight:bolder;
                color:red;">
                    Email
                </td>
```

```
                <td style="font:12px/16px Georgia;font-weight:bolder;
                color:red;">
                   Mobile
                </td>
                <td style="font:12px/16px Georgia;font-weight:bolder;
                color:red;">
                   Books
                </td>
             </tr>
          <%
             Iterator iterator = authors.iterator();
             while (iterator.hasNext()) {
                Authors objAuthors = (Authors) iterator.next();
          %>
             <tr>
                <td style="font:12px/16px Georgia; color:#786e4e;">
                   <%=objAuthors.getAuthorName()%>
                </td>
                <td style="font:12px/16px Georgia; color:#786e4e;">
                   <%=objAuthors.getAboutAuthor()%>
                </td>
                <td style="font:12px/16px Georgia; color:#786e4e;">
                   <%=objAuthors.getContactdetails().getEmail()%>
                </td>
                <td style="font:12px/16px Georgia; color:#786e4e;">
                   <%=objAuthors.getContactdetails().getMobileNumber()%>
                </td>
                <td style="font:12px/16px Georgia; color:#786e4e;">
                   <%
                      String bookone, booktwo;
                      Set<Books> books = objAuthors.getBookses();
                      String[] bookArray = new String[2];
                      int count = 0;

                      for(Books book : books)
                      {
                         bookArray[count] = book.getBookName();
                         count++;
```

```
                        }
                        bookone = bookArray[0];
                        booktwo = bookArray[1];
                        out.println(bookone);
                        out.println("<br/>");
                        out.println(booktwo);
                    %>
                </td>
                <td>
                    <a
                        href="View.jsp?AuthorNo=<%=objAuthors.getAuthorNo()%>">Delete</a>
                </td>
            </tr>
        <%
            }
        %>
        </table>
      </td>
    </tr>
  </table>
 </body>
</html>
<%
    hibSession.close();
%>
```

Explanation:

This is a server-side script that saves the captured data, fetches all the available entries and displays them.

Variable Declaration

The following variables are declared:

```
<%!
    SessionFactory sessionFactory;
    org.hibernate.Session hibSession;
```

```
    List<Authors> authors;
%>
```

- To represent the connections to the database, variable named **sessionFactory** is declared
- To create an instance of Session, variable named **hibSession** is declared
- A list of type **Authors** is created. This will hold the entries for view purposes

Application Logic

Creating A Configuration Instance And Building A Session Factory

```
sessionFactory = new Configuration().configure().buildSessionFactory();
```

An instance of the Configuration interface is created. Using it's **configure()** method, the session factory is built. This step indicates Hibernate to load the **hibernate.cfg.xml** file.

Obtaining A Session Object

After obtaining the SessionFactory, Hibernate org.hibernate.Session objects can be retrieved.

```
hibSession = sessionFactory.openSession();
```

The **openSession()** method of the SesisonFactory interface creates an instance of Session. This instance represents the primary interface to the Hibernate framework

Instantiating A Transaction

```
Transaction tx = null;
```

An empty instance of **Transaction** is created

Querying The Authors Class For View

```
try {
    hibSession.beginTransaction();
    authors = hibSession.createQuery("from Authors").list();
}
catch (RuntimeException e) {
    throw e;
}
```

Here, the Authors class is queried to retrieve the saved author details. This query also retrieves the associated data from the Contactdetails and Books classes.

This retrieved data is held in a List object which will be used later to produce a data grid as shown in diagram 9.1.2.

Saving Captured Data

When the user keys in the data and clicks **Submit:**

```
String submit = request.getParameter("btnSubmit");
if(submit != null && ("Submit").equals(submit)) {
```

Retrieving And Setting Author Details

```
Authors objAuthors = new Authors();
objAuthors.setAuthorName(request.getParameter("txtAuthorName"));
objAuthors.setAboutAuthor(request.getParameter("txtAboutAuthor"));
```

Retrieving And Setting Contact Details

```
Contactdetails objContactdetails = new Contactdetails(request.getParameter("txtEmailAddress"),
Integer.parseInt(request.getParameter("txtMobileNumber")));
objAuthors.setContactdetails(objContactdetails);
```

The retrieved contact detail is assigned to the Authors object using the setter method.

Retrieving And Setting Book Details

```
Books objBooks1 = new Books(objAuthors, request.getParameter("txtBookName1"),
request.getParameter("txtISBN1"), request.getParameter("txtAboutBook1"),
Integer.parseInt(request.getParameter("txtPrice1")));
Books objBooks2 = new Books(objAuthors, request.getParameter("txtBookName2"),
request.getParameter("txtISBN2"), request.getParameter("txtAboutBook2"),
Integer.parseInt(request.getParameter("txtPrice2")));
objAuthors.getBookses().add(objBooks1);
objAuthors.getBookses().add(objBooks2);
```

The retrieved book details are added to the Author's SET object using add() method.

Persisting Retrieved Data

To insert all the retrieved data:

```
tx = hibSession.beginTransaction();
hibSession.save(objAuthors);
tx.commit();
```

Here, an instance of the Transaction class is created by invoking the **beginTransaction()** method of the Session interface.

The session interface is used to save the Authors object i.e. **objAuthors** by invoking the **save()** method. More information on the Session can be found in *Chapter 12: Session*.

Since the **cascade="all"** was used when defining the associated objects, saving Authors object automatically fires the appropriate INSERT statements on the **associated tables** in this case **ContactDetails** and **Books**.

Finally, the transaction is committed.

Deleting Data

The data gird holds a hyper link which when clicked submits the page to this script.

This script receives **AuthorNo** in the query string. This AuthorNo is used to locate the appropriate Author object:

```
Authors objAuthor = new Authors();
objAuthor = (Authors) hibSession.load(Authors.class,
Integer.parseInt(authorno));
```

and delete it:

```
tx = hibSession.beginTransaction();
hibSession.delete(objAuthor);
tx.commit();
```

Displaying Retrieved Data

The displaying of the records fetched is handled by:

```
<%
    Iterator iterator = authors.iterator();
    while (iterator.hasNext()) {
```

```
    Authors objAuthors = (Authors) iterator.next();
%>
```

Here, an iterator is used to traverse through the List object called authors. This list object was populated earlier by:

```
authors = hibSession.createQuery("from Authors").list();
```

Using <TABLE>, <TR> and <TD> the elements of the List object are placed.

To retrieve the required values:

The **parent object** [**Authors**] is used as:

```
<%=objAuthors.getAuthorName()%>
```

The **associated child object** [**Contactdetails**] is used as:

```
<%=objAuthors.getContactdetails().getEmail()%>
```

The **associated child object** [**Books**] is used as:

```
Set<Books> books = objAuthors.getBookses();
```

Here, the multiple entries [in this case only 2 books] are retrieved and placed in the **SET** object.

```
for(Books book : books)
{
```

A FOR loop is used to iterate through the object and retrieve the required values:

```
bookone = bookArray[0];
booktwo = bookArray[1];
```

Editing The web.xml File

In NetBeans, by default, the web.xml file uses the index.jsp file as the welcome file i.e. whenever the application is run the web.xml file will display the index.jsp file.

This file needs to be edited to invoke the application's data entry form [Entry.jsp] every time it's invoked.

Refer to *Chapter 03: Writing The First Application* for the steps to Edit the web.xml file.

Now built and run the application to see it working.

Note the **cascading inserts** and **deletes** that are **automatically fired** on the database tables by this application. All this happens because of the associations and the cascade mode defined in the mapping documents.

The Book CDROM holds the complete application source code built using the NetBeans IDE for the following application:

- AuthorDetails_Chap09

This can be directly used by making appropriate changes [username/password] to the configuration file.

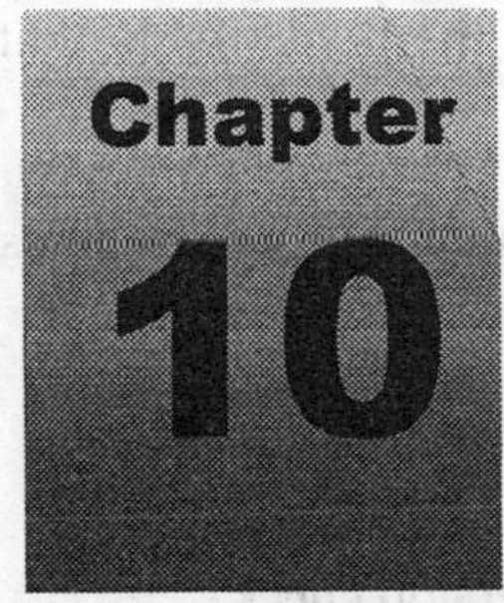

SECTION III: UNDERSTANDING CONFIGURATION AND MAPPING

Concurrency Control Using Versioning

<version> Element

Hibernate provides automatic versioning. Each entity instance has a version, which can be a number or a timestamp. Hibernate increments an object's version when it's modified, compares versions automatically and throws an exception, if a conflict is detected.

To have version support, all that needs to be done is:

- Add a version property to all the persistent entity classes to enable optimistic locking

```
public class Books
{
    ...
    private int version;
    ...
}
```

- Place the <version> element in the mapping document immediately after the identifier property mapping

```
<class name="Books" table="Books">
    <id .../>
    <version name="version" access="field" column="ObjectVersion"/>
    ...
</class>
```

The <version> element indicates that the table contains versioned data which is quite useful when dealing with **long transactions**. **ObjectVersion** is a column in the Books table that holds the version number.

It allows versioning the data in the object as opposed to having a unique ID thereby helps keeping the data up to date.

How Versioning Takes Place

After the versioning is implemented, every DML operation includes a version check.

For example,

1. In the Books table, a new book is added. This sets the **version to 1**
2. One of its value/property called Price of the same book is modified

   When the persistence context is flushed, Hibernate:

   a. Detects such modification and increments **the version of the Book to 2**

      Hibernate increments the version number whenever an entity instance is dirty

   b. Executes the **SQL UPDATE** to make this modification **permanent** in the database:

```
UPDATE Books SET Price = 750, ObjectVersion = 2
    WHERE BookNo = 2 AND ObjectVersion = 1
```

If another concurrent user attempts updating the same book and commits, since the ObjectVersion column no longer contains the value **1**, Hibernate does not update the row and throws a **StaleObjectStateException**.

By catching this exception, the developer can decide what to do about such a conflict.

This is how Hibernate makes it incredibly easy to manage versions for optimistic concurrency control.

Syntax:

```
<version column="<ColumnName>" name="<PropertyName>"
  type="<DataType>" access="<field | property | ClassName>"
  unsaved-value="<null | negative | undefained>"
  generated="<never | always>" insert="<true | false>"/>
```

The column Attribute

The column attribute specifies the name of the column holding the version number to use for identifier and is optional.

By default, this attribute takes the value of the name attribute.

The name Attribute

The name attribute specifies the name of the persistent class.

The type Attribute

The type attribute specifies the type of the version number and is optional.

By default, the value of this attribute is int.

Following are the valid data types:

- long
- integer
- short
- timestamp
- calendar

The access Attribute

The access attribute, informs Hibernate, the strategy to be used to access the properties and is optional.

If this attribute is set to **property**, then **get** and **set** methods are used to access the data.

If this attribute is set to **field**, then the data is accessed directly.

Alternatively, this attribute can also be set to a class name of a PropertyAccessor implementation which defines any other access mechanism.

By default, the value of this attribute is property.

The unsaved-value Attribute

The unsaved-value attribute indicates whether the object is newly instantiated, distinguishing it from detached instances that were saved or loaded in a previous session and is optional.

Hibernate uses the value to determine whether the object needs to be persisted.

By default, the value of this attribute is undefined, which specifies that the identifier property value should be used.

The generated Attribute

The generated attribute specifies that this version property value is generated by the database and is optional.

By default, the value of this attribute is never, which means that the database does not generate the property value.

If this attribute is set to always, then it states that the property value is generated both on INSERT and UPDATE.

The insert Attribute

The insert attribute informs Hibernate to not to include the column in an SQL INSERT statement and is optional.

By default, the value of this attribute is true.

WARNING

The value of this attribute can be set to false if and only if the database column is defined with a default value of 0 [zero].

<timestamp> Element

<timestamp> element indicates that the table contains time-stamped data.

This is intended as an alternative to versioning. Timestamps are by nature a less safe implementation of optimistic locking. However, sometimes the application might use the timestamps in other ways.

To have a timestamp support, all that needs to be done is:

- Add a timestamp property to all the persistent entity classes to enable optimistic locking

```
public class Books
{
   ...
   private Date lastUpdated;
   ...
}
```

- Place the <timestamp> element in the mapping document immediately after the identifier property mapping

```
<class name="Books" table="Books">
   <id .../>
   <timestamp name="lastUpdated" access="field" column="lastUpdated"/>
   ...
</class>
```

WARNING

A timestamp is always considered slightly less safe, because two concurrent transactions may both load and update the same record in the same millisecond. It is therefore, advisable to use version numbers and not timestamps.

Syntax:

```
<timestamp column="<ColumnName>" name="<PropertyName>"
  access="<field | property | ClassName>" source="<vm | db>"
  unsaved-value="<null | undefained>" generated="<never | always>"/>
```

The column Attribute

The column attribute specifies the name of the column holding the timestamp to use for identifier and is optional.

By default, this attribute takes the value of the name attribute.

The name Attribute

The name attribute specifies the name of a JavaBeans style property of Java data type Date or Timestamp of the persistent class.

The access Attribute

The access attribute, informs Hibernate, the strategy to be used to access the properties and is optional.

If this attribute is set to **property**, then **get** and **set** methods are used to access the data.

If this attribute is set to **field**, then the data is accessed directly.

Alternatively, this attribute can also be set to a class name of a PropertyAccessor implementation which defines any other access mechanism.

By default, the value of this attribute is property.

The source Attribute

From where does the Hibernate retrieve the timestamp value?

- From the database

OR

- From the current Java Virtual Machine

Database-based timestamps incur an overhead because Hibernate must hit the database in order to determine the next value, but will be safer for use in clustered environments.

REMINDER

Not all Dialects are known to support retrieving of the database's current timestamp, while others might be unsafe for usage in locking due to lack of precision, for example, Oracle 8

The source attribute informs Hibernate from where to retrieve the values and is optional.

By default, the value of this attribute is vm.

The unsaved-value Attribute

The unsaved-value attribute indicates whether the object is newly instantiated, distinguishing it from detached instances that were saved or loaded in a previous session and is optional.

Hibernate uses the value to determine whether the object needs to be persisted.

By default, the value of this attribute is null.

If the value of this attribute is set to undefined, then it specifies that the identifier property value should be used.

The generated Attribute

The generated attribute specifies that this version property value is generated by the database and is optional.

By default, the value of this attribute is never, which means that the database does not generate the property value.

If this attribute is set to always, then it states that the property value is generated both on INSERT and UPDATE.

Chapter

11

SECTION III: UNDERSTANDING CONFIGURATION AND MAPPING

Annotations

Annotations are a mechanism of passing information about the code spec [class, property, method]. This helps Java **tools** such as **ORM** to:

- Understand how the code spec is being used
- Enable automation that saves work

Any kind of **Object/Relation Mapping tool** requires metadata to transform one data representation to another. Prior to Hibernate 3, XML files were the only choice for defining the metadata/configuration. The database mappings were defined in a set of XML mapping files and loaded at startup time.

Hibernate 3 bought a new and more elegant configuration approach called **Annotations**. This approach permits taking advantage of the new Annotations feature of Java 5 to define database mappings inline with the POJO code spec.

Annotations provide a powerful and flexible way of declaring persistence mappings.

In this approach, the configuration that was defined earlier using mapping files can now be defined as annotations which are directly embedded in the Java classes [POJO].

HINT

Hibernate annotations also support the new EJB 3 persistence specifications. These specifications aim at providing a standardized Java persistence mechanism.

Why Annotations

Annotations based mappings are:

- More intuitive than the XML mapping file
- Less verbose than their XML equivalents [Diagram 11.1 and diagram 11.2 depict the differences]
- Embedded in the code spec along with the properties that they are associated with
- Compiled directly with the appropriate class files which reduces the risk of a missing or stale mapping file causing problems at deployment

Disadvantages Of Using Annotations

The following are a few disadvantages of using annotations:

Java 5 Is A Compulsion

Java 5 appeared in late 2004 as a major new release of the language.

Annotations are not supported by versions of Java prior to this, only XML mapping files are supported.

This means even though the core of Hibernate 3 is compatible with earlier Java versions, annotations cannot be used, unless the Java 5 is the version of choice.

Migration Issues

In Applications developed using Hibernate 2, XML-based mapping files will already be in place to support the code spec. Hence, when migrating, such applications to Hibernate 3, no one would desire spending time in re-expressing the mappings using annotations just because Hibernate 3 supports it.

Changes Require Rebuilding The Application

One disadvantage with using Annotations is that whenever any mapping details are changed to reflect business changes or schema alternations, the application needs to be rebuilt which is not the case with XML based mapping files. Here, the mapping details can be changed as and when the need arises to reflect business changes or schema alternations without rebuilding the application.

What To Use When

If annotations do not reduce the amount of metadata that needs to be provided [in most cases they do], then do not use annotations.

If there are regular changes to the application's business model, then the XML mapping files are the best place for the metadata as there is no need to recompile the application to make the changes.

Any changes made to the mapping details could be a potential risk. In case of annotations, the mapping details **cannot be changed dynamically** at runtime. Hence, annotations seem to be a better choice.

If the application requires mapping between classes and different databases with different schemas, the XML mapping file is preferred.

If the application needs to be portable to other EJB 3 compliant ORM applications, then annotations is recommended to represent the mapping details.

If a completely new application is being created, using annotations is recommended.

Diagram 11.1 and diagram 11.2 depict the visual differences between the two kinds of configurations.

```
package myApp;

public class Guestbook  implements java.io.Serializable {
    private Integer visitorNo;
    private String visitorName;
    private String message;
    private String messageDate;

    public Guestbook() {
    }

    public Guestbook(String visitorName, String message, String messageDate) {
       this.visitorName = visitorName;
       this.message = message;
       this.messageDate = messageDate;
    }

    public Integer getVisitorNo() {
        return this.visitorNo;
    }

    public void setVisitorNo(Integer visitorNo) {
        this.visitorNo = visitorNo;
    }
    public String getVisitorName() {
        return this.visitorName;
    }

    public void setVisitorName(String visitorName) {
        this.visitorName = visitorName;
    }
    public String getMessage() {
        return this.message;
    }

    public void setMessage(String message) {
        this.message = message;
    }
    public String getMessageDate() {
        return this.messageDate;
    }

    public void setMessageDate(String messageDate) {
        this.messageDate = messageDate;
    }
}
```

Mapping Document

```
<?xml version="1.0"?>
<IDOCTYPE hibernate-mapping PUBLIC "-//Hibernate/Hibernate Mapping DTD 3.0//EN"
"http://hibernate.sourceforge.net/hibernate-mapping-3.0.dtd">
<hibernate-mapping>
   <class name="myApp.Guestbook" table="guestbook" catalog="guestbook">
      <id name="visitorNo" type="java.lang.Integer">
         <column name="VisitorNo" />
         <generator class="identity" />
      </id>
      <property name="visitorName" type="string">
         <column name="VisitorName" length="50" />
      </property>
      <property name="message" type="string">
         <column name="Message" length="100" />
      </property>
      <property name="messageDate" type="string">
         <column name="MessageDate" length="40" />
      </property>
   </class>
</hibernate-mapping>
```

Diagram 11.1: POJO with XML Mapping Document

```
package myApp;
import javax.persistence.Column;
import javax.persistence.Entity;
import javax.persistence.GeneratedValue;
import static javax.persistence.GenerationType.IDENTITY;
import javax.persistence.Id;
import javax.persistence.Table;

@Entity
@Table(name="guestbook"
   ,catalog="guestbook"
)
public class Guestbook implements java.io.Serializable {


     private Integer visitorNo;
     private String visitorName;
     private String message;
     private String messageDate;

    public Guestbook() {
    }

    public Guestbook(String visitorName, String message, String messageDate) {
       this.visitorName = visitorName;
       this.message = message;
       this.messageDate = messageDate;
    }

     @Id @GeneratedValue(strategy=IDENTITY)

    @Column(name="VisitorNo", unique=true, nullable=false)
    public Integer getVisitorNo() {
        return this.visitorNo;
    }

    public void setVisitorNo(Integer visitorNo) {
        this.visitorNo = visitorNo;
    }

    @Column(name="VisitorName", length=50)
    public String getVisitorName() {
        return this.visitorName;
    }

    public void setVisitorName(String visitorName) {
        this.visitorName = visitorName;
    }

    @Column(name="Message", length=100)
    public String getMessage() {
        return this.message;
    }

    public void setMessage(String message) {
        this.message = message;
    }

    @Column(name="MessageDate", length=40)
    public String getMessageDate() {
        return this.messageDate;
    }

    public void setMessageDate(String messageDate) {
        this.messageDate = messageDate;
    }
}
```

Imports for Annotations

Annotations

Diagram 11.2: POJO with EJB 3 Annotations

Configuring Hibernate Annotations

To begin using Annotations, the Hibernate 3 annotations toolset needs to be downloaded and installed from http://www.hibernate.org/Download/DownloadOverview.

REMINDER

If JDK 5.0 is not available, an upgrade to it is required to use annotations.

Downloading Hibernate Annotations

From the download page, download the current latest release of Hibernate Annotations. At the time of writing this book, **3.4.0.GA** [available in this Book's accompanying CDROM] was the latest version that was available for download.

Click the **Download** link to begin the download and save the setup file to the machine.

After the file is downloaded, extract its contents to a directory.

Adding Hibernate Annotations Library Files

An application that requires using annotations needs to have a few annotation library files listed below.

Adding Library Files Using NetBeans IDE

These library files can be placed in the application's dedicated [explained earlier in *Chapter 03: Writing The First Application*] library directory [usually called **lib**].

Copy the following library files under **lib**:

- From the **hibernate-annotations-3.4.0.GA** directory
  - hibernate-annotations.jar
- From the **hibernate-annotations-3.4.0.GA → lib** directory
  - hibernate-commons-annotations.jar
  - ejb3-persistence.jar

Now that the files are available in the lib directory, add them to the project using the NetBeans IDE.

Right-click on the **Libraries** directory, click the **Add JAR/Folder...** menu item.

Clicking the **Add JAR/Folder** file displays the dialog box to choose the JAR files. Browse to the **lib** directory and select **JAR** files available in the lib directory of the project to add to the project.

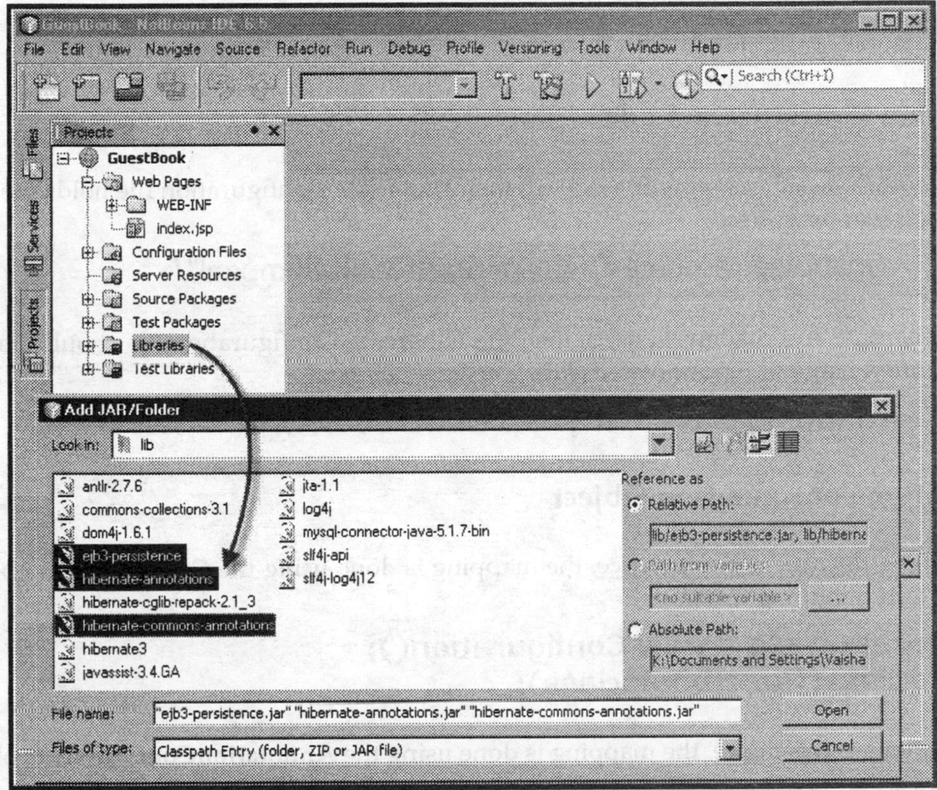

Diagram 11.3: Add Jar/Folder dialog box

Creating An Instance Of Annotation Configuration

If a Mapping document is the choice, an instance of **org.hibernate.cfg.Configuration** is created:

```
1  Configuration cfg = new Configuration();
```

If Annotations is the choice, then an instance of **AnnotationConfiguration** is created:

```
1  AnnotationConfiguration cfg = new AnnotationConfiguration();
```

Mapping The JavaBean Class Location

The persistent class POJO that now holds annotations should be indicated to Hibernate.

There are two ways to indicate this:

- Hibernate Configuration File
- AnnotationConfiguration object

Hibernate Configuration File

When the XML based mapping file is used, then Hibernate Configuration file holds the name of the XML mapping file:

```
<mapping resource="myApp/GuestBook.hbm.xml"/>
```

When Hibernate Annotations is used, then the Hibernate Configuration file should hold the fully qualified name of the annotated class [persistent class]:

```
<mapping class="myApp.Guestbook"/>
```

AnnotationConfiguration Object

If a Mapping document is the choice, the mapping is done using the **Configuration** object to load the XML mapping document:

```
Configuration cfg = new Configuration();
cfg.addClass(Guestbook.class);
```

If Annotations is the choice, the mapping is done using the **AnnotationConfiguration** object:

```
AnnotationConfiguration cfg = new AnnotationConfiguration();
cfg.addAnnotatedClass(Guestbook.class);
```

addAnnotatedClass() method reads the mapping from the class annotation metadata.

Obtaining A SessionFactory

When all the mappings have been parsed by the AnnotationConfiguration, the application must obtain a factory for org.hibernate.Session instance. The factory obtained is intended to be shared by all application threads.

The following code spec obtains a SessionFactory:

```
SessionFactory sessions = cfg.configure().buildSessionFactory();
```

configure() method returns an instance of AnnotationConfiguration object.

buildSessionFactory() method instantiates a new SessionFactory, using the properties and mappings in this configuration.

EJB 3 Annotations

Hibernate 3 uses the standard **EJB 3 annotations** along with several Hibernate specific annotations.

Hence to define the metadata mapping, Hibernate allows annotating **POJOs** with Hibernate 3/EJB 3 annotations.

EJB 3 annotations are contained in the **javax.persistence.*** package.

Hibernate 3 offers a variety of additional annotations that can be mixed with the EJB 3 entities. They have been designed as a natural extension of EJB3 annotations.

The javax.persistence.* package needs to be imported in the persistent class, where annotations are used:

```
import javax.persistence.*;
```

HINT

The IDEs such as NetBeans and Eclipse are JDK 5 complaint. That means these IDE will auto complete the annotation interfaces and attributes even without a specific EJB 3 module, since EJB 3 are plain JDK 5 annotations.

Each and every persistent POJO class is an entity bean. Hence, the first step is to annotate the POJO class as an EJB 3 **Entity** bean.

@Entity

The Entity Bean is declared using the @Entity annotation:

```
package myApp;

import javax.persistence.*;
```

```

@Entity
public class Guestbook {
...
}
```

@Entity declares the class as an entity bean i.e. a persistent POJO class.

The EJB 3 annotation in this case called Entity is available in the javax.persistence package, hence, the entire package is imported. However, it is recommended to use **explicit imports** such as:

- **import** javax.persistence.Entity;

instead of:

- **import** javax.persistence.*;

REMINDER

The POJO class that needs to be marked as an Entity bean needs to have a **no argument constructor** with at least protected scope.

@Entity annotation has the following attributes:

- **dynamicInsert:** Specifies whether the INSERT statement should be generated at runtime. It allows only the altered columns to be inserted. By default, the value of this attribute is disabled
- **dynamicUpdate:** Specifies whether the UPDATE statement should be generated at runtime. It allows only the altered columns to be updated. By default, the value of this attribute is disabled
- **mutable:** By default, the value of this attribute is true. If this attribute is set to false, then Hibernate allows the persistence engine to cache the values read from the database and the persistence engine will make no attempt to update them in response to changes
- **optimisticLock:** Allows an optimistic lock strategy to be selected from the OptimisticLockType enumeration values of ALL, DIRTY, NONE and VERSION. By default, the value of this attribute is VERSION
- **persister:** Allows a persister class other than the default Hibernate one to be selected for the entity. For example, allowing serialization to be used instead of relational persistence
- **polymorphism:** Allows the polymorphism strategy to be selected from the PolymorphismType enumeration values of EXPLICIT and IMPLICIT. By default, the value of this attribute is IMPLICIT

- **selectBeforeUpdate:** Allows the user to request that a SELECT be performed to retrieve the entity before any potential update

@Table

@Table allows specifying the details of the table, which will be used to persist the entity bean in the database.

HINT

If @Table is not defined, then Hibernate uses the default class name of the entity bean as the **table name.**

@Table annotation provides the following attributes:

- The name of the table
- The name of the catalog
- The name of the schema
- Enforce unique constraints on columns in the table

@Table at class level:

```
package myApp;

import javax.persistence.*;

@Entity
@Table(name="GuestbookMaster", catalog="guestbook")
public class Guestbook {
...
}
```

In the above example, name and catalog attributes of the @Table annotation are used to specify the name of the table and the database.

Unique Constraints

Unique constraints can also be declared in the @Table annotation using the @UniqueConstraint annotation:

```
package myApp;

import javax.persistence.*;
```

```

@Entity
@Table(name="CustomerMaster",
   uniqueConstraints = {@UniqueConstraint(columnNames="EmailAddress")})
public class Customers {
...
}
```

In the above example, unique constraint is applied to the EmailAddress column.

The same can be achieved using @Column [explained later]:

```
package myApp;

import javax.persistence.*;

@Entity
@Table(name="CustomerMaster")
public class Customers {
...
   @Column(name="EmailAddress", unique=true, nullable=false)
   public String getEmailAddress() {
      return this.emailAddress;
   }

   public void setEmailAddress(String emailAddress) {
      this.emailAddress= emailAddress;
   }

...
}
```

@UniqueConstraint can also be applied to multiple columns:

```
package myApp;

import javax.persistence.*;

@Entity
@Table(name="CustomerMaster",
   uniqueConstraints = {@UniqueConstraint(columnNames={"EmailAddress", "Username"})})
public class Customers {
...
}
```

In the above example, unique constraint is applied to the two table columns i.e. EmailAddress and Username.

@Id

Each entity bean must have a **Primary Key**, which can be annotated using the @Id annotation. The @Id annotation helps define the property as the identifier of the entity bean.

The @Id annotation's placement determines the default access strategy that Hibernate uses for the mapping.

Field Access

In the following code spec, @Id is applied to a field:

```
package myApp;

import javax.persistence.*;

@Entity
@Table(name="CustomerMaster")
public class Customers {
...
  @Id
  private int customerNo();

  public int getCustomerNo() {
     return this.customerNo;
  }

  public void setCustomerNo(String customerNo) {
     this.customerNo= customerNo;
  }

...
}
```

Here, @Id annotation is applied to the CustomerNo field, which means that the CustomerNo **field access** is used by Hibernate.

Property Access

In the following code spec, @Id is applied to a getter method:

```
package myApp;

import javax.persistence.*;
```

```
@Entity
@Table(name="CustomerMaster")
public class Customers {
...
    @Id
    public int getCustomerNo() {
        return this.customerNo;
    }

    public void setCustomerNo(String customerNo) {
        this.customerNo= customerNo;
    }

...
}
```

Here, @Id annotation is applied to the getter method of the CustomerNo field, which means that **property access** is used by Hibernate.

An identifier property [Primary Key] can be set by the application or generated by Hibernate using identifier generation strategies. By default, @Id automatically determines the most appropriate primary key generation strategy to use. However, this can be overridden by using the @GeneratedValue annotation.

@GeneratedValue

@GeneratedValue has the following attributes:

- strategy
- generator

The following are the types of primary key generators:

- **AUTO:** Is the default value. Hibernate decides which generator to use based on the database's support for primary key generation
- **TABLE:** It keeps a separate table with the primary key values
- **IDENTITY:** The database is responsible for determining and assigning the next primary key
- **SEQUENCE:** Some database support a SEQUENCE column type

The following code spec uses the default primary key generation:

```
package myApp;

import javax.persistence.*;

@Entity
@Table(name="CustomerMaster")
public class Customers {
...
    @Id
    @GeneratedValue
    public int getCustomerNo() {
        return this.customerNo;
    }

    public void setCustomerNo(String customerNo) {
        this.customerNo= customerNo;
    }

...
}
```

Here, Hibernate determines which generator type is to be used. This makes the code spec portable between different databases.

@SequenceGenerator

The primary key can be generated with the help of sequence.

HINT

A sequence is a database object that can be used as a source of primary key values.

The following code spec uses @SequenceGenerator annotation:

```
package myApp;

import javax.persistence.*;

@Entity
@Table(name="CustomerMaster")
```

```
public class Customers {
...
    @Id
    @SequenceGenerator(name="sequenceGen", sequenceName="CustomersSq")
    @GeneratedValue(generator="sequenceGen", strategy=GenerationType.SEQUENCE)
    public int getCustomerNo() {
       return this.customerNo;
    }

    public void setCustomerNo(String customerNo) {
       this.customerNo= customerNo;
    }

...
}
```

Here, a sequence generation annotation named **sequenceGen** is declared, which refers to the database sequence object called **CustomersSq**.

The sequence named sequenceGen is then referred as the generator of the @GeneratedValue annotation.

The following are the attributes of @SequenceGenerator annotation:

- **name:** It is mandatory. It is the name of the sequence generated
- **sequenceName:** Defines the sequence generator
- **initialValue:** Allows the starting primary value to be specified
- **allocationSize:** Allows the increment on the primary key value to be specified. The default allocation size is 50, so if a sequence is used and each time the value is picked up, set the allocation size to 1

@TableGenerator

@TableGenerator manipulates the standard database table to obtain its primary key values instead of using a vendor specific sequence object. This annotation is portable between database platforms.

Usually, the table used to hold the primary key values, may hold rows, each representing a value for an entity.

PrimaryKeys

Table Definition

Column Name	Datatype	NOT NULL
PKColumn	VARCHAR	✔
PKValue	INTEGER	✔

Sample Data

PKColumn	PKValue
Customers	5
Authors	7
Publishers	9
Employees	19

The following code spec uses @TableGenerator to generate the primary key value:

```
package myApp;

import javax.persistence.*;

@Entity
@Table(name="CustomerMaster")
public class Customers {
...
   @Id
   @TableGenerator(name="tableGen",table="PrimaryKeys", pkColumnName="PKColumn",
   valueColumnName="PKValue" )
   @GeneratedValue(generator="tableGen", strategy=GenerationType.TABLE)
   public int getCustomerNo() {
      return this.customerNo;
   }

   public void setCustomerNo(String customerNo) {
      this.customerNo= customerNo;
   }

...
}
```

Here, since the **PrimaryKeys** table holds primary key values for multiple entities:

- **pkColumnName** is used to indicate the column containing the next primary key for the **Customers** Entity
- **pkColumnValue** is used to indicate the column that holds the actual primary key value

The following are the attributes of the @TableGenerator annotation:

- **name:** It is mandatory. The name of the table generation primary key
- **table:** The name of the table containing the primary key values
- **schema:** Allows the schema that the table resides within to be specified
- **catalog:** Allows the catalog that the table resides within to be specified
- **initialValue:** Allows the starting primary value to be specified
- **allocationSize:** Allows the increment on the primary key value to be specified

- **pkColumnName:** Allows the primary key column of the table to be identified. The table can contain the details necessary for generating primary key values for multiple entities
- **pkColumnValue:** Allows the primary key for the row containing the primary key generation information to be identified
- **uniqueConstraints:** Allows additional constraints to be applied to the table for schema generation
- **valueColumnName:** Allows the column containing the primary key generation information for the current entity to be identified

@Column

The column(s) used for a property mapping can be defined using the @Column annotation. @Column annotation helps specifying the column details of columns to which a property is being mapped.

The following code spec using the @Column annotation on a property called username:

```
package myApp;

import javax.persistence.*;

@Entity
@Table(name="CustomerMaster")
public class Customers {
...

   @Column(name="Username", length=18, updatable=false, nullable=false)
   public String getUsername() {
      return this.username;
   }

   public void setUsername(String username) {
      this.username = username;
   }

...
}
```

In the above example, the **username** property is mapped to the **Username** column, which:

- Is **not nullable**
- Has a **length** of 18 characters
- Is **not updatable** i.e. making the property immutable

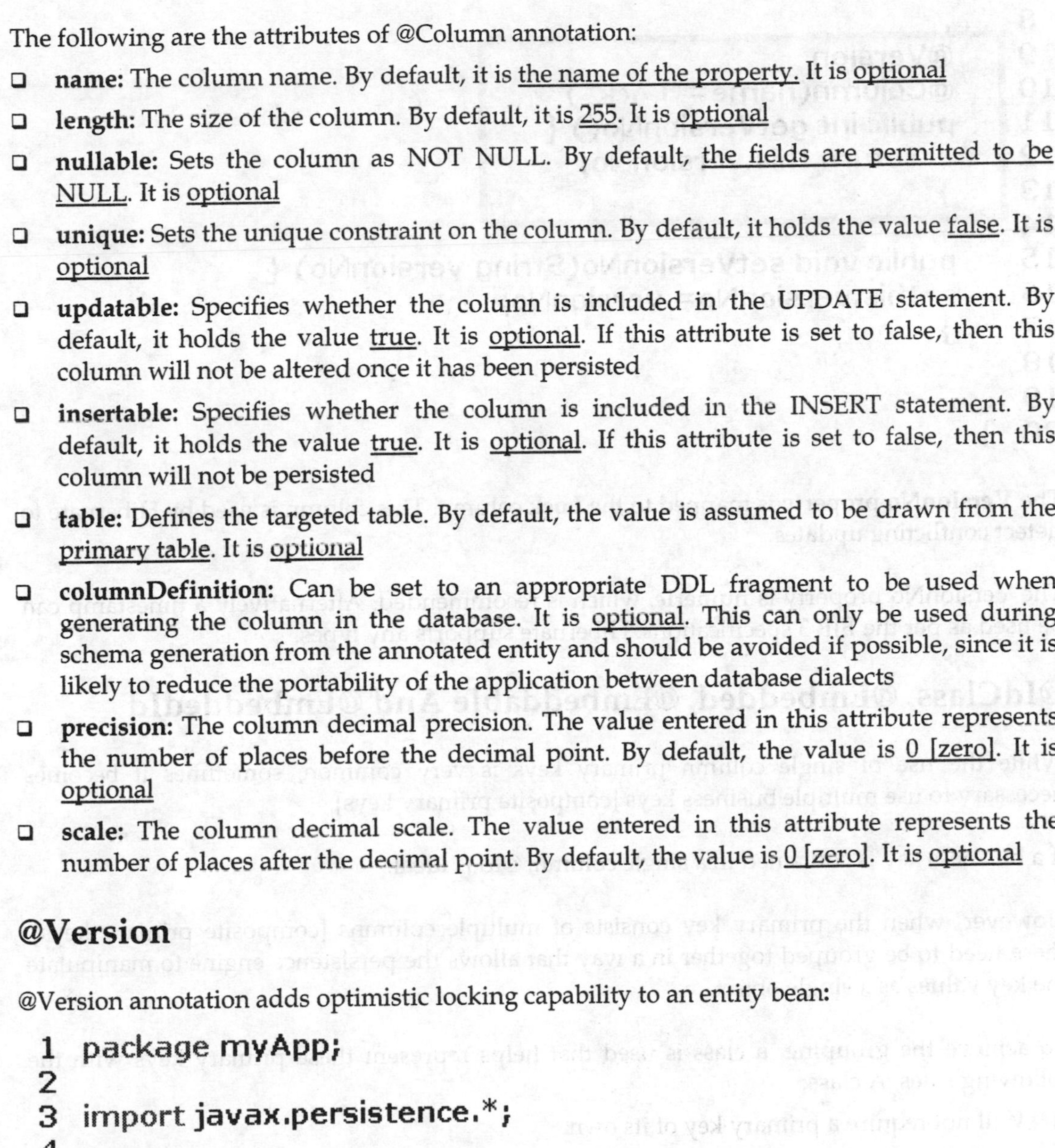

The following are the attributes of @Column annotation:

- **name:** The column name. By default, it is the name of the property. It is optional
- **length:** The size of the column. By default, it is 255. It is optional
- **nullable:** Sets the column as NOT NULL. By default, the fields are permitted to be NULL. It is optional
- **unique:** Sets the unique constraint on the column. By default, it holds the value false. It is optional
- **updatable:** Specifies whether the column is included in the UPDATE statement. By default, it holds the value true. It is optional. If this attribute is set to false, then this column will not be altered once it has been persisted
- **insertable:** Specifies whether the column is included in the INSERT statement. By default, it holds the value true. It is optional. If this attribute is set to false, then this column will not be persisted
- **table:** Defines the targeted table. By default, the value is assumed to be drawn from the primary table. It is optional
- **columnDefinition:** Can be set to an appropriate DDL fragment to be used when generating the column in the database. It is optional. This can only be used during schema generation from the annotated entity and should be avoided if possible, since it is likely to reduce the portability of the application between database dialects
- **precision:** The column decimal precision. The value entered in this attribute represents the number of places before the decimal point. By default, the value is 0 [zero]. It is optional
- **scale:** The column decimal scale. The value entered in this attribute represents the number of places after the decimal point. By default, the value is 0 [zero]. It is optional

@Version

@Version annotation adds optimistic locking capability to an entity bean:

```
package myApp;

import javax.persistence.*;

@Entity
@Table(name="CustomerMaster")
public class Customers {
```

```
...
    @Version
    @Column(name="Lock")
    public int getVersionNo() {
        return this.versionNo;
    }

    public void setVersionNo(String versionNo) {
        this.versionNo= versionNo;
    }

    ...
}
```

The **VersionNo** property is mapped to the **Lock** column. This column is used by Hibernate to detect conflicting updates.

The VersionNo property is **numeric**, which is recommended. Alternatively a timestamp can be used as per the EJB 3 specifications. Hibernate supports any types.

@IdClass, @Embedded, @Embeddable And @EmbeddedId

While the use of single column primary keys is very common, sometimes it becomes necessary to use multiple business keys [composite primary keys].

If a business key is contained in a single column, @Id is ideal.

However, when the primary key consists of multiple columns [composite primary keys], these need to be grouped together in a way that allows the persistence engine to manipulate the key values as a single object.

To achieve the grouping, a class is used that helps represent these primary keys with the following rules. A class:

- Will not require a primary key of its own
- Must be a public class
- Must have a default constructor
- Must be serializable

- Must implement hashCode() and equals() methods to allow the Hibernate code to test for primary key collisions i.e. they must be implemented with the appropriate database semantics for the primary key values

Hibernate allows defining composite primary keys using one of the following approaches:

- Annotate the component property as @Id and make the component class @Embeddable
- Annotate the component property as @EmbeddedId
- Annotate the class as @IdClass and annotate each property of the entity involved in the primary key with @Id

Component Property As @Id And Component class @Embeddable

```
package myApp;
import javax.persistence.*;

@Entity
@Table(name="CustomerMaster")
public class Customers {
    private CustomersPk ID;
    private String Address;

    public Customers() {
    }

    @Id
    public CustomersPk getID() {
        return ID;
    }
    public void setID(CustomersPk ID) {
        this.ID = ID;
    }

    public String getAddress() {
        return Address;
    }
    public void setAddress(String Address) {
        this.Address = Address;
    }
```

```

@Embeddable
public static class CustomersPk {
    private String CustomerName;
    private String Username;

    public CustomersPk() {
    }

    public String getCustomerName() {
        return CustomerName;
    }
    public void setCustomerName(String CustomerName) {
        this.CustomerName = CustomerName;
    }

    public String getUsername() {
        return Username;
    }
    public void setUsername(String Username) {
        this.Username = Username;
    }

    public int hashCode() {
        . . .
    }
    public boolean equals(Object obj) {
        . . .
    }
  }
}
```

Here, the **CustomerName** and the **Username** form the **composite primary key** for the **Customers** entity.

Both these properties are contained in a separate **Embeddable** class called **CustomersPk**.

A component property of type **CustomersPk** is annotated as @Id.

```
@Id
public CustomersPk getID() {
   return ID;
}
```

The component class **CustomersPk** is annotated as @Embeddable.

```
@Embeddable
public static class CustomersPk {
```

The @Embeddable annotation treats the compound primary key as a single property.

Component Property As @EmbeddedId

```
package myApp;
import javax.persistence.*;

@Entity
@Table(name="CustomerMaster")
public class Customers {
    private CustomersPk ID;
    private String Address;

   public Customers() {
   }

   @EmbeddedId
   public CustomersPk getID() {
      return ID;
   }
   public void setID(CustomersPk ID) {
      this.ID = ID;
   }

   public String getAddress() {
      return Address;
   }
   public void setAddress(String Address) {
```

```
        this.Address = Address;
    }

    public static class CustomersPk {
        private String CustomerName;
        private String Username;

        public CustomersPk() {
        }

        public String getCustomerName() {
            return CustomerName;
        }
        public void setCustomerName(String CustomerName) {
            this.CustomerName = CustomerName;
        }

        public String getUsername() {
            return Username;
        }
        public void setUsername(String Username) {
            this.Username = Username;
        }

        public int hashCode() {
            . . .
        }
        public boolean equals(Object obj) {
            . . .
        }
    }
}
```

Here, the **CustomerName** and the **Username** form the **composite primary key** for the **Customers** entity.

Both these properties are contained in a separate class called **CustomersPk**.

A component property of type **CustomersPk** is annotated as @EmbeddedId.

```
@EmbeddedId
public CustomersPk getID() {
  return ID;
}
```

The @EmbeddedId annotation treats the key as a single attribute of the Customers class.

Class As @IdClass And Property @Id

```
package myApp;
import javax.persistence.*;

@Entity
@Table(name="CustomerMaster")
@IdClass(Customers.CustomersPk.class)
public class Customers {
    private String CustomerName;
    private String Username;
    private String Address;

   public Customers() {
   }

   @Id
   public String getCustomerName() {
      return CustomerName;
   }
   public void setCustomerName(String CustomerName) {
      this.CustomerName = CustomerName;
   }

   @Id
   public String getUsername() {
      return Username;
   }
   public void setUsername(String Username) {
      this.Username = Username;
```

```
    }

    public String getAddress() {
        return Address;
    }
    public void setAddress(String Address) {
        this.Address = Address;
    }

    public static class CustomersPk {
        private String CustomerName;
        private String Username;

        public CustomersPk() {
        }

        public String getCustomerName() {
            return CustomerName;
        }
        public void setCustomerName(String CustomerName) {
            this.CustomerName = CustomerName;
        }

        public String getUsername() {
            return Username;
        }
        public void setUsername(String Username) {
            this.Username = Username;
        }
        public int hashCode() {
            . . .
        }

        public boolean equals(Object obj) {
            . . .
        }
    }
}
```

Here, the **CustomerName** and the **Username** form the **composite primary key** for the **Customers** entity.

The fields that correspond to the properties of the primary key class to be used must all be annotated with @Id.

Both these properties are placed in the entity class **Customers** and annotated using @Id.

```
@Id
public String getCustomerName() {
   return CustomerName;
}

@Id
public String getUsername() {
   return Username;
}
```

The entity class Customers is annotated as @IdClass.

```
@IdClass(Customers.CustomersPk.class)
public class Customers {
```

The @IdClass annotation accepts a value parameter of Class type, which must be the class to be used as the compound primary key.

The only advantage to using this method is its ability to hide the use of the primary key class from the interface of the enclosing entity.

Irrespective of the approach chosen, to declare the composite compound primary key, the underlying database table will still use the same set of columns.

Column Name	Datatype
CustomerName	VARCHAR
Username	VARCHAR(18)
Address	VARCHAR(100)

@OneToOne

Entity beans can be associated through a one-to-one relationship using @OneToOne annotation.

Example

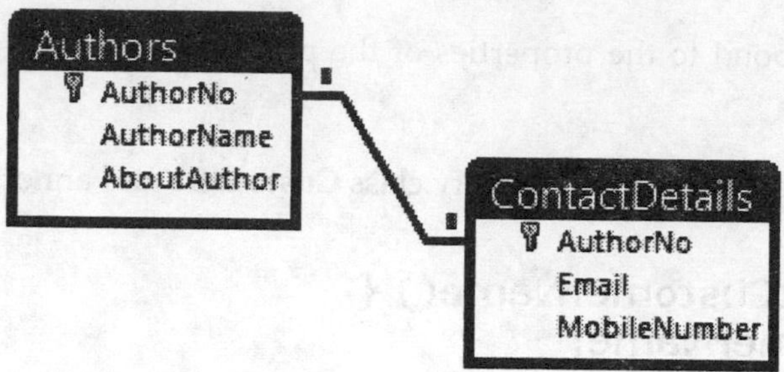

From the perspective of the Authors class [ONE-TO-ONE]:

```
import javax.persistence.*;
import org.hibernate.annotations.*;

@Entity
@Table(name = "authors", catalog = "associations")
public class Authors implements java.io.Serializable {
    private int authorNo;
    private String authorName;
    private String aboutAuthor;
    private Contactdetails contactdetails;

    public Authors() {
    }

    public Authors(int authorNo) {
        this.authorNo = authorNo;
    }

    public Authors(Contactdetails contactdetails, int authorNo, String
    authorName, String aboutAuthor) {
        this.contactdetails = contactdetails;
        this.authorNo = authorNo;
```

```
        this.authorName = authorName;
        this.aboutAuthor = aboutAuthor;
    }

    @Id
    @GeneratedValue(generator = "genForeign")
    @GenericGenerator(name = "genForeign", strategy = "foreign",
    parameters = {@Parameter(name = "property", value = "contactdetails")})
    @Column(name = "AuthorNo", unique = true, nullable = false)
    public int getAuthorNo() {
        return this.authorNo;
    }
    public void setAuthorNo(int authorNo) {
        this.authorNo = authorNo;
    }

    @Column(name = "AuthorName", length = 25)
    public String getAuthorName() {
        return this.authorName;
    }
    public void setAuthorName(String authorName) {
        this.authorName = authorName;
    }

    @Column(name = "AboutAuthor", length = 50)
    public String getAboutAuthor() {
        return this.aboutAuthor;
    }
    public void setAboutAuthor(String aboutAuthor) {
        this.aboutAuthor = aboutAuthor;
    }

```

```
    @OneToOne(cascade = CascadeType.ALL, targetEntity =
    myApp.Contactdetails.class)
    @JoinColumn(name="AuthorNo")
    public Contactdetails getContactdetails() {
        return contactdetails;
    }
    public void setContactdetails(Contactdetails contactdetails) {
        this.contactdetails = contactdetails;
    }
}
```

@ManyToOne

The simplest way to maintain a many-to-one relationship between two entities is by managing the foreign key of the entity at the **one end** of the one-to-many relationship as a column in the **many entity's table**.

The @OneToMany annotation can be applied to a field or property value for a collection or an array representing the mapped **many end** of the association.

Example

From the perspective of the States class [MANY-TO-ONE]:

```
import javax.persistence.*;
import org.hibernate.annotations.*;

@Entity
@Table(name="states",catalog="associations")
```

```
public class States implements java.io.Serializable {
    private int stateNo;
    private Countries countries;
    private String stateName;

    public States() {
    }

    public States(int stateNo) {
        this.stateNo = stateNo;
    }

    public States(int stateNo, Countries countries, String stateName) {
        this.stateNo = stateNo;
        this.countries = countries;
        this.stateName = stateName;
    }

    @Id
    @Column(name="StateNo", unique=true, nullable=false)
    public int getStateNo() {
        return this.stateNo;
    }
    public void setStateNo(int stateNo) {
        this.stateNo = stateNo;
    }

    @ManyToOne(fetch=FetchType.LAZY)
    @JoinColumn(name="CountryNo")
    public Countries getCountries() {
        return this.countries;
    }
    public void setCountries(Countries countries) {
```

```
        this.countries = countries;
    }

    @Column(name="StateName", length=25)
    public String getStateName() {
        return this.stateName;
    }
    public void setStateName(String stateName) {
        this.stateName = stateName;
    }
}
```

From the perspective of the Countries class [ONE-TO-MANY]:

```
import java.util.*;
import javax.persistence.*;
import org.hibernate.annotations.*;

@Entity
@Table(name="countries",catalog="associations")
public class Countries implements java.io.Serializable {
    private int countryNo;
    private String countryName;
    private Set stateses = new HashSet(0);

    public Countries() {
    }

    public Countries(int countryNo) {
        this.countryNo = countryNo;
    }

    public Countries(int countryNo, String countryName, Set stateses) {
```

```
        this.countryNo = countryNo;
        this.countryName = countryName;
        this.stateses = stateses;
    }

    @Id
    @Column(name="CountryNo", unique=true, nullable=false)
    public int getCountryNo() {
        return this.countryNo;
    }
    public void setCountryNo(int countryNo) {
        this.countryNo = countryNo;
    }

    @Column(name="CountryName", length=25)
    public String getCountryName() {
        return this.countryName;
    }
    public void setCountryName(String countryName) {
        this.countryName = countryName;
    }

    @OneToMany(cascade=CascadeType.ALL, fetch=FetchType.LAZY,
    mappedBy="countries")
    public Set getStateses() {
        return this.stateses;
    }
    public void setStateses(Set stateses) {
        this.stateses = stateses;
    }
}
```

@ManyToMany

Example

From the perspective of the Authors class [MANY-TO-MANY]:

```
import java.util.*;
import javax.persistence.*;
import org.hibernate.annotations.*;

@Entity
@Table(name="authors",catalog="associations")
public class Authors  implements java.io.Serializable {
    private int authorNo;
    private String authorName;
    private String aboutAuthor;
    private Set bookses = new HashSet(0);

    public Authors() {
    }


    public Authors(int authorNo) {
        this.authorNo = authorNo;
    }

```

```
    public Authors(int authorNo, String authorName, String aboutAuthor, Set bookses) {
        this.authorNo = authorNo;
        this.authorName = authorName;
        this.aboutAuthor = aboutAuthor;
        this.bookses = bookses;
    }

    @Id
    @Column(name="AuthorNo", unique=true, nullable=false)
    public int getAuthorNo() {
        return this.authorNo;
    }
    public void setAuthorNo(int authorNo) {
        this.authorNo = authorNo;
    }

    @Column(name="AuthorName", length=25)
    public String getAuthorName() {
        return this.authorName;
    }
    public void setAuthorName(String authorName) {
        this.authorName = authorName;
    }

    @Column(name="AboutAuthor", length=50)
    public String getAboutAuthor() {
        return this.aboutAuthor;
    }
    public void setAboutAuthor(String aboutAuthor) {
        this.aboutAuthor = aboutAuthor;
    }
```

```

    @ManyToMany(cascade=CascadeType.ALL, fetch=FetchType.LAZY, mappedBy="authorses")
    public Set getBookses() {
        return this.bookses;
    }
    public void setBookses(Set bookses) {
        this.bookses = bookses;
    }
}
```

The following are the attributes of all the three annotations:

- **targetEntity:** Can be set to the class of an entity storing the association. If this attribute is not set, then the appropriate type will be inferred from the field type or the return type of the property's getter method
- **cascade:** Can be set to any of the members of the javax.persistence.CascadeType enumeration. It defaults to none. Following are the members of the CascadeType enumeration:
    - **ALL:** Requires all operations to be cascaded to dependent entities
    - **MERGE:** Cascades updates to the entity's state in the database i.e. UPDATE
    - **PERSIST:** Cascades the initial storing of the entity's state in the database i.e. INSERT
    - **REFRESH:** Cascades the updating of the entity's state from the database i.e. SELECT
    - **REMOVE:** Cascades deletion of the entity from the database i.e. DELETE
    - If no cascade type is specified, no operations will be cascaded through the association
- **fetch:** Can be set to the EAGER or LAZY members of FetchType
- **optional:** Indicates whether the value being mapped can be null
- **mappedBy:** Indicates that a bidirectional one-to-one relationship is owned by the named entity. The owning entity contains the primary key of the subordinate entity

Guest Book Application

Example

Now that the fundamentals of annotations are in place, let's learn how to use annotations in the GuestBook application created earlier.

To create the GuestBook application from scratch, refer to *Chapter 03: Writing The First Application*. The following only depicts the steps involved in adding the annotations to the application.

Open the GuestBook application in the NetBeans IDE.

This application currently uses mapping documents.

Remove/Delete the already existing files from the **myApp** package:

- **Mapping Document** [Guestbook.hbm.xml]
- **POJO** [Guestbook.java].

After they are removed, add a new POJO class with annotations. Instead of hand coding the POJO class, use the Hibernate Tools provided by NetBeans IDE and reverse engineer the POJO from the available database table.

Right-click the **myApp** package. Select **New → Hibernate Mapping Files and POJOs from Database...** as shown in diagram 11.4.1.

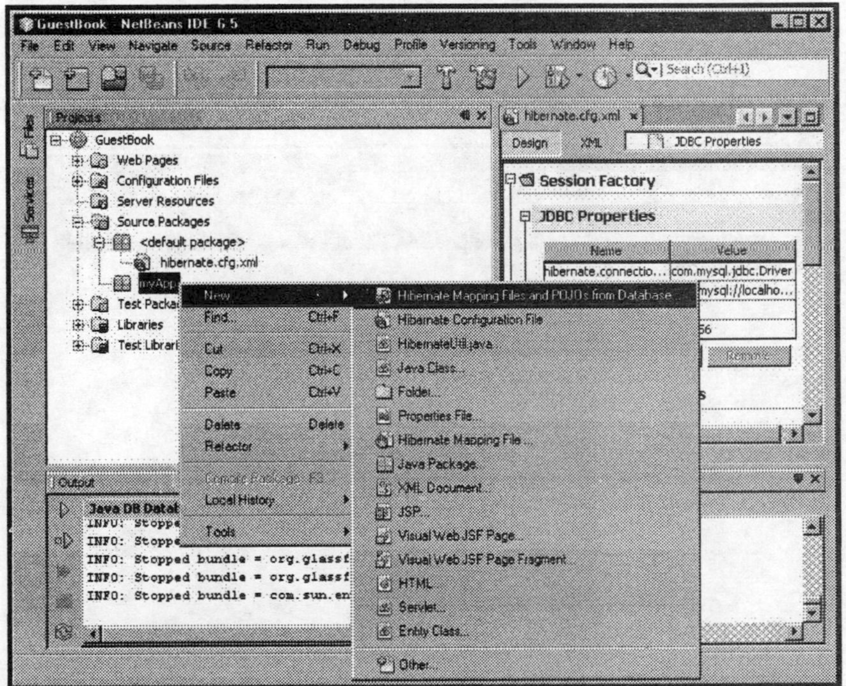

Diagram 11.4.1: Creating Hibernate mapping file

Click [Next >]. This shows the **New Hibernate Mapping Files and POJOs from Database** dialog box as shown in diagram 11.4.2.

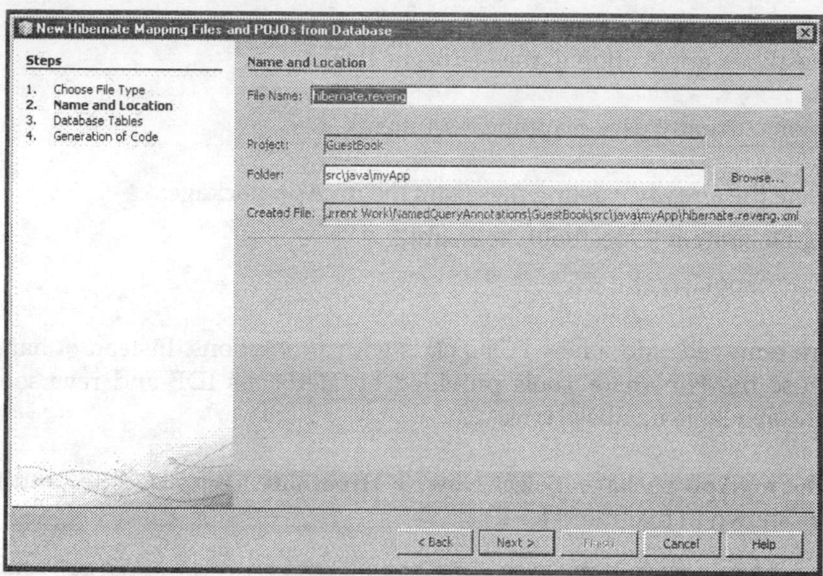

Diagram 11.4.2

Keep the defaults and click [Next >]. This brings up the screen as shown in diagram 11.4.3.

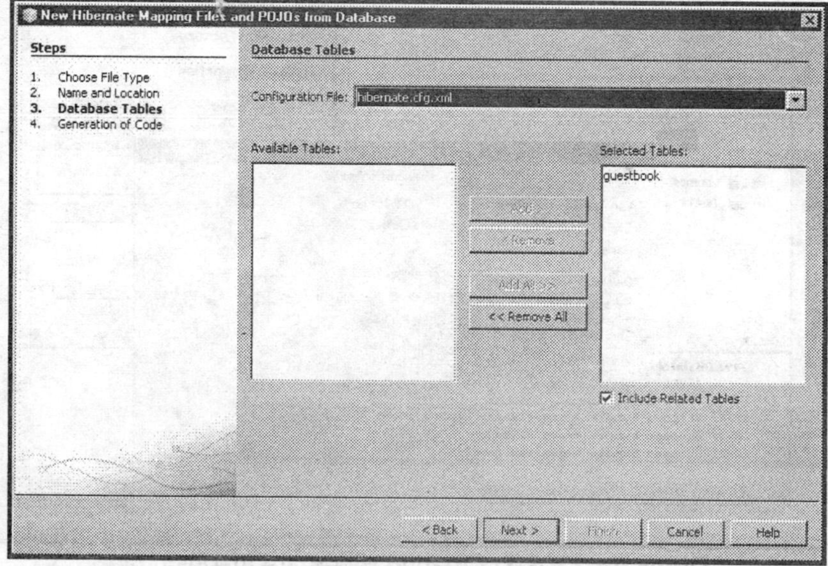

Diagram 11.4.3

Choose the table GuestBook from the **Available Tables** lists and add it to the **Selected Tables** list using [Add >].

Click [Next >] when done. This brings up the screen as shown in diagram 11.4.4.

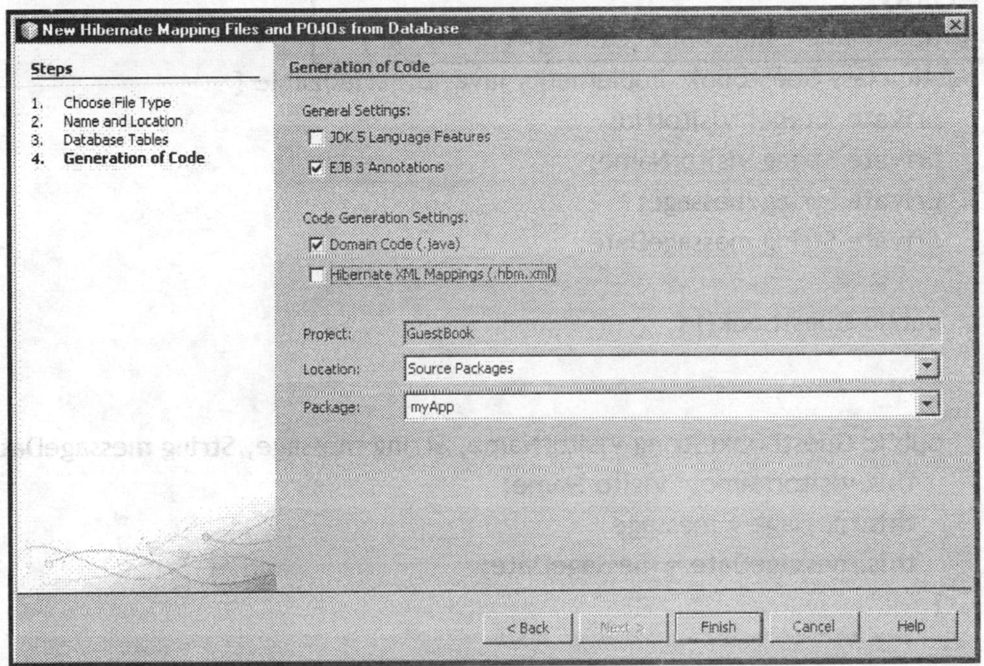

Diagram 11.4.4

Choose **EJB 3 Annotations** as shown in diagram 11.4.4.

Since, annotations are to be used, de-select **Hibernate XML Mappings (.hbm.xml)**.

Click [Finish] when done. This begins the file creation process and the progress is indicated using a progress bar.

The POJO file [automatically created] holds the following code spec:

```
package myApp;

import javax.persistence.Column;
import javax.persistence.Entity;
import javax.persistence.GeneratedValue;
```

```
import static javax.persistence.GenerationType.IDENTITY;
import javax.persistence.Id;
import javax.persistence.Table;

@Entity
@Table(name="guestbook",catalog="guestbook")
public class Guestbook  implements java.io.Serializable {
   private Integer visitorNo;
   private String visitorName;
   private String message;
   private String messageDate;

   public Guestbook() {
   }

   public Guestbook(String visitorName, String message, String messageDate) {
      this.visitorName = visitorName;
      this.message = message;
      this.messageDate = messageDate;
   }

   @Id @GeneratedValue(strategy=IDENTITY)

   @Column(name="VisitorNo", unique=true, nullable=false)
   public Integer getVisitorNo() {
      return this.visitorNo;
   }
   public void setVisitorNo(Integer visitorNo) {
      this.visitorNo = visitorNo;
   }

   @Column(name="VisitorName", length=50)
   public String getVisitorName() {
      return this.visitorName;
   }
```

```
    public void setVisitorName(String visitorName) {
        this.visitorName = visitorName;
    }

    @Column(name="Message", length=100)
    public String getMessage() {
        return this.message;
    }
    public void setMessage(String message) {
        this.message = message;
    }

    @Column(name="MessageDate", length=40)
    public String getMessageDate() {
        return this.messageDate;
    }
    public void setMessageDate(String messageDate) {
        this.messageDate = messageDate;
    }
}
```

The wizard automatically updates the **hibernate.cfg.xml** file to now include the POJO class as a reference.

```
<?xml version="1.0" encoding="UTF-8"?>
<!DOCTYPE hibernate-configuration PUBLIC "-//Hibernate/Hibernate Configuration DTD 3.0//EN"
"http://hibernate.sourceforge.net/hibernate-configuration-3.0.dtd">
<hibernate-configuration>
  <session-factory>
    <property name="hibernate.dialect">org.hibernate.dialect.MySQLDialect</property>
    <property name="hibernate.connection.driver_class">com.mysql.jdbc.Driver</property>
    <property name="hibernate.connection.url">jdbc:mysql://localhost:3306/GuestBook</property>
    <property name="hibernate.connection.username">root</property>
    <property name="hibernate.connection.password">123456</property>
    <mapping class="myApp.Guestbook"/>
  </session-factory>
</hibernate-configuration>
```

Since this application is going to use annotations, it is required to spawn an instance of the Annotations Configuration instead of the standard Configuration.

In the GuestBook application, the spawning of the Configuration object takes place in GuestBookView.jsp. Hence, edit this file.

Edit the GuestBookView.jsp file:

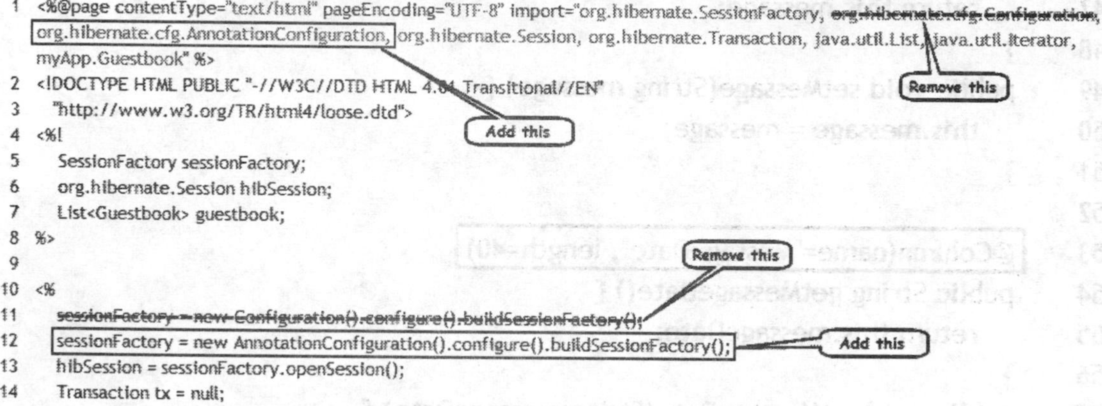

```
<%@page contentType="text/html" pageEncoding="UTF-8" import="org.hibernate.SessionFactory, org.hibernate.cfg.Configuration,
org.hibernate.cfg.AnnotationConfiguration, org.hibernate.Session, org.hibernate.Transaction, java.util.List, java.util.Iterator,
myApp.Guestbook" %>
<!DOCTYPE HTML PUBLIC "-//W3C//DTD HTML 4.01 Transitional//EN"
  "http://www.w3.org/TR/html4/loose.dtd">
<%!
  SessionFactory sessionFactory;
  org.hibernate.Session hibSession;
  List<Guestbook> guestbook;
%>

<%
  sessionFactory = new Configuration().configure().buildSessionFactory();
  sessionFactory = new AnnotationConfiguration().configure().buildSessionFactory();
  hibSession = sessionFactory.openSession();
  Transaction tx = null;
```


Only the section that needs change is shown, the rest remains the same.

Run the application to see this working.

This book's accompanying CDROM holds the code spec.

Author Details Using Associations [Annotations]

Example

Let's use the web application that was built in *Chapter 09: Collections* and convert the POJOs → Mapping documents to POJOs → Annotations.

Open the application using the NetBeans IDE.

Since annotations are being used add the required library files to this application using the NetBeans IDE as shown earlier.

Currently this application holds the following POJOs and the associated mapping documents:

- Authors.java
  - Authors.hbm.xml
- Books.java
  - Books.hbm.xml
- Contactdetails.java
  - Contactdetails.hbm.xml

Delete the mapping documents.

Edit the POJOs to now include annotations.

Contactdetails [Contactdetails.java]

Edit the **Contactdetails.java** file with the following contents.

```
package myApp;

import javax.persistence.Column;
import javax.persistence.Entity;
import javax.persistence.GeneratedValue;
import static javax.persistence.GenerationType.IDENTITY;
import javax.persistence.Id;
import javax.persistence.Table;

@Entity
@Table(name="contactdetails",catalog="associations")
public class Contactdetails  implements java.io.Serializable {
    private Integer authorNo;
    private String email;
    private Integer mobileNumber;

    public Contactdetails() {
    }
```

```

    public Contactdetails(String email, Integer mobileNumber) {
        this.email = email;
        this.mobileNumber = mobileNumber;
    }

    @Id @GeneratedValue(strategy=IDENTITY)
    @Column(name="AuthorNo", unique=true, nullable=false)
    public Integer getAuthorNo() {
        return this.authorNo;
    }
    public void setAuthorNo(Integer authorNo) {
        this.authorNo = authorNo;
    }

    @Column(name="Email", length=50)
    public String getEmail() {
        return this.email;
    }
    public void setEmail(String email) {
        this.email = email;
    }

    @Column(name="MobileNumber")
    public Integer getMobileNumber() {
        return this.mobileNumber;
    }
    public void setMobileNumber(Integer mobileNumber) {
        this.mobileNumber = mobileNumber;
    }
}
```

Books [Books.java]

Edit the **Books.java** file with the following contents.

```
package myApp;

import javax.persistence.Column;
import javax.persistence.Entity;
import javax.persistence.FetchType;
import javax.persistence.GeneratedValue;
import static javax.persistence.GenerationType.IDENTITY;
import javax.persistence.Id;
import javax.persistence.JoinColumn;
import javax.persistence.ManyToOne;
import javax.persistence.Table;

@Entity
@Table(name="books",catalog="associations")
public class Books  implements java.io.Serializable {
   private Integer bookNo;
   private Authors authors;
   private String bookName;
   private String isbn;
   private String aboutBook;
   private Integer price;

   public Books() {
   }

   public Books(Authors authors, String bookName, String isbn, String aboutBook, Integer price) {
      this.authors = authors;
      this.bookName = bookName;
```

```
        this.isbn = isbn;
        this.aboutBook = aboutBook;
        this.price = price;
    }

    @Id @GeneratedValue(strategy=IDENTITY)
    @Column(name="BookNo", unique=true, nullable=false)
    public Integer getBookNo() {
        return this.bookNo;
    }
    public void setBookNo(Integer bookNo) {
        this.bookNo = bookNo;
    }

    @ManyToOne(fetch=FetchType.LAZY)
    @JoinColumn(name="AuthorNo")
    public Authors getAuthors() {
        return this.authors;
    }
    public void setAuthors(Authors authors) {
        this.authors = authors;
    }

    @Column(name="BookName", length=25)
    public String getBookName() {
        return this.bookName;
    }
    public void setBookName(String bookName) {
        this.bookName = bookName;
    }

```

```
    @Column(name="ISBN", length=25)
    public String getIsbn() {
        return this.isbn;
    }
    public void setIsbn(String isbn) {
        this.isbn = isbn;
    }

    @Column(name="AboutBook", length=50)
    public String getAboutBook() {
        return this.aboutBook;
    }
    public void setAboutBook(String aboutBook) {
        this.aboutBook = aboutBook;
    }

    @Column(name="Price")
    public Integer getPrice() {
        return this.price;
    }

    public void setPrice(Integer price) {
        this.price = price;
    }
}
```

Authors [Authors.java]

Edit the **Authors.java** file with the following contents.

```
package myApp;

import java.util.HashSet;
```

```
import java.util.Set;
import javax.persistence.CascadeType;
import javax.persistence.Column;
import javax.persistence.Entity;
import javax.persistence.FetchType;
import javax.persistence.GeneratedValue;
import javax.persistence.Id;
import javax.persistence.JoinColumn;
import javax.persistence.OneToMany;
import javax.persistence.OneToOne;
import javax.persistence.Table;
import org.hibernate.annotations.GenericGenerator;
import org.hibernate.annotations.Parameter;

@Entity
@Table(name = "authors", catalog = "associations")
public class Authors implements java.io.Serializable {
    private int authorNo;
    private String authorName;
    private String aboutAuthor;
    private Set bookses = new HashSet(0);
    private Contactdetails contactdetails;

    public Authors() {
    }

    public Authors(int authorNo) {
        this.authorNo = authorNo;
    }

    public Authors(Contactdetails contactdetails, int authorNo, String
    authorName, String aboutAuthor, Set bookses) {
```

```
        this.contactdetails = contactdetails;
        this.authorNo = authorNo;
        this.authorName = authorName;
        this.aboutAuthor = aboutAuthor;
        this.bookses = bookses;
    }

    @Id
    @GeneratedValue(generator = "genForeign")
    @GenericGenerator(name = "genForeign", strategy = "foreign",
    parameters = {@Parameter(name = "property", value =
    "contactdetails")})
    @Column(name = "AuthorNo", unique = true, nullable = false)
    public int getAuthorNo() {
        return this.authorNo;
    }
    public void setAuthorNo(int authorNo) {
        this.authorNo = authorNo;
    }

    @Column(name = "AuthorName", length = 25)
    public String getAuthorName() {
        return this.authorName;
    }
    public void setAuthorName(String authorName) {
        this.authorName = authorName;
    }

    @Column(name = "AboutAuthor", length = 50)
    public String getAboutAuthor() {
        return this.aboutAuthor;
    }
```

```
    public void setAboutAuthor(String aboutAuthor) {
        this.aboutAuthor = aboutAuthor;
    }

    @OneToMany(cascade = CascadeType.ALL, fetch = FetchType.LAZY,
    mappedBy = "authors", targetEntity=myApp.Books.class)
    public Set getBookses() {
        return this.bookses;
    }
    public void setBookses(Set bookses) {
        this.bookses = bookses;
    }

    @OneToOne(cascade = CascadeType.ALL, targetEntity =
    myApp.Contactdetails.class)
    @JoinColumn(name="AuthorNo")
    public Contactdetails getContactdetails() {
        return contactdetails;
    }
    public void setContactdetails(Contactdetails contactdetails) {
        this.contactdetails = contactdetails;
    }
}
```

Hibernate Configuration File [hibernate.cgf.xml]

Edit the hibernate.cfg.xml to include the annotated classes:

```
<?xml version="1.0" encoding="UTF-8"?>
<!DOCTYPE hibernate-configuration PUBLIC "-//Hibernate/Hibernate Configuration DTD 3.0//EN"
"http://hibernate.sourceforge.net/hibernate-configuration-3.0.dtd">
<hibernate-configuration>
  <session-factory>
    <property name="hibernate.dialect">org.hibernate.dialect.MySQLDialect</property>
    <property name="hibernate.connection.driver_class">com.mysql.jdbc.Driver</property>
```

```
    <property name="hibernate.connection.url">jdbc:mysql://localhost:3306/associations</property>
    <property name="hibernate.connection.username">root</property>
    <property name="hibernate.connection.password">123456</property>
    <mapping class="myApp.Authors"/>
    <mapping class="myApp.Contactdetails"/>
    <mapping class="myApp.Books"/>
  </session-factory>
</hibernate-configuration>
```

Since annotations are used the AnnotationConfiguration interface needs to be used instead of the Configuration interface.

Hence, edit the View.jsp to use the AnnotationConfiguration interface.

View.jsp

Edit the **View.jsp** file with the following contents.

```
<%@page contentType="text/html" pageEncoding="UTF-8" import="org.hibernate.SessionFactory,
org.hibernate.cfg.Configuration, org.hibernate.cfg.AnnotationConfiguration,
org.hibernate.Session, org.hibernate.Transaction, java.util.*, myApp.*" %>
<!DOCTYPE HTML PUBLIC "-//W3C//DTD HTML 4.01 Transitional//EN"
  "http://www.w3.org/TR/html4/loose.dtd">
<%!
   SessionFactory sessionFactory;
   org.hibernate.Session hibSession;
   List<Authors> authors;
%>

<%
   sessionFactory = new Configuration().configure().buildSessionFactory();
   sessionFactory = new AnnotationConfiguration().configure().buildSessionFactory();
   hibSession = sessionFactory.openSession();
   Transaction tx = null;

   try {
      hibSession.beginTransaction();
      authors = hibSession.createQuery("from Authors").list();
```

Remove this

Add this

Remove this

Add this

That's it!

Now built and run the application to see it working.

The Book CDROM holds the complete application source code built using the NetBeans IDE for the following applications:

- GuestBook_Chap11
- AuthorDetails_Chap11

These can be directly used by making appropriate changes [username/password] to the configuration file.

SECTION IV: WORKING WITH HIBERNATE

Session

In the examples seen so far, a Session object always existed to allow interaction with the database.

In Hibernate sense, a session is a single unit of work [usually data operations]. It can also be referred as:

- A gateway to the database
- A cache or collection of loaded objects relating to a single unit of work
- The main runtime interface between a Java application and Hibernate
- An agent between the application and the data store

To begin a unit of work, a Session is opened. To end a unit of work, a Session is closed.

From the programming perspective, a Session object can be used to:

- Create new database entities
- Read objects from the database

- Update objects in the database
- Delete objects from the database

Hibernate provides a simple API for CREATING, RETRIEVING, UPDATING and DELETING objects from a relational database through the Session interface.

A typical hibernate code spec:

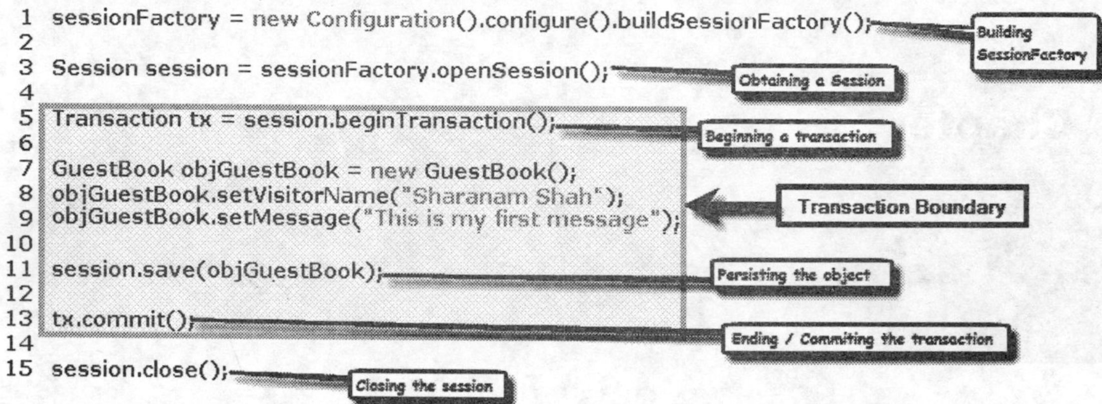

In order to make use of Hibernate's persistence mechanisms, the Hibernate environment needs to be initialized [using the **configure()** method] and a Session object must be obtained from Hibernate's SessionFactory class [using the **openSession()** method].

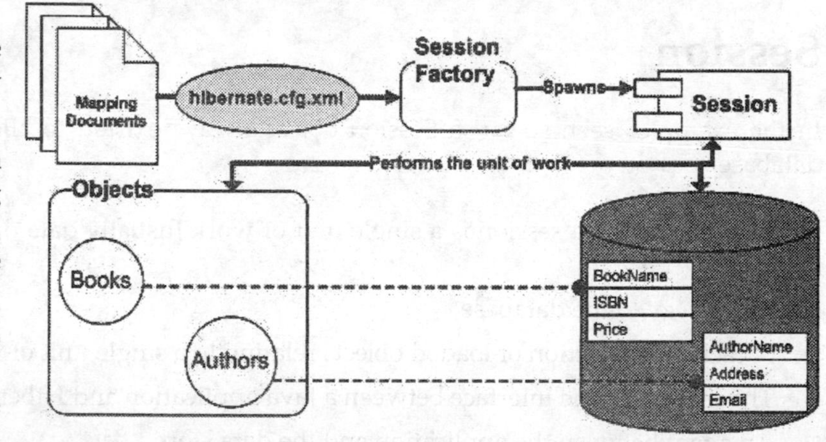

A typical Hibernate application usually does the following:

- Building a session factory by reading hibernate configuration file [hibernate.cfg.xml]

  The call to **Configuration().configure()** loads the **hibernate.cfg.xml** configuration file and initializes the Hibernate environment.

  An instance of **SessionFactory** is typically created once and used to create all sessions related to a given context.

- Retrieving and opening a Hibernate Session

- Beginning a transaction
- Performing the desired database operations such as persisting an object
- Ending a transaction / committing the transaction
- Closing the session

A SessionFactory helps open a Session, which in turn helps start a transaction.

When compared to traditional JDBC, a Session object can be thought of as a JDBC connection, whereas the SessionFactory [which provides Session objects] can be thought of as a ConnectionPool [which provides Connection objects].

Kind Of Objects

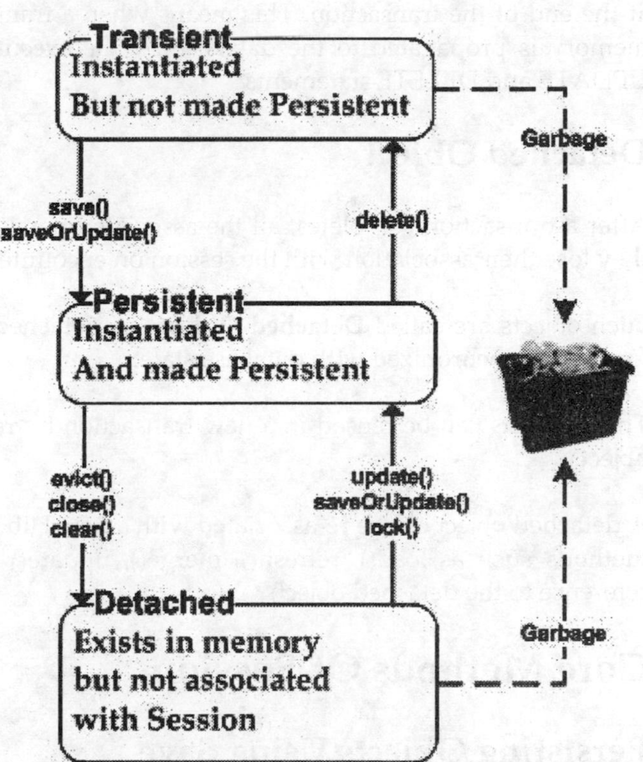

Hibernate works with normal Java objects that the application creates using the new operator. These objects are mapped to actual database tables using Hibernate Mapping mechanism.

An instance of an object that is mapped to Hibernate can be in any one of three different states i.e. **Transient**, **Persistent** or **Detached**.

Before beginning with the core methods of the session object, let's take a quick look at the different terminology the object states.

Transient Object

Transient Objects are those that are instantiated by the application but not yet made persistent by calling the **save()** method of the session object.

This kind of object is instantiated using the new operator but is not immediately persistent. Hence such an object is not associated with any database table row.

To convert a transient object to persistent state, the save() method of the session object is invoked.

Persistent Object

Persistent Objects are those that are instantiated by the application and then made persistent by calling the **save()** method of the session object.

Persistent objects are always associated with a Session and are transactional.

Persistent objects participate in transactions and their state is synchronized with the database at the end of the transaction. This means when a transaction is committed, the state held in memory is propagated to the database by the execution of the appropriate SQL INSERT, UPDATE and DELETE statements.

Detached Object

After a transaction completes, all the associated persistent objects still exists in memory but they lose their association with the session on encountering a **session.close()**.

Such objects are called **Detached Objects.** A detached object indicates that its state will no longer be synchronized with database state.

These objects can be reused in a new transaction by re-associating them with a new session object.

A detached object can be re-associated with a new Hibernate session by invoking one of these methods such as load(), refresh(), merge(), update() or save() on the new session with a reference to the detached object.

Core Methods Of Session

Persisting Objects Using Save

Creating an instance of a class [mapped to database table using Hibernate mapping] does not automatically persist the object to the database. This has to be done explicitly by saving the object using a valid Hibernate session.

The first step a typical hibernate application usually performs using a Session object is making a new **[transient]** object **persistent**.

To do so, the **save()** method is used. The most typical method is to create a new object in Java, set a few of its properties and then save it through the session.

Example

```
GuestBook objGuestBook = new GuestBook();      New object
objGuestBook.setVisitorName("Sharanam Shah");
objGuestBook.setMessage("This is my first message");

session.save(objGuestBook);      Making the new object persistent
```

Here, the new object called objGuestBook is spawned and instantiated.

Using the session object's **save()** method, the new object instance is made **persistent**. It's now associated with the current Session.

However, the SQL INSERT has not yet been fired. This means the changes made to persistent object are yet to be synchronized with the database. This happens when the **commit()** method of the Hibernate Transaction object is fired.

Example

```
Transaction tx = session.beginTransaction();

GuestBook objGuestBook = new GuestBook();
objGuestBook.setVisitorName("Sharanam Shah");
objGuestBook.setMessage("This is my first message");

session.save(objGuestBook);

tx.commit();      Transaction commited
```

On commit, Hibernate obtains a JDBC connection and issues a single **SQL INSERT** statement.

Example

```
Transaction tx = session.beginTransaction();

GuestBook objGuestBook = new GuestBook();
```

```
objGuestBook.setVisitorName("Sharanam Shah");
objGuestBook.setMessage("This is my first message");

session.save(objGuestBook);

tx.commit();

session.close();
```

Session closed

Finally, the Session is closed and the JDBC connection is released.

Syntax:

```
public Serializable save(Object object) throws HibernateException

public void save(Object object, Serializable id) throws HibernateException

public Serializable save(String entityName, Object object)
  throws HibernateException
```

The **save()** method accepts a **transient** object as an argument. It is mandatory to have a mapping for the transient object's class. Hibernate cannot persist arbitrary unmapped objects.

Persisting Objects Using SaveOrUpdate

It is not appropriate to save an object that has already been persisted.

Similarly, it is not appropriate to update a transient object.

Sometimes it's not possible to determine the state of the object whether it's transient or persistent.

In such a scenario, the **saveOrUpdate()** method can be used.

```
session.saveOrUpdate(objGuestBook);
```

Hibernate uses the identifier [Primary Key] of the object to determine whether to insert a new row into the database table or update an existing row.

Hibernate assumes that an object is an unsaved transient object, if:

- The identifier property [if it exists] is null
- The version property [if it exists] is null

- An unsaved value is supplied in the mapping document for the class and the value of the identifier property matches
- An unsaved value is supplied in the mapping document for the version property and the value of the version property matches

Syntax:

```
public void saveOrUpdate(Object object) throws HibernateException
```

Retrieving Objects Using Load

The Session is also used to query the database and retrieve existing persistent objects.

The load() method allows retrieving persistent objects from the database.

The load() method requires the object's primary key value as an identifier as well as the class or entity name to use to find the object with that identifier.

Syntax:

```
public Object load(Class theClass, Serializable id) throws HibernateException

public Object load(String entityName, Serializable id)
  throws HibernateException
```

Another variation of the load() method accepts an empty object of the class that is desired to be loaded. Hibernate populates that object with the object requested based on the identifier supplied as the second argument.

Syntax:

```
public void load(Object object, Serializable id) throws HibernateException
```

Example

```
sessionFactory = new Configuration().configure().buildSessionFactory();
Session session = sessionFactory.openSession();
Transaction tx = session.beginTransaction();
long VisitorNo = 1;
GuestBook objGuestBook = (GuestBook) session.load(GuestBook, VisitorNo);
```

```
tx.commit();

session.close();
```

Explanation:

Here, the details belonging to the visitor no 1 are loaded into the GuestBook object.

Hibernate actually fires an SQL SELECT query to retrieve the record where Visitor No = 1. The record contents [column values] are loaded into the object [properties].

The retrieved object [GuestBook] may be passed to the presentation layer for using it as a detached object.

Retrieving Objects Using Get

If the developer is not certain about the existence of the object, then get() method should be used, instead of the load() method.

If the object does not exist because the unique identifier is not found in the database table:

- The get() method returns a **null** reference
- The load() methods throws an exception

The get() method also allows retrieving persistent objects from the database. Similar to the load() method, the get() method also requires the object's primary key as an identifier as well as the class or entity name to use to find the object with that identifier.

Syntax:

```
public Object get(Class theClass, Serializable id) throws HibernateException
public Object get(String entityName, Serializable id)
  throws HibernateException
```

This method is useful in situation where an application user chooses to view the details of a particular customer identified by the Customer Number.

In such a scenario, the get() method can be used to determine, whether the record exists and if not, then displays an appropriate error message to the application user.

Example

```
sessionFactory = new Configuration().configure().buildSessionFactory();

Session session = sessionFactory.openSession();
```

```
Transaction tx = session.beginTransaction();

long CustomerNo = 1;

Customer objCustomer = (Customer) session.get(Customer, CustomerNo);

if (objCustomer == null)
{
   System.out.println("Details of the customer identified as: " + CustomerNo + " is not available.");
}

tx.commit();

session.close();
```

Refreshing Objects Using Refresh

Hibernate provides a method called refresh() which when invoked refreshes the persistent object from their database representation.

Syntax:

```
public void refresh(Object object) throws HibernateException

public void refresh(Object object, LockMode lockMode)
  throws HibernateException
```

The most ideal scenario where a refresh would be used is to undo changes that were made to a persistent object in memory. In such a situation, refresh() when called, reloads the in memory objects from their database representation.

Updating Objects

In a situation where, any persistent object is returned by **get()** or **load()** or any other kind of query is associated with **the current Session and transaction context**, such an object can be modified and its state is automatically synchronized with the database.

This mechanism is called automatic dirty checking. Here, Hibernate tracks and saves the changes made to an object inside a session.

Example

```
sessionFactory = new Configuration().configure().buildSessionFactory();

Session session = sessionFactory.openSession();

Transaction tx = session.beginTransaction();

long CustomerNo = 1;
```

```
Customer objCustomer = (Customer) session.get(Customer, CustomerNo);
if (objCustomer == null)
{
   System.out.println("Details of the customer identified as: " + CustomerNo + " is not available.");
}
objCustomer.setName("Vaishali Shah");
tx.commit();
session.close();
```

Explanation:

Here, an object is retrieved from the database with the given identifier.

The object is then modified in **the current Session and transaction context**. Hibernate propagates these modifications to the database when **tx.commit()** is invoked.

The update() Method

If an object is modified after the session is closed, it is not persisted in the database.

When the session is closed, the object is detached. It needs to be re-associated with a new Session by calling the **update()** method.

The **update()** method **forces** an update to the persistent state of the object in the database, scheduling an SQL UPDATE.

Syntax:

```
public void update(Object object) throws HibernateException

public void update(String entityName, Object object)
  throws HibernateException
```

Example

```
sessionFactory = new Configuration().configure().buildSessionFactory();
Session session = sessionFactory.openSession();
Transaction tx = session.beginTransaction();
long CustomerNo = 1;
Customer objCustomer = (Customer) session.get(Customer, CustomerNo);
```

```
objCustomer.setName("Vaishali Shah");

tx.commit();
session.close();

objCustomer.setUserName("vaishalis");

Session session2 = sessionFactory.openSession();
tx = session2.beginTransaction();

session2.update(objCustomer);

objCustomer.setPassword("123456");

tx.commit();
session2.close();
```

It does not matter if the object is modified before or after it is passed to **update()**.

update() when invoked re-associates the detached object to the new Session [session2] and informs Hibernate to treat that object as dirty. Hibernate propagates the modifications to the database when **tx.commit()** is invoked.

Deleting Persistent Objects

Deleting a persistent object [making it transient] means removing its persistent state from the database. This is achievable using the **delete()** method.

Syntax:

```
public void delete(Object object) throws HibernateException
```

This method accepts a persistent object as an argument.

REMINDER

The argument can also be a transient object with the identifier set to the id of the object that needs to be erased.

Example

```
sessionFactory = new Configuration().configure().buildSessionFactory();

Session session = sessionFactory.openSession();
```

```
Transaction tx = session.beginTransaction();
long CustomerNo = 1;
Customer objCustomer = (Customer) session.get(Customer, CustomerNo);
session.delete(objCustomer);
tx.commit();
session.close();
```

After the transaction is committed using tx.commit(), Hibernate fires an SQL DELETE statement.

After the Session is closed, the object [objCustomer] is an ordinary transient object.

HINT

The transient objects are automatically destroyed by the garbage collector, if they are no longer referenced by any other object.

SECTION IV: WORKING WITH HIBERNATE

Transactions

Now that the basics of the object/relational mapping and session management with Hibernate are in place, let's take a look at how transactions are managed by Hibernate.

Transactions In General

Transactions allow grouping several operations into a <u>single unit of work</u>. Since the operations are wrapped in a transaction, the behavior of other system users does not affect the data being referred to by the transaction.

A transaction can be:

- **Started**
- **Ended** by either
    - <u>**Committing**</u> to write the data permanently to the database

- o **Rolling back** to undo all the changes that took placed right from the beginning of the transaction [i.e. when the transaction was started]

If even a single operation within the transaction fails, all the previous operations belonging to that transaction are rolled back and the unit of work simply terminates.

For example:

Let's consider a typical banking transaction where an amount of Rs. 500/- has to be moved from Customer A's savings account to Customer B's saving account.

From the banking perspective, this transaction looks like a single operation, but from the application's perspective, it involves two separate operations:

- **Debiting** Customer A's savings account by Rs. 500 /-
- **Crediting** Customer B's savings account by Rs. 500/-

If the debit operation succeeds but the credit operation fails [or vice versa], the books of the bank will not balance at the end of the day.

Hence, it is required to ensure that either both the operations succeed or both of them fail. This, thus, eliminates any inconsistency in the bank's database as a whole.

To achieve this, Transactions are required.

With the help of Transactions, multiple individual operations can be linked together as a single, indivisible transaction. This ensures that either all operations in that transaction are completed without errors or none of them.

Transactions In Hibernate

Transaction management in a Hibernate application is exposed via the Hibernate Transaction interface [**org.hibernate.transaction**]. The core of transactions in Hibernate is the transaction interface which is accessible from the Session interface. A transaction object is always associated with a Session object.

Transaction Interface Implementations

Hibernate does make it mandatory to use this API. Hibernate also allows to **begin** and **end** a transaction using JDBC transaction demarcation or the JTA interface or Container Managed Transactions with EJBs.

Hibernate provides the following three implementations of the transaction interface:

- JDBCTransaction [The default interface, if hibernate.transaction_factory is not set]
- JTATransaction
- CMTTransaction

To keep things simple, this chapter focuses on the Hibernate Transaction API.

The Hibernate Transaction API is the most unified transaction strategy for Hibernate applications. It works in plain JDBC environment as well as in an application server with JTA as the underlying system transaction service.

The most classical approach when dealing with transactions is to:

→ **Create Hibernate Session**
→ **Start Transaction**
→ **Perform the desired operations**
→ **Finalize [Commit or Rollback]**
→ **Close Hibernate Session**

Each transaction is wrapped in a session. A session can have multiple transactions.

Since multiple transactions can take place within a session, the concept of savepoints is not required and thus not available. The savepoint functionality is provided by the concept of multiple transactions within a session.

To instantiate a transaction object, **beginTransaction()** is called on the session object.

```
Transaction tx = session.beginTransaction();
```

This statement instantiates a transaction object [**tx**]. Many instances of transactions can be obtained using the same session object.

Transaction Interface Methods

The following are the methods of the transaction interface:

begin()

This method begins a new transaction and returns void.

commit()

This method flushes the associated Session and ends the unit of work. It ends a transaction.

commit() internally commits the underlying transaction. Simply calling the **save()** method on the session object does not persist the data contained in the Bean object to the database, the transaction has to be committed for the actual save to happen.

Example

```
Transaction tx = session.beginTransaction();
/* The save, update, delete and retrieve operations will be placed here */
tx.commit();
```

isActive()

This method indicates if the transaction is still active and returns Boolean.

HINT

The value it returns is in respect to the local transaction and not the actual underlying transaction.

registerSynchronization(Synchronization synchronization)

This method registers a user synchronization callback for this transaction and returns void.

rollback()

This method forces the underlying transaction to roll back.

Example

```
try {
    Transaction tx = session.beginTransaction();
/* The save, update, delete and retrieve operations will be placed here */
    tx.commit();
}
catch (RuntimeException e) {
```

```
    tx.rollback();
    throw e;
}
```

setTimeout(int seconds)

This method sets the transaction timeout for any transaction started by a subsequent call to begin() on this instance and returns void.

wasCommitted()

This method checks if this transaction was successfully committed and returns Boolean.

wasRolledBack()

This method indicates if the transaction was rolled back or only set to rollback and returns a Boolean. The value it returns is in respect to the actions initiated from the local transaction.

Example

The following example shows a method called insert which accepts a bean class object [GuestBook].

This method:

- Spawns a session object
- Instantiates a transaction
- Begins a transaction
- Inserts data in the GuestBook table using the save method
- Commits the transaction

Whilst performing this operation, if a runtime exception occurs, the transaction is rolled back.

Code spec:

```
public void insert(GuestBook gb)
{
    Session session = HibernateUtil.getSession();
    Transaction tx=null;
```

```
try
{
    tx = session.beginTransaction();
    session.save(gb);
    tx.commit();
}
catch (RuntimeException e)
{
    if(tx != null) tx.rollback();
    throw e;
}
finally
{
    session.close();
}
}
```

The GuestBook instance is persisted to the database table, only after the transaction is committed.

The call to **session.beginTransaction()** marks the beginning of a database transaction.

The call to **tx.commit()** synchronizes the Session state with the database.

HINT

It is important to close the Session in a finally block in order to ensure that the JDBC connection is released and returned to the connection pool.

SECTION IV: WORKING WITH HIBERNATE

Implementing Connection Pooling

Opening a connection to a database is always expensive than executing an SQL statement.

The most standard practice is to:

- Manually open a database connection either directly or using a database abstraction API/layer
- Perform the required database operations
- Close the connection

Most of the times, the closing of connection does not take place. This leaves several open connections to the database server clogging up resources which in turn degrades the application's performance.

Hence, it is highly recommended to manage these connections efficiently which can be achieved using connection pooling.

A connection pool is a group of connections already running and ready to go. It is used to minimize the number of connections opened between application and database. It opens and closes connections on behalf of developers.

How Does Connection Pooling Work

The data provider [in this case Hibernate] automatically opens a minimum number of connections for the application.

The developer does not need to worry about spawning a connection and destroying it.

All that the developer has to do is:

- Put in the request to the data provider [Hibernate] which in turn grabs a connection from the pool and returns
- Perform the desired database operations
- Put the connection back in the pool, which makes that connection ready for another request

Pooling allows multiple connections to be running different requests at the same time without having to open and close multiple connections constantly.

This allows the application to grow, thereby, allowing more requests to be generated.

In case, if the number of requests increase more than the number of available connections in the pool, the data provider [Hibernate] automatically increases the size of the connection pool for as many requests as are required.

Similarly, the data provider also automatically decreases the size of the pool, after certain amount of time, when they are not required.

There is a minimum size that is always maintained which ensures that x number of connections will always be available.

There is a maximum size that sets an upper limit of the pool to cope with a large surge, if required.

Hibernate's Connection Pooling System - C3P0

Hibernate supports a variety of connection pooling mechanisms. If an application server is being used, Hibernate allows using the server's built-in pool where a connection is obtained using JNDI.

If getting an application server is an issue, Hibernate allows using several other connection pools such as **Apache DBCP** and **Proxool**.

Hibernate not only allows integration with these connection pools but also provides a built in connection pooling system called **C3P0**. This pooling can be setup by simply adding a few lines in the **hibernate.properties** or **hibernate.cfg.xml** file.

The following are the properties that need to be set in the Hibernate configuration file.

Property	Default	Description
initialPoolSize	3	Initial number of connections to be spawned.
minPoolSize	1	The minimum number of connections to be maintained in the pool.
maxPoolSize	100	The maximum number of connections i.e. the upper limit.
idleTestPeriod	0	If this is a number greater than 0, c3p0 will test all idle, pooled but unchecked-out connections, every this number of seconds.
timeout	0	The seconds a Connection can remain pooled but unused before being discarded. Zero means idle connections never expire.
maxStatements	0	The size of c3p0's PreparedStatement cache. Zero means statement caching is turned off.
acquireIncrement	1	Determines how many connections at a time, c3p0 will try to acquire when the pool is exhausted.

Connection Pooling In GuestBook

Let's add connection pooling to the GuestBook application. To do so, edit hibernate.cfg.xml file as:

```
<?xml version="1.0" encoding="UTF-8"?>
<!DOCTYPE hibernate-configuration PUBLIC "-//Hibernate/Hibernate Configuration DTD 3.0//EN"
"http://hibernate.sourceforge.net/hibernate-configuration-3.0.dtd">
<hibernate-configuration>
  <session-factory>
    <property name="hibernate.dialect">org.hibernate.dialect.MySQLDialect</property>
    <property name="hibernate.connection.driver_class">com.mysql.jdbc.Driver</property>
    <property name="hibernate.connection.url">jdbc:mysql://localhost:3306/GuestBook</property>
    <property name="hibernate.connection.username">root</property>
```

```
<property name="hibernate.connection.password">123456</property>
<!-- configuration pool via c3p0 -->
<property name="hibernate.c3p0.acquire_increment">1</property>
<property name="hibernate.c3p0.idle_test_period">100</property> <!-- seconds -->
<property name="hibernate.c3p0.max_size">50</property>
<property name="hibernate.c3p0.max_statements">0</property>
<property name="hibernate.c3p0.min_size">10</property>
<property name="hibernate.c3p0.timeout">100</property> <!-- seconds -->
<mapping resource="myApp/Guestbook.hbm.xml"/>
</session-factory>
</hibernate-configuration>
```

To use the built-in connection pool, a library file is required.

Add the library file called **c3p0-0.9.1.jar** using the NetBeans IDE. This file is available under **lib\optional\c3p0** of **hibernate-distribution-3.3.1.GA**.

This enables connection pooling in the GuestBook application. Run the application to see it working.

Connection Pooling Using JNDI

Hibernate also allows using an application server's connection pooling using JNDI.

Let's implement it in the GuestBook application, using Glassfish v2 as the Application Server.

Glassfish v2 comes bundled with the NetBeans IDE 6.5.

To setup a connection pool under the Glassfish application server, the JDBC driver needs to be added in the application server. Add the MySQL JDBC Driver to the **lib** folder of the Glassfish Application Server under <Drive Name>:\Program Files\glassfish-v2ur2\lib as show in diagram 14.1.

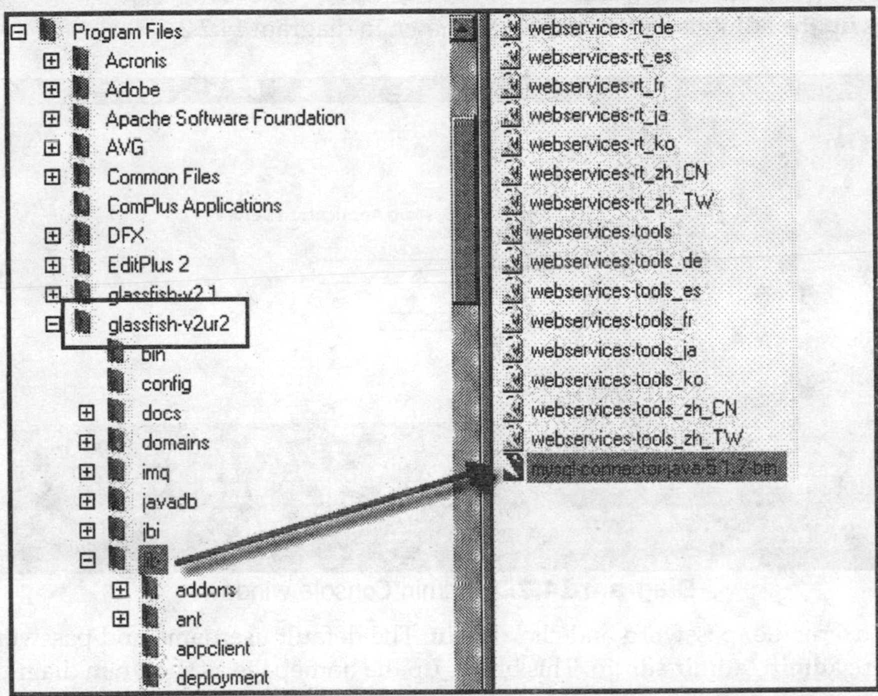

Diagram 14.1: Adding the MySQL database driver

Using the NetBeans IDE, open the **Admin Console** of the Glassfish v2 Application Server, as show in diagram 14.2.1.

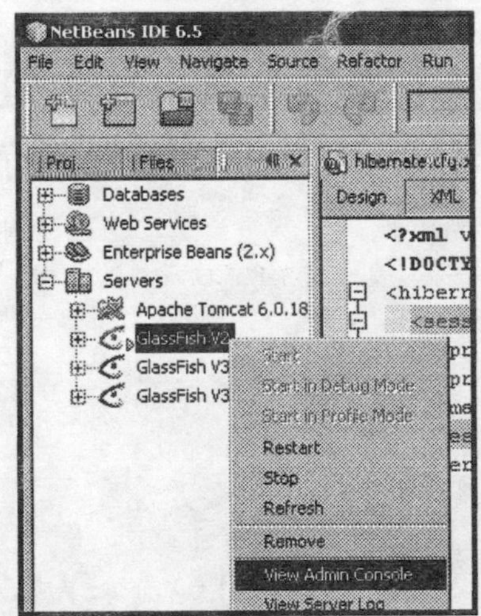

Diagram 14.2.1: Opening Admin Console

This brings up the administration console as shown in diagram 14.2.2.

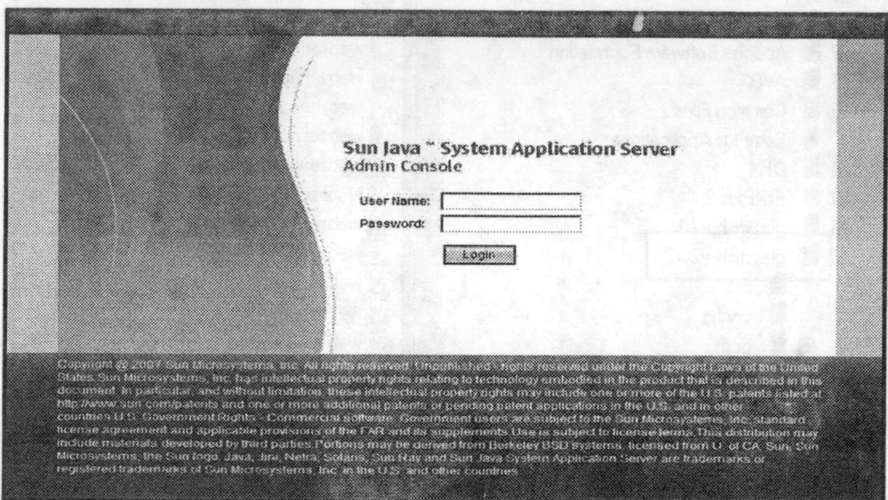

Diagram 14.2.2: Admin Console window

Key in the username/password and click **Login**. The default username and password [if not changed] are **admin/adminadmin**. This brings up the homepage as shown in diagram 14.2.3.

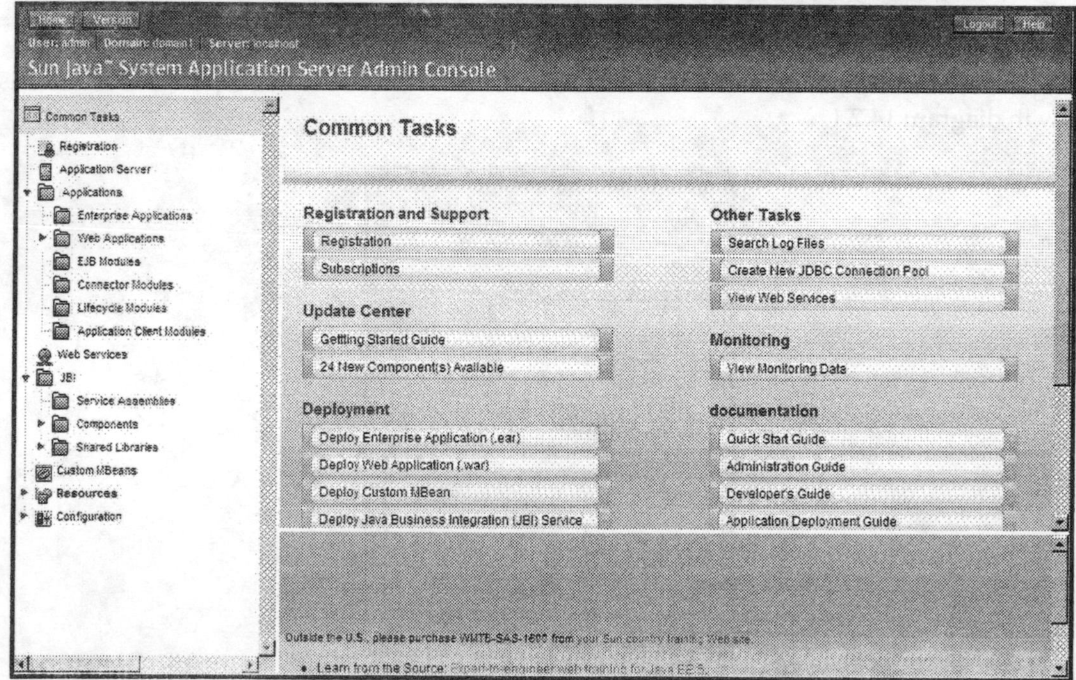

Diagram 14.2.3: Homepage

Choose **Resources → JDBC → Connection Pools**. This brings up the screen as shown in diagram 14.2.3.

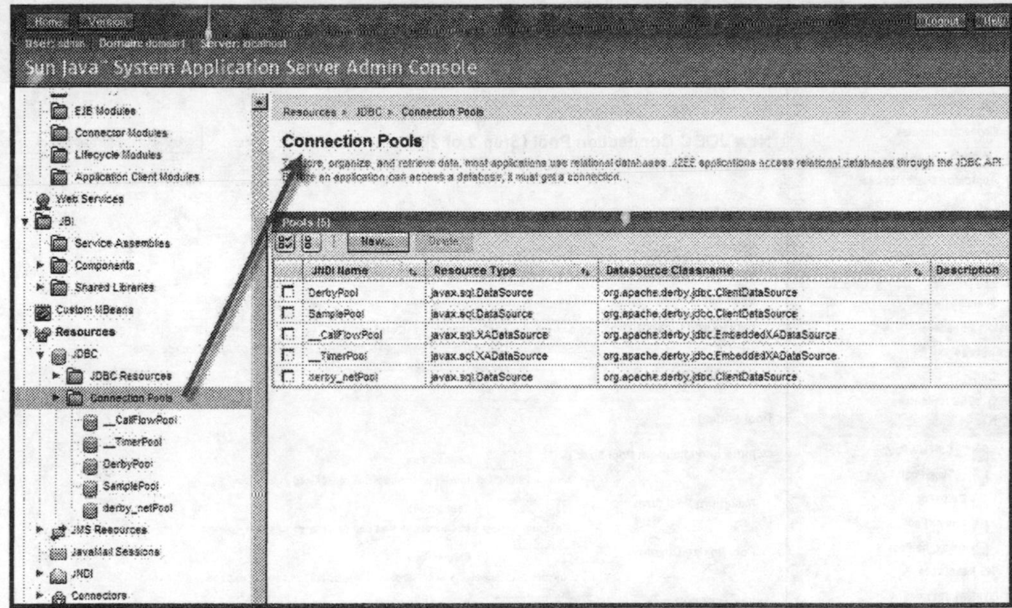

Diagram 14.2.3: Connection Pools page

Create a new connection pool by clicking **New**. Key in the details as shown in diagram 14.2.4.

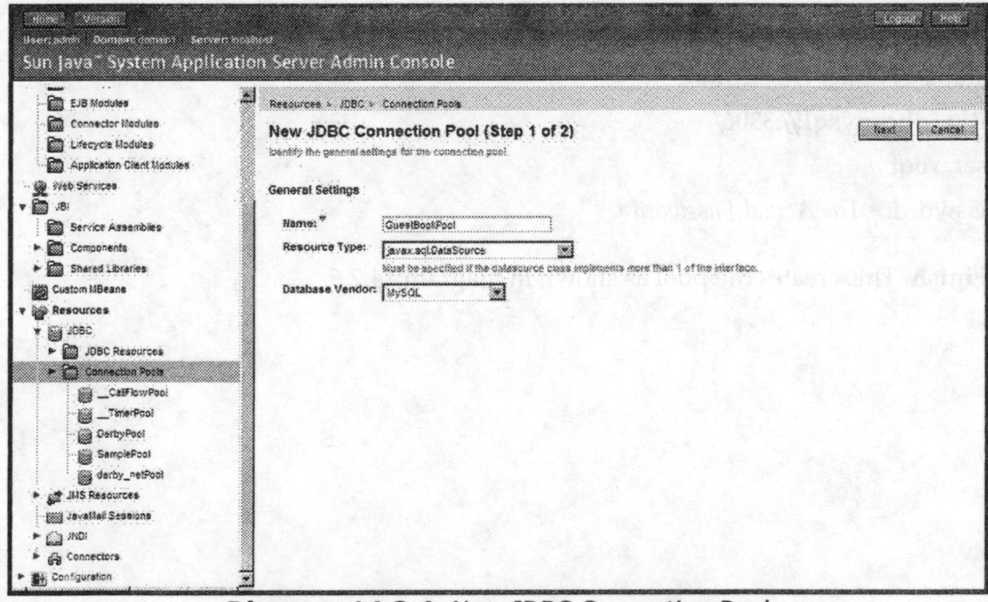

Diagram 14.2.4: New JDBC Connection Pool

Click **Next**. This brings a screen as shown in diagram 14.2.5.

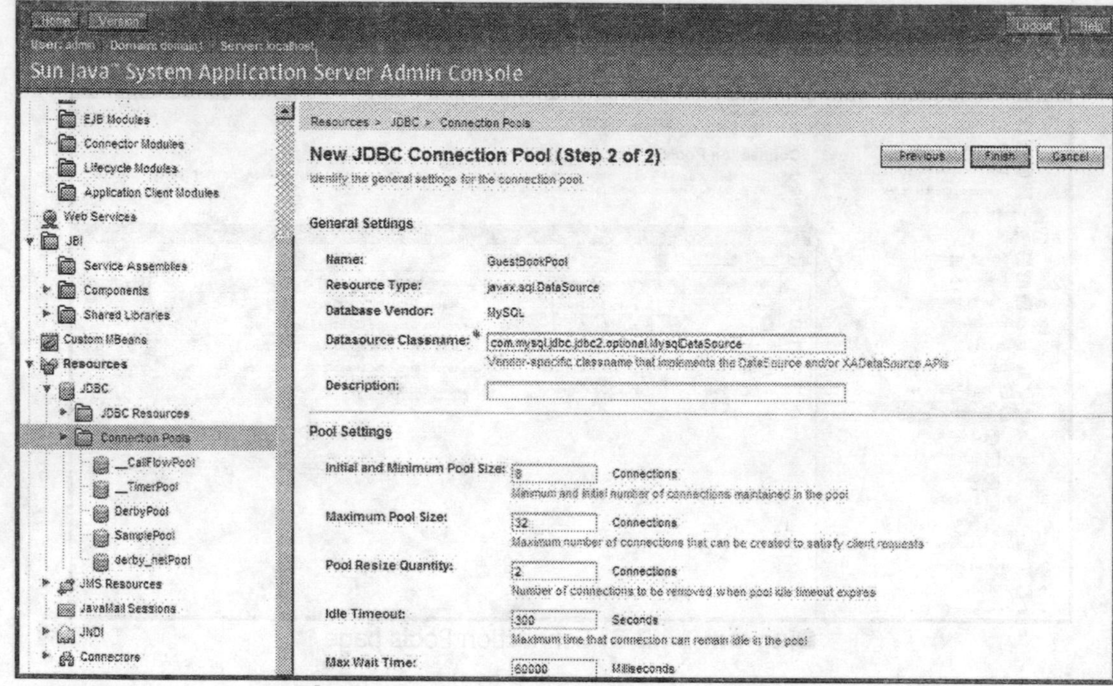

Diagram 14.2.5: New JDBC Connection Pool

Scroll down and set the following properties using checkboxes:

- DatabaseName: **GuestBook**
- URL: **jdbc:mysql://:3306/**
- User: **root**
- Password: <*The Actual Password*>

Click **Finish**. This creates the pool as shown in diagram 14.2.6.

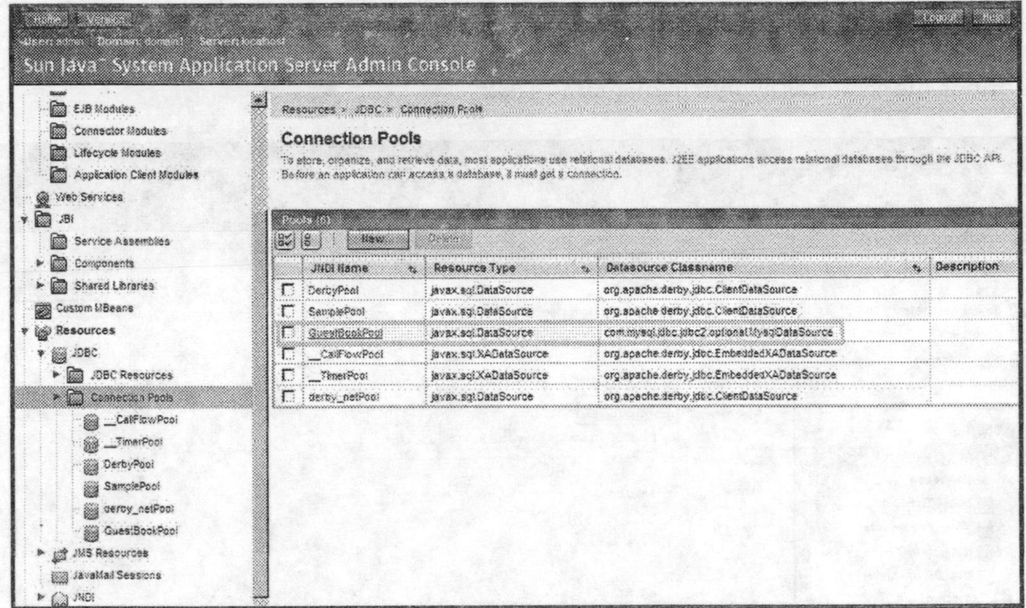

Diagram 14.2.6: New Connection Pool added

Click **Resource → JDBC Resources** as shown in diagram 14.3.1.

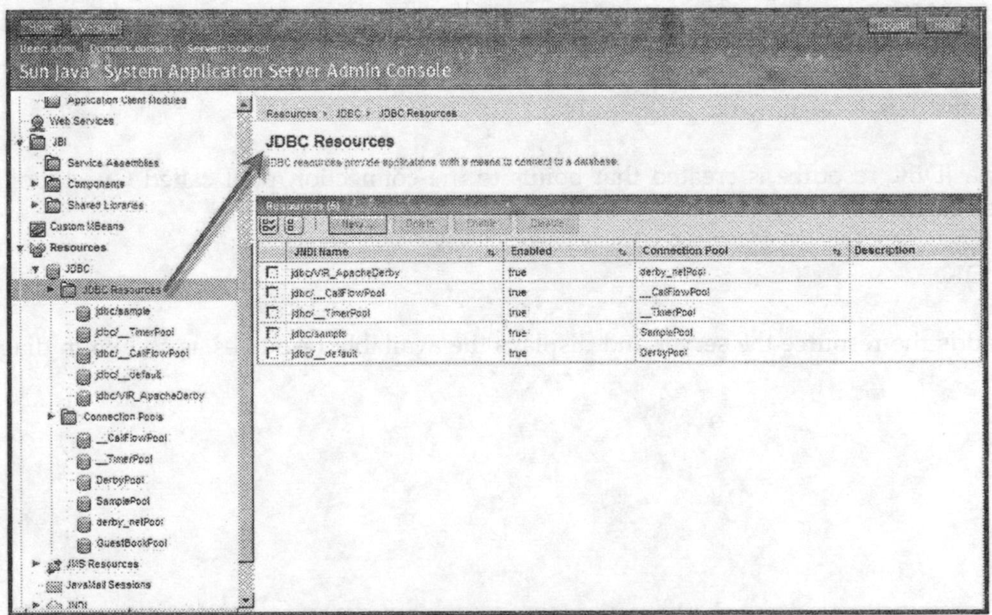

Diagram 14.3.1: JDBC Resources

Click **New** to create a new resource.

This brings the screen as shown in diagram 14.3.2.

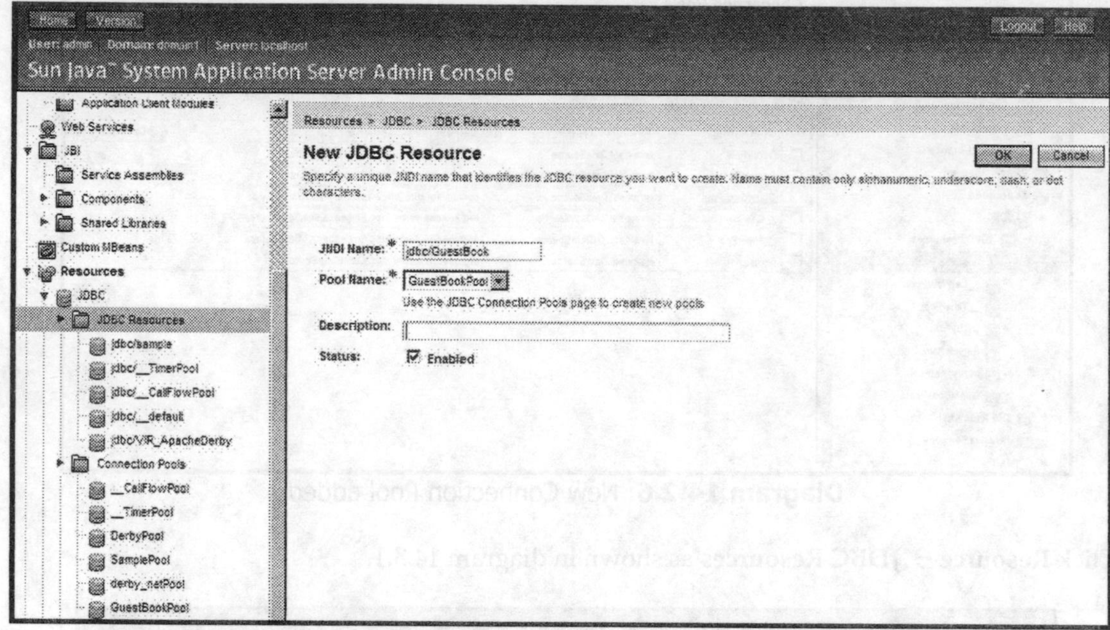

Diagram 14.3.2: New JDBC Resource

Key in the details as shown in diagram 14.3.2.

Here, a JDBC resource is created that points to the connection pool called GuestBookPool created earlier.

Click **OK**.

This adds the resource the server and displays the available resources as shown in diagram 14.3.3.

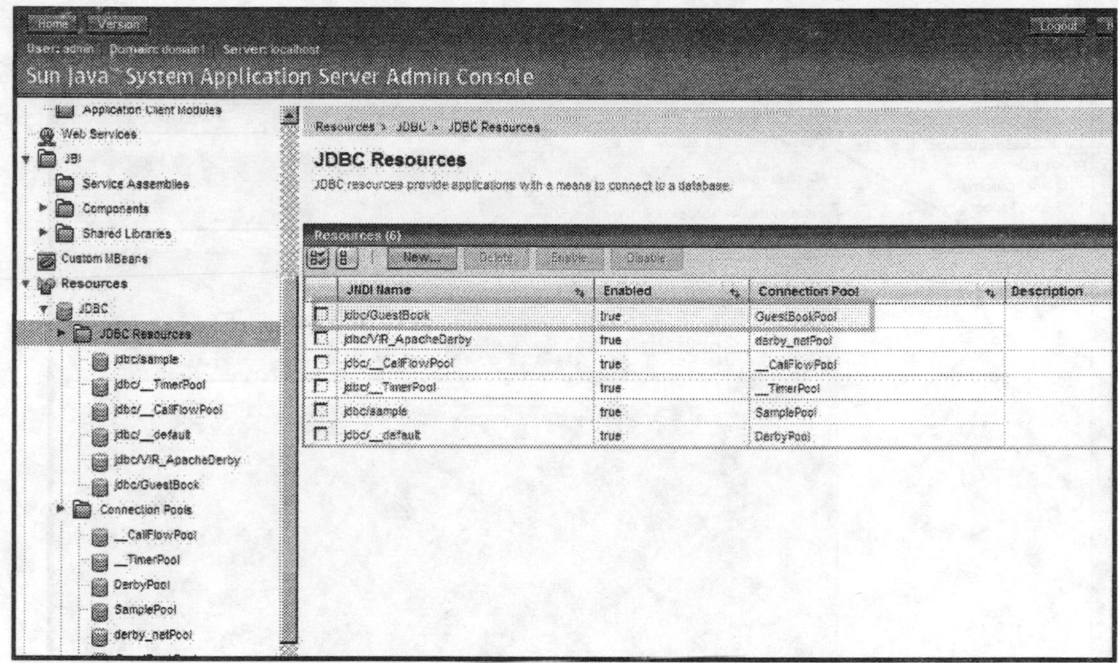

Diagram 14.3.3: New JDBC Resource added

This completes the creation of a connection pool.

Change the Hibernate configuration file to use this connection pool as:

```
<?xml version="1.0" encoding="UTF-8"?>
<!DOCTYPE hibernate-configuration PUBLIC "-//Hibernate/Hibernate Configuration DTD 3.0//EN"
"http://hibernate.sourceforge.net/hibernate-configuration-3.0.dtd">
<hibernate-configuration>
  <session-factory>
    <property name="hibernate.dialect">org.hibernate.dialect.MySQLDialect</property>
    <property name="hibernate.connection.datasource">jdbc/GuestBook</property>
    <mapping resource="myApp/Guestbook.hbm.xml"/>
  </session-factory>
</hibernate-configuration>
```

Here, datasource property points to the **JDBC resource** created using the Glassfish as shown in diagram 14.3.2.

That's it. Run the application [**using Glassfish v2**] to see it working.

The application server can be chosen in NetBeans by right clicking the project, choosing **Properties → Run** as shown in diagram 14.4.

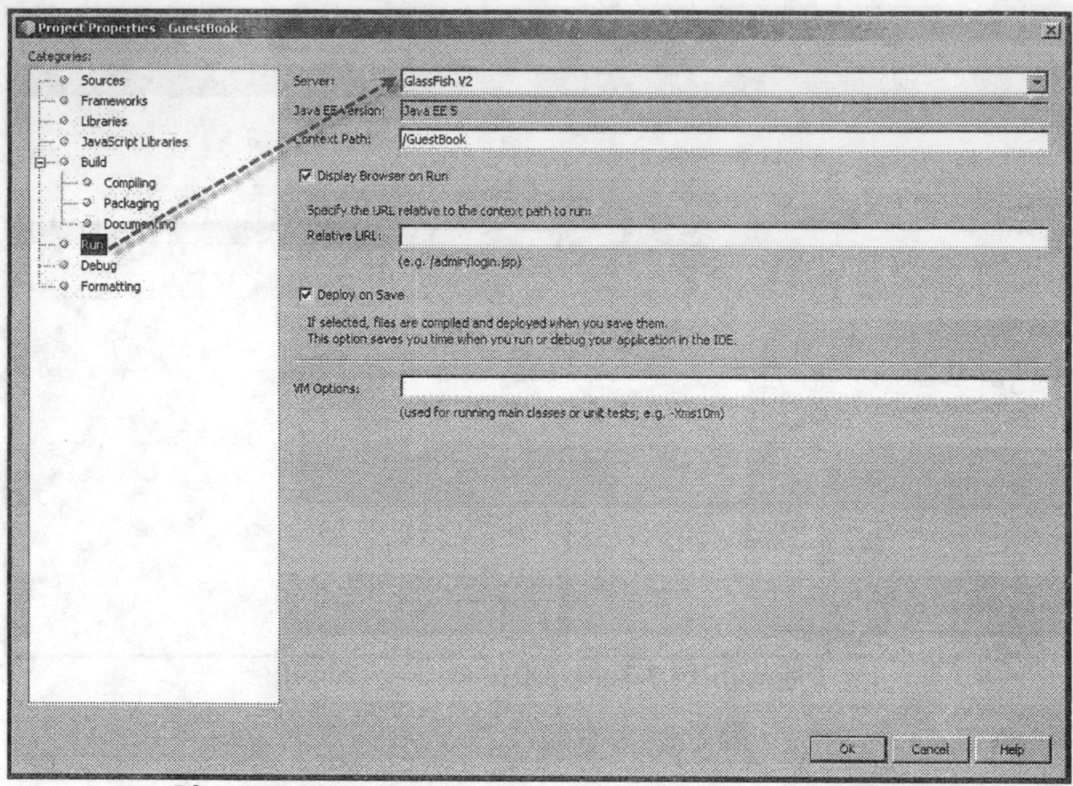

Diagram 14.4: Choosing the Application Server in NetBeans IDE

The Book CDROM holds the complete application source code built using the NetBeans IDE for the following applications:

- GuestBook_Chap14_C3P0
- GuestBook_Chap14_JNDI

These can be directly used by making appropriate changes [username/password] to the configuration file.

SECTION V: THE HIBERNATE QUERY LANGUAGE

The Basics Of Hibernate Query Language [HQL]

Hibernate allows representing an underlying database by using simple Java objects. In order to retrieve objects from the underlying database, Hibernate provides:

- Hibernate Query Language [HQL]
- Query By Criteria [QBC] and Query By Example [QBE] using Criteria API
- Native SQL queries

HQL is much like SQL. The only difference is that SQL operates on relations, whereas HQL operates on objects. HQL is an extremely powerful query language and is considered the most preferred way.

The examples in the last few chapters have already used HQL [Hibernate Query Language] queries. Now let's spend some time understanding what HQL is and how it differs from SQL.

HQL queries:

- Are based on the relational object models
- Have syntax and keywords/clauses very similar to SQL
- Uses classes and properties instead of tables and columns
- Are case insensitive except for the names of the Java Classes and properties
- Support several SQL kind of features such as aggregate functions [sum(), max()] and clauses such as GROUP BY and ORDER BY
- Makes the SQL object oriented

Using Hibernate Query Language, queries can be executed against the database. Hibernate automatically generates the appropriate SQL query and executes it against underlying database.

Why Hibernate Query Language

Hibernate allows using native SQL queries with a Hibernate based persistence layer. However, it is more efficient to use HQL instead, because of the following reasons:

HQL is easy to learn and implement, as its syntax and features are very similar to SQL.

HQL is fully object oriented, understands inheritance, polymorphism and association. It, thus, allows representing SQL queries in the form of objects by using classes and properties instead of tables and columns like SQL does.

Queries written using HQL are database independent queries. These queries are actually converted to the native SQL dialect of the underlying database at runtime. This brings in portability to the application across multiple supported databases.

SQL when used returns the query results in form of plain data, however, HQL when used, returns the query result in the form of object(s), that are ready to be accessed, operated upon and manipulated programmatically. This approach does away with the routine task of creating and populating objects from scratch with the result-set retrieved from database queried.

HQL fully supports polymorphic queries. This means, along with the object to be returned as a query result, all child objects [objects of subclasses], if any, of the given object are returned along.

HQL supports pagination, fetch join with dynamic profiling, Inner, Outer, Full joins, Cartesian products, Projection, Aggregation [such as max(), avg() and so on], Grouping, Ordering, Sub queries and SQL function calls.

The simplest possible Hibernate query is:

```
FROM Customers
```

The SQL equivalent query would be:

```
SELECT * FROM CustomerMaster
```

Here, **Customers** is a **POJO** class **mapped** to the database table **CustomerMaster**.

```
package myApp;

public class Customers
{
   public Customers(String name, int age, String address)
   {
      this.name = name;
      this.age = age;
      this.address = address;
   }

   public Customers()
   {
   }

   private int customerno;
   private String name;
   private int age;
   private String address;

   public int getCustomerNo()
   {
      return customerno;
   }

   public void setCustomerno(int customerno)
   {
      this.customerno = customerno;
   }

   public String getName()
   {
      return name;
   }

   public void setName(String name)
   {
      this.name = name;
   }

   public int getAge()
   {
      return age;
   }

   public void setAge(int age)
   {
      this.age = age;
   }

```

POJO

Mapping Document

```
<?xml version="1.0" encoding="UTF-8"?>
<!DOCTYPE hibernate-mapping PUBLIC '-//Hibernate/Hibernate Mapping DTD 3.0//EN'
'http://hibernate.sourceforge.net/hibernate-mapping-3.0.dtd'>
<hibernate-mapping>
   <class name="myApp.Customers" table="CustomerMaster">
      <id name="customerno" type="integer" column="CustomerNo">
         <generator class="native" />
      </id>
      <property name="name" type="string" column="CustomerName" />
      <property name="age" type="integer" column="Age" />
      <property name="address" type="string" column="Address" />
   </class>
</hibernate-mapping>
```

Table

Column Name	Datatype	NOT NULL	AUTO INC
CustomerNo	INTEGER	✔	✔
CustomerName	VARCHAR(45)	✔	
Age	INTEGER	✔	
Address	VARCHAR(45)	✔	

```
    public String getAddress()
    {
      return address;
    }

    public void setAddress(String address)
    {
      this.address = address;
    }
}
```

The HQL is executed using the following code spec:

```
Query query = session.createQuery("FROM Customers");
List customers = query.list();
```

Here, HQL is used to query the Customers → CustomerMaster to retrieve all the customers. The query result is retrieved using the **list()** method that returns a list containing customer objects.

HINT

Queries written using HQL are case insensitive, barring the Java class and property names. Hence, **SELECT** and **select** are the same, but **CustomerMaster** and **customermaster** are not.

REMINDER

Although SQL statements can be directly used with Hibernate, it is recommended to use HQL [or criteria] whenever possible to avoid database portability hassles and to take advantage of Hibernate's SQL generation and caching strategies.

The Elements Of HQL

An HQL query consists of the following elements:

- Clauses
- Aggregate functions
- Sub-queries

Clauses

The FROM Clause

The **FROM** clause is the simplest form of an HQL query.

Syntax:

```
FROM <Object> [AS <ObjectAlias>]
```

It allows specifying the OBJECT [Customers] whose instances are to be returned as the query result. This clause is commonly used with the SELECT clause.

Example

```
FROM myApp.Customers
```

It is not required to qualify the object name with the class name.

Example

```
FROM Customers
```

Assigning Alias

An alias can be assigned to the object name, so that it can be used later in the query.

Example

```
FROM Customers AS c
```

The **AS** keyword is optional, the same assignment can also be done using:

```
FROM Customers c
```

Multiple Objects

The FROM clause can also accept multiple object names. In such a scenario, the query result will hold a list of type Object[].

Example

```
FROM Customers c, Orders o
```

This query produces a cross join [since the WHERE clause is absent] of the Customers and Orders objects.

The SELECT Clause

The SELECT clause allows specifying Objects and Properties to be returned in the query result set. This clause is used along with the FROM clause.

Syntax:

```
SELECT [<Object>.]<Property>
  FROM <Object> [AS <ObjectAlias>]
```

The FROM clause allows querying whole Objects. The SELECT clause when used together with the FROM clause allows querying particular properties of the objects in the FROM clause.

Example

```
SELECT c.name FROM Customers c
```

Multiple properties can be queried using a comma to separate the property names.

Example

```
SELECT c.name, c.age FROM Customers c
```

The query result will be a list of type Object[].

SQL Aggregate Functions

The SELECT clause also allows using SQL aggregate functions such as count(), sum(), avg(), max(), min(). These functions when used via HQL are translated into the resulting SQL on runtime.

Example

```
SELECT COUNT(c.name) FROM Customers c
```

The DISTINCT Keyword

Syntax:

```
SELECT [DISTINCT] [<Object>.]<Property>
  FROM <Object> [AS <ObjectAlias>]
```

To obtain distinct results, the keyword **DISTINCT** can be used.

Example

```
SELECT DISTINCT c.age FROM Customers c
```

Encapsulating Results In Collections

The query results can also be encapsulated in collections such as LISTS and MAPS.

List

Example

```
SELECT new list(c.name, c.age, c.address) FROM Customers c
```

The query result is a list of collections.

Map

Example

```
SELECT new map(c.name AS customerName, c.age AS customerAge,
        c.address AS customerAddress) FROM Customers c
```

Here, to map the key for each property, the **AS** keyword is used. The query result is a map of collections.

Custom Type

The SELECT clause also allows using custom types.

For example, a class called CustomerAddresses [with a parameterized constructor] can be created to hold Customer Name and Address:

```
public class CustomerAddresses
{
   private String customerName;
   private String customerAddress;

   // Parameterized Constructor
   public CustomerAddresses(String customerName, String customerAddress)
   {
      this.customerName = customerName;
      this.customerAddress = customerAddress;
```

```
    }
    // Getters and Setters
    ...
    ...
}
```

HQL to query customer address using a custom type:

```
SELECT new CustomerAddresses(c.name, c.address)
  FROM Customers c
```

The WHERE Clause

The WHERE clause allows specifying the conditions that should be satisfied prior the query result is retuned. It allows filtering the results similar to SQL

This clause is used with SELECT and/or FROM clause.

Syntax:

```
[SELECT [<Object>.]<Property>]
  FROM <Object> [AS <ObjectAlias>]
     WHERE <condition>
```

The following expressions can be used as the condition:

- **Logic operators:** OR, AND, NOT
- **Equality operators:** =, <>, !=, ^=
- **Comparison operators:** <, >, <=, >=, like, not like, between, not between
- **Math operators:** +, -, *, /
- **Concatenation operator:** ||
- **Cases:** Case when <logical expression> then <unary expression> else _<unary expression> end
- **Collection expressions:** some, exists, all, any

The condition holds a combination of these operators.

Example

```
SELECT c.name, c.age FROM Customers c
  WHERE c.age > 18
```

Multiple Conditions

Example

```
SELECT c.name, c.age FROM Customers c
   WHERE c.age > 18 AND c.age < 60
```

Using BETWEEN And LIKE Operators

Example

```
SELECT c.name, c.age FROM Customers c
   WHERE c.name LIKE '%Sh%'
      AND c.age BETWEEN 18 AND 60
```

Comparing NULL Values

Example

```
SELECT c.name, c.age FROM Customers c
   WHERE c.address IS NOT NULL
```

Using IN Operator

Example

```
SELECT c.name, c.age FROM Customers c
   WHERE c.name IN ('Sharanam', 'Vaishali')
```

Using Unique Identifier

HQL provides a special property called **id** which can be used to reference the unique identifier of an object.

Example

```
SELECT c.name, c.age FROM Customers c
   WHERE c.id = 1
```

This will be equivalent to the following SQL query:

```
SELECT c.name, c.Age FROM Customers c
   WHERE c.CustomerNo = 1
```

Using Composite Unique Identifiers

HQL also allows using the properties of composite identifiers.

For example, a table called CityStates has the following columns:

- CityStateNo
- CityName
- StateName
- CityDetails

The columns CityName and StateName are composite identifiers. This table is mapped to a class called Citystates with properties named as citystateno, cityname, statename and citydetails.

In such a scenario, the query would be:

```
SELECT cs.citydetails FROM Citystates cs
   WHERE c.id.cityname = 'Mumbai' AND c.id.statename = 'Maharashtra'
```

The ORDER BY Clause

The ORDER BY clause allows specifying the order [Ascending or Descending] in which the properties of objects should be returned as query results.

This clause is used with SELECT and/or FROM clause.

Syntax:

```
[SELECT [<Object>.]<Property>]
  FROM <Object> [AS <ObjectAlias>]
     WHERE <condition>
        ORDER BY <Object1>.<Property1> [ASC|DESC]
                 [, <Object2>.<Property2>]. . .
```

The ORDER BY clause sorts the HQL query's results by any property of the objects either in the ascending [ASC] or descending [DESC] order.

Example

```
FROM Customers c ORDER BY c.age
```

HINT

By default, the order is ascending unless specified otherwise.

Example

```
FROM Customers c ORDER BY c.age DESC
```

The ordering can be specified on more than one property in the query.

Example

```
FROM Customers c ORDER BY c.age DESC, c.name ASC
```

The GROUP BY Clause

The GROUP BY clause allows specifying the grouping criteria using objects properties, by which the list of objects returned as a query result should be grouped together.

This clause is used with SELECT and/or FROM clause.

Syntax:

```
[SELECT [<Object>.]<Property>]
  FROM <Object> [AS <ObjectAlias>]
     WHERE <condition>
        GROUP BY <Object1>.<Property1> [, <Object2>.<Property2>] . .
        ORDER BY <Object1>.<Property1> [ASC|DESC]
                 [, <Object2>.<Property2>] . . .
```

A query that returns aggregated values can be grouped by any property of a returned class or components:

```
SELECT COUNT(c.name) FROM Customers c
  GROUP BY c.age
```

The HAVING Clause

Syntax:

```
[SELECT [<Object>.]<Property>]
  FROM <Object> [AS <ObjectAlias>]
    WHERE <condition>
      GROUP BY <Object1>.<Property1> [, <Object2>.<Property2>] . .
        HAVING <condition>
      ORDER BY <Object1>.<Property1> [ASC|DESC]
               [, <Object2>.<Property2>] . . .
```

HQL also allows using a HAVING clause.

Example

```
SELECT COUNT(c.name) FROM Customers c
  GROUP BY c.age
    HAVING c.age >18
```

Sub-Queries

Hibernate also supports executing sub-queries within queries, if the underlying database supports it.

A sub-query must be surrounded by parentheses.

Example

```
FROM Customers c
  WHERE c.age > (SELECT AVG(c1.age) FROM Customers c1)
```

REMINDER

HQL sub-queries may occur only in the SELECT or WHERE clauses.

The result of a sub-query might contain either a single row or multiple rows. Typically, sub-queries that return single rows perform aggregation.

If a sub-query returns multiple rows, it can be combined with quantification.

HQL provides the following quantifiers:

- any
- all
- some [a synonym for any]
- in [a synonym for = any]

Example

```
FROM Customers c
   WHERE c.Age > ALL(SELECT e.EmployeeName FROM Employees e);
```

Example

```
FROM Customers c
   WHERE c.Age < ANY(SELECT e.EmployeeName FROM Employees e);
```

Example

```
FROM Customers c
   WHERE c.CustomerName = SOME
      (SELECT odDtls.CustomerName FROM OrderDetails odDtls);
```

Example

```
FROM Books b
   WHERE b.AuthorNo IN(SELECT a.AuthorNo FROM Authors a
      WHERE a.AuthorName = 'Sharanam Shah'
         OR a.AuthorName = 'Vaishali Shah');
```

Invoking SQL Functions

HQL also provides the ability to call arbitrary SQL functions in the **WHERE** clause.

If the database supports user-defined functions, they can be invoked.

For example, the following query uses an ANSI SQL function lower() to perform case-insensitive searching:

```
FROM Customers c WHERE LOWER(c.name) = 'sharanam'
```

Similarly, it is also possible for some Hibernate SQL dialects to call database specific SQL functions from the **SELECT** clause.

For example, for Oracle dialect, the following query retrieves the current date and time:

```
SELECT c.name, sysdate, UPPER(c.name) FROM Customers c
```

The HQL UPDATE

HQL provides the UPDATE clause which allows altering the details of existing objects in the database.

In-memory entities will not be updated to reflect changes resulting from issuing UPDATE statements.

Syntax:

```
UPDATE [VERSIONED] [FROM] <Object> [[AS] <Alias>] [, . . .]
  SET <Property> = <Value> [, . . .]
     [WHERE <condition>]
```

Object can be given an alias name to abbreviate references to specific objects or their properties and must be used when property names used in the query would otherwise be ambiguous.

Example

```
UPDATE Customers c
   SET c.name = :newName
      WHERE c.name = :oldName
```

:newName and **:oldName** will be passed using the setString() method of the query interface [explained later].

The HQL DELETE

HQL provides the DELETE clause that allows removing the details of existing objects from the database.

In-memory entities will not be updated to reflect changes resulting from DELETE statements.

This also means that cascade rules will not be followed for deletions carried out using HQL.

This approach to deletion is commonly referred to as bulk deletion, since it is the most efficient way to remove large numbers of entities from the database.

Syntax:

```
DELETE [FROM] <Path> [[AS] <Alias>]
  [WHERE <condition>]
```

Object can be given an alias name to abbreviate references to specific objects or their properties and must be used when property names used in the query would otherwise be ambiguous.

Example

```
DELETE Customers c WHERE c.name = :oldName
```

:oldName will be passed using the setString() method of the query interface [explained later].

The HQL INSERT

HQL provides the HQL INSERT clause. This clause cannot be used to insert arbitrary entities.

HQL INSERT can only be used to insert data constructed from information obtained from SELECT queries. This means INSERT INTO (...) VALUES (...) is not supported only INSERT INTO (...) SELECT ... is supported.

Syntax:

```
INSERT
  INTO <Object> (<Property> [, . . .])
     SELECT
```

The **SELECT** query is an **HQL SELECT** clause explained earlier.

Example

```
INSERT
   INTO Customers (customerno, name, age, address)
      SELECT oc.id, oc.name, oc.age, oc.address FROM OldCustomers oc
```

This chapter covers the basics of HQL. The next chapter begins with Joins using HQL.

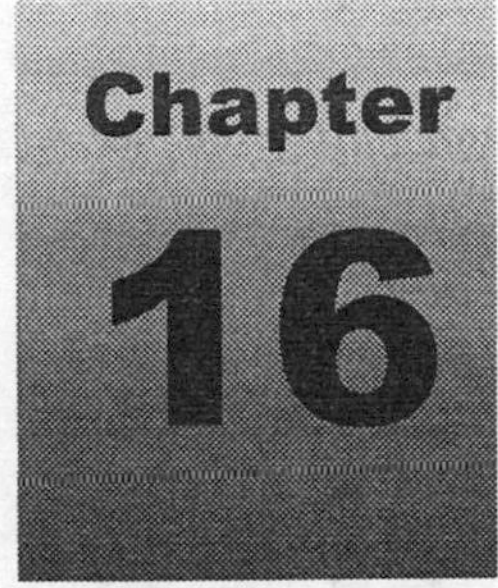

SECTION V: THE HIBERNATE QUERY LANGUAGE

Joins In HQL

One of the fundamental strengths of relational data access is the ability to arbitrarily join data from multiple tables, which is possible using SQL Joins. In the same manner, HQL allows fetching more than one class in a single query.

In HQL, the **JOIN** keyword is used to join the associated objects. Join allows combining data in two or more relations.

Example

The following query retrieves all the book details of those books that are authored by "Sharanam Shah":

```
FROM Books b
    JOIN b.Authors a
        WHERE a.AuthorName = 'Sharanam Shah'
```

The query result contains a list of object pairs in the form of Object[]. Each pair consists of Books object and Authors object.

Example

```
FROM States state
   JOIN state.Countries country
      WHERE country.Country = 'India'
```

The above query retrieves all those states that belong to the country named **India**.

The query result contains a list of object pairs in the form of Object[]. Each pair consists of States object and Countries.

States is given an alias called **state**. Hence, States can be referenced anywhere in the query, using **state**. state.Countries is given an alias called **country**. Hence, state.Countries can be referenced anywhere in the query, using **country**.

In Hibernate, the name of a mapped Java class association is specified to create a Join.

Example

Table Representation

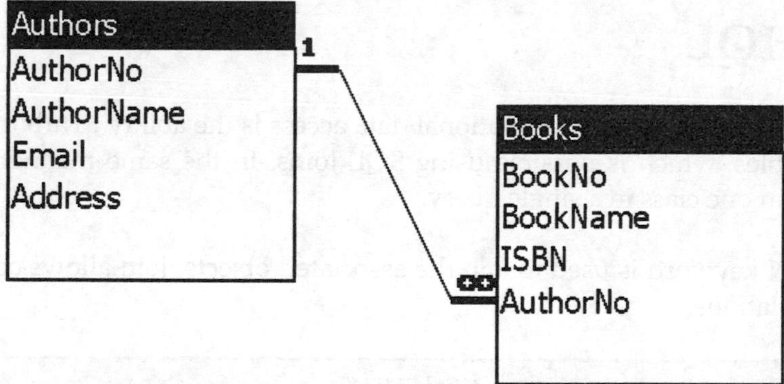

Class Representation

```
public class Books {

    private Integer bookNo;
    private Authors authors;
    private String bookName;
    private String isbn;
```

```
public class Authors {
    private Integer authorNo;
    private String authorName;
    private String email;
    private String address;
    private Set<Books> bookses
        = new HashSet<Books>(0);
```

Mapping Document

```
<?xml version="1.0"?>
<!DOCTYPE hibernate-mapping PUBLIC "-//Hibernate/Hibernate Mapping DTD 3.0//EN"
"http://hibernate.sourceforge.net/hibernate-mapping-3.0.dtd">
<hibernate-mapping>
  <class name="myApp.Books" table="books" catalog="bms">
    <id name="bookNo" type="java.lang.Integer">
      <column name="BookNo" />
      <generator class="identity" />
    </id>
    <many-to-one name="authors" class="myApp.Authors" fetch="select">
      <column name="AuthorNo" not-null="true" />
    </many-to-one>
    <property name="bookName" type="string">
      <column name="BookName" />
    </property>
    <property name="isbn" type="string">
      <column name="ISBN" length="20" />
    </property>
  </class>
</hibernate-mapping>
```

Here, the **Books** class has an association [many-to-one] named **authors** with the **Authors** class.

Hibernate has enough information in the mapping document to figure out the table join expression.

```
FROM Books b
   JOIN b.Authors a
      WHERE a.AuthorName = 'Sharanam Shah'
```

Implicit And Explicit Joins

HQL supports two forms of association joining:

- Implicit

- Explicit

In the above examples of joins, JOIN keyword was used to join associated objects. This kind of join is knows as **Explicit Joins**. This is the most recommended form.

In the **Implicit Join**, the JOIN keyword is missing i.e. the JOIN keyword is not used. The associations are dereferenced using the dot notation. The associations are referenced by its name directly.

Example

Implicit Join:

```
FROM Books b
   WHERE b.Authors.AuthorName = 'Sharanam Shah'
```

Explicit Join:

```
FROM Books b
   JOIN b.Authors a
      WHERE a.AuthorName = 'Sharanam Shah'
```

In case of an implicit join, the result contains **a list of Books objects only** since no JOIN is specified in the **FROM** clause.

For a collection association, an implicit join occurs each time when it is navigated. This means, if the same collection is navigated for two times, the same table will also be joined two times.

Example

Implicit Join:

```
FROM Books b
   WHERE b.Authors.FirstName = 'Sharanam'
      AND b.Authors.LastName = 'Shah'
```

So, be careful while using implicit joins with collection association. For the collection to be referenced more than one time, use Explicit Join to avoid duplicate joins.

Example

Explicit Join:

```
FROM Books b JOIN b.Authors a
   WHERE a.FirstName = 'Sharanam'
      AND a.LastName = 'Shah'
```

Types Of Joins

Hibernate supports the following types of Joins:

- Inner Join
- Left Outer Join
- Right Outer Join
- Full Outer Join

The ones that are commonly used are Inner and Outer [Left or Right]. The Full Join is rarely a choice.

INNER JOIN

The INNER JOIN is used in situations where two tables having common columns needs to be joined. This is the **default** join type, if a join type is not specified.

For example, consider the following tables:

- Books
  - BookNo
  - BookName
  - ISBN
  - Price
  - **PublisherNo**
- Publishers
  - **PublisherNo**
  - PublisherName
  - Address

Example

Implicit Join:

```
FROM Books b JOIN b.Publishers
```

Both these tables have PublisherNo as a common column.

These two tables can be joined using **PublisherNo**. When such tables are joined, the result of the join is those rows from both tables where the PublisherNo is the same for each table.

The result of this Join will not include those rows with **null PublisherNo.**

LEFT OUTER JOIN

The LEFT OUTER JOIN is designed to join tables that have common column between them. The result of the join is rows containing value from both the tables matched on the common column. Rows in the source table that do not match a row in the joined table are also included in the result. The values for the joined table in these unmatched rows have null values.

The LEFT part of the clause says that the table on the left is the source table and all of its rows are included in the result regardless of a match.

To retrieve all the books irrespective of null **PublisherNo**, LEFT OUTER JOIN can be used:

```
FROM Books b LEFT OUTER JOIN b.Publishers
```

The LEFT OUTER JOIN can be abbreviated:

```
FROM Books b LEFT JOIN b.Publishers
```

RIGHT OUTER JOIN

The RIGHT OUTER JOIN has the same functionality as the LEFT OUTER JOIN. But the only difference is that the table on the right is the source and all of its rows [that do not match a row in the joined table] are included in the result.

To retrieve all the books irrespective of null **PublisherNo**, LEFT OUTER JOIN can be used:

```
FROM Publishers p RIGHT OUTER JOIN p.Books
```

The RIGHT OUTER JOIN can be abbreviated:

```
FROM Publishers p RIGHT JOIN p.Books
```

FULL JOIN

A FULL JOIN is a kind of outer join that combines the results of both LEFT and RIGHT outer joins.

The result of this join is rows containing value from both the tables matched where it can.

The following query retrieves all the books and the Publishers:

```
FROM Books b FULL OUTER JOIN b.Publishers
```

This query results hold:

- Each book which is published
- Each publisher that has published a book
- Each book that is not published
- Each publisher that has not published any book

The FULL OUTER JOIN can be abbreviated:

```
FROM Books b FULL JOIN b.Publishers
```

WARNING

Use this join with caution, due to the total number of rows in the result.

Fetching Associations

Hibernate follows a fetching strategy. This strategy is used for retrieving associated objects, if the application needs to navigate the association.

By default, Hibernate 3 uses **Lazy SELECT fetching** for collections and **Lazy PROXY fetching** for single-valued associations. These defaults make sense for almost all associations in almost all applications.

In Lazy collection fetching, a collection is fetched when the application invokes an operation upon that collection.

These fetching strategies may be declared in the O/R mapping metadata, or over-ridden by a particular HQL or Criteria query.

However, at times, this kind of behavior may not be desired. Hibernate allows overriding this behavior, where, FETCH JOIN [non-lazy behavior] can be used instead of SELECT fetching in a particular transaction.

FETCH JOIN is one of the fetching strategies that Hibernate follows.

FETCH JOIN allows fully initializing an object along with its associated collection. It forces a lazy association to be initialized.

In a normal JOIN, only the parent objects are included in the result, whereas, in the FETCH JOIN, all the parent objects along with and all child objects are retrieved, in a single SELECT.

This is particularly useful in the case of a collection. It effectively overrides the OUTER JOIN and lazy declarations of the mapping file for associations and collections.

```
FROM Books B
   JOIN FETCH B.AuthorNo Authors
```

This query returns all Books and all the authors, in a single SELECT.

When executed, it returns a list of Books instances, with their Authors collections **fully initialized**.

The above query will not return Books objects with NULL Authors.

In case, if the NULL Authors need to be included, then the following query can be used:

```
FROM Books B
   LEFT JOIN FETCH B.AuthorNo Authors
```

SECTION V: THE HIBERNATE QUERY LANGUAGE

The Query Interface

Any application that needs to interact with the database requires Queries. Queries form the most interesting part of writing good data access code.

When working with Hibernate querying happens on persistent objects. Hibernate supports an easy-to-use but powerful object oriented query language called **H**ibernate **Q**uery **L**anguage [HQL].

HQL queries can be written and represented by the instance of org.hibernate.Query [The Query Interface].

This interface offers methods that allow:

- Execution of the actual query
- Binding parameters to the query
- Handling result set

The Session interface allows creating Query objects to retrieve persistent objects by invoking the **createQuery()** method of the Session object.

Example

```
List authors = session.createQuery("FROM Authors).list();
```

Typical Usage Of Query:

A query is usually executed by invoking the **list()** method.

The results of the query are loaded completely into a collection [in this case **authors**] in the memory.

Importing Query Interface

To use the query interface, it has to be imported into the module that requires it.

```
import org.hibernate.Query;
```

Technically, this interface offers methods for:

- Binding Query parameters
- Result set handling [Limit the number of results returned by the query]
- Managing JDBC timeouts
- Managing JDBC fetch sizes
- Executing the actual query
- Returning the query results as:
    - Java List
    - Iterator
    - Unique result

Forming An HQL Query

An HQL query can be formed and stored in a memory variable:

```
String hqlQuery = "FROM Books";
```

Here, the query returns objects of type Books. There is no need to have a SELECT clause. It is optional.

Creating A New Instance Of Query Interface

After the HQL query is formed and held in a memory variable, an instance of the Query interface is required. This has to be obtained by invoking the **createQuery()** method of the Session interface:

```
Query qry = session.createQuery(hqlQuery);
```

In the above code spec, **hqlQuery** is the memory variable that holds the HQL query.

The Query interface is always obtained via the current Session object.

The createQuery() method:

- Accepts a valid HQL statement/query

  and

- Returns an org.hibernate.Query object

Hibernate returns a newly instantiated Query object that may be used to specify exactly how a particular query should be executed.

An HQL query can also be passed directly to the **createQuery()** method:

```
Query query = session.createQuery("FROM Books");
```

Executing Queries

After a Query object is available, the next step is to execute the query.

The list() method

Usually a query is executed by invoking the list() method.

The following code spec declares a list object to execute the query and hold the results in the list object:

```
List books = query.list();
```

The list() method can also be used while creating a new instance of Query:

```
List books = session.createQuery("FROM Books").list();
```

The list() method executes the HQL query and returns the query result as a **List**.

The uniqueResult() method

In situations, where the HQL query is sure to return a single object, the **uniqueResult()** method of the Query interface can be used.

uniqueResult() obtains just one object from an HQL query.

A HQL query executed by invoking the uniqueResult() method:

```
Books book = (Books) session.createQuery("FROM Books WHERE BookNo = 1").uniqueResult();
```

The uniqueResult() method returns only one object or **null** if there are zero results. If there is more than one result, the uniqueResult() method throws a NonUniqueResultException.

Do not use the uniqueResult() method to pick the first result and return it. To achieve this, set the maximum results of the HQL query to 1:

```
String hqlQuery = "FROM Books WHERE Cost > 500";
Query query = session.createQuery(hqlQuery );
query.setMaxResults(1);
Books book = (Books) session.query.uniqueResult();
```

Here, since the HQL query may return more than one result, the maximum results of the HQL query is restricted to 1 and then uniqueResult() is applied.

The iterate() method

Sometimes, a HQL query is expected to return a very large number of objects where not all the retrieved objects may be used.

In such a scenario, to gain better performance, the iterate() method can be used. This method returns a java.util.Iterator object.

The advantage here is that, instead of loading all the objects, the iterator loads objects on demand, using the identifiers returned by an initial HQL query.

When the iterate() method is invoked:

- Hibernate retrieves only the primary key values

- Then on demand, Hibernate retrieves the rest. Even when retrieving the rest, Hibernate first tries to find them in the cache before reaching the database

Example

```
Query query = session.createQuery("FROM Customers");
Iterator results = query.iterate();
while (results.hasNext())
{
    Customers cust = (Customers) results.next();
    if (cust.getActivateStatus())
    {
        System.out.println(cust.getUsername() + " is activated.");
    }
}
```

Here, Customers is queried and the query is executed using **iterate()**.

Each collection of Customers is an uninitialized collection wrapper.

Whilst iterating through the collection, if the customer is found active, the Username is extracted and displayed.

This technique can be used to optimize loading, in cases, where the actual entity instances returned by the query are already in the session or second-level cache. If they are not, then iterate() method is slower than list() and might require several database hits for a simple query, usually 1 for the initial select which only returns identifiers and an additional SELECT statements to initialize the actual instances on demand.

Binding Query Parameters

The query interface also provides methods for binding values to named parameters or in JDBC manner[?].

Named parameters are identifiers of the form **:name** in the query string.

The advantages of named parameters are:

- Named parameters are insensitive to the order they occur in the query string

- They may occur multiple times in the same query
- They are self-documenting

Example

```
String hqlQuery = "FROM Books book WHERE
      book.Author1No = :AuthorNo
      AND book.Author2No = :AuthorNo
      AND book.Author3No = :AuthorNo
      AND book.Author4No = :AuthorNo";
Query query = session.createQuery(hqlQuery);
query.setString("AuthorNo", AuthorNo);
List books = query.list;
```

Here, the query intends retrieving all those books that have been authored [Author1No] or co-authored [Author2No or Author3No or Author4No,] by a particular author.

In the above code spec, the **colon** followed by a parameter name, indicates a named parameter.

This named parameter is populated with a value using:

```
query.setString("AuthorNo", AuthorNo);
```

Since, AuthorNo is a user-supplied string variable, the setString() method of the Query interface is used to bind it to the named parameter [AuthorNo].

The above code is cleaner, much safer and performs better, because a single compiled HQL statement can be reused, if only bind parameters change.

JDBC Style Positional Parameter

The Query interface also supports binding JDBC style positional parameters.

Example

```
String hqlQuery = "FROM Books book WHERE
      book.PublisherNo = ?";
```

```
Query query = session.createQuery(hqlQuery);
query.setString(0, "1");
List books = query.list;
```

Here, the query intends retrieving all those books that have been published by a particular publisher [in this case 1].

In the above code spec, the ? indicates a positional parameter.

This positional parameter is populated with a value using:

```
query.setString(0, "1");
```

Since, this is the first positional parameter, 0 is used to indicate it. Hence, the second positional parameter would be indicated using 1 and so on.

Named List Parameters

The Query interface also supports binding named list [multiple] parameters.

Example

```
String hqlQuery = "FROM Books book WHERE
      book.BookName IN (:namesList)";
List names = new ArrayList();
names.add("Oracle");
names.add("PHP");
Query query = session.createQuery(hqlQuery);
query.setParameterList("namesList", names);
List books = query.list;
```

Here, the query intends retrieving all those books that are named Oracle or PHP.

In the above code spec, the **colon** followed by a parameter name indicates a named list parameter.

This named parameter is populated with a List object using:

```
query.setParameterList("namesList", names);
```

This List object is populated with the desired values using:

```
List names = new ArrayList();
names.add("Oracle");
names.add("PHP");
```

Commenting The SQL

Sometimes, it is required to trace through the application log whilst debugging errors. Since an application may have several HQL statements, determining the right one becomes quite difficult.

Hibernate allows commenting HQL queries using the Query instance. This makes it possible to apply a comment to a specific query.

The Query interface provides a **setComment()** method, which accepts a String object as an argument:

```
public Query setComment(String comment)
```

The setComment() method helps identify the right SQL output in the application's logs, if SQL logging is enabled.

Example

```
String hqlQuery = "FROM Books";
Query query = session.createQuery(hqlQuery);
query.setComment("Retrieving all the book's details: " + hqlQuery);
List rs = query.list();
```

Output: [In the application' log]

```
Hibernate: /* Retrieving all the book's details: from Books*/
select book0_.id as id, book0_.name as name2_ from Books book0_
```

Here, the application's log holds a Java style comment before the SQL query. This helps identify the purpose of the query when going through the log.

To enable SQL logging, place the following line in hibernate.cfg.xml:

```
<hibernate.show.sql>true</hibernate.show.sql>
```

In the output,

```
select book0_.id as id, book0_.name as name2_ from Books book0_
```

Indicates the SQL query that is generated by Hibernate and it appears after show.sql is switched on.

```
Hibernate: /* Retrieving all the book's details: from Books*/
```

Indicates the actual comment that was set using the **setComment()** method.

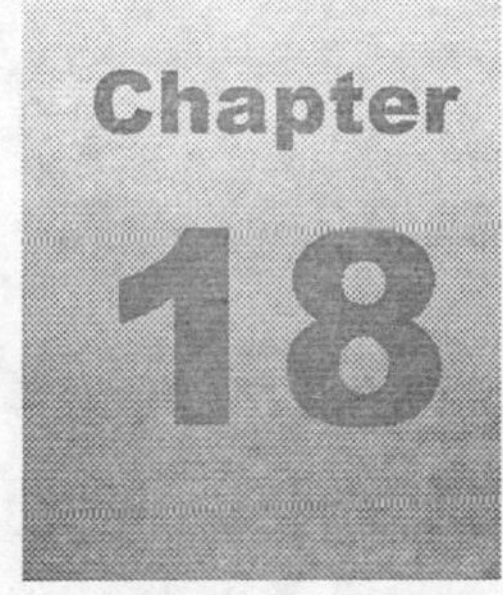

SECTION V: THE HIBERNATE QUERY LANGUAGE

The Criteria API

HQL works very well with objects but it still requires some prior knowledge about SQL to form the HQL queries for CRUD operations. To overcome this obstacle, Hibernate provides an alternative called **Criteria Query API**.

Hibernate Criteria Query API is a powerful and elegant alternative to HQL. It is ideal for dynamic search functionalities where complex Hibernate queries have to be generated **on-the-fly**.

Criteria Query is used mostly in case of multi criteria search screens, where HQL is not very effective.

Criteria API:

- Is a simplified API for retrieving entities by composing Criterion objects
- Provides a set of Java objects for constructing queries

- Allows building nested structured query expressions in Java programming language
- Supports Query By Example [QBE] i.e. Performs a query by providing an example object, which contains properties that need to be retrieved
- Supports aggregation methods

Core Classes Of Criteria

There are five core APIs that are commonly used. Each class of the Criteria Query API represents an aspect of the relational approach.

Criteria Class

The Criteria class provides a gateway to working with criteria APIs.

It is an interface that provides a simplified API for retrieving objects containing or composed of Criterion objects.

Criteria interface provides the following methods:

- **add(Criterion criterion):** Adds a Criterion to constrain the results to be retrieved
- **addOrder(Order order):** Adds an Order to the result set
- **createAlias(String associationPath, String alias):** Joins an association, assigning an alias to the joined entity
- **createCriteria(String associationPath):** Used to create new Criteria, **rooted** at the associated entity
- **setFetchSize(int fetchSize):** Sets a fetch size for the underlying JDBC query
- **setFirstResult(int first Result):** Sets the first result to be retrieved
- **setMaxResults(int maxResults):** Sets a limit upon the number of objects to be retrieved
- **uniqueResult():** Returns a single instance that matches the query or null if the query returns no results

Example

```
Criteria criteria = session.createCriteria(Books.class);
List results = criteria.list();
```

The HQL equivalent of this query:

```
FROM Books
```

Criterion Class

In the relational approach, conditions placed on retrieving data are known as criterion.

The Criterion class is the object-oriented representation of the relational criterion. It can be used as restrictions on the criteria query.

In other words, Criterion is the object-oriented representation of the **WHERE** clause of an SQL query.

The conditions to be applied [also known as restrictions] can be provided by the Restrictions class.

Restrictions Class

Restrictions allow filtering the query result. It is very similar to using the WHERE clause in HQL.

The Restrictions class provides a variety of methods for restriction building. Each restriction added is treated as a logical conjunction.

The Restriction API provides the built-in types for Criterion.

Example

```
Criteria criteria = session.createCriteria(Books.class);
Criterion criterion = Restriction.eq("BookNo", "5");
criteria.add(criterion);
List results = criteria.list();
```

The HQL equivalent of this query:

```
FROM Books b WHERE b.BookNo = 5
```

Here:

- The Criterion is the **WHERE** clause, which, when added to the Criteria object, provides a complete query with restrictions
- Here the built-in Restriction type **eq()** for testing equality is used

Most of the methods in the Criteria class return the instance, hence the same query can be re-written as:

```
Criteria criteria = session.createCriteria(Books.class);
criteria.add(Restriction.eq("BookNo", "5"));
List results = criteria.list();
```

Projection Class

The Projection class is an object-oriented representation of query resultset projection in a Criteria query. It refers to the fields mentioned in the SELECT clause of a query.

The SELECT clause performs projection. Projection allows specifying which objects or properties are needed in the query result.

It is used to customize the fields of the result by specifying the fields to be returned.

Example

```
Criteria criteria = session.createCriteria(Book.class)
        .setProjection(Projections.property("ISBN"));
List books = criteria.list();
```

The HQL equivalent of this query:

```
SELECT b.ISBN FROM Books b
```

Order Class

The Order class represents the **ORDER BY** clause of an SQL query. By using the ASC() and DESC() methods of this class, order can be imposed upon the Criteria resultset.

Example

```
Criteria criteria = session.createCriteria(Books.class)
   .addOrder(Order.asc("BookName"))
   .addOrder(Order.desc("PublishDate"));
List books = criteria.list();
```

The HQL equivalent of this query:

```
FROM Book b ORDER BY b.BookName ASC, b.PublishDate DESC
```

Creating An Instance Of Criteria

The Criteria API allows building up a criteria query object programmatically. The **org.hibernate.Criteria** interface defines the available methods for one of these objects.

To retrieve a reference to the Criteria interface, the **createCriteria()** method of the Session class is used.

The createCriteria() method accepts the persistent object's class or its entity name. Hibernate then creates a Criteria object that returns instances of the persistence object's class when the application executes a criteria query.

Syntax:

```
Criteria criteria = session.createCriteria(<ClassName>.class);
```

Example

The following query returns **every object** that corresponds to the Books class:

```
Criteria criteria = session.createCriteria(Books.class);
List rs = criteria.list();
```

The above query retrieves all the objects that are instances of the Books class which means it retrieves **all the rows** from the **Books** table.

Projections

Projections can be used by retrieving a **Projection object** from the **org.hibernate.criterion.Projections**.

After retrieving Projection object, add it to the Criteria object with the **setProjection() method**.

When the Criteria object executes, the list contains object references that can be casted to the appropriate type.

Example

```
Criteria criteria = session.createCriteria(Books.class);
criteria.setProjection(Projections.property("BookName"));
List rs = criteria.list();
```

In the above example, BookName is passed as an argument to the property() method of the **Projections** class.

The Projection instance returned in turn becomes an argument to the **setProjection()** method.

Example

Similarly, to retrieve two fields, a ProjectionList can be used:

```
Criteria criteria = session.createCriteria(Books.class)
    .setProjection(Projections.propertyList()
        .add(Projection.property("ISBN"))
        .add(Projection.property("BookName"))
    ).list();
```

To add multiple projections, the projectionList() method is used on the Projections class.

The **org.hibernate.criterion.ProjectionList** object has an **add()** method, which accepts a Projection object.

Projection properties are added to a project list which in turn is passed as an argument to the to the **setProjection()** method on the Criteria object.

Projections are useful when the network traffic needs to be cut down between the application servers and the database servers. For example:

- If the table has a large number of columns, this can slim down the results
- There might be a large set of joins that would return a very wide result set, but the developer is only interested in a few columns
- Lastly, if the users have limited memory, this can save the trouble with large datasets

Aggregation

Aggregation helps retrieve data based on the group of values of a column. The Criteria API provides aggregation functionality through the Projection class.

The following aggregate functions can be used with Projections:

- **rowCount():** Is the property value count
- **avg(String PropertyName):** Retrieves the average of a property's value
- **count(String PropertyName):** Counts the number of times a property occurs
- **countDistinct(String PropertyName):** Counts the number of unique values the property contains
- **max(String PropertyName):** Calculates the maximum value of the property values
- **min(String PropertyName):** Calculates the minimum value of the property values
- **sum(String PropertyName):** Calculates the sum total of the property values

Example

The following query retrieves a count of all the rows present in the Books table based on the ISBN column:

```
List rs = session.createCriteria(Books.class)
    .setProjection(Projections.projectionList()
        .add(Projections.count("ISBN"))
    ).list();
```

When the aggregation functions are used, the values may have to be grouped according to a particular field.

Grouping always operates on a dataset.

In Criteria Query API, grouping is provided by the Projection class. The **groupProperty() method** of the Projections class provides the grouping functionality.

Example

The following query groups the query results using the groupProperty() projection to determine cost wise number of books:

```
Criteria criteria = session.createCriteria(Books.class)
```

```
    .setProjection(Projections.propertyList()
        .add(Projection.groupProperty("Cost"))
        .add(Projection.count("ISBN"))
    ).list();
```

The HQL equivalent of this query:

```
SELECT book.Cost, count(book.ISBN)
    FROM Books book
        GROUP BY book.Cost
```

Joins

createCriteria() can also be used to specify constraints upon related entities by navigating associations.

A Join using HQL:

```
SELECT B.*, P.*
    FROM Books B, Publishers P
        WHERE B.PublisherNo = P.PublisherNo;
```

A Join using Criteria:

```
List rs = session.createCriteria(Books.class)
    .setFetchMode("Publishers", FetchMode.JOIN)
    .list();
```

The only thing to be done is to invoke the **setFetchMode() method** of the Criteria class with two parameters:

- The **name** of the class with which the current class has to be joined
- The **mode** of the fetching of the data from the associated class

In the above case, the class name is actually the instance variable provided within the Books class and the fetching strategy [**mode** of fetching] is **Join**.

Restrictions can also be applied with joins.

Example

The following SQL query:

```
SELECT B.*, P.*
  FROM Books B, Publishers P
    WHERE B.PublisherNo = P.PublisherNo
      AND B.BookName = "Oracle For Professionals";
```

Can be written using Criteria, Join and Restrictions as:

```
List rs = session.createCriteria(Books.class)
  .setFetchMode("Publishers", FetchMode.JOIN)
  .add(Restrictions.eq("BookName", "Oracle For Professionals"))
  .list();
```

Restrictions

To retrieve data based on certain conditions, Restriction must be used. All the conditions provided by SQL are available in Criteria.

The following are the conditions used in Criteria class:

- **Restriction.allEq:** Is used to apply an **EQUALS** constraint to each property in the key set of a Map
- **Restriction.between:** Is used to apply a **BETWEEN** constraint to the field
- **Restriction.eq:** Is used to apply an **EQUAL** constraint to the field
- **Restriction.ge:** Is used to apply a **GREATER THAN OR EQUAL** constraint to the field
- **Restriction.gt:** Is used to apply a **GREATER THAN** constraint to the field
- **Restriction.idEq:** Is used to apply an **EQUAL** constraint to the identifier property
- **Restriction.ilike:** Is case-insensitive **LIKE**, similar to Postgres ilike operator
- **Restriction.in:** Is used to apply an **IN** constraint to the field
- **Restriction.isNotNull:** Is used to apply an **IS NOT NULL** constraint to the field
- **Restriction.isNull:** Is used to apply an **IS NULL** constraint to the field
- **Restriction.le:** Is used to apply a **LESS THAN OR EQUAL** constraint to the field
- **Restriction.like:** Is used to apply a **LIKE** constraint to the field
- **Restriction.lt:** Is used to apply a **LESS THAN** constraint to the field

- **Restriction.ltProperty:** Is used to apply **LESS THAN** constraint to two properties
- **Restriction.ne:** Is used to apply a **NOT EQUAL** constraint to the field
- **Restriction.neProperty:** Is used to apply a **NOT EQUAL** constraint to two properties
- **Restriction.not:** Returns the negation of an expression
- **Restriction.or:** Returns the disjuction of two expressions

The restrictions can be added to a Criteria object with the **add()** method.

The add() method accepts an org.hibernate.criterion.Criterion object that represents an individual restriction.

Example

The following SQL query:

```
SELECT * FROM Books WHERE BookName='Oracle For Profesionals';
```

Can be written using Criteria and Restrictions as:

```
List rs = session.createCriteria(Books.class)
    .add(Restrictions.eq("BookName", "Oracle For Professionals"))
    .list();
```

Example

```
Criteria criteria = session.createCriteria(Books.class)
    .add(Restrictions.like("BookName", "Ora%"));
    .list();
```

OR

```
Criteria criteria = session.createCriteria(Books.class)
    .add(Restrictions.ilike("BookName", "Ora%", MatchMode.END));
    .list();
```

In the above example, % character is used as wildcard to match parts of the string.

The like() and ilike() methods of Restrictions class uses an **org.hibernate.criterion.MatchMode** object to specify how to match the specified value to the stored data.

The following are the matches of the MatchMode object:

- **ANYWHERE:** Anyplace in the string
- **END:** The end of the string
- **EXACT:** An exact match
- **START:** The beginning of the string

The isNull() and isNotNull() restrictions allows to do a search for objects that have or do not have NULL property values.

Example

Retrieve all those books which do not have an ISBN.

Solution:

```
Criteria criteria = session.createCriteria(Books.class)
    .add(Restrictions.isNull("ISBN"))
    .list();
```

Example

Retrieve all those books that cost more than 350.

Solution:

```
Criteria criteria = session.createCriteria(Books.class)
    .add(Restrictions.gt("cost", new int(350)))
    .list();
```

Example

```
Criteria criteria = session.createCriteria(Books.class)
    .add(Restrictions.gt("Cost", new int(350)))
    .add(Restrictions.like("bookName", "Ora%"))
    .list();
```

Here, two restrictions are added, both of which are automatically interpreted as AND.

Disjunction

If an OR expression needs to be created with more than two different criteria, use an org.hibernate.criterion.Disjunction object to represent a disjunction.

Disjunction object can be obtained from the **disjunction()** factory method on the Restrictions class.

The disjunction is more convenient than building a tree of OR expressions in the code spec.

Example

```
Criteria criteria = session.createCriteria(Books.class);
Criterion bookCost = Restrictions.gt("Cost", new int(350));
Criterion bookName = Restrictions.like("BookName", "Oracle%");
Criterion bookSynopsis = Restrictions.ilike("Synopsis", "%Oracle%");
Disjunction disjunction = Restrictions.disjunction();
disjunction.add(bookCost);
disjunction.add(bookName);
disjunction.add(bookSynopsis);
criteria.add(disjunction);
List results = criteria.list();
```

This query retrieves all books whose:

- Cost is more than 350

OR

- Name begins with Oracle

OR

- Synopsis holds the word Oracle [case insensitive]

Conjunction

To represent an AND expression with more than two criteria, use the conjunction() method even though one can easily just add those to the Criteria object. The conjunction is also more convenient than building a tree of AND expressions in the code spec.

Example

```
Criteria criteria = session.createCriteria(Books.class);
Criterion bookCost = Restrictions.gt("Cost", new int(350));
Criterion bookName = Restrictions.like("BookName", "Oracle%");
Criterion bookSynopsis = Restrictions.ilike("Synopsis", "%Oracle%");
Conjunction conjunction = Restrictions.conjunction();
conjunction.add(bookCost);
conjunction.add(bookName);
conjunction.add(bookSynopsis);
criteria.add(conjunction);
List results = criteria.list();
```

This query retrieves all books whose:

- Cost is more than 350

AND

- Name begins with Oracle

AND

- Synopsis holds the work Oracle [case insensitive]

Order

The results can be sorted in the ascending or descending order.

Sorting the query's results works much the same way with criteria as it would with HQL or SQL. The Criteria API provides the org.hibernate.criterion.Order class to sort the result set in either ascending or descending order according to one of the object's properties.

To order results, an **Order object** is created using:

- **asc()** for ascending
- **desc()** for descending

Both the methods accept the name of the property as their only argument.

After an Order object is created, the **addOrder() method** is used on the Criteria object to add it to the query.

More than one Order object can be added to the Criteria object. Hibernate then passes them through to the underlying SQL query.

Example

```
Criteria criteria = session.createCriteria(Books.class)
    .add(Restrictions.gt("cost", new Integer(350)))
    .addOrder(Order.asc("BookName"))
    .addOrder(Order.desc("Cost"))
    .list();
```

OR

```
Criteria criteria = session.createCriteria(Books.class)
    .add(Restrictions.gt("cost", new Integer(350)))
    .addOrder(Property.forName("BookName").asc())
    .addOrder(Property.forName("Cost").desc())
    .list();
```

The HQL equivalent:

```
FROM Books book
    WHERE book.Cost = 350
        ORDER BY book.BookName ASC, book.Cost DESC
```

Restrictions On Associations

In HQL, an association property can be referenced by its name to trigger an implicit join.

To add a restriction on a class that is associated with the criteria's class, another Criteria object has to be created and then restrictions have to be added to criteria.

Example

The following query retrieves all those books whose name begin with **Oracle** and are published by a publisher whose name begin with **Sh**.

Solution:

```
Criteria criteria = session.createCriteria(Books.class)
    .add(Restrictions.like("BookName", "Oracle%"))
        .createCriteria("Publishers")
            .add(Restrictions.like("PublisherName", "Sh%"))
    .list();
```

In the above example, the second createCriteria() method returns a new instance of Criteria, which refers to the elements of the Publishers collection.

The above criteria as HQL:

```
FROM Books book
   WHERE book.BookName = "Oracle%"
      AND book.Publishers.PublisherName = "Sh%"
```

Example

Ordering the query results by BookName in the ascending order.

Solution:

```
Criteria criteria = session.createCriteria(Books.class)
    .add(Restrictions.like("BookName", "Ora%"))
        .createCriteria("Publishers")
            .add(Restrictions.like("PublisherName", "Sh%"))
    .addOrder(Order.asc("BookName"))
    .list();
```

Using An Alias

An alias may optionally be assigned to a projection, so that the projected value may be referred to in restrictions or orderings.

Here are the two different ways to do this:

```
List rs = session.createCriteria(Books.class)
    .setProjection(Projections.alias(
        Projections.groupProperty("BookName"), "name"))
    .addOrder(Order.asc("name"))
    .list();
```

OR

```
List rs = session.createCriteria(Books.class)
    .setProjection(Projections.groupProperty("BookName").as("name"))
    .addOrder(Order.asc("name"))
    .list();
```

The **alias()** and **as()** methods simply wrap a projection instance in another aliased instance of Projection.

As a shortcut, an alias can be assigned when the projection is added to a projection list.

Example

```
List rs = session.createCriteria(Books.class)
    .setProjection(Projections.projectionList()
        .add(Projections.rowCount(), "books")
        .add(Projections.max("cost"), "maxCost")
        .add(Projections.groupProperty("BookName"), "name")
    )
    .addOrder(Order.desc("books"))
    .addOrder(Order.desc("maxCost"))
    .list();
```

Query By Example [QBE]

Query By Example [QBE] allows locating information quickly within a database by providing an example of the record being looked for before searching for it.

Basically, a Java object is instantiated with the corresponding values coming from the search screen. Hibernate then builds the corresponding query using the non-null field values to partially populate the instance of that object.

For example, for the Books table:

- An instance of a Books object is created
- The property value for Cost is set

The Criteria API is used to run a QBE query on this object. Hibernate returns a result set containing all books objects that match the property value [Cost].

The org.hibernate.criterion.Example class contains the QBE functionality.

To use QBE:

- Construct an object
- Set the desired properties of that object
- Create an instance of the object using the create() method on the Example class
  The create() accepts the object as its argument
- Add the Example object to the Criteria object [just like any other Criterion object]

Example

The following example searches for books that match the cost on the Books object:

```
Criteria criteria = session.createCriteria(Books.class);
Books b = new Books();
b.setCost(350);
criteria.add(Example.create(b));
List results = criteria.list();
```

When Hibernate translates the Example object into an SQL query, all the properties on the object gets examined.

Some columns can be excluded or some behavior can be changed as:

Example

```
Criteria criteria = session.createCriteria(Books.class);
Books b = new Books();
b.setCost(350);
Example example = Example.create(b)
    .excludeZeroes()              /* Exclude zero valued properties. */
    .excludeProperty("Year")      /* Exclude the property named "year". */
    .ignoreCase()                 /* Perform case insensitive string comparisons. */
    .enableLike();                /* Use like for string comparisons. */
criteria.add(example);
List results = criteria.list();
```

The QBE API is ideal for search forms with multiple search inputs [advanced search]. QBE makes it easier to set values on business objects than to manipulate restrictions with the Criteria API.

The GuestBook Application

The Criteria API

The GuestBook application [Created in *Chapter03: Writing The First Application*] currently uses HQL, let's convert it to Criteria.

The only change that will be required is the GuestBookView.jsp:

```
            gb.setVisitorName(guest);
            gb.setMessage(message);
            gb.setMessageDate(messageDate);

            hibSession.save(gb);
            tx.commit();
        }
        catch (RuntimeException e) {
            if(tx != null) tx.rollback();
            throw e;
```

```
        }
        response.sendRedirect("GuestBookView.jsp");
    }

    try {
        hibSession.beginTransaction();
        guestbook = hibSession.createQuery("from Guestbook").list();
        guestbook = hibSession.createCriteria(Guestbook.class).list();
    }
    catch (RuntimeException e) {
        throw e;
    }
    hibSession.close();
%>
<html>
```

Remove this

Add this

The Query By Example API

Let's build a search form for the GuestBook application. This form will accept the following as the search criteria:

- VistorName
- Message
- Message Date

Search Guest Book

Visitor Name:

Message:

Message Date:

Search

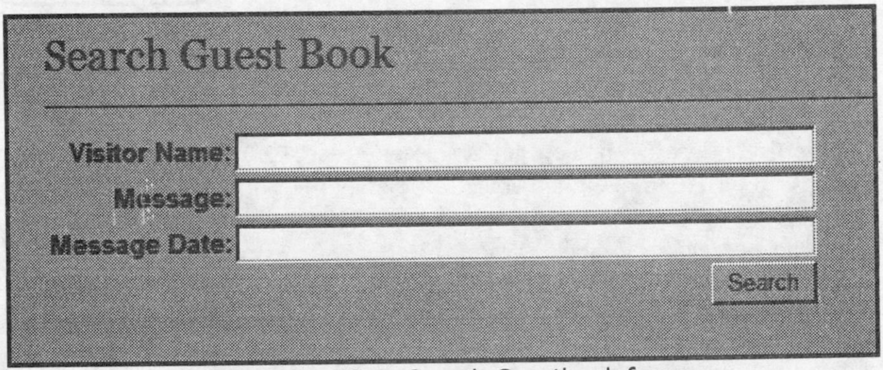

Diagram 18.1: Search Guestbook form

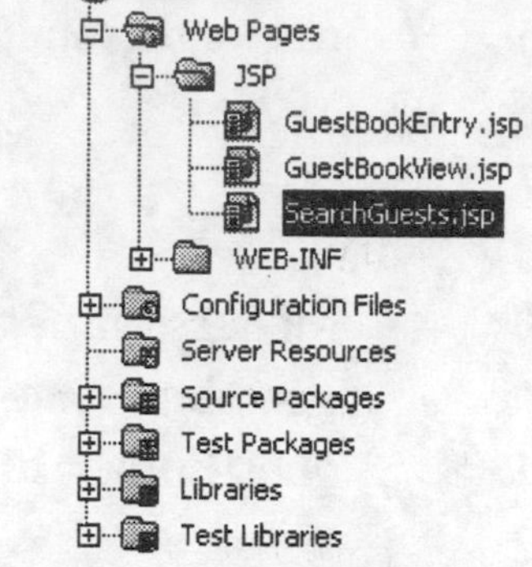

The user can key in either of them or all and click **Search**.

Search when clicked should search and retrieve all the records based on the search criteria keyed in.

To achieve this, open the GuestBook application in the NetBeans IDE.

Add a new JSP called SearchGuests.jsp.

Add the following code spec to that file:

```
<%@page contentType="text/html" pageEncoding="UTF-8" import="org.hibernate.SessionFactory,
org.hibernate.cfg.Configuration, org.hibernate.Session, org.hibernate.Transaction, java.util.List,
java.util.Iterator, myApp.Guestbook, org.hibernate.Criteria, org.hibernate.criterion.Example" %>
<!DOCTYPE html PUBLIC "-//W3C//DTD HTML 4.01 Transitional//EN"
"http://www.w3.org/TR/html4/loose.dtd">
<%!
   SessionFactory sessionFactory;
   org.hibernate.Session hibSession;
   List<Guestbook> guestbook;
%>

<%
   sessionFactory = new Configuration().configure().buildSessionFactory();
   hibSession = sessionFactory.openSession();
   Transaction tx = null;

   String submit = request.getParameter("btnSubmit");
   if(submit != null && ("Search").equals(submit)) {
      try {
         hibSession.beginTransaction();
         Criteria criteria = hibSession.createCriteria(Guestbook.class);
         Guestbook g = new Guestbook();
         g.setVisitorName("%"+request.getParameter("guest")+"%");
         g.setMessage("%"+request.getParameter("message")+"%");
         g.setMessageDate("%"+request.getParameter("messageDate")+"%");
         Example example = Example.create(g)
            .excludeZeroes()          //exclude zero valued properties
            .ignoreCase()             //perform case insensitive string comparisons
            .enableLike();            //use like for string comparisons
         criteria.add(example);
         guestbook = criteria.list();
```

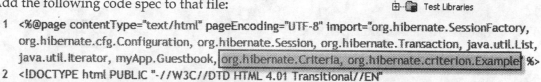

Example By Query

```
        }
        catch (RuntimeException e) {
            throw e;
        }
    }
    hibSession.close();
%>
<html>
    <head>
        <meta http-equiv="Content-Type" content="text/html;charset=ISO-8859-1">
        <title>Guest Book</title>
    </head>
    <body bgcolor="pink">
        <table border="0" cellpadding="0" cellspacing="0" align="center" width="760">
            <tr>
                <td>
                    <table border="0" cellpadding="0" cellspacing="0" width="100%">
                        <tr>
                            <td valign="top" align="left" style="padding-right:0px; padding-left:0px;
                            padding-bottom:0px; font:24px/30px Georgia; width:228px; color:#786e4e;
                            padding-top:0px; height:37px;">
                                Search Guest Book
                            </td>
                        </tr>
                    </table>
                </td>
            </tr>
            <tr align="left" valign="top">
                <td height="20">
                    <hr />
                </td>
            </tr>
            <tr>
                <td>
                    <form method="post">
                        <table border="0" cellpadding="0" cellspacing="2">
                            <tr>
                                <td align="right">
                                    <font style="font-size:15px; font-family:Arial,Times,serif;
                                    font-weight:bold;">Visitor Name:</font>
                                </td>
                                <td>
```

```
                        <input name="guest" maxlength="25" size="50" />
                    </td>
                </tr>
                <tr>
                    <td align="right">
                        <font style="font-size:15px; font-family:Arial,Times,serif;
                        font-weight:bold;">Message:</font>
                    </td>
                    <td>
                        <input name="message" maxlength="25" size="50" />
                    </td>
                </tr>
                <tr>
                    <td align="right">
                        <font style="font-size:15px; font-family:Arial,Times,serif;
                        font-weight:bold;">Message Date:</font>
                    </td>
                    <td>
                        <input name="messageDate" maxlength="25" size="50" />
                    </td>
                </tr>
                <tr>
                    <td colspan="2" align="right">
                        <input type="submit" name="btnSubmit" value="Search" />
                    </td>
                </tr>
            </table>
        </form>
    </td>
  </tr>
</table>
<table border="0" cellpadding="0" cellspacing="0" align="center" width="100%">
  <%
    if(guestbook != null){
      Iterator iterator = guestbook.iterator();
      while (iterator.hasNext()) {
        Guestbook objGb = (Guestbook) iterator.next();
  %>
  <tr>
    <td style="font:12px/16px Georgia; color:#786e4e;">
      On <%=objGb.getMessageDate()%>,<br />
      <b><%=objGb.getVisitorName()%>:</b>
```

Search Results

```
            <%=objGb.getMessage()%>
            <br /><br />
          </td>
        </tr>
        <%
            }
          }
        %>
      </table>
    </body>
</html>
```

Run this file using the NetBeans IDE:

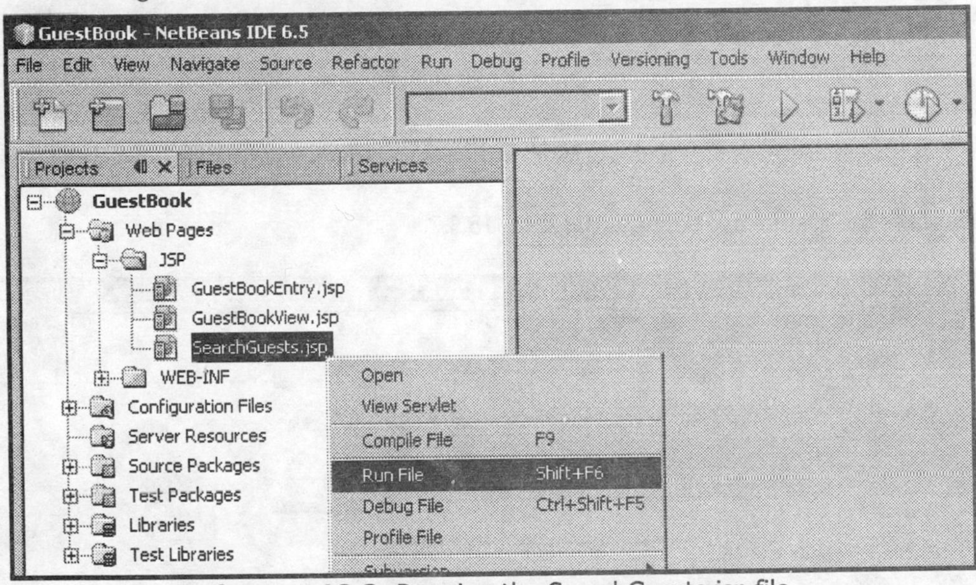

Diagram 18.2: Running the SearchGuests.jsp file

This brings up the JSP as shown in diagram 18.3.1.

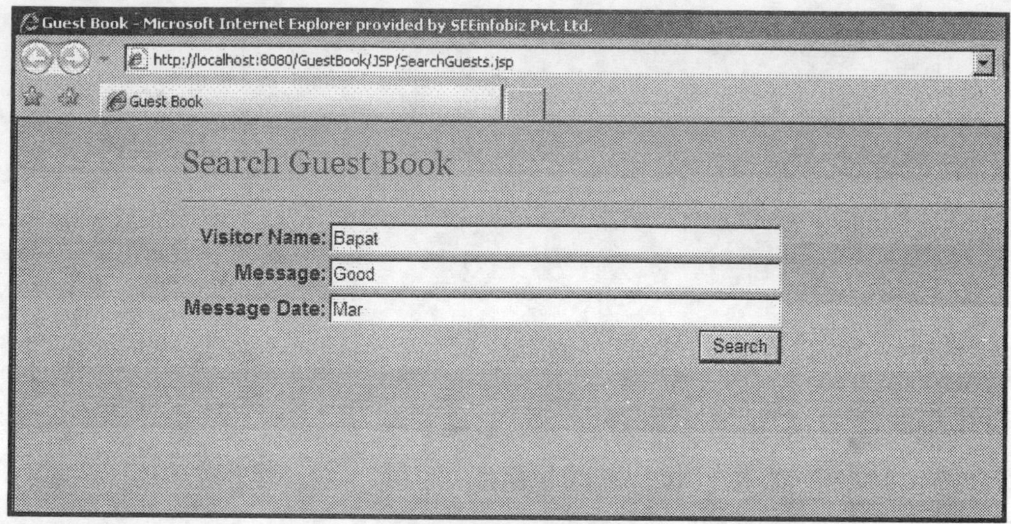

Diagram 18.3.1

Key in the search criteria and click Search.

This displays the results as shown in diagram 18.3.2.

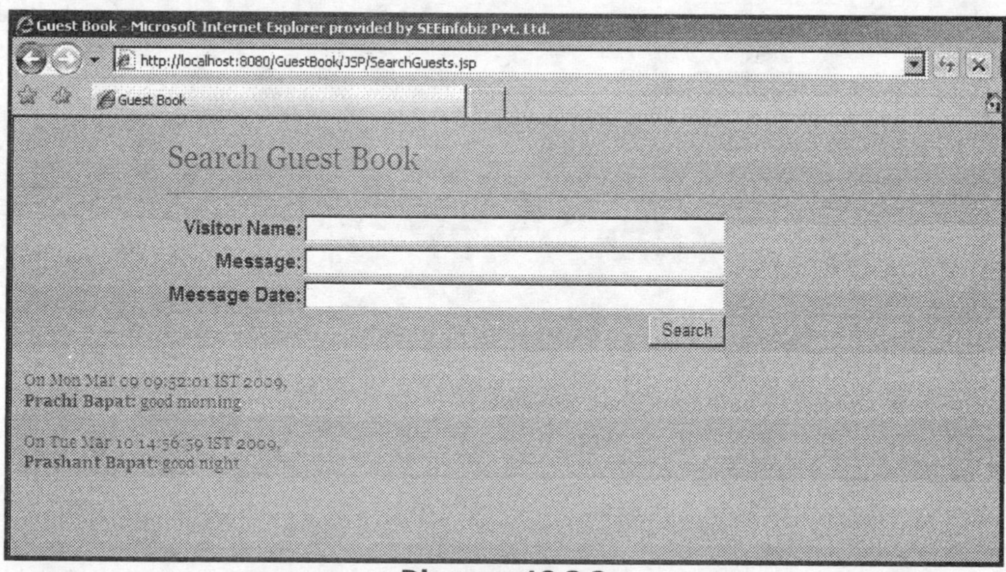

Diagram 18.3.2

The Book CDROM holds the complete application source code built using the NetBeans IDE for the following applications:

- GuestBook_Chap18_Criteria
- GuestBook_Chap18_QBE

These can be directly used by making appropriate changes [username/password] to the configuration file.

SECTION V: THE HIBERNATE QUERY LANGUAGE

Pagination

Pagination is the very common requirement for a lot of enterprise Web applications.

A typical requirement of pagination would be when thousands of records are retrieved from the database. If all these records are loaded by the application into memory and displayed at the same time, the application would be very slow. The application therefore requires to:

- Page through the database query result set
- Retrieve only the results to be displayed one chunk at a time
- Return an appropriate page to the user

Hibernate provides a pagination solution that works well on most major databases.

For example,

- In MySQL, the LIMIT keyword allows providing an offset and a length in the query and MySQL can provide a window of the data
- In Oracle, ROWNUM can be used to achieve the same

- In HSQLDB database, TOP and LIMIT can be used to achieve the same

A typical LIMIT query in MySQL:

```
SELECT * FROM Books LIMIT 100 10
```

This query retrieves 10 records beginning from 100 up to 109.

A typical Web application that requires pagination would:

- Provide a page selection [1 2 3]
- Based on the page number the user selects
  - Change the query's LIMIT clause

  For example, the user chooses the second page:

  ```
  SELECT * FROM Books LIMIT 10 10
  ```
- Run the query
- Return the appropriate records to the client

Every time the records are returned to the user, a typical pagination feature will also display the total result size:

```
SELECT COUNT(*) FROM Books
```

This count also helps the developer to calculate the total number of pages based on the total number of records.

For example, if the application chooses to display 10 records per page and the count of total records is 100, then the total number of pages would be calculated as:

Pages = No. Of Records / Records Per Page [Pages = 100 / 10 which results in 10 pages]

This calculation is done on every user request to ensure that the user is provided an up-to-date result.

Unfortunately, not all databases support pagination [LIMIT or ROWNUM] functionality.

Hibernate comes in help for pagination. The Query as well as the Criteria interface supports pagination.

Methods Of Pagination

In Hibernate, there are two methods of the Query [as well as the Criteria] interface that allow pagination.

The setFirstResult() Method

The setFirstResult() method represents the first row in the result set. It takes an integer as its parameter and starts displaying the records from that particular record of the table.

Suppose, a table contains 100 records and the developer wants to display data from the 20th record:

```
query.setFirstResult(20);
```

The above code spec returns records starting from the twentieth row. This is the first parameter of the **LIMIT** clause:

```
SELECT * FROM Books LIMIT 20 10
```

The setMaxResults() Method

The setMaxResults() method allows retrieving a fix number of records. It takes an integer as its parameter and retrieves only that many records.

Suppose, a table contains 100 records and the developer wants to display only 10 records at a time, the following code spec is written:

```
query.setMaxResults(10);
```

The above code spec returns only 10 records in a page at a time. This is the second parameter of the **LIMIT** clause:

```
SELECT * FROM Books LIMIT 20 10
```

Example

Using the Query interface:

```
Query query = session.createQuery("FROM Books");
query.setFirstResult(20);
```

```
query.setMaxResults(10);
List booksPage = query.list();
```

Using the Criteria interface:

```
Criteria criteria = session.createCriteria(Books.class);
criteria.setFirstResult(20);
criteria.setMaxResults(10);
List booksPage = criteria.list();
```

In either case, the HQL query remains unchanged, only the values need to be modified. In the application, the values are changed dynamically based on the user selection.

Building Web Application With Pagination Support

Let's bring in the pagination support in the Guestbook application [created earlier in *Chapter 03: Writing The First Application*].

The pagination after it is applied, fetches first ten records and provides links to other pages for the remaining records.

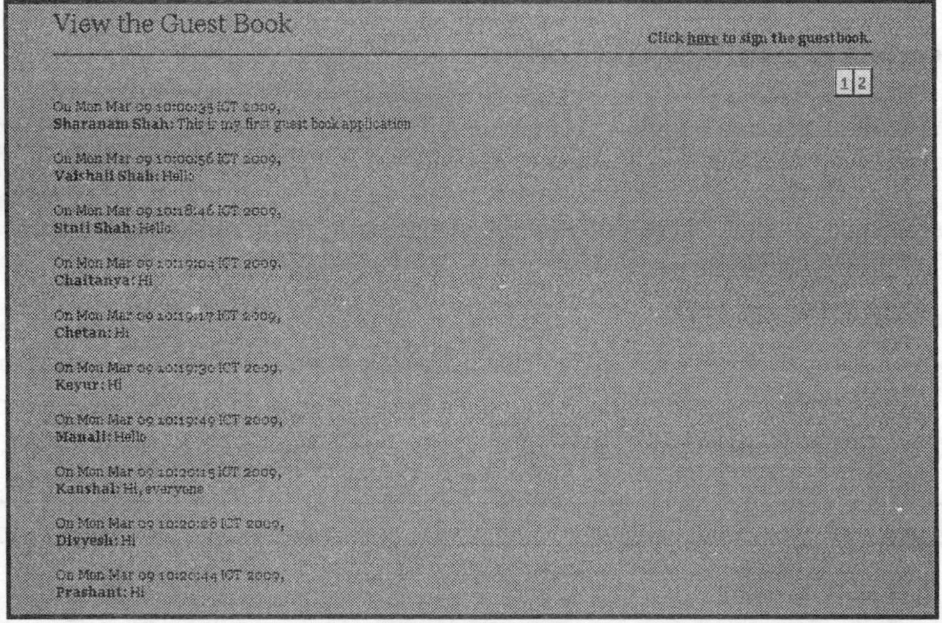

Diagram 19.1

The pages are identified using page numbers which are hyperlinks for allowing the user to navigate across pages.

To create the GuestBook application from scratch, refer to *Chapter 03: Writing The First Application*.

In the GuestBook application, the code spec for pagination is written in the GuestBookView.jsp file. Hence, this file needs to be edited to now include the pagination code spec.

Edit the GuestBookView.jsp as shown below:

```
<%@page contentType="text/html" pageEncoding="UTF-8" import="org.hibernate.SessionFactory,
org.hibernate.cfg.Configuration, org.hibernate.Session, org.hibernate.Transaction, java.util.List,
java.util.Iterator, myApp.Guestbook" %>
<!DOCTYPE HTML PUBLIC "-//W3C//DTD HTML 4.01 Transitional//EN"
  "http://www.w3.org/TR/html4/loose.dtd">
<%!
   SessionFactory sessionFactory;
   org.hibernate.Session hibSession;
   List<Guestbook> guestbook;
%>

<%
   sessionFactory = new Configuration().configure().buildSessionFactory();
   hibSession = sessionFactory.openSession();
   Transaction tx = null;

   String submit = request.getParameter("btnSubmit");
   if(submit != null && ("Submit").equals(submit)) {
      Guestbook gb = new Guestbook();
      try {
         tx = hibSession.beginTransaction();

         String guest = request.getParameter("guest");
         String message = request.getParameter("message");
         String messageDate = new java.util.Date().toString();
         gb.setVisitorName(guest);
         gb.setMessage(message);
         gb.setMessageDate(messageDate);

```

```
            hibSession.save(gb);
            tx.commit();
        }
        catch (RuntimeException e) {
            if(tx != null) tx.rollback();
            throw e;
        }
        response.sendRedirect("GuestBookView.jsp");
    }

    try {
        String pageNo = request.getParameter("page");
        if(pageNo == null)
            pageNo = "1";

        hibSession.beginTransaction();
        guestbook = hibSession.createQuery("from Guestbook")
                .setFirstResult((Integer.parseInt(pageNo)-1)*10)
                .setMaxResults(10)
                .list();
    }
    catch (RuntimeException e) {
        throw e;
    }
    hibSession.close();
%>
<html>
    <head>
        <meta http-equiv="Content-Type" content="text/html;charset=ISO-8859-1">
        <title>Guest Book</title>
    </head>
    <body bgcolor="pink">
        <table border="0" cellpadding="0" cellspacing="0" align="center" width="760">
            <tr>
                <td>
                    <table border="0" cellpadding="0" cellspacing="0" width="100%">
                        <tr>
                            <td width="60%" valign="top" align="left" style="padding-right:0px;
                            padding-left:0px; padding-bottom:0px; font:24px/30px Georgia; width:228px;
                            color:#786e4e; padding-top:0px; height:37px;">
                                View the Guest Book
                            </td>
                            <td valign="bottom" align="right" style="font:12px/16px Georgia, serif;
                            color:#786e4e;">
```

Add this

Remove this

```
                    <b>Click <a href="<%=request.getContextPath()%>/JSP/GuestBookEntry.jsp">
                    here</a> to sign the guestbook.</b>
                </td>
            </tr>
        </table>
    </td>
</tr>
<tr align="left" valign="top">
    <td height="20">
        <hr />
    </td>
</tr>
```

Add this

```
<tr>
    <td align="right">
        <%
            int totalPages = 0;
            try {
                hibSession.beginTransaction();
                String totalRecords = hibSession.createSQLQuery("SELECT COUNT(*) AS Total
                FROM GuestBook")
                        .addScalar("Total")
                        .uniqueResult()
                        .toString();
                totalPages = (int) Math.ceil(Double.parseDouble(totalRecords)/10);
            }
            catch(Exception e) {
                out.println("Error while fetching " + e);
            }
        %>
        <table border="1" cellpadding="4" cellspacing="0">
            <tr>
            <%
                for(int i=1; i<=totalPages; i++) {
            %>
                <td align="center" width="2px" style="border:#c3bca4 1px solid;
                background:#efebde; font-family:sans-serif; font-size:12px; font-weight:bolder;
                text-align:center; vertical-align:middle;">
                    <a href="GuestBookView.jsp?page=<%=i%>"><%=i%></a>
                </td>
            <%
                }
            %>
            </tr>
        </table>
```

```
            </td>
        </tr>
        <tr>
            <td>
                <table border="0" cellpadding="0" cellspacing="0" align="center" width="100%">
                <%
                    Iterator iterator = guestbook.iterator();
                    while (iterator.hasNext()) {
                        Guestbook objGb = (Guestbook) iterator.next();
                %>
                    <tr>
                        <td style="font:12px/16px Georgia; color:#786e4e;">
                            On <%=objGb.getMessageDate()%>,<br />
                            <b><%=objGb.getVisitorName()%>:</b>
                            <%=objGb.getMessage()%>
                            <br /><br />
                        </td>
                    </tr>
                <%
                    }
                %>
                </table>
            </td>
        </tr>
    </table>
  </body>
</html>
<%
    hibSession.close();
%>
```

Add this

REMINDER

The **GuestBook** code spec is available on this book's accompanying CDROM.

Explanation:

```
hibSession.beginTransaction();
String totalRecords = hibSession.createSQLQuery("SELECT COUNT(*) AS Total FROM GuestBook")
    .addScalar("Total")
    .uniqueResult()
    .toString();
totalPages = (int) Math.ceil(Double.parseDouble(totalRecords)/10);
```

Here, using an HQL query, the total number of records available in the GuestBook table is retrieved.

Based on this value, the total number of pages is calculated.

```
totalPages = (int) Math.ceil(Double.parseDouble(totalRecords)/10);
```

Using an HTML TABLE, the page links are created.

```
<table border="1" cellpadding="4" cellspacing="0">
  <tr>
  <%
    for(int i=1; i<=totalPages; i++) {
  %>
    <td align="center" width="2px" style="border:#c3bca4 1px solid; background:#efebde; font-family:sans-serif;
    font-size:12px; font-weight:bolder; text-align:center; vertical-align:middle;">
      <a href="GuestBookView.jsp?page=<%=i%>"><%=i%></a>
    </td>
  <%
    }
  %>
  </tr>
</table>
```

The columns of the table are dynamically created using a FOR loop, which iterates through the total number of pages calculated earlier.

For every page number, a column is created that holds the page number as a hyper link that points to **GuestBookView.jsp**. This page is invoked on the click of the hyper link.

The hyperlink passes page number [page] to **GuestBookView.jsp** as the additional information. This information helps **GuestBookView.jsp** to understand the page that has to be retrieved and displayed.

```
String pageNo = request.getParameter("page");
if(pageNo == null)
  pageNo = "1";
```

The above code spec retrieves the page number, if it was passed.

If it was not passed, then page number is set to retrieve the first page. This happens when **GuestBookView.jsp** is invoked for the very first time, after the user enters the data and submits.

Based on the page number, the pagination is done, using setFirstResult() and setMaxResults().

```
guestbook = hibSession.createQuery("from Guestbook")
        .setFirstResult((Integer.parseInt(pageNo)-1)*10)
        .setMaxResults(10)
        .list();
```

Running The GuestBook Application

Now that the application is ready, let's run this application.

To run the GuestBook application, refer to *Chapter 03: Writing The First Application*.

The GuestBookEntry.jsp page is served in the Web browser as shown in diagram 19.2.1.

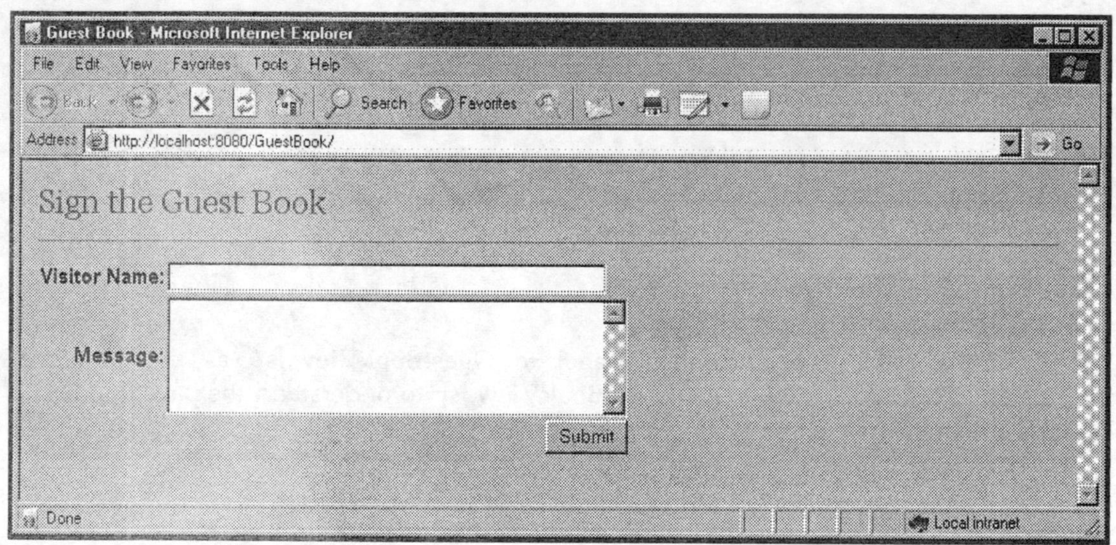

Diagram 19.2.1: The application run in the Web browser

Enter the name and the comments in the Name and Message fields as shown in diagram 19.2.2.

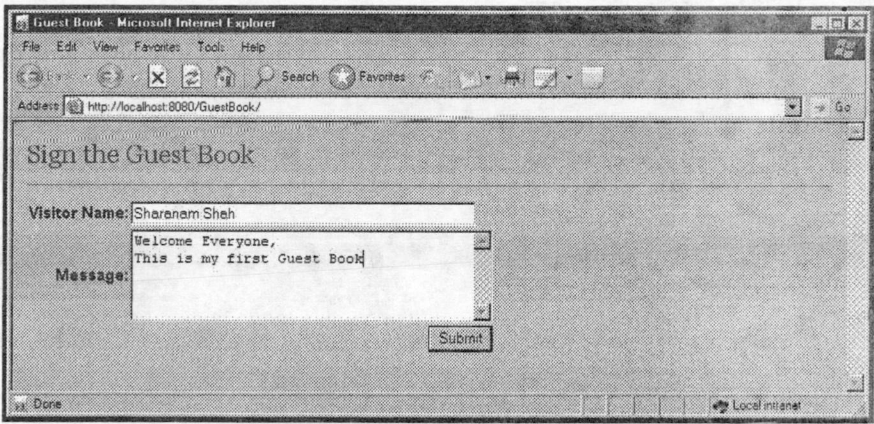

Diagram 19.2.2: Entering data

Click Submit. This displays the already existing messages [entered by others who visited the site before] along with the newly added message.

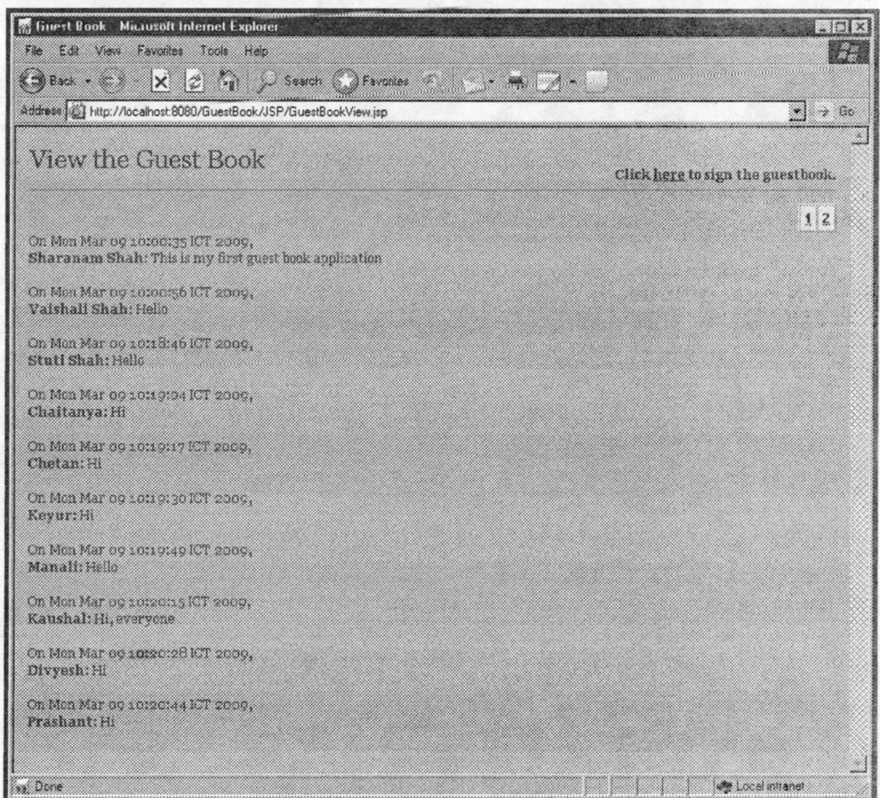

Diagram 19.2.3: Viewing data

The GuestBook now displays page numbers 1 2 as hyperlinks for allowing the user to navigate across the pages.

The database holds more than 10 records so the second page number link appears. When the second page number link is clicked, the page content changes as shown in diagram 19.2.4.

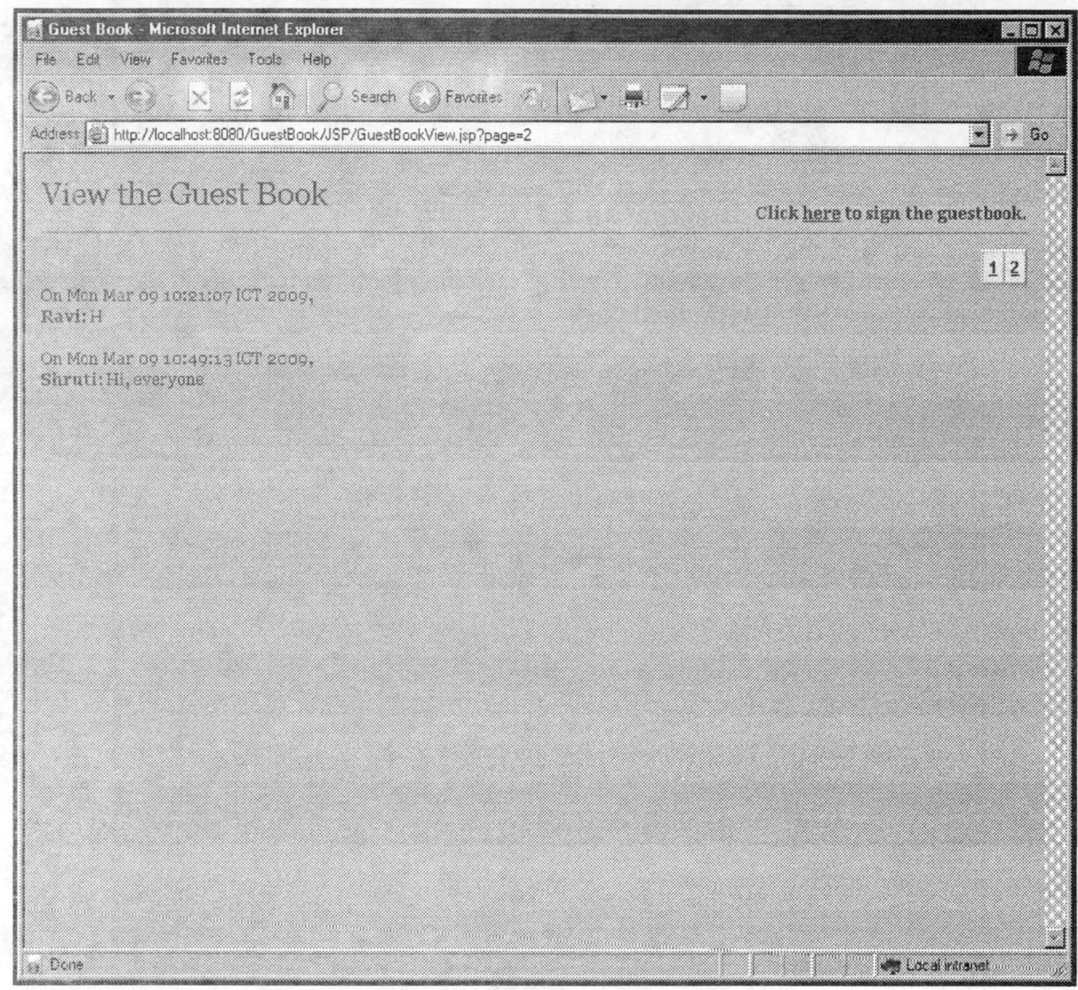

Diagram 19.2.4: Viewing data

Click **here** link available on the top right corner of the page to go back to the Guest Book data entry form.

The Book CDROM holds the complete application source code built using the NetBeans IDE for the following application:

- GuestBook_Chap19

This can be directly used by making appropriate changes [username/password] to the configuration file.

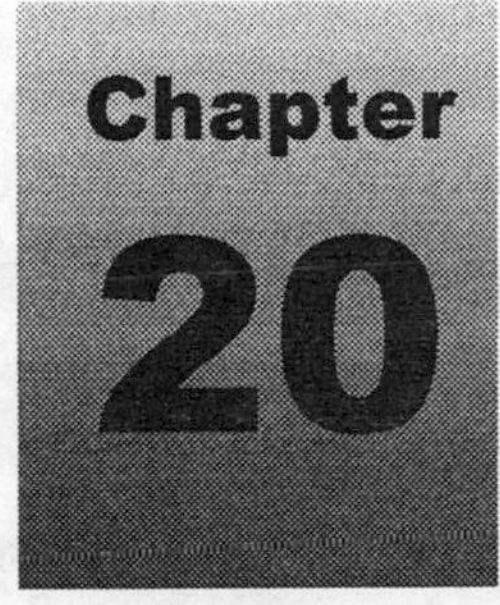

SECTION V: THE HIBERNATE QUERY INTERFACE

Named Queries

Sometimes it is required to store queries outside the application to:

- Avoid query string literals scattered all over the Java code
- Make the Java code spec a lot cleaner and more compact
- Make application maintenance easier
- Share queries amongst several objects

This can be easily achieved using Hibernate.

Hibernate supports a feature called **Named Queries**. This allows writing **queries** in the mapping document(s) and use them in the Java code spec by a **name**.

Named queries may contain HQL as well as the native SQL queries. The Java code spec calling the named query need not know the kind of query [SQL or HQL].

Defining The Query In The Mapping Document

The queries can be defined either inside the <hibernate-mapping> element or inside a <class> element.

If the query is defined inside the <hibernate-mapping> element, then the name of the query requires a **global** unique name.

If the query is defined inside the <class> element, the query is automatically made unique by preceding the query name with the fully qualified name of the class.

For example, **com.development.**Books.

Using The <query> Element

The query is defined by using the <query> element in the mapping document.

Example

Retrieve the details of all the available Books.

Solution:

```
<query name="findAllBooks">
   FROM Books
</query>
```

The above code spec defines a named query **findAllBooks** which can be invoked by the application's code spec using this name.

Example

Retrieve the Book details of all those books written by a particular Author

Solution:

```
<query name="findBooksByAuthor">
<! [CDATA[
   FROM Books book WHERE book.AuthorNo = :AuthorNo
]]></query>
```

OR

The WHERE clause can also be specified using positional parameters.

Solution:

```
<query name="findBooksByAuthor">
<! [CDATA[
   FROM Books book WHERE book.AuthorNo = ?
]]></query>
```

In the above code spec, HQL query is embedded in the CDATA section.

XML does not accept characters such as <, > and &. These characters need to be escaped. Hence, CDATA is used which protects the queries from inferring with the XML parser and the developer is free from worries about these characters breaking the XML.

Using The <sql-query> Element

The native SQL query can also be defined using the <sql-query> element in the mapping document.

When HQL query is used, Hibernate handles that mapping behind the scenes, as it knows which objects went in.

With SQL, the return types need to be specified. <return-scalar> or <return> elements can be used to define the return type.

Hibernate converts the JDBC result set into an array of objects, just like the HQL query. Functionally, both of these are identical.

Example

Retrieve the highest book price.

Solution:

```
<sql-query name="findBooksByCost">
   <return-scalar column="maxPrice" type="int"/>
   <! [CDATA[
      SELECT MAX(book.PRICE) AS maxPrice
```

```
  ]]>
</sql-query>
```

In the above example, <return-scalar> element is used to return the type as a column named **maxPrice** with a type of **int**.

Example

Retrieve the details of Books of a particular Author

Solution:

```
<sql-query name="findBooksByAuthors">
  <return alias="1" class="Books"/>
  <! [CDATA[
    SELECT {1.*} FROM Books {1} WHERE AuthorNo = :AuthorNo
  ]]>
</sql-query>
```

In the above example, the **<return>** element is used to describe the resulting objects.

Invoking The Query In the Application Code Spec

Once the query has been named in the mapping document, it has to be invoked in the application code spec.

The **getNamedQuery()** method is used to obtain a Query interface for a named query.

Example

If the query is a simple one which holds no WHERE clause or any other clauses, then the following code spec is used:

```
List allBooks = session.getNamedQuery("findAllBooks").list();
```

The getNamedQuery() method accepts a string that identifies the name of the query defined in mapping document.

Once the query is invoked from the mapping document, the Query object can be used as it's normally used.

Example

If the query holds a named parameter, then the following code spec is used:

```
Query query = session.getNamedQuery("findBooksByAuthor")
List authorBooks = query.setString("AuthorNo", AuthorNo).list();
```

If the parameter was positional, then:

```
Query query = session.getNamedQuery("findBooksByAuthor")
List authorBooks = query.setString(0, AuthorNo).list();
```

GuestBook Using Named Queries

Let's implement named queries in the GuestBook application created earlier [Guestbook created in *Chapter 03: Writing The First Application*]. Open the application in the NetBeans IDE.

Edit the Mapping document [Guestbook.hbm] as:

```
<?xml version="1.0"?>
<!DOCTYPE hibernate-mapping PUBLIC "-//Hibernate/Hibernate Mapping DTD 3.0//EN"
"http://hibernate.sourceforge.net/hibernate-mapping-3.0.dtd">
<hibernate-mapping>
   <class name="myApp.Guestbook" table="guestbook">
      <id name="visitorNo" type="java.lang.Integer">
         <column name="VisitorNo" />
         <generator class="identity" />
      </id>
      <property name="visitorName" type="string">
         <column name="VisitorName" length="50" />
      </property>
      <property name="message" type="string">
         <column name="Message" length="100" />
      </property>
      <property name="messageDate" type="string">
         <column name="MessageDate" length="40" />
      </property>
   </class>
   <query name="findAllGuests">from Guestbook</query>
</hibernate-mapping>
```

Named Query

To invoke this named query edit the JSP [GuestBookView.jsp] as:

```
try {
    tx = hibSession.beginTransaction();

    String guest = request.getParameter("guest");
    String message = request.getParameter("message");
    String messageDate = new java.util.Date().toString();
    gb.setVisitorName(guest);
    gb.setMessage(message);
    gb.setMessageDate(messageDate);

    hibSession.save(gb);
    tx.commit();
}
catch (RuntimeException e) {
    if(gb != null) tx.rollback();
    throw e;
}
response.sendRedirect("GuestBookView.jsp");
}

try {
    hibSession.beginTransaction();
    guestbook = hibSession.createQuery("FROM Guestbook").list();
    guestbook = hibSession.getNamedQuery("findAllGuests").list();
}
catch (RuntimeException e) {
    throw e;
}
```

Remove this

Add this

Run the application to see this working. This book's accompanying CDROM holds the code spec.

Named Queries Using Annotations

Named queries can also be defined using annotations.

Example

@NamedQuery(name="findAllGuests", query="from Guestbook")

Let's try this in the annotations based application created earlier [Guestbook created in *Chapter 11: Annotations*].

Open the application in the NetBeans IDE.

Edit the POJO [Guestbook.java] as:

```
package myApp;

import javax.persistence.Column;
import javax.persistence.Entity;
import javax.persistence.GeneratedValue;
import static javax.persistence.GenerationType.IDENTITY;
import javax.persistence.Id;
import javax.persistence.Table;
import org.hibernate.annotations.NamedQuery;

@Entity
@NamedQuery(name="findAllGuests",query="from Guestbook")
@Table(name="guestbook",catalog="guestbook")
public class Guestbook  implements java.io.Serializable {
    private Integer visitorNo;
    private String visitorName;
    private String message;
    private String messageDate;

    public Guestbook() {
    }

    public Guestbook(String visitorName, String message, String messageDate) {
        this.visitorName = visitorName;
```

Import required to support Named Queries

Edit the JSP [GuestBookView.jsp] to invoke this named query [as shown earlier].

Run the application to see this working.

The Book CDROM holds the complete application source code built using the NetBeans IDE for the following applications:

- GuestBook_Chap20_Mapping
- GuestBook_Chap20_Annotations

These can be directly used by making appropriate changes [username/password] to the configuration file.

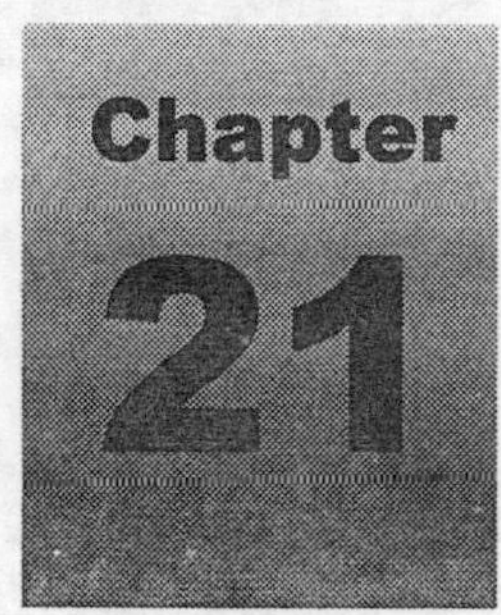

SECTION V: THE HIERNATE QUERY LANGUAGE

Native SQL Queries

Hibernate does not force the developer to use HQL as the only way to perform database operations. **Native SQL** can also be used as an alternative using the **createSQLQuery()** method. In this case, Hibernate takes care of the mapping from result sets to the objects.

Native SQL is handwritten SQL code spec for database operations. Using the Native SQL support, stored procedures can also be invoked. The Native SQL support can be very useful when migrating SQL/JDBC based application [that uses handwritten SQL] to Hibernate.

The following are a few reasons why native SQL is required:

- A lot of databases support special features such as query hints or the CONNECT keyword in Oracle. These features are not supported via the dialect in HQL
- Invoking stored procedures is not supported by HQL which can be easily done using native SQL support

The native SQL support is provided by the **org.hibernate.SQLQuery interface**. This interface controls the execution of native SQL queries.

To use native SQL queries, the **createSQLQuery() method** of the Session interface is used.

Syntax:

```
public SQLQuery createSQLQuery(String queryString)
  throws HibernateException
```

Example:

```
session.createSQLQuery("SELECT * FROM Books");
```

Here, an SQL SELECT query is passed to the createSQLQuery method. This query retrieves all the records from the Books table.

After the SQL query is passed as a string to the createSQLQuery() method, the SQL result has to be associated with one of the following:

- A scalar result
- An existing Hibernate entity
- A Join

The SQLQuery interface provides addEntity(), addJoin() and addScalar() methods to achieve the association.

Scalar Queries

The most basic SQL query is to retrieve a list of values.

Example:

```
session.createSQLQuery("SELECT * FROM Books").list();
```

Example:

```
session.createSQLQuery("SELECT BookNo, BookName, ISBN, Synopsis
                FROM Books").list();
```

Both the above queries will return a List of Object arrays with scalar values for each column in the Books table.

Hibernate uses ResultSetMetadata to assume the actual order and types of the returned scalar values.

REMINDER

ResultSetMetadata is an object that can be used to retrieve information about the types and properties of the columns in a ResultSet object.

To avoid the overhead of using ResultSetMetadata or simply to be more explicit in what is returned, use **addScalar()** method.

Example:

```
session.createSQLQuery("SELECT * FROM Books")
        .addScalar("BookNo", Hibernate.LONG)
        .addScalar("BookName", Hibernate.STRING)
        .addScalar("ISBN", Hibernate.STRING)
        .addScalar("Synopsis", Hibernate.STRING).list();
```

In the above example, the query specifies:

- The SQL query
- The columns and types to return

In the above example:

```
SELECT * FROM Books
```

Is the regular SQL query.

```
session.createSQLQuery()
```

An object of SQLQuery is created.

```
.addScalar("BookNo", Hibernate.LONG)
.addScalar("BookName", Hibernate.STRING)
.addScalar("ISBN", Hibernate.STRING)
.addScalar("Synopsis", Hibernate.STRING)
```

A scalar mapping is added with the built in **LONG** and **STRING** types.

```
.list()
```

The result is a List with four objects.

Hibernate explicitly retrieves the BookNo, BookName, ISBN and Synopsis column as Long, String, String and String, respectively from the underlying ResultSet.

Hibernate returns four columns even though the SQL query holds * [asterix] to retrieve all columns from the Books table.

The type information can also be skipped for all or some of the scalars.

Example:

```
session.createSQLQuery("SELECT * FROM Books")
        .addScalar("BookNo", Hibernate.LONG)
        .addScalar("BookName")
        .addScalar("ISBN")
        .addScalar("Synopsis").list();
```

This is the same previous example, but with a difference in the addScalar() method.

Only BookNo is explicitly set as LONG.

In such a scenario, Hibernate uses the ResultSetMetaData to determine the type of BookName, ISBN and Synopsis.

Entity Queries

The earlier examples were all about returning scalar values i.e. basically returning the raw values from the ResultSet.

It is also possible to map an entity to the SQL query. To retrieve entity objects from a native SQL query, the addEntity() method is used.

The addEntity() method accepts either a class name or an entity name.

Example:

```
session.createSQLQuery("SELECT * FROM Books")
        .addEntity(Books.class).list();
```

Hibernate reads the result-set of the SQL query and tries to discover the column names and types as defined in the mapping metadata. If the column BookName is returned and it's mapped to the Name property of the Books class, Hibernate knows how to populate that property and finally returns fully loaded business object.

Example:

```
session.createSQLQuery("SELECT BookNo, BookName, ISBN, Synopsis
                        FROM Books").addEntity(Books.class).list();
```

Here, **Books** is mapped as a class with the columns BookNo, BookName, ISBN and Synopsis.

Both the above queries return a List where each element is a Books entity.

If all the columns in the result have the same names as in the mapping definition of Books, simply specifying an alias - {books.*} in the SELECT clause also works. This alias allows Hibernate to map the database columns back to the object properties.

Hibernate replaces {books.*} with all the column names in the mapping definition.

Example:

```
String sqlQuery = "SELECT {books.*} FROM Books books";
Query query = session.createSQLQuery(sqlQuery)
                     .addEntity("books", Books.class).list();
```

Here, the SQL SELECT query includes a placeholder which names the table alias books and considers all columns of this table into the result.

```
.addEntity("books", Books.class).list();
```

This informs Hibernate that the placeholder for alias **book** refers to all columns that are needed to populate the **Books** entity **class**.

The column names and types are automatically determined by Hibernate during query execution and result assembling.

Join Queries

The native SQL support also allows Joins. This is useful as it helps avoid the possible extra roundtrip for initializing the proxy.

A Join can be specified using the addJoin() method. This method allows joining in an association or collection.

The addJoin() methods accepts an alias argument and a path to join.

Example:

```
String sqlQuery = "SELECT {books.*},
                    books.AuthorNo as {author.AuthorNo},
                    books.FirstName as {author.FirstName},
                    books.LastName as {author.LastName},
                    books.EmailAddress as {author.EmailAddress}
                    FROM Books books";
Query query = session.createSQLQuery(sqlQuery)
                    .addEntity("books", Books.class)
                    .addJoin("author", "books.author").list();
```

This SQL query extracts:

- All the Book table's columns values {book.*}
- The following associated Author table's column values:
    - AuthorNo [book.AuthorNo as {author.AuthorNo}]
    - FirstName [book.FirstName as {author.FirstName}]
    - LastName [book.LastName as {author.LastName}]
    - EmailAddress [book.EmailAddress as {author.EmailAddress}]

The Books table is associated to the Authors table using:

```
.addJoin("author", "books.author").list();
```

The addJoin() method informs Hibernate, that the author alias refers to columns that can be used to immediately populate the associated books of each author.

The addJoin() method accepts:

- **author** [the first argument] as the alias
- **books.author** [the second argument] as a path to join with

Since a Join is added, Hibernate ensures that the returned values of Book's have their associated Author properties fully initialized without any extra roundtrip to the database.

Aliases And Property

Hibernate allows using aliases in SQL queries:

- **{ObjectName.*}** - All properties on an object
- **{ObjectName.Property}** - A particular property on an object

For most queries the above two aliases are used. However, for advanced queries that deal with complex mappings such as composite properties, inheritance discriminators, collections and so on, Hibernate, provides specific aliases.

The following table shows the different aliases and their possible usages:

Simple Property	
Syntax	{[AliasName].[PropertyName]
Usage	{book.BookName}
Composite Property	
Syntax	{[aliasname].[componentname].[propertyname]}
Usage	{author.AuthorName.FirstName}
Discriminator of an Entity	
Syntax	{[aliasname].class}
Usage	{book.class}
All properties of an Entity	
Syntax	{[aliasname].*}
Usage	{book.*}
A Collection key	
Syntax	{[aliasname].key}
Usage	{book.key}
ID of the Collection	
Syntax	{[aliasname].if}
Usage	{bookID.id}

Element of the Collection	
Syntax	{[aliasname].element}
Usage	{book.element}
Property of the element in the Collection	
Syntax	{[aliasname].element.[PropertyName]}
Usage	{book.element.BookName}
All properties of the element in the Collection	
Syntax	{[aliasname].element.*}
Usage	{book.element.*}
All properties of the Collection	
Syntax	{[aliasname].*}
Usage	{book.*}

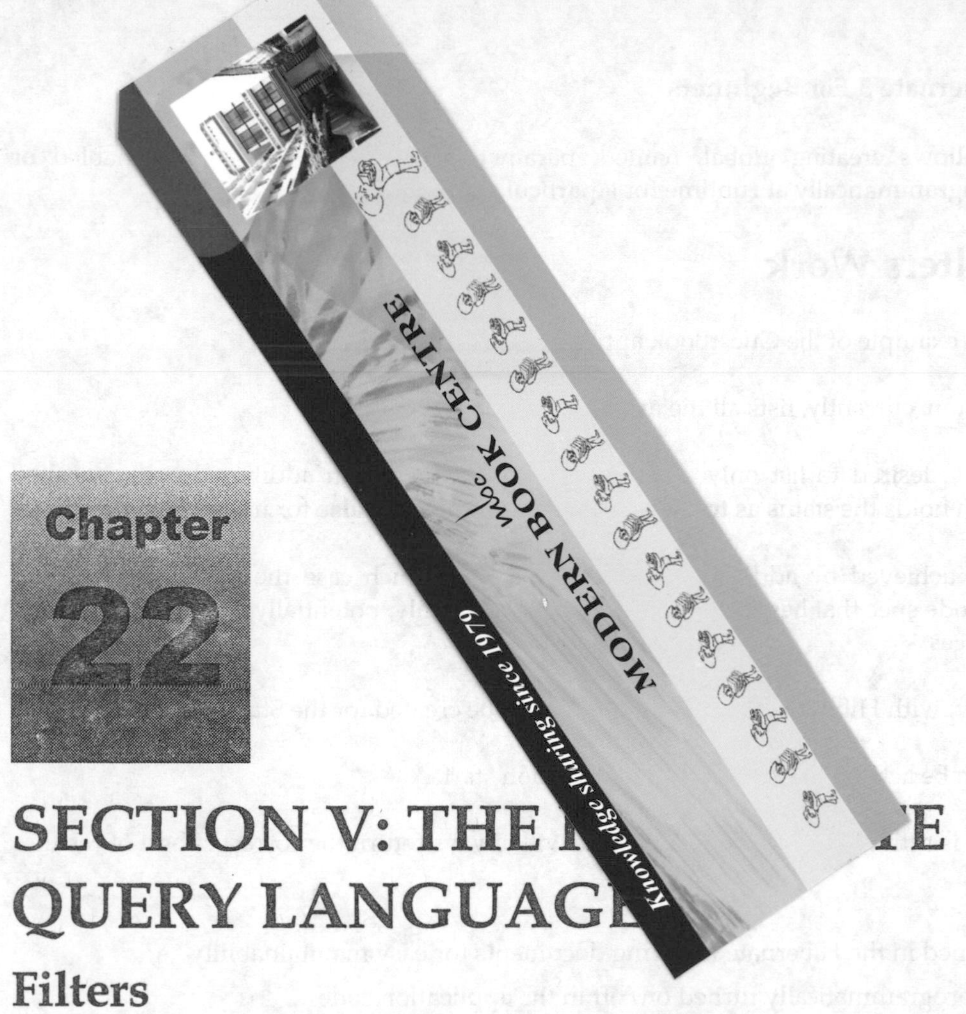

Chapter 22

SECTION V: THE [illegible]E QUERY LANGUAGE

Filters

Hibernate Filters provide something similar to what Database Views provide. Filters allow an application to programmatically restrict the view of the data in the database.

A typical use of Filters would be to make available only a subset of data to the application. For example, the application may only see:

- Data that belongs to the current date
- Users who are active
- Currently logged in user's data

The same subset can be achieved without using filters, but filters are an excellent solution to the following two problems:

- Security
- Personalization

Hibernate allows creating global, named, parameterized filters that can be enabled or disabled programmatically at runtime for a particular Hibernate session.

How Filters Work

Let's take an example of the GuestBook application created earlier.

The application, currently, lists all the available entries in the table.

Suppose it is desired to list only approved entries based on an additional column called **Status** which holds the status as **true** for approved entries and **false** for un-approved entries.

This can be achieved by adding a WHERE clause, in which case the developer ends up modifying code spec that has already been tested thoroughly, potentially changing it in many different places.

Alternatively, with Hibernate, a filter restriction can be created for the Status column.

The filter can be activated as soon as the application starts.

After a filter is activated, any SELECT queries will always return the correct subset of results.

Filters:

- Are defined in the Hibernate mapping documents for easy maintainability
- Can be programmatically turned on/off in the application code
- Can be parameterized
- Cannot be created at run time

Defining Filters

In order to use filters, they must first be defined and then attached to the appropriate mapping elements.

To define a filter, the <filter-def> element is used in the mapping document. These filter definitions must contain the name of the filter and the names and types of any filter parameters.

Filter parameters must be declared in the <filter-param> element. Filter parameters are similar to named parameters for HQL queries, as both require : **[colon]** before the parameter name.

The use of <filter-def> element within a <hibernate-mapping> element:

```
<hibernate-mapping>
  . . .
  <filter-def name="ApprovedState">
      <filter-param name="paramStatus" type="boolean" />
  </filter-def>
  . . .
</hibernate-mapping>
```

After defining the filter, it needs to be attached to:

- Either to a **class:**

```
<class name="Guestbook">
  . . .
  <filter name="ApprovedState" condition=":paramStatus = Status"/>
</class>
```

- Or a **collection:**

```
<set . . .>
  <filter name="ApprovedState" condition=":paramStatus = Status"/>
</set>
```

- Or even to both [or multiples of each] at the same time

The <filter> element is added inside a <class> and/or <set> element(s). This element has two attributes:

- **name:** It references a filter definition
- **condition:** It represents the WHERE clause in HQL

HINT

Each <filter> element must correspond to a <filter-def> element.

There can be more than one filter for each filter definition and each class can have more than one filter.

This extra level of abstraction allows defining all the filter parameters in one place. They, then, can be referred in the individual filter conditions.

Filter Interface

Whenever a Filter is used, org.hibernate.Filter interface needs to be imported:

```
import org.hibernate.Filter;
```

The Filter interface defines the user's view into enabled dynamic filters, allowing them to set filter parameter values.

The following are the methods of Filter interface:

The getFilterDefinition() Method

Syntax:

```
public FilterDefinition getFilterDefinition()
```

The getFilterDefinition() method retrieves a FilterDefinition object representing the filter metadata.

A FilterDefinition defines the global attributes of a dynamic filter. This information includes its name, its parameter's names and the parameter types.

The getName() Method

Syntax:

```
public String getName()
```

The getName() method retrieves the name of the filter.

The setParameter() Method

Syntax:

```
public Filter setParameter(String name, Object value)
```

The setParameter() method sets the named parameter's value for the filter.

The setParameter() method takes two arguments:

- **name:** Is the name of the parameter
- **value:** Is the value to be applied to the named parameter

The setParameterList() Method

Syntax:

```
public Filter setParameterList(String <Name>, Collection <Values>)
public Filter setParameterList(String <Name>, Object[] <Values>)
```

The setParameterList() methods sets the named parameter's value list for the filter.

The setParameterList() methods are useful for using IN clauses in the filters.

The setParameterList() method takes two arguments:

- **name:** Is the name of the parameter
- **values:** Is the value to be expanded into an SQL IN list

The validate() Method

Syntax:

```
public void validate() throws HibernateException
```

The validate() method performs validation of the filter state.

This is used to verify the state of the filter after its enablement and before its use.

The validate() method throws an HibernateException, if the state is not currently valid.

Enabling Or Disabling Filters

After the Filter interface is imported, the application has to programmatically activate or deactivate a filter for a given Hibernate session. Each session can have a different set of filters with different parameter values.

By default, sessions do not have any active filters. Filters must be explicitly enabled programmatically for each session.

The Session interface contains several methods for working with filters:

```
public Filter enableFilter(String <FilterName>)
public Filter getEnabledFilter(String <FilterName>)
public void disableFilter(String <FilterName>)
```

The **enableFilter() method** activates a specific filter and returns an instance of the Filter interface.

The **getEnableFilter() method** retrieves an already activated filter.

The **disableFilter() method** deactivates a specific filter.

The following code spec enables the **ApprovedState** filter defined earlier:

```
session.enableFilter("ApprovedState")
   .setParameter("paramStatus", new Boolean(true));
```

Implementing Filters In GuestBook

Let's use the GuestBook application created earlier. The application currently displays all the captured entries without any approval system. This is not a good practice. Usually, an administrator would view each and every entry and approve them prior they are shown to the visitors.

To implement this, add an additional column called **Status** in the **Guestbook** table.

This column will hold **true** for **approved** entries and **false otherwise.**

Column Name	Datatype	NOT NULL	AUTO INC	Flags		Default Value
VisitorNo	INTEGER	✔	✔	UNSIGNED	ZEROFILL	NULL
VisitorName	VARCHAR(50)			BINARY		NULL
Message	VARCHAR(100)			BINARY		NULL
MessageDate	VARCHAR(40)			BINARY		NULL
Status	TINYINT(1)			UNSIGNED	ZEROFILL	0

Note that the default value of this column is set to false i.e. **0**. Hence, all the new entries that will be inserted in this table will have Status as **false**. The administrator will have to manually update the Status to **true** for approving the desired entries.

Open the Guestbook application in the NetBeans IDE.

Defining And Attaching Filter

Edit the Guestbook.java file to hold the following code spec:

```
package myApp;

```

```
public class Guestbook  implements java.io.Serializable {
    private Integer visitorNo;
    private String visitorName;
    private String message;
    private String messageDate;
    private Boolean status;

    public Guestbook() {
    }

    public Guestbook(String visitorName, String message,
    String messageDate, Boolean status) {
      this.visitorName = visitorName;
      this.message = message;
      this.messageDate = messageDate;
      this.status = status;
    }

    public Integer getVisitorNo() {
       return this.visitorNo;
    }
    public void setVisitorNo(Integer visitorNo) {
       this.visitorNo = visitorNo;
    }

    public String getVisitorName() {
       return this.visitorName;
    }
    public void setVisitorName(String visitorName) {
       this.visitorName = visitorName;
    }

```

```
public String getMessage() {
    return this.message;
}
public void setMessage(String message) {
    this.message = message;
}

public String getMessageDate() {
    return this.messageDate;
}
public void setMessageDate(String messageDate) {
    this.messageDate = messageDate;
}

public Boolean getStatus() {
    return this.status;
}
public void setStatus(Boolean status) {
    this.status = status;
}
}
```

Edit the Guestbook.hbm.xml file to hold the following code spec:

```
<?xml version="1.0"?>
<!DOCTYPE hibernate-mapping PUBLIC "-//Hibernate/Hibernate Mapping DTD 3.0//EN"
"http://hibernate.sourceforge.net/hibernate-mapping-3.0.dtd">
<hibernate-mapping>
   <class name="myApp.Guestbook" table="guestbook" catalog="guestbook">
      <id name="visitorNo" type="java.lang.Integer">
         <column name="VisitorNo" />
         <generator class="identity" />
      </id>
      <property name="visitorName" type="string">
         <column name="VisitorName" length="50" />
```

```
        </property>
        <property name="message" type="string">
            <column name="Message" length="100" />
        </property>
        <property name="messageDate" type="string">
            <column name="MessageDate" length="40" />
        </property>
        <property name="status" type="java.lang.Boolean">
            <column name="Status" />
        </property>
        <filter name="ApprovedState" condition=":paramStatus = Status"/>
    </class>
    <filter-def name="ApprovedState">
        <filter-param name="paramStatus" type="boolean"/>
    </filter-def>
</hibernate-mapping>
```

New column and Filter Attachment

Filter Defined

Enabling Filter

After the filter is defined and attached, enable it. In the Guestbook application, **GuestBookView.jsp** holds the query.

Hence edit GuestBookView.jsp to enable filter:

```
<%@page contentType="text/html" pageEncoding="UTF-8" import="org.hibernate.SessionFactory,
org.hibernate.cfg.Configuration, org.hibernate.Session, org.hibernate.Transaction,
org.hibernate.Filter, java.util.List, java.util.Iterator, myApp.Guestbook" %>
<!DOCTYPE HTML PUBLIC "-//W3C//DTD HTML 4.01 Transitional//EN"
  "http://www.w3.org/TR/html4/loose.dtd">
<%!
    SessionFactory sessionFactory;
    org.hibernate.Session hibSession;
    List<Guestbook> guestbook;
%>

<%
    sessionFactory = new Configuration().configure().buildSessionFactory();
    hibSession = sessionFactory.openSession();
    Transaction tx = null;

    String submit = request.getParameter("btnSubmit");
```

Importing the Filter Interface

```
    if(submit != null && ("Submit").equals(submit))
    {
        Guestbook gb = new Guestbook();
        try
        {
            tx = hibSession.beginTransaction();

            String guest = request.getParameter("guest");
            String message = request.getParameter("message");
            String messageDate = new java.util.Date().toString();
            gb.setVisitorName(guest);
            gb.setMessage(message);
            gb.setMessageDate(messageDate);

            hibSession.save(gb);
            tx.commit();
        }
        catch (RuntimeException e)
        {
            if(tx != null) tx.rollback();
            throw e;
        }
        response.sendRedirect("GuestBookView.jsp");
    }

    try
    {
        hibSession.beginTransaction();
        Filter filter = hibSession.enableFilter("ApprovedState");
        filter.setParameter("paramStatus", new Boolean(true));
        guestbook = hibSession.createQuery("from Guestbook").list();
    }
    catch (RuntimeException e)
    {
        throw e;
    }

  hibSession.close();
%>
<html>
    <head>
        <meta http-equiv="Content-Type" content="text/html;charset=ISO-8859-1">
        <title>Guest Book</title>
```

Enabling Filter and passing

Now run this application. Key in an entry and click **Submit**. Doing so saves the current entry as **unapproved** [Status = **False**]. The view page shows only those records that are approved as shown in diagram 22.1.

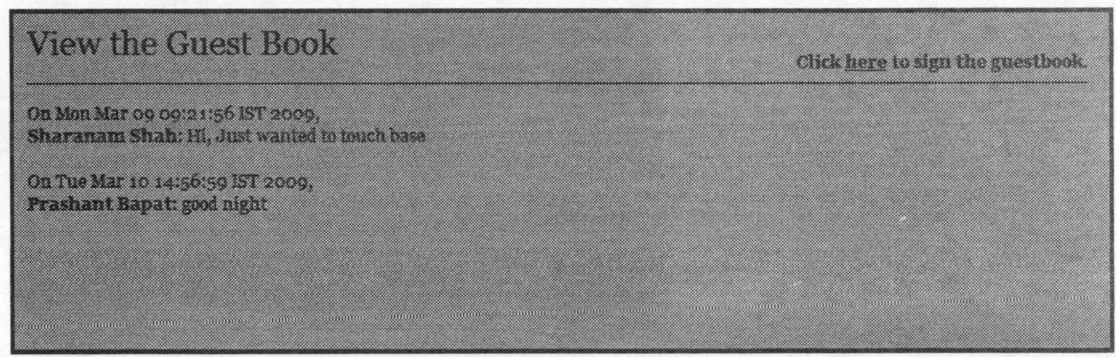
View the Guest Book
Click here to sign the guestbook.
On Mon Mar 09 09:21:56 IST 2009,
Sharanam Shah: Hi, Just wanted to touch base
On Tue Mar 10 14:56:59 IST 2009,
Prashant Bapat: good night

Diagram 22.1

Currently the Guestbook table holds the following entries:

VisitorNo	VisitorName	Message	MessageDate	Status
1	Sharanam Shah	Hi, Just wanted to touch base	Mon Mar 09 09:21:56 IST 2009	1
2	Vaishali Shah	My message	Mon Mar 09 09:21:56 IST 2009	0
3	Stuti Shah	checking this out	Mon Mar 09 09:23:51 IST 2009	0
4	Gopi Shah	hey hi	Mon Mar 09 09:50:43 IST 2009	0
5	Chaitanya Shah	hello	Mon Mar 09 09:51:53 IST 2009	0
6	Prachi Bapat	good morning	Mon Mar 09 09:52:01 IST 2009	0
7	Prashant Bapat	good night	Tue Mar 10 14:56:59 IST 2009	1

Only visitors **Sharanam Shah** and **Prashant Bapat** are approved [Status = 1] and hence visible in the application.

The Book CDROM holds the complete application source code built using the NetBeans IDE for the following application:

- GuestBook_Chap22

This can be directly used by making appropriate changes [username/password] to the configuration file.

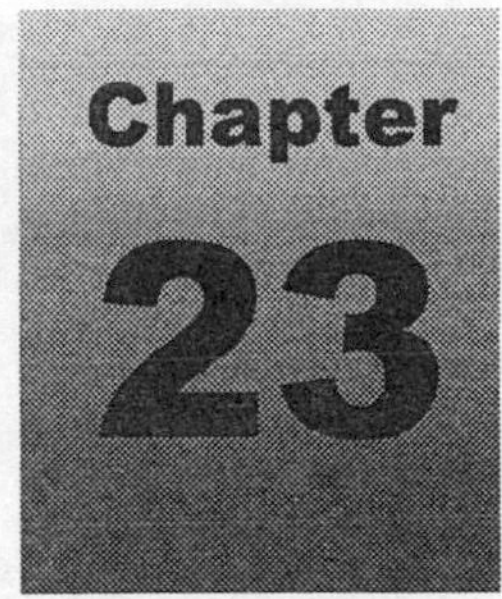

SECTION VI: APPLICATION DEVELOPMENT WITH HIBERNATE

Customer Database Using JSP

Now that concepts are in place, let's build an application that helps re-enforce the learning that took place.

Hibernate can be used in just about any kind of Java application. It may run inside a Servlet, JSP, JSF, a Swing client and so on. It can also be used along with Model-View-Controller [MVC] Web application frameworks such as Struts, Spring, Tapestry and so on.

This chapter uses JSP to demonstrate building an application with Hibernate as the ORM tool. Chapter 25 demonstrates integrating this application with Web application framework.

The application to be built is called **Customer Database**.

It will:

- Provide a data entry form to accept customer details
- Allow viewing, editing and deleting existing customers

This application will use:

- **JSP/Servlets** as the delivery mechanism
- **Hibernate** as the ORM tool
- **DAO** as the design pattern
- **MySQL** as the database
- **Ajax** wherever required

All the code spec will be built and deployed using the **NetBeans IDE**.

Database Tables

Entity Relationship Diagram

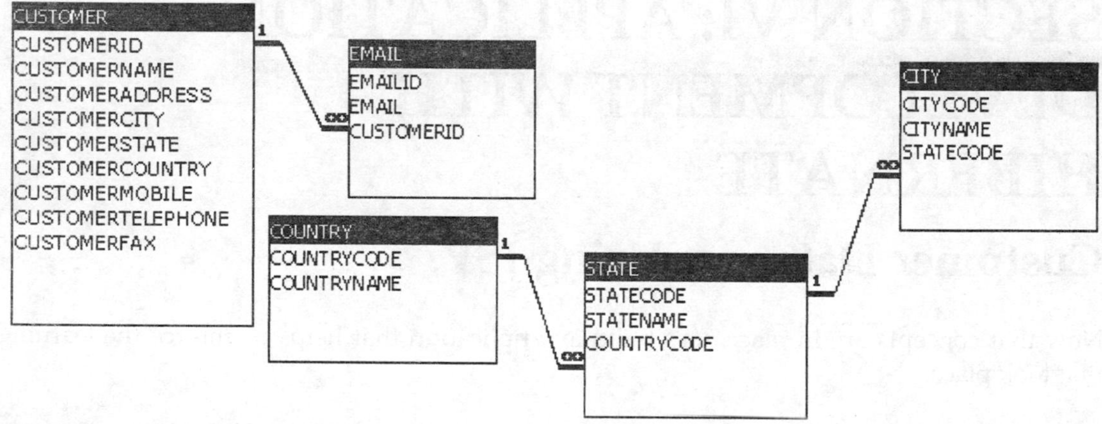

Table Specifications

CITY

Column Name	Datatype	NOT NULL	AUTO INC	Flags	Default Value
CITYCODE	INTEGER	✔	✔	UNSIGNED ZEROFILL	NULL
CITYNAME	VARCHAR(50)			BINARY	NULL
STATECODE	INTEGER			UNSIGNED ZEROFILL	NULL

STATE

Column Name	Datatype	NOT NULL	AUTO INC	Flags	Default Value
STATECODE	INTEGER	✔	✔	UNSIGNED ZEROFILL	NULL
STATENAME	VARCHAR(50)			BINARY	NULL
COUNTRYCODE	INTEGER			UNSIGNED ZEROFILL	NULL

COUNTRY

Column Name	Datatype	NOT NULL	AUTO INC	Flags	Default Value
COUNTRYCODE	INTEGER	✔	✔	UNSIGNED ZEROFILL	NULL
COUNTRYNAME	VARCHAR(50)			BINARY	NULL

CUSTOMER

Column Name	Datatype	NOT NULL	AUTO INC	Flags	Default Value
CUSTOMERID	INTEGER	✔	✔	UNSIGNED ZEROFILL	NULL
CUSTOMERNAME	VARCHAR(50)			BINARY	NULL
CUSTOMERADDRESS	VARCHAR(150)			BINARY	NULL
CUSTOMERCITY	VARCHAR(25)			BINARY	NULL
CUSTOMERSTATE	VARCHAR(25)			BINARY	NULL
CUSTOMERCOUNTRY	VARCHAR(25)			BINARY	NULL
CUSTOMERMOBILE	VARCHAR(10)			BINARY	NULL
CUSTOMERTELEPHONE	VARCHAR(15)			BINARY	NULL
CUSTOMERFAX	VARCHAR(15)			BINARY	NULL

EMAIL

Column Name	Datatype	NOT NULL	AUTO INC	Flags		Default Value
EMAILID	INTEGER	✔	✔	UNSIGNED	ZEROFILL	NULL
EMAIL	VARCHAR(75)			BINARY		NULL
CUSTOMERID	INTEGER			UNSIGNED	ZEROFILL	NULL

The table creation code spec is available as an SQL script [**CustomerDBMySQL.sql**] in this Book's accompanying CDROM.

These tables allow holding:

- Multiple Customers [CUSTOMER]
- Each customer may have multiple email addresses [EMAIL]
- Each customer's address is made up of a COUNTRY, STATE and CITY

Using MySQL's command line utility:

- Create a database called CustomerDB
- Create the above defined tables within this database

Data Entry Form

The application holds a single data entry form as shown in diagram 23.1 which is also the entry point to this application.

This form allows:

- Accepting the customer details
- Editing an existing customer's details
- Deleting an existing customer

Customer Database

It is mandatory to enter information in all information capture boxes which have a * adjacent

Name

Customer Name*:

Mailing Address

Address:
Country: -- Please Select --
State: -- Please Select --
City: -- Please Select --

Contact Details

Mobile Number:
Telephone Number*:
Fax Number:

Email

First Email Address*:
Second Email Address:
Third Email Address:

SAVE CLEAR

2 items found, displaying all items. 1

Customer Name	Address	Mobile
Sharanam Shah	Bhakti Pride	9898989898
Vaishali Shah	Bhakti Pride	8989898989

Export options: CSV | Excel | XML | PDF | RTF

Copyright © 2009, Sharanam And Vaishali Shah

Diagram 23.1: The Customer Database Data Entry Form

As soon as the application is executed, this form is delivered.

To insert a new customer, the user can key in the customer details using the data entry form and click SAVE.

The data grid [created using the **Display Tag library**] on this form allows viewing existing records. Every record in this grid provides links that allow editing or deleting that record. The edit icon when clicked populates the data entry form with that customer's details. The user can make the desired changes and click SAVE.

✖ when clicked deletes that customer and all the associated email addresses from the underlying database tables.

Building The Application Using NetBeans

Until now, all the Hibernate code spec was placed inside JSP. This is fine for learning purpose.

In this approach, the presentation logic and data access logic are mixed.

This is absolutely not a good practice.

In a multi tier application, the presentation logic and data access logic should be separate for better reusability and maintainability. To achieve this separation a design pattern called **D**ata **A**ccess **O**bject [DAO] needs to be used for encapsulating the data access logic.

A standard industry practice that is followed is to have **one DAO per persistent class**. This DAO should hold the code spec that deals with all the data operations related to that class.

Applying the Data Access Object pattern enables separating the low-level data access logic from the business logic. DAO classes are basically used to provide CRUD [**C**reate, **R**ead, **U**pdate, **D**elete] operations for each data source.

Creating Web Application

Since NetBeans is the IDE of choice throughout this book. Use it to create a new Web Application Project called CustomerDatabase.

Run the NetBeans IDE and create a new **Web Application** project, as shown in diagram 23.2.1.

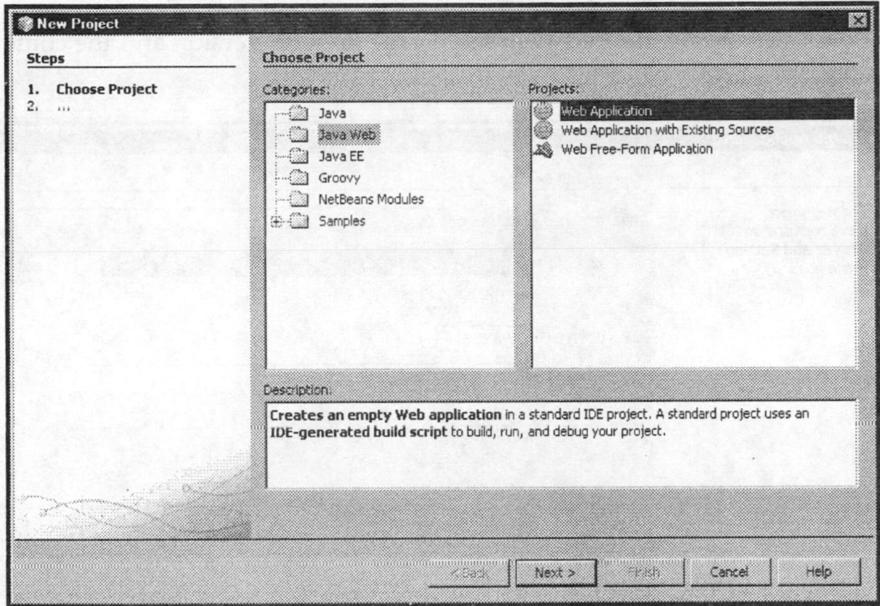

Diagram 23.2.1: New Project

Click [Next >]. Name this Web application as **CustomerDatabase** as shown in diagram 23.2.2.

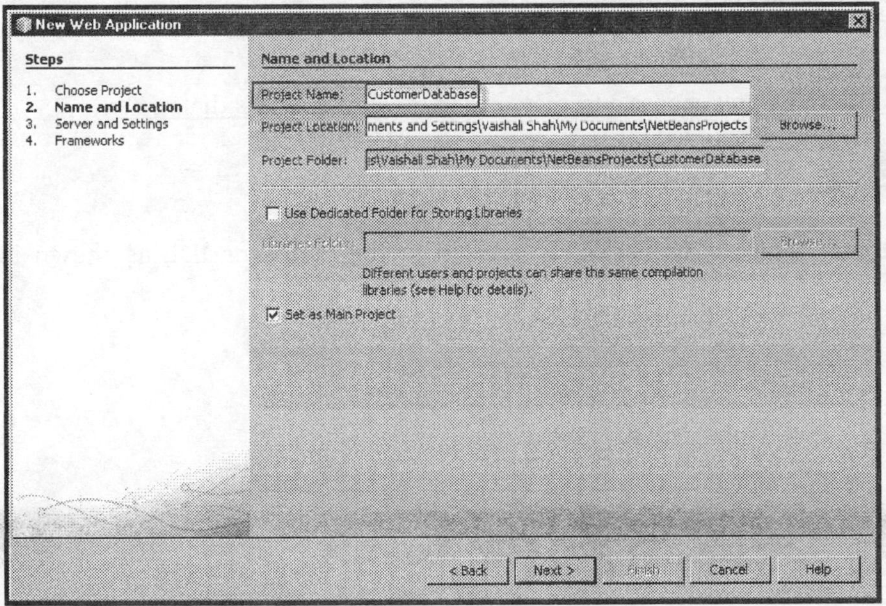

Diagram 23.2.2: Name and Location

Click Next >. Choose the desired Web server, the Java EE version and the context path as shown in diagram 23.2.3.

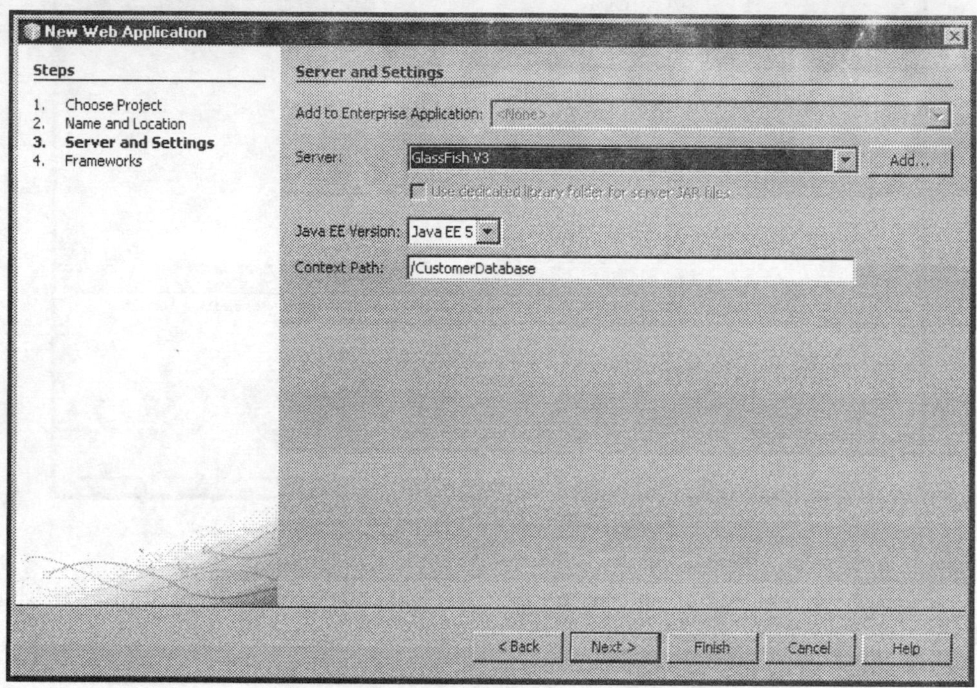

Diagram 23.2.3: Server and Settings

Click Next >. Do not choose a framework, in the Frameworks dialog box.

Click Finish.

The CustomerDatabase application is created in the NetBeans IDE as shown in diagram 23.2.4.

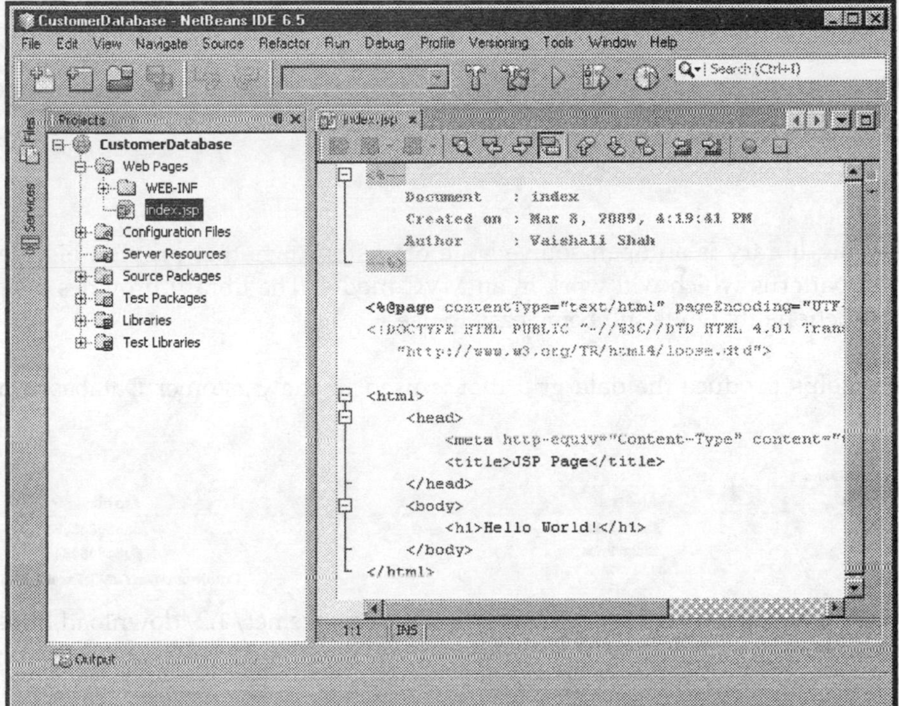

Diagram 23.2.4: CustomerDatabase in NetBeans IDE

Once the NetBeans IDE brings up the CustomerDatabase application, the next step is to add the required library files [JDBC driver, Hibernate, DisplayTag] to the CustomerDatabase application.

Adding The Library Files To The Project

This application uses Hibernate, a JDBC driver and Display Tag. Hence, appropriate library files have to be added to the project.

Downloading The Required Library Files

This application requires the following:

Hibernate

The Hibernate ORM tool. This can be downloaded from http://www.hibernate.org → Download.

MySQL JDBC Driver

The JDBC driver to interact with the MySQL database. This can be downloaded from http://dev.mysql.com/downloads/connector/j/5.1.html.

Display Tag

The display tag library is an open source suite of custom tags that provide high-level web presentation patterns which will work in an MVC model. The library provides a significant amount of functionality while still being easy to use.

This library helps produce the data grid that is used in the Customer Database data entry form.

2 items found, displaying all items. 1

Customer Name	Address	Mobile	
Sharanam Shah	Bhakti Pride	9898989898	
Vaishali Shah	Bhakti Pride	8989898989	

Export options: CSV | Excel | XML | PDF | RTF

This can be downloaded from http://displaytag.sourceforge.net/1.2/download.html

iText

iText is a free and open source library for creating and manipulating PDF, RTF and HTML files in Java.

In this application, this library is required by the **Display Tag** to support **PDF export**.

2 items found, displaying all items. 1

Customer Name	Address	Mobile	
Sharanam Shah	Bhakti Pride	9898989898	
Vaishali Shah	Bhakti Pride	8989898989	

Export options: CSV | Excel | XML | PDF | RTF

This can be downloaded from http://www.lowagie.com/iText/download.html

Common Library Files Required By The Display Tag

The Display Tag requires the following libraries to operate correctly.

Commons BeanUtils

Commons BeanUtils provide dynamic access to Java object properties without compiled-in knowledge of the property getter and setter methods to be called.

This can be downloaded from http://commons.apache.org/beanutils/

Commons Lang

The Lang Component provides a host of helper utilities for the java.lang API such as:

- String manipulation methods
- Basic numerical methods
- Object reflection, creation and serialization
- System properties
- Basic enhancements to java.util.Date

This can be downloaded from http://commons.apache.org/lang/

The Logging Component

The Logging package is an ultra-thin bridge between different logging implementations.

It is a library that uses the commons-logging API. It comes with support for a number of popular logging implementations and writing adapters for others is a reasonably simple task.

This can be downloaded from http://commons.apache.org/downloads/download_logging.cgi

REMINDER

All of these library files are available in this book's accompanying CDROM.

A Dedicated Library Directory

It's a good practice to manually create a dedicated **lib** folder with all the required library files in the project folder and then using NetBeans add libraries from this folder as the source.

To do so,

Create a directory called **lib** under <Drive>:**NetBeansProjects**\CustomerDatabase. [**NetBeansProjects** is the folder where NetBeans places the projects created]

Copying Library Files To The Dedicated Directory

Copy the following library files to the lib directory:

- From the **hibernate-distribution-3.3.1.GA** directory

- hibernate3.jar

- From the **hibernate-distribution-3.3.1.GA → lib → required** directory
  - antlr-2.7.6.jar
  - jta-1.1.jar
  - javassist-3.4.GA.jar
  - commons-collections-3.1.jar
  - dom4j-1.6.1.jar
- From the **hibernate-distribution-3.3.1.GA → lib → bytecode → cglib** directory
  - hibernate-cglib-repack-2.1_3.jar
- From the **hibernate-annotations-3.4.0.GA** directory
  - hibernate-annotations.jar
- From the **hibernate-annotations-3.4.0.GA → lib** directory
  - hibernate-commons-annotations.jar
  - slf4j-api.jar
  - slf4j-log4j12.jar
- From the **hibernate-annotations-3.4.0.GA → lib → test** directory
  - asm.jar
  - asm-attrs.jar
  - log4j.jar
- From the **mysql-connector-java-5.1.7** directory [MySQL **JDBC Driver**]
  - mysql-connector-java-5.1.7-bin.jar
- From the **Display tags** directory **[explanation and donwload]**
  - displaytag-1.2.jar
  - displaytag-export-poi-1.2.jar
  - displaytag-portlet-1.2.jar
- For **PDF** export support for the **Display tag**
  - itext-1.4.7.jar
- From the **commons** directory [commons.apache.org]
  - commons-beanutils-1.7.0.jar
  - commons-lang-2.1.jar
  - commons-logging-1.0.4.jar

HINT

Now add these libraries to the application using NetBeans. Refer to *Chapter 03: Writing The First Application* for the steps to add libraries using the NetBeans IDE.

The Hibernate Configuration

Since Hibernate is the ORM of choice for this application, it is necessary to have a configuration file that defines connection and the mapping resources.

Using NetBeans IDE, create an XML based configuration file named hibernate.cfg.xml with the following code spec:

```
<?xml version="1.0" encoding="UTF-8"?>
<!DOCTYPE hibernate-configuration PUBLIC "-//Hibernate/Hibernate Configuration DTD 3.0//EN"
"http://hibernate.sourceforge.net/hibernate-configuration-3.0.dtd">
<hibernate-configuration>
  <session-factory>
    <property name="hibernate.dialect">org.hibernate.dialect.MySQLDialect</property>
    <property name="hibernate.connection.driver_class">com.mysql.jdbc.Driver</property>
    <property name="hibernate.connection.url">jdbc:mysql://localhost:3306/CustomerDB</property>
    <property name="hibernate.connection.username">root</property>
    <property name="hibernate.connection.password">123456</property>
    <property name="hibernate.default_catalog">CustomerDB</property>
    <!-- Mapping resources will be placed here. -->

  </session-factory>
</hibernate-configuration>
```

This file informs Hibernate to use **MySQL** as the **dialect** and **CustomerDB** as the **database**.

The resource mappings will be inserted later.

HINT

Refer to *Chapter 03: Writing The First Application* for the steps to create the configuration file using the NetBeans IDE.

The Hibernate Utility Class [com.development.utils]

The SessionFactory is considered one of the most important components in the Hibernate API. It is responsible for the generation of Hibernate Session objects that are required to interact with database.

For learning purpose, till now, this component was being created over and over again and placed in the module [JSP] that required it.

For example, in the GuestBook application, GuestBookView.jsp holds the SessionFactory code spec:

```
<%@page contentType="text/html" pageEncoding="UTF-8" import="org.hibernate.SessionFactory,
org.hibernate.cfg.Configuration, org.hibernate.Session, org.hibernate.Transaction, java.util.List, java.util.Iterator,
myApp.Guestbook, org.hibernate.cfg.AnnotationConfiguration;
" %>
<!DOCTYPE HTML PUBLIC "-//W3C//DTD HTML 4.01 Transitional//EN"
  "http://www.w3.org/TR/html4/loose.dtd">
<%!
  SessionFactory sessionFactory;
  org.hibernate.Session hibSession;
  List<Guestbook> guestbook;
%>

<%
  sessionFactory = new AnnotationConfiguration().configure().buildSessionFactory();
  hibSession = sessionFactory.openSession();
  Transaction tx = null;

  String submit = request.getParameter("btnSubmit");
  if(submit != null && ("Submit").equals(submit))
  {
      Guestbook gb = new Guestbook();
      try
      {
          tx = hibSession.beginTransaction();

          String guest = request.getParameter("guest");
          String message = request.getParameter("message");
          String messageDate = new java.util.Date().toString();
          gb.setVisitorName(guest);
          gb.setMessage(message);
          gb.setMessageDate(messageDate);
```

The standard and the most recommended practice is to have a <u>helper class</u> called **HibernateUtil** that manages the SessionFactory component for the entire application.

Create a Java class called **HibernateUtil** under the package com.development.utils with the following code spec:

```
package com.development.utils;

import org.hibernate.cfg.AnnotationConfiguration;
import org.hibernate.SessionFactory;

public class HibernateUtil {
   private static final SessionFactory sessionFactory;

   static {
      try {
         sessionFactory = new AnnotationConfiguration().configure().buildSessionFactory();
      }
      catch (Throwable ex) {
         System.err.println("Initial SessionFactory creation failed." + ex);
         throw new ExceptionInInitializerError(ex);
      }
   }
```

```

    public static SessionFactory getSessionFactory() {
        return sessionFactory;
    }
}
```

This class declares, initializes, configures and subsequently returns a session factory.

The SessionFactory is bound to a static and final variable [**sessionFactory**]. This allows all the threads to share this variable, because SessionFactory is threadsafe.

```
private static final SessionFactory sessionFactory;
```

The SessionFactory is created in a static **initializer code block**. This code block is executed when the **classloader** loads the class.

```
static {
    try {
        sessionFactory = new
        AnnotationConfiguration().configure().buildSessionFactory();
    } catch (Throwable ex) {
        System.err.println("Initial SessionFactory creation failed." + ex);
        throw new ExceptionInInitializerError(ex);
    }
}
```

The method **getSessionFactory()** is the method that returns the session factory which is used by the entire application.

```
public static SessionFactory getSessionFactory() {
    return sessionFactory;
}
```

Using the NetBeans IDE, add a new **Java class** [as shown in diagram 23.3.1] named **HibernateUtil.java** under a **package** called **com.development.utils** as shown in diagram 23.3.2.

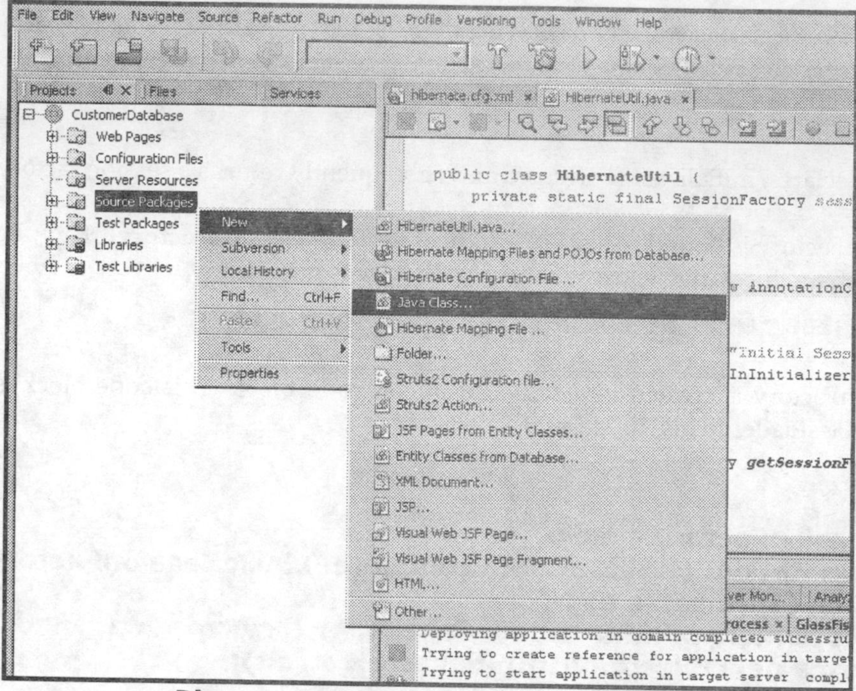

Diagram 23.3.1: Adding a new Java class

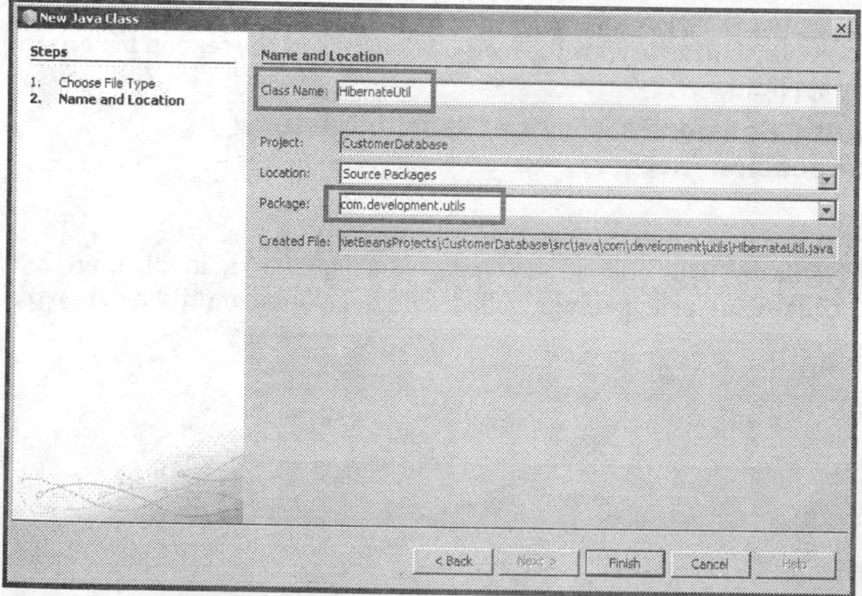

Diagram 23.3.2: Creating HibernateUtil class

The Base Hibernate DAO Interface [com.development.utils]

To perform any kind of database operation a Hibernate Session object is required.

With the configuration object initialized and the SessionFactory in place, let's work towards obtaining a Session object.

To achieve this via the DAO design pattern, create an interface called **IBaseHibernateDAO**. This interface will define WHAT to do. The HOW to do will be defined in the class called **BaseDAO** [explained later] that implements this interface.

This interface defines the required methods in this case being **getSession()**. This method when implemented by **BaseDAO** will return a Session object on being invoked.

Create a Java class called **IBaseHibernateDAO** under the package com.development.utils with the following code spec:

```
package com.development.utils;

import org.hibernate.Session;

public interface IBaseHibernateDAO {
   public Session getSession();
}
```

HINT

Using the NetBeans IDE, add a new **Java class** [as shown in diagram 24.3.1] named **IBaseHibernateDAO.java** under a **package** called **com.development.utils** as shown earlier.

The Base Hibernate DAO [com.development.utils]

Now that the interface is ready, the implementation class needs to be created.

Create a Java class called **BaseDAO** under the package com.development.utils with the following code spec:

```
package com.development.utils;

import org.hibernate.Session;
```

```
import org.hibernate.Transaction;

public class BaseDAO implements IBaseHibernateDAO {
    private Session session;
    private Transaction trans;

    public BaseDAO() {
        session = HibernateUtil.getSessionFactory().openSession();
        trans = session.beginTransaction();
    }

    public Session getSession() {
        return session;
    }

    public void beginTransaction() {
        trans.begin();
    }

    public void commitTransaction() {
        trans.commit();
    }
}
```

Obtaining Session Object

This class's constructor obtains a session object with the help of the SessionFactory object using **HibernateUtil** created earlier and also instantiates the Transaction object.

```
public BaseDAO() {
    session = HibernateUtil.getSessionFactory().openSession();
    trans = session.beginTransaction();
}
```

The **openSession()** method of the SessionFactory object returns a Session object.

This Session object is made available to the application using the **getter** method called **getSession()** [defined earlier in the interface called **IBaseHibernateDAO]**.

```
public Session getSession() {
    return session;
}
```

Managing Transactions

An application should be able to begin a transaction and subsequently, ask the Hibernate framework to commit any changes that have occurred during the scope of that transaction.

To achieve this, this class holds two more methods that help manage transactions [begin and commit].

This class allows managing transactions with the help of a publicly accessible method called **beginTransaction()**, along with a corresponding publicly accessible method called **commitTransaction()**.

```
public void beginTransaction() {
    trans.begin();
}

public void commitTransaction() {
    trans.commit();
}
```

This class's methods will then be used by application's DAO classes to perform database operations as:

```
package com.development.hibernate.customer;

import com.development.utils.BaseDAO;
import java.util.List;

public class CustomerDAO extends BaseDAO {
    public void save(Customer customer) {
```

```
        try {
            beginTransaction();
            getSession().save(customer);
            commitTransaction();
        }
        catch (RuntimeException re) {
            re.printStackTrace();
            throw re;
        }
    }
```

HINT

Using the NetBeans IDE, add a new **Java class** [as shown in diagram 23.3.1] named **BaseDAO.java** under a **package** called **com.development.utils** as shown earlier.

POJOs, Mapping Documents And DAOs

This application uses the following tables:

- City
- State
- Country
- Customer
    - Email

The customer data entry form holds drop down list boxes where the user can choose a country, state and a city to define the customer's address.

Appropriate POJO that represent these tables have to be created. For each POJO an XML based mapping document will be created.

All the code spec that allows performing database operations such as **C**reate, **R**ead, **U**pdate and **D**elete will be placed in the DAO. POJOs and Mapping Document can be created manually by typing the code spec or by using a wizard [Hibernate Tools → Reverse Engineering] using the NetBeans IDE.

City [com.development.hibernate.city]

POJO

Create a Java class called **City** under the package **com.development.hibernate.city** with the following code spec:

```
package com.development.hibernate.city;

public class City  implements java.io.Serializable {
     private Integer citycode;
     private State state;
     private String cityname;

    public City() {
    }

    public City(State state, String cityname) {
       this.state = state;
       this.cityname = cityname;
    }

    public Integer getCitycode() {
        return this.citycode;
    }
    public void setCitycode(Integer citycode) {
        this.citycode = citycode;
    }
    public State getState() {
        return this.state;
    }
    public void setState(State state) {
        this.state = state;
    }
```

```

    public String getCityname() {
        return this.cityname;
    }
    public void setCityname(String cityname) {
        this.cityname = cityname;
    }
}
```

Mapping Document

Create a XML Mapping file called **City.hbm.xml** under the package **com.development. hibernate.city** with the following code spec:

```
<?xml version="1.0"?>
<!DOCTYPE hibernate-mapping PUBLIC "-//Hibernate/Hibernate Mapping DTD 3.0//EN"
"http://hibernate.sourceforge.net/hibernate-mapping-3.0.dtd">
<hibernate-mapping>
    <class name="com.development.hibernate.city.City" table="city"
    catalog="customerdb">
        <id name="citycode" type="java.lang.Integer">
            <column name="CITYCODE" />
            <generator class="identity" />
        </id>
        <many-to-one name="state" class="com.development.hibernate.city.State"
        fetch="select">
            <column name="STATECODE" />
        </many-to-one>
        <property name="cityname" type="string">
            <column name="CITYNAME" length="50" />
        </property>
    </class>
</hibernate-mapping>
```

DAO

Create a Java class called **CityDAO** under the package **com.development.hibernate.city** with the following code spec:

```
package com.development.hibernate.city;

import com.development.utils.BaseDAO;
import java.util.List;

public class CityDAO extends BaseDAO {
    public void save(City city) {
        try {
            beginTransaction();
            getSession().save(city);
            commitTransaction();
        }
        catch (RuntimeException re) {
            re.printStackTrace();
            throw re;
        }
    }

    public List<City> findAll() {
        beginTransaction();
        List<City> list = getSession().createQuery("from City").list();
        commitTransaction();
        return list;
    }

    public List<City> findByStateCode(Integer stateCode) {
        beginTransaction();
```

```
        List<City> list = getSession().createQuery("select c from City c
        where c.state.statecode = :stateCode")
                .setParameter("stateCode", stateCode)
                .list();
        commitTransaction();
        return list;
    }
}
```

Explanation:

The **CityDAO** class extends another DAO class i.e. **BaseDAO** and thus gains access to the methods such as **getSession()**, **beginTransaction()** and **commitTransaction()**.

This class provides the following methods that allow database operations:

- **save():** This method accepts an object of the **City** POJO. This method when invoked, begins a transaction, saves the object it receives using the **save()** method of the Session object and finally commits the transaction
- **findAll():** This method fires an HQL SELECT query on the City object and returns the query result as a list
- **findByStateCode():** This method accepts StateCode, fires an HQL SELECT query with a condition using a WHERE clause on the City object and returns the query result as a list

HINT

To automatically create the **POJO** and the **Mapping document** using **Hibernate Tools** → Reverse Engineering using Tables refer the topic: *Creating POJO And Mapping Documents Automatically* [explained later]. These can be created manually as well.

After the POJO and the mapping documents are created, using the NetBeans IDE, add a new **Java class** [as shown in diagram 23.3.1] named **CityDAO.java** under a **package** called **com.development.hibernate.city** as shown earlier.

State [com.development.hibernate.city]

POJO

Create a Java class called **State** under the package **com.development.hibernate.city** with the following code spec:

```
package com.development.hibernate.city;
```

```
import java.util.HashSet;
import java.util.Set;

public class State  implements java.io.Serializable {
     private Integer statecode;
     private Country country;
     private String statename;
     private Set<City> cities = new HashSet<City>(0);

    public State() {
    }

    public State(Country country, String statename, Set<City> cities) {
       this.country = country;
       this.statename = statename;
       this.cities = cities;
    }

    public Integer getStatecode() {
        return this.statecode;
    }
    public void setStatecode(Integer statecode) {
        this.statecode = statecode;
    }
    public Country getCountry() {
        return this.country;
    }
    public void setCountry(Country country) {
        this.country = country;
    }

```

```
    public String getStatename() {
        return this.statename;
    }
    public void setStatename(String statename) {
        this.statename = statename;
    }

    public Set<City> getCities() {
        return this.cities;
    }
    public void setCities(Set<City> cities) {
        this.cities = cities;
    }
}
```

Mapping Document

Create a XML Mapping file called **State.hbm.xml** under the package **com.development.hibernate.city** with the following code spec:

```
<?xml version="1.0"?>
<!DOCTYPE hibernate-mapping PUBLIC "-//Hibernate/Hibernate Mapping DTD 3.0//EN"
"http://hibernate.sourceforge.net/hibernate-mapping-3.0.dtd">
<hibernate-mapping>
    <class name="com.development.hibernate.city.State" table="state" catalog="customerdb">
        <id name="statecode" type="java.lang.Integer">
            <column name="STATECODE" />
            <generator class="identity" />
        </id>
        <many-to-one name="country" class="com.development.hibernate.city.Country" fetch="select">
            <column name="COUNTRYCODE" />
        </many-to-one>
        <property name="statename" type="string">
            <column name="STATENAME" length="50" />
```

```
        </property>
        <set name="cities" inverse="true">
            <key>
                <column name="STATECODE" />
            </key>
            <one-to-many class="com.development.hibernate.city.City" />
        </set>
    </class>
</hibernate-mapping>
```

Explanation:

One state can have multiple cities. This association is depicted using:

```
<set name="cities" inverse="true">
    <key>
        <column name="STATECODE" />
    </key>
    <one-to-many class="com.development.hibernate.city.City" />
</set>
```

DAO

Create a Java class called **StateDAO** under the package **com.development.hibernate.city** with the following code spec:

```
package com.development.hibernate.city;

import com.development.utils.BaseDAO;
import java.util.List;

public class StateDAO extends BaseDAO {
    public void save(State state) {
        try {
            beginTransaction();
            getSession().save(state);
            commitTransaction();
        }
```

```
        catch (RuntimeException re) {
            re.printStackTrace();
            throw re;
        }
    }

    public List<State> findAll() {
        beginTransaction();
        List<State> list = getSession().createQuery("from State").list();
        commitTransaction();
        return list;
    }

    public List<State> findByCountryCode(Integer countryCode) {
        beginTransaction();
        List<State> list = getSession().createQuery("select s from State s where
        s.country.countrycode = :countryCode")
                .setParameter("countryCode", countryCode)
                .list();
        commitTransaction();
        return list;
    }
}
```

Explanation:

The **StateDAO** class extends another DAO class i.e. **BaseDAO** and thus gains access to the methods such as **getSession()**, **beginTransaction()** and **commitTransaction()**.

This class provides the following methods that allow database operations:

- **save():** This method accepts an object of the **State** POJO. This method when invoked, begins a transaction, saves the object it receives using the **save()** method of the Session object and finally commits the transaction
- **findAll():** This method fires an HQL SELECT query on the State object and returns the query result as a list

- **findByCountryCode():** This method accepts CountryCode fires an HQL SELECT query with a condition using a WHERE clause on the State object and returns the query result as a list

HINT

To automatically create the **POJO** and the **Mapping document** using **Hibernate Tools** → Reverse Engineering using Tables refer the topic: *Creating POJO And Mapping Documents Automatically* [explained later]. These can be created manually as well.

After the POJO and the mapping documents are created, using the NetBeans IDE, add a new **Java class** [as shown in diagram 23.3.1] named **StateDAO.java** under a **package** called **com.development.hibernate.city** as shown earlier.

Country [com.development.hibernate.city]

POJO

Create a Java class called **Country** under the package **com.development.hibernate.city** with the following code spec:

```
package com.development.hibernate.city;

import java.util.HashSet;
import java.util.Set;

public class Country  implements java.io.Serializable {
     private Integer countrycode;
     private String countryname;
     private Set<State> states = new HashSet<State>(0);

    public Country() {
    }

    public Country(String countryname, Set<State> states) {
       this.countryname = countryname;
       this.states = states;
    }
```

```

    public Integer getCountrycode() {
        return this.countrycode;
    }
    public void setCountrycode(Integer countrycode) {
        this.countrycode = countrycode;
    }
    public String getCountryname() {
        return this.countryname;
    }
    public void setCountryname(String countryname) {
        this.countryname = countryname;
    }

    public Set<State> getStates() {
        return this.states;
    }
    public void setStates(Set<State> states) {
        this.states = states;
    }
}
```

Mapping Document

Create a XML Mapping file called **Country.hbm.xml** under the package **com.development.hibernate.city** with the following code spec:

```
<?xml version="1.0"?>
<!DOCTYPE hibernate-mapping PUBLIC "-//Hibernate/Hibernate Mapping DTD 3.0//EN"
"http://hibernate.sourceforge.net/hibernate-mapping-3.0.dtd">
<hibernate-mapping>
    <class name="com.development.hibernate.city.Country" table="country"
    catalog="customerdb">
        <id name="countrycode" type="java.lang.Integer">
            <column name="COUNTRYCODE" />
```

```
            <generator class="identity" />
        </id>
        <property name="countryname" type="string">
            <column name="COUNTRYNAME" length="50" />
        </property>
        <set name="states" inverse="true">
            <key>
                <column name="COUNTRYCODE" />
            </key>
            <one-to-many class="com.development.hibernate.city.State" />
        </set>
    </class>
</hibernate-mapping>
```

Explanation:

One country can have multiple states. This association is depicted using:

```
<set name="states" inverse="true">
    <key>
        <column name="COUNTRYCODE" />
    </key>
    <one-to-many class="com.development.hibernate.city.State" />
</set>
```

DAO

Create a Java class called **CountryDAO** under the package **com.development.hibernate.city** with the following code spec:

```
package com.development.hibernate.city;

import com.development.utils.BaseDAO;
import java.util.List;

public class CountryDAO extends BaseDAO {
    public void save(Country country) {
        try {
```

```
            beginTransaction();
            getSession().save(country);
            commitTransaction();
        }
        catch (RuntimeException re) {
            re.printStackTrace();
            throw re;
        }
    }

    public List<Country> findAll() {
        beginTransaction();
        List<Country> list = getSession().createQuery("from Country").list();
        commitTransaction();
        return list;
    }
}
```

Explanation:

The **CountryDAO** class extends another DAO class i.e. **BaseDAO** and thus gains access to the methods such as **getSession()**, **beginTransaction()** and **commitTransaction()**.

This class provides the following methods that allow database operations:

- **save():** This method accepts an object of the **Country** POJO. This method when invoked, begins a transaction, saves the object it receives using the **save()** method of the Session object and finally commits the transaction
- **findAll():** This method fires an HQL SELECT query on the Country object and returns the query result as a list

HINT

To automatically create the **POJO** and the **Mapping document** using **Hibernate Tools** → Reverse Engineering using Tables refer the topic: *Creating POJO And Mapping Documents Automatically* [explained later]. These can be created manually as well.

After the POJO and the mapping documents are created, using the NetBeans IDE, add a new **Java class** [as shown in diagram 23.3.1] named **StateDAO.java** under a **package** called **com.development.hibernate.city** as shown earlier.

Creating POJO And Mapping Documents Automatically

If the required POJOs and the mapping documents were not created manually, they can be created automatically using **Reverse Engineering**, since the database tables already exists.

Using NetBeans, create the package called **com.development.hibernate.city**. Right click on this package and choose **New → Hibernate Mapping Files and POJOs from Database...**

This brings up the wizard as shown in diagram 23.4.1.

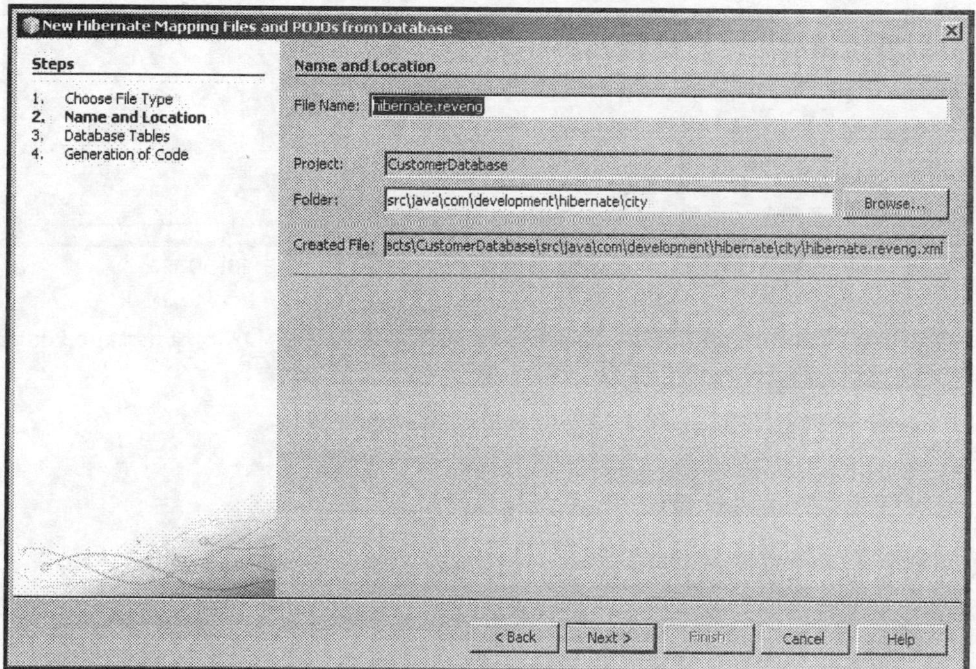

Diagram 23.4.1: New Hibernate Mapping Files and POJOs from Database

Keep the default values and Click Next >. Doing so reads the database using the values from the **hibernate.cfg.xml** file and displays the available tables under the CustomerDB database as shown in diagram 23.4.2.

WARNING

Ensure that the database and the appropriate tables are created prior running this wizard.

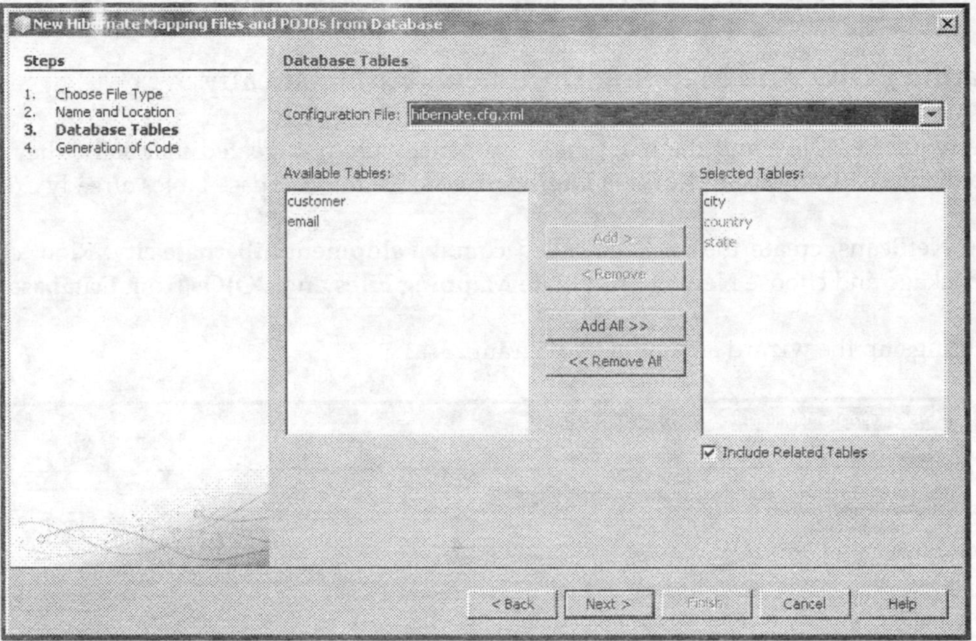

Diagram 23.4.2: Selecting the tables from the database

Choose the City, Country and State tables. Click Next >. Select **JDK 5 Language Features** as shown in diagram 23.4.3.

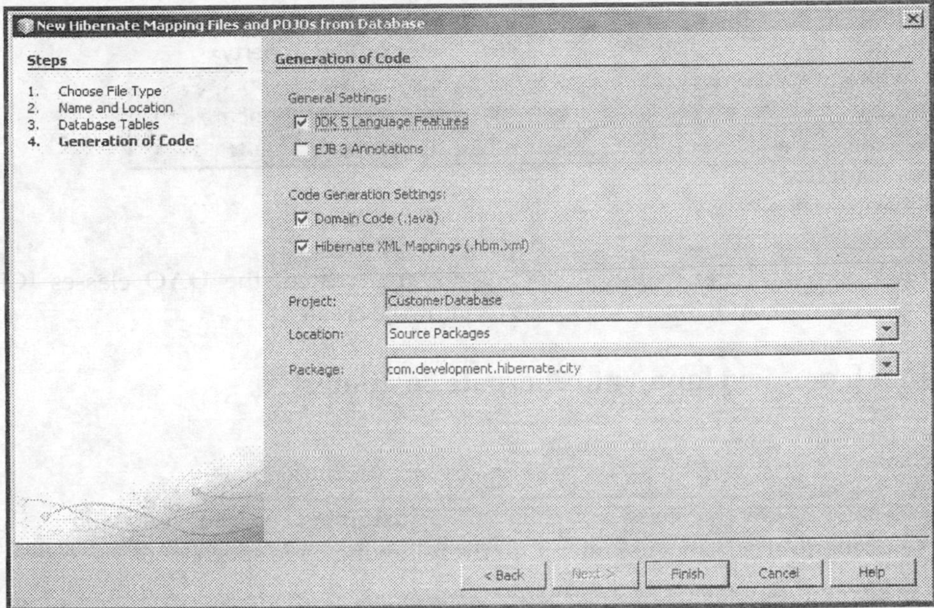

Diagram 23.4.3

Click Finish. This creates the POJOs and the appropriate mapping documents.

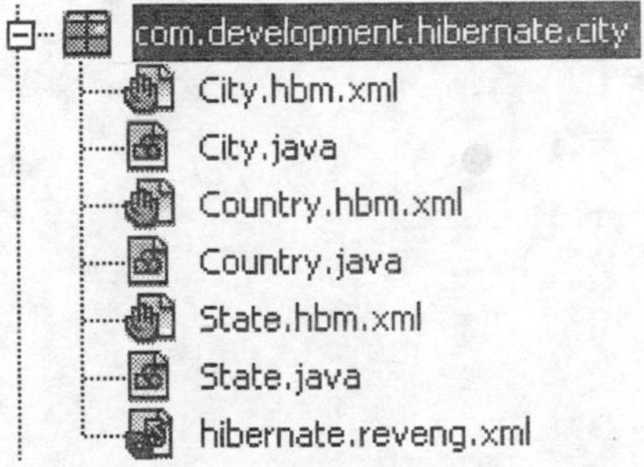

The wizard also adds the appropriate mapping resources in the **hibernate.cfg.xml** file.

```
<?xml version="1.0" encoding="UTF-8"?>
<!DOCTYPE hibernate-configuration PUBLIC "-//Hibernate/Hibernate Configuration DTD 3.0//EN" "http://hibernate.sourceforge.net/hibernate-configuration-3.0.dtd">
<hibernate-configuration>
  <session-factory>
    <property name="hibernate.dialect">org.hibernate.dialect.MySQLDialect</property>
    <property name="hibernate.connection.driver_class">com.mysql.jdbc.Driver</property>
    <property name="hibernate.connection.url">jdbc:mysql://localhost:3306/CustomerDB</property>
    <property name="hibernate.connection.username">root</property>
```

```
    <property name="hibernate.connection.password">123456</property>
    <property name="hibernate.default_catalog">CustomerDB</property>
    <mapping resource="com/development/hibernate/city/State.hbm.xml"/>
    <mapping resource="com/development/hibernate/city/Country.hbm.xml"/>
    <mapping resource="com/development/hibernate/city/City.hbm.xml"/>
  </session-factory>
</hibernate-configuration>
```

Since the POJOs and the mapping documents are created, the **DAO** classes [CityDAO, StateDAO, CountryDAO] for these **POJOs** can now be created.

Customer [com.development.hibernate.customer]

POJO

Create a Java class called **Customer** under the package **com.development.hibernate.customer** with the following code spec:

```
package com.development.hibernate.customer;

import java.util.HashSet;
import java.util.Set;

public class Customer implements java.io.Serializable {
    private Integer customerid;
    private String customername;
    private String customeraddress;
    private String customercity;
    private String customerstate;
    private String customercountry;
    private String customermobile;
    private String customertelephone;
    private String customerfax;
    private Set<Email> emails = new HashSet<Email>(0);

    public Customer() {
    }

    public Customer(String customername, String customeraddress, String customercity,
    String customerstate, String customercountry, String customermobile, String
    customertelephone, String customerfax, Set<Email> emails) {
```

```
        this.customername = customername;
        this.customeraddress = customeraddress;
        this.customercity = customercity;
        this.customerstate = customerstate;
        this.customercountry = customercountry;
        this.customermobile = customermobile;
        this.customertelephone = customertelephone;
        this.customerfax = customerfax;
        this.emails = emails;
    }

    public Integer getCustomerid() {
        return this.customerid;
    }
    public void setCustomerid(Integer customerid) {
        this.customerid = customerid;
    }

    public String getCustomername() {
        return this.customername;
    }
    public void setCustomername(String customername) {
        this.customername = customername;
    }

    public String getCustomeraddress() {
        return this.customeraddress;
    }
    public void setCustomeraddress(String customeraddress) {
        this.customeraddress = customeraddress;
    }

    public String getCustomercity() {
        return this.customercity;
    }
    public void setCustomercity(String customercity) {
        this.customercity = customercity;
    }
```

```

public String getCustomerstate() {
    return this.customerstate;
}
public void setCustomerstate(String customerstate) {
    this.customerstate = customerstate;
}

public String getCustomercountry() {
    return this.customercountry;
}
public void setCustomercountry(String customercountry) {
    this.customercountry = customercountry;
}

public String getCustomermobile() {
    return this.customermobile;
}
public void setCustomermobile(String customermobile) {
    this.customermobile = customermobile;
}

public String getCustomertelephone() {
    return this.customertelephone;
}
public void setCustomertelephone(String customertelephone) {
    this.customertelephone = customertelephone;
}

public String getCustomerfax() {
    return this.customerfax;
}
public void setCustomerfax(String customerfax) {
    this.customerfax = customerfax;
}

public Set<Email> getEmails() {
    return this.emails;
}
```

```
    public void setEmails(Set<Email> emails) {
        this.emails = emails;
    }
}
```

Mapping Document

Create a XML Mapping file called **Customer.hbm.xml** under the package **com.development.hibernate.customer** with the following code spec:

```
<?xml version="1.0"?>
<!DOCTYPE hibernate-mapping PUBLIC "-//Hibernate/Hibernate Mapping DTD 3.0//EN"
"http://hibernate.sourceforge.net/hibernate-mapping-3.0.dtd">
<hibernate-mapping>
    <class name="com.development.hibernate.customer.Customer" table="customer">
        <id name="customerid" type="java.lang.Integer">
            <column name="CUSTOMERID" />
            <generator class="identity" />
        </id>
        <property name="customername" type="string">
            <column name="CUSTOMERNAME" length="50" />
        </property>
        <property name="customeraddress" type="string">
            <column name="CUSTOMERADDRESS" length="150" />
        </property>
        <property name="customercity" type="string">
            <column name="CUSTOMERCITY" length="25" />
        </property>
        <property name="customerstate" type="string">
            <column name="CUSTOMERSTATE" length="25" />
        </property>
        <property name="customercountry" type="string">
            <column name="CUSTOMERCOUNTRY" length="25" />
        </property>
        <property name="customermobile" type="string">
            <column name="CUSTOMERMOBILE" length="10" />
        </property>
        <property name="customertelephone" type="string">
            <column name="CUSTOMERTELEPHONE" length="15" />
```

```
        </property>
        <property name="customerfax" type="string">
            <column name="CUSTOMERFAX" length="15" />
        </property>
        <set name="emails" cascade="all">
            <key>
                <column name="CUSTOMERID" />
            </key>
            <one-to-many class="com.development.hibernate.customer.Email" />
        </set>
    </class>
</hibernate-mapping>
```

Explanation:

One customer can have multiple emails. This association is depicted using:

```
<set name="emails" cascade="all">
    <key>
        <column name="CUSTOMERID" />
    </key>
    <one-to-many class="com.development.hibernate.customer.Email" />
</set>
```

cascade="all" is used to cascade both **save-update** and **delete**.

This application will save the customer data [along with email addresses] using the Customer **POJO** and **DAO**, the email addresses will be automatically saved using **cascade mechanism**. **cascade="all"**, achieves this.

DAO

Create a Java class called **CustomerDAO** under the package **com.development.hibernate.customer** with the following code spec:

```
package com.development.hibernate.customer;

import com.development.utils.BaseDAO;
import java.util.List;
```

```
public class CustomerDAO extends BaseDAO {
    public void save(Customer customer) {
        try {
            beginTransaction();
            getSession().save(customer);
            commitTransaction();
        }
        catch (RuntimeException re) {
            re.printStackTrace();
            throw re;
        }
    }

    public void update(Customer customer) {
        try {
            beginTransaction();
            getSession().update(customer);
            commitTransaction();
        }
        catch (RuntimeException re) {
            re.printStackTrace();
            throw re;
        }
    }

    public void delete(Customer customer) {
        try {
            beginTransaction();
            getSession().delete(customer);
            commitTransaction();
        }
        catch (RuntimeException re) {
            re.printStackTrace();
            throw re;
        }
    }
```

```

    public List<Customer> findAll() {
        beginTransaction();
        List<Customer> list = getSession().createQuery("select c from Customer c").list();
        commitTransaction();
        return list;
    }

    public Customer findByCustomerCode(Integer customerCode) {
        beginTransaction();
        Customer customer = new Customer();
        customer = (Customer) getSession().load(Customer.class, customerCode);
        commitTransaction();
        return customer;
    }
}
```

Explanation:

The **CustomerDAO** class extends another DAO class i.e. **BaseDAO** and thus gains access to the methods such as **getSession()**, **beginTransaction()** and **commitTransaction()**.

This class provides the following methods that allow database operations:

- **save():** This method accepts an object of the **Customer** POJO. This method when invoked, begins a transaction, saves the object it receives using the **save()** method of the Session object and finally commits the transaction
- **update():** This method accepts an object of the **Customer** POJO. This method when invoked, begins a transaction, saves the object it receives using the **update()** method of the Session object and finally commits the transaction
- **delete():** This method accepts an object of the **Customer** POJO. This method when invoked, begins a transaction, deletes the object it receives using the **delete()** method of the Session object and finally commits the transaction
- **findAll():** This method fires an HQL SELECT query on the Customer object and returns the query result as a list
- **findByCustomerCode():** This method accepts CustomerCode fires an HQL SELECT query with a condition using a WHERE clause on the Customer object and returns the query result as a list

HINT

To automatically create the **POJO** and the **Mapping document** using **Hibernate Tools → Reverse Engineering using Tables** refer the topic: *Creating POJO And Mapping Documents Automatically* [explained later]. These can be created manually as well.

After the POJO and the mapping documents are created, using the NetBeans IDE, add a new **Java class** [as shown in diagram 23.3.1] named **CustomerDAO.java** under a **package** called **com.development.hibernate.customer** as shown earlier.

Email [com.development.hibernate.customer]

POJO

Create a Java class called **Email** under the package **com.development.hibernate.customer** with the following code spec:

```
package com.development.hibernate.customer;

public class Email  implements java.io.Serializable {
    private Integer emailid;
    private Customer customer;
    private String email;

    public Email() {
    }

    public Email(Customer customer, String email) {
       this.customer = customer;
       this.email = email;
    }

    public Integer getEmailid() {
        return this.emailid;
    }
    public void setEmailid(Integer emailid) {
        this.emailid = emailid;
```

```
    }

    public Customer getCustomer() {
        return this.customer;
    }
    public void setCustomer(Customer customer) {
        this.customer = customer;
    }

    public String getEmail() {
        return this.email;
    }
    public void setEmail(String email) {
        this.email = email;
    }
}
```

Mapping Document

Create a XML Mapping file called **Email.hbm.xml** under the package **com.development.hibernate.customer** with the following code spec:

```
<?xml version="1.0"?>
<!DOCTYPE hibernate-mapping PUBLIC "-//Hibernate/Hibernate Mapping DTD 3.0//EN"
"http://hibernate.sourceforge.net/hibernate-mapping-3.0.dtd">
<hibernate-mapping>
    <class name="com.development.hibernate.customer.Email" table="email"
    catalog="customerdb">
        <id name="emailid" type="java.lang.Integer">
            <column name="EMAILID" />
            <generator class="identity" />
        </id>
        <many-to-one name="customer"
        class="com.development.hibernate.customer.Customer" fetch="select">
            <column name="CUSTOMERID" />
        </many-to-one>
```

```
        <property name="email" type="string">
            <column name="EMAIL" length="75" />
        </property>
    </class>
</hibernate-mapping>
```

Explanation:

One customer can have multiple emails. This association is depicted using:

```
<many-to-one name="customer"
class="com.development.hibernate.customer.Customer" fetch="select">
   <column name="CUSTOMERID" />
</many-to-one>
```

DAO

Create a Java class called **EmailDAO** under the package **com.development.hibernate.customer** with the following code spec:

```
package com.development.hibernate.customer;

import com.development.utils.BaseDAO;

public class EmailDAO extends BaseDAO {
    public void deleteAll(int customerid) {
        try {
            beginTransaction();
            getSession().createQuery("DELETE FROM Email
            WHERE customerid = :customerid")
                    .setInteger("customerid", customerid)
                    .executeUpdate();
            commitTransaction();
        }
        catch (RuntimeException re) {
            re.printStackTrace();
            throw re;
```

```
        }
    }
}
```

Explanation:

The **EmailDAO** class extends another DAO class i.e. **BaseDAO** and thus gains access to the methods such as **getSession(), beginTransaction()** and **commitTransaction()**.

This class provides the following methods that allow database operations:

- **deleteAll():** This method accepts the customerid. This method when invoked, begins a transaction, creates and fires a query that deletes all the email addresses belonging to a particular customer and finally commits the transaction

This DAO holds only a single method [**deleteAll()**] which is called when a customer's data is being updated. Whenever the user edits the customer data and clicks **Save**, all the existing email addresses of that customer are deleted and the fresh email addresses available in the data entry form are re-inserted in the Email table. This process emulates the Email update operation.

The standard **save, update** and **delete** operations will happen in cascade manner via the Customer's DAO. This means the Customer POJO will hold the customer data along with the **email addresses** [Set<Email> emails] which will be passed to the Customer DAO's **save()** or **update()** or **delete()** method as the case may be.

HINT

To create the **POJO** and the **Mapping document** using **Hibernate Tools →** Reverse Engineering using Tables refer the topic: *Creating POJO And Mapping Documents Automatically* [explained later]. These can be created manually as well.

After the POJO and the mapping documents are created, using the NetBeans IDE, add a new **Java class** [as shown in diagram 23.3.1] named **EmailDAO.java** under a **package** called **com.development.hibernate.customer** as shown earlier.

Creating POJO And Mapping Documents Automatically

Use the same steps as explained earlier to create POJO and Mapping documents for the Customer and Email tables as shown in diagram 23.5.1.

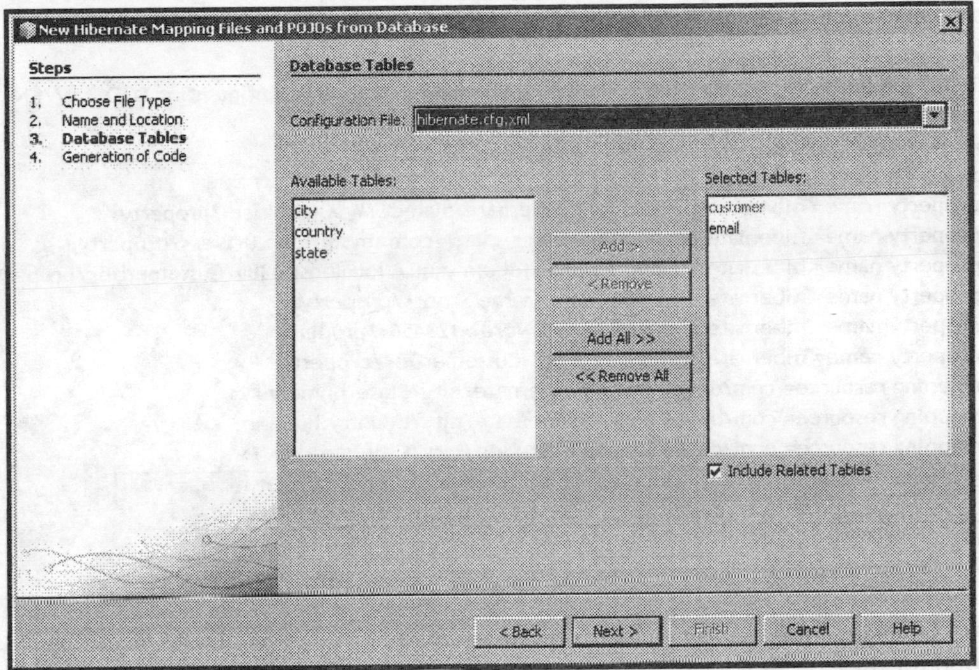

Diagram 23.5.1: New Hibernate Mapping Files and POJOs from Database

This wizard creates the POJOs and mapping documents.

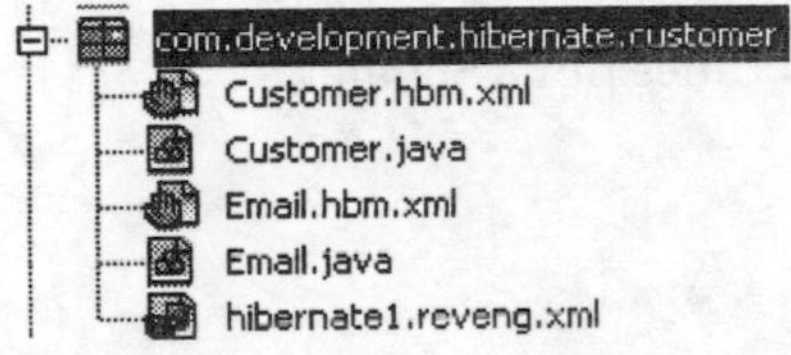

Cascade All

If the mapping documents were automatically created then the cascade option needs to be manually added as by default these files do not have the cascade option that is required in this application. Hence, edit the Customer.hbm.xml file and add the **cascade** attribute.

```
<set name="emails" cascade="all">
    <key>
        <column name="CUSTOMERID" />
    </key>
    <one-to-many class="com.development.hibernate.customer.Email" />
</set>
```

The wizard also adds the appropriate mapping resources in the **hibernate.cfg.xml** file.

```
<?xml version="1.0" encoding="UTF-8"?>
<!DOCTYPE hibernate-configuration PUBLIC "-//Hibernate/Hibernate Configuration DTD 3.0//EN"
"http://hibernate.sourceforge.net/hibernate-configuration-3.0.dtd">
<hibernate-configuration>
  <session-factory>
    <property name="hibernate.dialect">org.hibernate.dialect.MySQLDialect</property>
    <property name="hibernate.connection.driver_class">com.mysql.jdbc.Driver</property>
    <property name="hibernate.connection.url">jdbc:mysql://localhost:3306/CustomerDB</property>
    <property name="hibernate.connection.username">root</property>
    <property name="hibernate.connection.password">123456</property>
    <property name="hibernate.default_catalog">CustomerDB</property>
    <mapping resource="com/development/hibernate/city/State.hbm.xml"/>
    <mapping resource="com/development/hibernate/city/Country.hbm.xml"/>
    <mapping resource="com/development/hibernate/city/City.hbm.xml"/>
    <mapping resource="com/development/hibernate/customer/Customer.hbm.xml"/>
    <mapping resource="com/development/hibernate/customer/Email.hbm.xml"/>
  </session-factory>
</hibernate-configuration>
```

Since the POJOs and the mapping documents are created, the **DAO** classes [CountryDAO, EmailDAO] for these **POJOs** can now be created.

Servlets

This application uses Ajax to retrieve States [for a Country] and Cities [for a State].

The retrieval is done by Servlets.

GetStateList [com.development.servlet]

This Servlet:

- Receives the CountryCode as a request parameter via Ajax
- Passes the CountryCode to the StateDAO object's findByCountryCode()
  - findByCountryCode() returns a list of states for that country
- Prints the list to the PrintWriter for Ajax to receive

Create a Java class called **GetStateList** under the package **com.development.servlet** with the following code spec:

```
package com.development.servlet;

```

```
import com.development.hibernate.city.State;
import com.development.hibernate.city.StateDAO;
import java.io.IOException;
import java.io.PrintWriter;
import java.util.List;
import javax.servlet.ServletException;
import javax.servlet.http.HttpServlet;
import javax.servlet.http.HttpServletRequest;
import javax.servlet.http.HttpServletResponse;

public class GetStateList extends HttpServlet {
    private String outstr = "";

    @Override
    protected void doGet(HttpServletRequest request, HttpServletResponse response)
    throws ServletException, IOException {
        PrintWriter out = response.getWriter();
        String searchValue = request.getParameter("searchValue");

        if (searchValue.length() > 0) {
            List<State> stateList = null;
            StateDAO stateDao = new StateDAO();

            try {
                stateList = stateDao.findByCountryCode(Integer.parseInt(searchValue));

                if (stateList != null && !stateList.isEmpty()) {
                    outstr = "";
                    for (State state : stateList) {
                        Integer val = state.getStatecode();
                        String str = state.getStatename();

                        if (outstr.length() == 0) {
                            outstr = val + "|" + str;
                        }
                        else {
                            outstr += "," + val + "|" + str;
```

```
                    }
                }
            }
        }
        catch (Exception e) {
            e.printStackTrace();
        }

        out.print(outstr);
        out.flush();
        out.close();
    }
  }
}
```

GetCityList [com.development.servlet]

This Servlet:

- Receives the StateCode as a request parameter via Ajax
- Passes the StateCode to the CityDAO object's findByStateCode()
    - findByStateCode() returns a list of cities for that state
- Prints the list to the PrintWriter for Ajax to receive

Create a Java class called **GetCityList** under the package **com.development.servlet** with the following code spec:

```
package com.development.servlet;

import com.development.hibernate.city.City;
import com.development.hibernate.city.CityDAO;
import java.io.IOException;
import java.io.PrintWriter;
import java.util.List;
import javax.servlet.ServletException;
import javax.servlet.http.HttpServlet;
import javax.servlet.http.HttpServletRequest;
import javax.servlet.http.HttpServletResponse;

```

```
public class GetCityList extends HttpServlet {
    private String outstr = "";

    @Override
    protected void doGet(HttpServletRequest request, HttpServletResponse response)
    throws ServletException, IOException {
        PrintWriter out = response.getWriter();
        String searchValue = request.getParameter("searchValue");

        if (searchValue.length() > 0) {
            List<City> cityList = null;
            CityDAO cityDao = new CityDAO();

            try {
                cityList = cityDao.findByStateCode(Integer.parseInt(searchValue));

                if (cityList != null && !cityList.isEmpty()) {
                    outstr = "";
                    for (City city : cityList) {
                        Integer val = city.getCitycode();
                        String str = city.getCityname();

                        if (outstr.length() == 0) {
                            outstr = val + "|" + str;
                        }
                        else {
                            outstr += "," + val + "|" + str;
                        }
                    }
                }
            }
            catch (Exception e) {
                e.printStackTrace();
            }

            out.print(outstr);
            out.flush();
```

```
            out.close();
        }
    }
}
```

JSP

Customer.jsp [jsp/customer]

Now that all the required functionality is in place, let's build the view.

The JSP:

- Holds a data entry form
  - To accept fresh customer data
  - To edit existing customer's data
- Holds a data grid
  - To view existing customers
  - To initiate
    - Edit
    - Delete
- Holds a footer [jsp/footer.jsp]

Technically, this JSP will allow:

- Insert
- Update
- Delete
- View

All these actions are submitted to the same JSP for processing. This means the FORM ACTION points to the same JSP file.

These actions are bifurcated as:

- Application Initialization & View Operation
- Save Operation
- Edit Operation
- Delete Operation

Once the action is determined, the DAO object's methods are invoked to perform the appropriate database operation.

Create a JSP called **Customer** under the directory **jsp/customer** with the following code spec:

```
<%@ page contentType="text/html; charset=UTF-8" import="java.util.*, com.development.hibernate.city.*, com.development.hibernate.customer.*" %>
<%@ taglib uri="http://displaytag.sf.net" prefix="display"%>

<%!
   private Customer customer = new Customer();
   private String emailone, emailtwo, emailthree;
   private CustomerDAO customerDao = new CustomerDAO();
   private EmailDAO emailDao = new EmailDAO();
   private List<Customer> customerList = new ArrayList<Customer>();
%>

<%
   customerList = customerDao.findAll();
   request.getSession().setAttribute("list", customerList);

   String editFlag = request.getParameter("editFlag");
   String deleteFlag = request.getParameter("deleteFlag");
   String submit = (request.getParameter("btnSubmit")!= null ? request.getParameter("btnSubmit") : "");

   if(submit.equals("Save")){
      Customer customerForSave = new Customer();

      if(editFlag!= null && editFlag.equals("Y")){
         customerForSave.setCustomerid(Integer.parseInt(request.getParameter("customerid")));
      }
      customerForSave.setCustomername(request.getParameter("customername"));
      customerForSave.setCustomeraddress(request.getParameter("customeraddress"));
      customerForSave.setCustomercity(request.getParameter("customercity"));
      customerForSave.setCustomercountry(request.getParameter("customercountry"));
      customerForSave.setCustomerfax(request.getParameter("customerfax"));
      customerForSave.setCustomermobile(request.getParameter("customermobile"));
      customerForSave.setCustomerstate(request.getParameter("customerstate"));
      customerForSave.setCustomertelephone(request.getParameter("customertelephone"));
      customerForSave.getEmails().add(new Email(customerForSave, request.getParameter("emailone")));
      customerForSave.getEmails().add(new Email(customerForSave, request.getParameter("emailtwo")));
      customerForSave.getEmails().add(new Email(customerForSave, request.getParameter("emailthree")));

      if (editFlag != null && editFlag.equals("Y")) {
         emailDao.deleteAll(Integer.parseInt(request.getParameter("customerid")));
         customerDao.update(customerForSave);
      }
      else {
```

Required for Display Tag

View Operation

Application Initialization

Save Operation

```
        customerDao.save(customerForSave);
    }

    editFlag = "";

    response.sendRedirect("Customer.jsp");
}

```

Edit Operation

```
if(editFlag!= null && editFlag.equals("Y")){
    customer = new Customer();
    customer = customerDao.findByCustomerCode(Integer.parseInt(request.getParameter("customerid")));

    Set<Email> emails = customer.getEmails();
    String[] mailArray = new String[3];
    int count = 0;

    if (!emails.isEmpty()) {
        for (Email mail : emails) {
            if (mail.getEmail() != null && !mail.getEmail().equals("")) {
                mailArray[count] = mail.getEmail();
            }
            else {
                mailArray[count] = "";
            }
            count++;
        }
    }
    emailone = mailArray[0];
    emailtwo = mailArray[1];
    emailthree = mailArray[2];
}

```

Delete

```
if(deleteFlag!= null && deleteFlag.equals("Y")){
    Customer customerForDelete =
    customerDao.findByCustomerCode(Integer.parseInt(request.getParameter("customerid")));
    customerDao.delete(customerForDelete);

    response.sendRedirect("Customer.jsp");
}
%>
<html>
    <head>
        <title>Customer Database</title>
        <script language="JavaScript" type="text/JavaScript" src="../../javaScript/ajax/jquery2.js"></script>
        <script language="JavaScript" type="text/JavaScript" src="../../javaScript/customer/customer.js"></script>
        <link href="../../css/stylesheet.css" type="text/css" rel="stylesheet">
    </head>
    <body>
        <div id="header"></div>
```

```
<form name="frmCustomerDatabase" method="post">
    <input type="hidden" name="customerid" value="<%=(customer.getCustomerid() != null ?
    customer.getCustomerid() : "")%>" />
    <table width="100%" border="0" align="center" cellpadding="0" cellspacing="0">
        <tr>
            <td>
                <table border="0" cellpadding="0" cellspacing="0" width="100%">
                    <tr>
                        <td valign="top" align="left" class="spanHeader">
                            <span>Customer Database</span>
                        </td>
                        <td class="treb13blacknormal" valign="top" align="right">
                            It is mandatory to enter information in all information <br>capture boxes which have a
                            <span class="mandatory">*</span> adjacent
                        </td>
                    </tr>
                </table>
            </td>
        </tr>
        <tr align="left" valign="top">
            <td height="20" style="background:url('../../images/hr.jpg') repeat-x;"> </td>
        </tr>
        <tr align="left" valign="top">
            <td>
                <table width="90%" border="0" align="center" cellpadding="0" cellspacing="0">
                    <tr>
                        <td>
                            <table width="100%" border="0" cellpadding="0" cellspacing="0">
                                <tr>
                                    <td class="Arial13BrownB" colspan="2" align="left">
                                        <br />Name<br /><br />
                                    </td>
                                </tr>
                                <tr>
                                    <td>
                                        Customer Name<span class="mandatory">*</span>:
                                    </td>
                                    <td>
                                        <input type="text" name="customername"
                                        value="<%=(customer.getCustomername() != null ?
                                        customer.getCustomername() : "")%>" title="Enter the customer name"
                                        maxLength="25" size="55"/>
                                    </td>
                                </tr>
                                <tr>
                                    <td class="Arial13BrownB" colspan="2" align="left">
                                        <br />Mailing Address<br /><br />
                                    </td>
                                </tr>
```

```
<tr>
  <td>
    Address:
  </td>
  <td>
    <input type="text" name="customeraddress"
    value="<%=(customer.getCustomeraddress() != null ?
    customer.getCustomeraddress() : "")%>" title="Enter the street address"
    maxLength="50" size="55"/>
  </td>
</tr>
<tr>
  <td>
    Country:
  </td>
  <td>
    <select id="SaveCustomer_customer_customercountry" name="customercountry"
    onchange="getStateList()">
      <option value="">-- Please Select --</option>
        <%
          String code = "";
          String name = "";
          CountryDAO countryDao = new CountryDAO();
          List<Country> countryList = countryDao.findAll();
          for (Country country : countryList) {
            code = country.getCountrycode().toString();
            name = country.getCountryname();
        %>
      <option value="<%=code%>"><%=name%></option>
        <%
          }
        %>
    </select>
    <script>
      document.frmCustomerDatabase.customercountry.value =
      "<%=(customer.getCustomercountry() != null ?
      customer.getCustomercountry() : "")%>";
    </script>
  </td>
</tr>
<tr>
  <td>
    State:
  </td>
  <td>
    <select id="SaveCustomer_customer_customerstate" name="customerstate"
    onchange="getCityList()">
      <option value="">-- Please Select --</option>
    </select>
```

```
<script>
  <%
    if(customer.getCustomerstate() != null) {
  %>
    getStateList();          Invoking GetStateList.java Servlet via Ajax
  <%
    }
  %>
  document.frmCustomerDatabase.customerstate.value =
  "<%=(customer.getCustomerstate() != null ? customer.getCustomerstate() :
  "")%>";
</script>
</td>
</tr>
<tr>
  <td>
    City:
  </td>
  <td>
    <select id="SaveCustomer_customer_customercity" name="customercity" >
      <option value="">-- Please Select --</option>
    </select>
    <script>
      <%
        if(customer.getCustomerstate() != null) {
      %>
        getCityList();          Invoking GetCityList.java Servlet via Ajax
      <%
        }
      %>
      document.frmCustomerDatabase.customercity.value =
      "<%=(customer.getCustomercity() != null ? customer.getCustomercity() :
      "")%>";
    </script>
  </td>
</tr>
<tr>
  <td class="Arial13BrownB" colspan="2" align="left">
    <br />Contact Details<br /><br />
  </td>
</tr>
<tr>
  <td>
    Mobile Number:
  </td>
  <td>
    <input type="text" name="customermobile"
    value="<%=(customer.getCustomermobile() != null ?
    customer.getCustomermobile() : "")%>" title="Enter the mobile number" />
```

```
        </td>
    </tr>
    <tr>
        <td>
            Telephone Number<span class="mandatory">*</span>:
        </td>
        <td>
            <input type="text" name="customertelephone"
            value="<%=(customer.getCustomertelephone() != null ?
            customer.getCustomertelephone() : "")%>" title="Enter the telephone number"
            />
        </td>
    </tr>
    <tr>
        <td>
            Fax Number:
        </td>
        <td>
            <input type="text" name="customerfax" value="<%=(customer.getCustomerfax()
            != null ? customer.getCustomerfax() : "")%>" title="Enter the fax number" />
        </td>
    </tr>
    <tr>
        <td class="Arial13BrownB" colspan="2" align="left">
            <br />Email<br /><br />
        </td>
    </tr>
    <tr>
        <td>
            First Email Address<span class="mandatory">*</span>:
        </td>
        <td>
            <input type="text" name="emailone" value="<%=(emailone != null ? emailone :
            "")%>" title="Enter the first email address" />
        </td>
    </tr>
    <tr>
        <td>
            Second Email Address:
        </td>
        <td>
            <input type="text" name="emailtwo" value="<%=(emailtwo != null ? emailtwo :
            "")%>" title="Enter the second email address" />
        </td>
    </tr>
    <tr>
        <td>
            Third Email Address:
```

```
                        </td>
                        <td>
                            <input type="text" name="emailthree" value="<%=(emailthree != null ? emailthree : "")%>" title="Enter the third email address" />
                        </td>
                    </tr>
                </table>
            </td>
        </tr>
        <tr>
            <td>
                <input type="submit" style="background:url(../../images/submit_bg.gif) no-repeat scroll 37px 0px;" class="buttonText" name="btnSubmit" value="Save" />
            </td>
            <td>
                <input type="reset" style="background:url(../../images/submit_bg.gif) no-repeat scroll 37px 0px;" class="buttonText" name="btnReset" value="Clear" onclick="javascript:document.location.href='Customer.jsp'" />
            </td>
        </tr>
    </table>
    </td>
  </tr>
  <tr align="left" valign="top">
    <td height="20" style="background:url('../../images/hr.jpg') repeat-x;"> </td>
  </tr>
</table>

<table width="100%" border="0" cellspacing="0" cellpadding="0">

    <display:table name="sessionScope.list" pagesize="5"
            excludedParams="*" export="true" cellpadding="0"
            cellspacing="0"
            requestURI="">
      <display:column property="customername" title="Customer Name" maxLength="35" headerClass="gridheader" class="griddata" style="width:30%" sortable="true"/>
      <display:column property="customeraddress" title="Address" maxLength="35" headerClass="gridheader" class="griddata" style="width:50%"/>
      <display:column property="customermobile" title="Mobile" headerClass="gridheader" class="griddata" style="width:15%"/>
      <display:column paramId="customerid" paramProperty="customerid" href="../../jsp/customer/Customer.jsp?editFlag=Y" headerClass="gridheader" class="griddata" media="html">
        <img align="right" src="../../images/edit.jpg" border="0" alt="Edit" style="cursor:pointer;"/>
      </display:column>
      <display:column paramId="customerid" paramProperty="customerid" href="../../jsp/customer/Customer.jsp?deleteFlag=Y" headerClass="gridheader" class="griddata" media="html">
```

Display Tag for Data Grid

```
                <img align="left" src="../../images/TrashIcon.png" border="0" alt="Delete"
                style="cursor:pointer;"/>
            </display:column>
        </display:table>

        </table>
    </form>
    <jsp:include page="../../jsp/footer.jsp" />
    <%
        customer = new Customer();
        emailone = "";
        emailtwo = "";
        emailthree = "";
    %>
  </body>
</html>
```

Cleanup

footer.jsp [jsp/]

Create a JSP called **footer** under the directory **jsp** with the following code spec:

```
<table align="center" width="100%" border="0" cellspacing="0" cellpadding="0">
    <tr height="50px">
        <td align="center"> </td>
    </tr>
    <tr height="50px" id="footer">
        <td align="center">
            <strong>Copyright © 2009, <a href="http://www.sharanamshah.com">Sharanam</a> And <a
            href="http://www.vaishalishahonline.com">Vaishali</a> Shah</strong>
        </td>
    </tr>
</table>
```

This file is included in the Customer.jsp.

```
<jsp:include page="../../jsp/footer.jsp" />
```

JavaScript

Customer.js [javaScript\customer]

This script holds two functions:

- getStateList()
- getCityList()

These functions are invoked by the Customer.jsp to populate:

- States when the user chooses a Country
- Cities when the user chooses a State

```
<script language="JavaScript" type="text/JavaScript" src="../../javaScript/customer/customer.js"></script>
```

Create a JavaScript file called customer under the directory **javaScript\customer** with the following code spec:

```
function getStateList() {
    var searchValue =
    document.getElementById("SaveCustomer_customer_customercountry").value;

    if (searchValue != "") {
        var msg = $.ajax({
            url:"/CustomerDatabase/stateList?searchValue=" + searchValue,
            async:false
        }).responseText;
        var listText = unescape(msg);
        var TypeArray = new Array();
        var TypeArrayInfo = new Array();
        TypeArray = listText.split(",");
        document.getElementById("SaveCustomer_customer_customerstate").options.length = 0;
        document.getElementById("SaveCustomer_customer_customerstate").options.add(new
        Option("-- Please Select --", ""));

        for (i = 0; i < TypeArray.length; i++) {
            TypeArrayInfo = TypeArray[i].split("|");
            document.getElementById("SaveCustomer_customer_customerstate").options.add(new
            Option(TypeArrayInfo[1], TypeArrayInfo[0]));
        }
    }
    else{
        document.getElementById("SaveCustomer_customer_customerstate").options.length = 0;
        document.getElementById("SaveCustomer_customer_customerstate").options.add(new
        Option("-- Please Select --", ""));
        document.getElementById("SaveCustomer_customer_customercity").options.length = 0;
        document.getElementById("SaveCustomer_customer_customercity").options.add(new
        Option("-- Please Select --", ""));
    }
}
```

```
function getCityList() {
    var searchValue = document.getElementById("SaveCustomer_customer_customerstate").value;

    if (searchValue != "") {
        var msg = $.ajax({
            url:"/CustomerDatabase/cityList?searchValue=" + searchValue,
            async:false
        }).responseText;
        var listText = unescape(msg);
        var TypeArray = new Array();
        var TypeArrayInfo = new Array();
        TypeArray = listText.split(",");
        document.getElementById("SaveCustomer_customer_customercity").options.length = 0;
        document.getElementById("SaveCustomer_customer_customercity").options.add(new
        Option("-- Please Select --", ""));

        for (i = 0; i < TypeArray.length; i++) {
            TypeArrayInfo = TypeArray[i].split("|");
            document.getElementById("SaveCustomer_customer_customercity").options.add(new
            Option(TypeArrayInfo[1], TypeArrayInfo[0]));
        }
    }
    else{
        document.getElementById("SaveCustomer_customer_customercity").options.length = 0;
        document.getElementById("SaveCustomer_customer_customercity").options.add(new
        Option("-- Please Select --", ""));
    }
}
```

jquery2 [javaScript\ajax]

jQuery is a lightweight JavaScript library that emphasizes interaction between JavaScript and HTML. It is great library for developing Ajax based application.

This file can be downloaded [available in this book's accompanying CDROM] from: http://docs.jquery.com/Downloading_jQuery#Current_Release.

Download it and place it under **javaScript\ajax**.

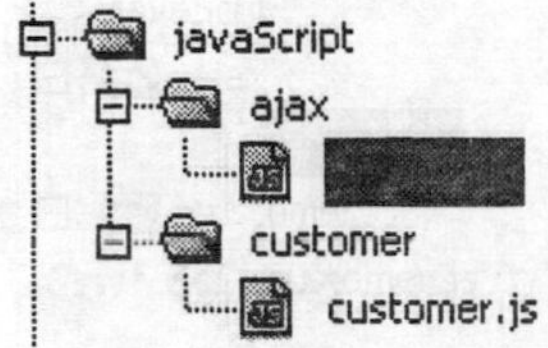

CSS

The application uses a CSS file stylesheet.css to style the JSP.

Customer.jsp uses it.

```
<link href="../../css/stylesheet.css" type="text/css" rel="stylesheet">
```

This file is available on this book's accompanying CDROM. Place it under css.

Images

The application uses a few images to style the JSP. Customer.jsp uses it. These files are available on this book's accompanying CDROM.

Copy those files and place them under **images.**

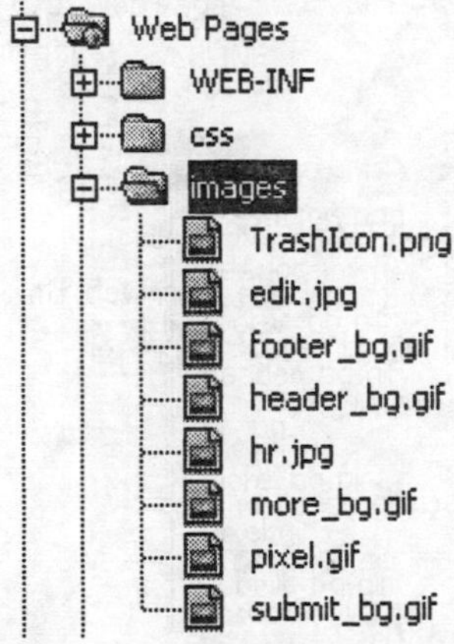

Index Page

Edit the index.jsp file to include the following code spec:

```
<% response.sendRedirect("jsp/customer/Customer.jsp"); %>
```

Display Tag Properties

Since this application uses Display Tag to produce a data grid to display the existing customers, a few properties need to be set.

This can be done using a properties file called **displaytag.properties**.

Create a properties file called **displaytag.properties** under the directory **src\java** with the following code spec:

```
export.types=csv excel xml pdf rtf
export.excel=true
export.csv=true
export.xml=true
export.pdf=true
export.rtf=true
export.pdf.class=org.displaytag.export.DefaultPdfExportView
export.rtf.class=org.displaytag.export.DefaultRtfExportView
export.excel.filename=customer.xls
export.pdf.filename=customer.pdf
export.xml.filename=customer.xml
export.csv.filename=customer.csv
export.rtf.filename=customer.rtf
```

Editing Web.XML

This application uses Servlets and Display Tag library which require creating a few Servlet mappings [for Servlets] and filters [for Display Tag].

Edit the web.xml file available under WEB-INF with the following code spec:

```
<?xml version="1.0" encoding="UTF-8"?>
<web-app version="2.5" xmlns="http://java.sun.com/xml/ns/javaee"
xmlns:xsi="http://www.w3.org/2001/XMLSchema-instance"
```

```
xsi:schemaLocation="http://java.sun.com/xml/ns/javaee
http://java.sun.com/xml/ns/javaee/web-app_2_5.xsd">
```

For Display Tag

```
<filter>
   <filter-name>ResponseOverrideFilter</filter-name>
   <filter-class>org.displaytag.filter.ResponseOverrideFilter</filter-class>
</filter>
<filter-mapping>
<filter-name>ResponseOverrideFilter</filter-name>
   <url-pattern>*.do</url-pattern>
</filter-mapping>
<filter-mapping>
<filter-name>ResponseOverrideFilter</filter-name>
   <url-pattern>*.jsp</url-pattern>
</filter-mapping>
```

For Servlets

```
<servlet>
   <servlet-name>StateList</servlet-name>
   <servlet-class>com.development.servlet.GetStateList</servlet-class>
</servlet>
<servlet>
   <servlet-name>CityList</servlet-name>
   <servlet-class>com.development.servlet.GetCityList</servlet-class>
</servlet>
<servlet-mapping>
   <servlet-name>StateList</servlet-name>
   <url-pattern>/stateList</url-pattern>
</servlet-mapping>
<servlet-mapping>
   <servlet-name>CityList</servlet-name>
   <url-pattern>/cityList</url-pattern>
</servlet-mapping>
<session-config>
   <session-timeout>30</session-timeout>
```

```
    </session-config>
    <welcome-file-list>
        <welcome-file>index.jsp</welcome-file>
    </welcome-file-list>
</web-app>
```

This completes building the application using the NetBeans IDE.

Running The Application

Run the application. To do so, right click the application and choose **Clean and Build**.

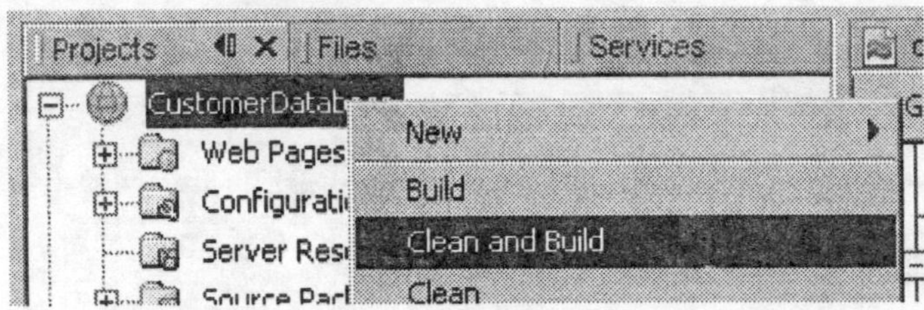

Once done, Run the application.

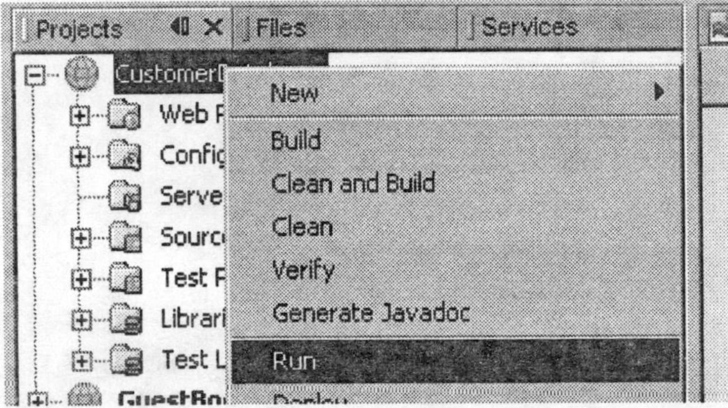

This brings up the application in the default web browser as shown in diagram 23.6.1.

Customer Database

It is mandatory to enter information in all information capture boxes which have a * adjacent

Name

Customer Name*:

Mailing Address

Address:
Country: – Please Select –
State: – Please Select –
City: – Please Select –

Contact Details

Mobile Number:
Telephone Number*:
Fax Number:

Email

First Email Address*:
Second Email Address:
Third Email Address:

SAVE CLEAR

Nothing found to display.

Copyright © 2009, Sharanam And Vaishali Shah

Diagram 23.6.1

Since there are no records, the data grid does not appear and a message indicates the same.

Nothing found to display.

Add a record by keying in the customer data and click Save. This saves the record and the data grid [Display Tag] begins displaying the records inserted as shown in diagram 23.6.2.

9 items found, displaying 1 to 5. [First/Prev] 1, 2 [Next/Last]

Customer Name	Address	Mobile	
Sharanam Shah	Bhakti Pride	9898989898	
Vaishali Shah	Bhakti Pride	878787878	
Stuti Shah	Shivaji Park	9988998	
Chaitanya Shah	Makanji Mansion	6655445566	
Gopi Shah	Makanji Mansion	474747474	

Export options: CSV | Excel | XML | PDF | RTF

Diagram 23.6.2

Edit

The user can edit the desired record by clicking ✎. ✎ when clicked populates the data entry form with the customer's data. The user can make the desired changes and click SAVE ▶.

Delete

The user can delete the desired record by clicking ✖. ✖ when clicked deletes the customer's data along with the emails associated [if any].

Export

The user can choose to export the available records to one of the following formats:

- CSV
- Excel
- XML
- PDF
- RTF

The Book CDROM holds the complete application source code built using the NetBeans IDE for the following application:

- CustomerDatabase_Chap23

This can be directly used by making appropriate changes [username/password] to the configuration file.

Chapter

24

SECTION VI: APPLICATION DEVELOPMENT WITH HIBERNATE

Using Java Persistence API With Hibernate

Till now, the API that was used through out the book, was native to Hibernate and designed by the Hibernate developers.

The same stands true for:

- Query interfaces
- Query language

Using the native API is not the only possibility. Hibernate can also be used with a standardized programming interface such as Java Persistence API.

This chapter is dedicated to JPA. It shows how Java Persistence API can be plugged in an application that uses Hibernate as the ORM.

Java Persistence API is a standardized programming interface that helps simplify application development. Designing and linking to standardized interfaces is an advantage especially when porting or deploying an application on a different runtime environment.

To understand the practical differences between Hibernate's API and JPA, let's re-use the Customer Database application built in *Chapter 23: Customer Database Using JSP*.

This exercise will help understand how JPA differs from Hibernate.

What Is JPA

The **J**ava **P**ersistence Architecture **A**PI [JPA] is a Java specification for accessing, persisting and managing data between Java objects / classes and the relational database.

JPA is:

- Just a specification
- **Not** a product

JPA cannot perform persistence by itself. It is a set of interfaces and requires:

- An implementation to perform persistence
- A database to persist to

There are several open source and commercial JPA **implementations** [such as Hibernate, JDO, TopLink] to choose from.

JPA allows POJO [**P**lain **O**ld **J**ava **O**bjects] to be persisted. The object's object-relational mappings can be defined through:

- Standard annotations
- XML based Mapping document

JPA comprises of:

- **Entities:** Persistent objects that are stored in a relational database
- **The EntityManager API:** The API for performing actual persistence operations such as saving, deleting and retrieving entities
- **The Java Persistence Query Language [JPQL]:** An SQL-like language used to retrieve and manipulate entities

REMINDER

JPA was defined as part of the EJB 3.0 specification as a replacement to the EJB 2 CMP Entity Beans specification. It is now considered the standard industry approach for Object to Relational Mapping [ORM] in the Java Industry.

JPA is meant to unify the ORMs such as EJB 2 CMP, JDO, **Hibernate** and TopLink and seems to have been very successful in doing so.

Why JPA

To perform persistence, either **proprietary** API [POJO API] solutions provided by the ORM tools such as Hibernate, TopLink and so on or **JPA** can be used. Currently most of the persistence vendors have released implementations of JPA. These include Hibernate, TopLink and JDO.

Using JPA as the API solution makes the application code spec standard and portable.

Portable code spec means the persistence provider [Hibernate, Toplink, JDO and so on] can be changed without changing the code spec.

For example Hibernate persistence can be switched to TopLink persistence without any modifications in the Java files.

The only change that is required is:

- The configuration file i.e. persistence.xml
- The new persistence provider's library files

JPA's Requirements

To use JPA as the persistence API, the following is needed:

- One or more **entity classes**
- **EntityManagerFactory** and **EntityManager** instance
- **EntityTransaction** instance
- **Persistence unit** written in XML
- **Database** engine

Once all of these are organized, a persistence solution can be implemented.

Most of this is already in place in the Customer Database application. Let's use that application and modify it to use JPA **instead of** Hibernate's native/proprietary API.

The Customer Database Application

Open the Customer Database Application [created earlier in *Chapter 23: Customer Database Using JSP*] using the NetBeans IDE. This application has the following in place:

- **JSP** for data entry form to allow Insert, Update, Delete and View
- **POJOs** for Country, State, City, Customer, Email
- **Mapping Documents** for all the POJOs
- **SessionFactory** and **Session** Instance
- **Transaction** Instance
- **DAO** for performing database operations [**C**reate, **R**ead, **U**pdate, **D**elete]
- Hibernate **Configuration** File

Based on the JPA requirements [defined earlier], the following is how the modifications will take place.

Hibernate's native API	Java Persistence API [JPA]
JSP	Will remain the same
POJO	Will remain the same
Mapping Documents	Will remain the same
SessionFactory Instance	Will be **replaced** with **EntityManagerFactory** Instance
Session Instance	Will be **replaced** with **EntityManager** Instance
Transaction Instance	Will be **replaced** with **EntityTransaction** Instance
Instance Methods in the **DAO** classes: ❑ beginTransaction() ❑ save() ❑ update() ❑ delete() ❑ begin() ❑ commit() ❑ createQuery() ❑ list() ❑ load()	Will be **replaced** with new Instance's methods: ❑ getTransaction() ❑ persist() ❑ merge() ❑ remove() ❑ begin() ❑ commit() ❑ createQuery() ❑ getResultList() ❑ find()
Hibernate **Configuration** File	Will be edited and a new configuration file called a **Persistence Unit** [XML] will be created that references Hibernate **Configuration** File

In this application, the Session Factory and the Transaction Instances are spawned in the BaseDAO.java and IBaseHibernateDAO.java. Hence these will be edited.

EntityManager And Transaction Instances [BaseDAO.java]

Edit the IBaseHibernateDAO.java as:

```
package com.development.utils;

import org.hibernate.Session;                  Remove this
import javax.persistence.EntityManager;        Add this

public interface IBaseHibernateDAO {
    public Session getSession();               Remove this
    public EntityManager getSession();         Add this
}
```

Explanation:

Here:

The following programming interface is imported:

- **javax.persistence.EntityManager:** The equivalent to a Hibernate Session. This single-threaded, non-shared object represents a particular unit of work for data access. It provides methods to manage the lifecycle of entity instances and to create Query instances

The Session instance used by Hibernate is replaced with EntityManager instance provided by JPA.

JPA uses many interfaces and annotation types defined in the **javax.persistence package** available with Java EE 5.

Edit the BaseDAO.java as:

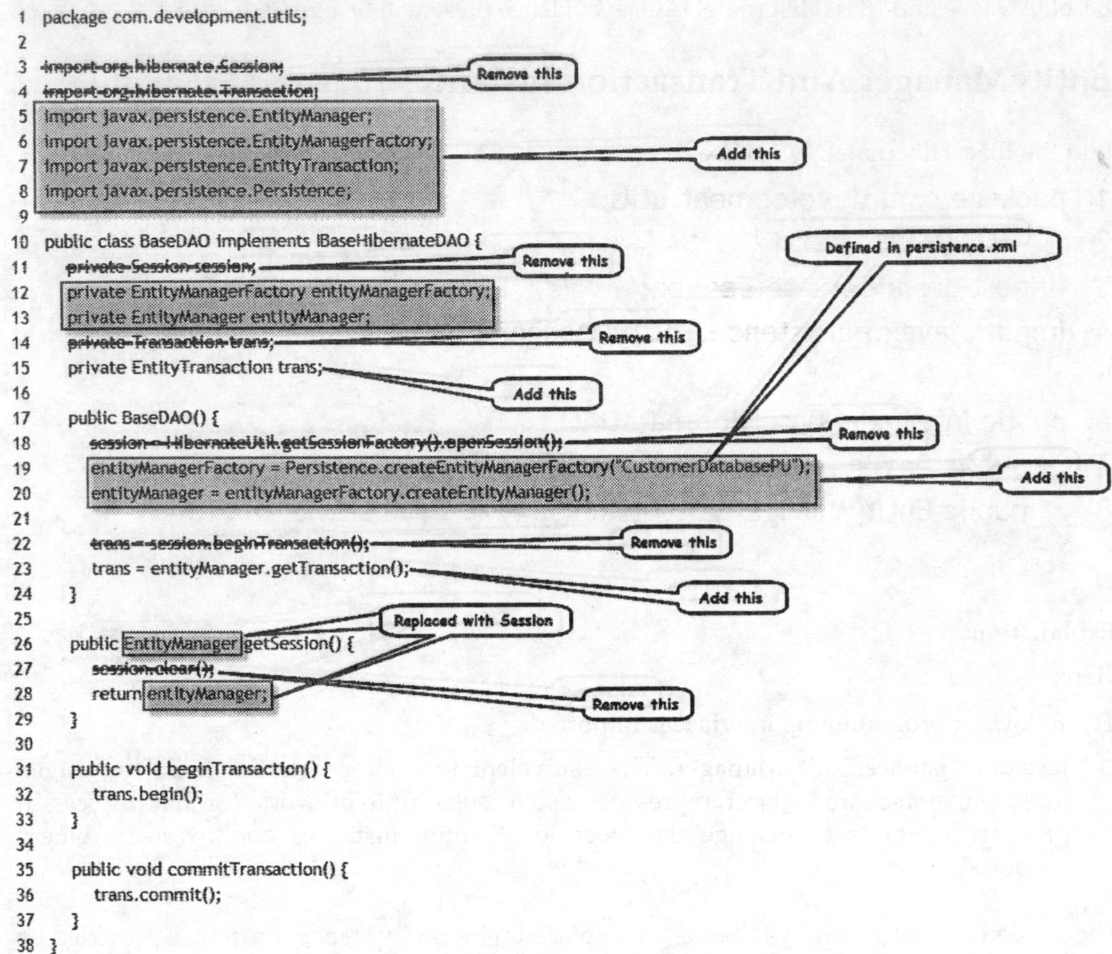

```
package com.development.utils;

import org.hibernate.Session;
import org.hibernate.Transaction;
import javax.persistence.EntityManager;
import javax.persistence.EntityManagerFactory;
import javax.persistence.EntityTransaction;
import javax.persistence.Persistence;

public class BaseDAO implements IBaseHibernateDAO {
    private Session session;
    private EntityManagerFactory entityManagerFactory;
    private EntityManager entityManager;
    private Transaction trans;
    private EntityTransaction trans;

    public BaseDAO() {
        session = HibernateUtil.getSessionFactory().openSession();
        entityManagerFactory = Persistence.createEntityManagerFactory("CustomerDatabasePU");
        entityManager = entityManagerFactory.createEntityManager();

        trans = session.beginTransaction();
        trans = entityManager.getTransaction();
    }

    public EntityManager getSession() {
        session.clear();
        return entityManager;
    }

    public void beginTransaction() {
        trans.begin();
    }

    public void commitTransaction() {
        trans.commit();
    }
}
```


Explanation:

Here:

The following programming interfaces are imported:

- **javax.persistence.Persistence:** A startup class that provides a static method for the creation of an EntityManagerFactory
- **javax.persistence.EntityManagerFactory:** The equivalent to a Hibernate SessionFactory. This runtime object represents a particular persistence unit. It is thread-safe and is usually handled as a singleton and provides methods for the creation of EntityManager instances

- **javax.persistence.EntityManager:** The equivalent to a Hibernate Session. This single-threaded, non-shared object represents a particular unit of work for data access. It provides methods to manage the lifecycle of entity instances and to create Query instances
- **javax.persistence.EntityTransaction:** This is the equivalent to a Hibernate Transaction, used for the demarcation of transactions

EntityManager is created using an EntityManagerFactory.

```
entityManagerFactory = Persistence.createEntityManagerFactory("CustomerDatabasePU");
entityManager = entityManagerFactory.createEntityManager();
```

The life cycle of JPA entities is managed by the entity manager, which is an instance of **javax.persistence.EntityManager**. Each such entity manager is associated with a persistence context. This context can be either propagated across all application components or managed by the application.

CustomerDatabasePU indicates the persistence unit's name defined in the persistence.xml file [will be created later].

```
trans = entityManager.getTransaction();
```

The Transaction object is instantiated using getTransaction() method of the EntityManager instance.

getSession() now returns an EntityManager [JPA] object instead of a Session [Hibernate] object.

The remaining code spec is quite self-explanatory. JPA is used very similar to Hibernate with a few minor differences in the API and the method names.

Removing The HibernateUtil Helper Class

Since, the EntityManagerFactory and EntityManager instances are used, the HibernateUtil helper class is no more required. Hence, **delete this class**.

In this application, the infrastructure initialization code spec is written directly in the BaseDAO.java class. However, a similar helper class such as **JPAUtil** can be created which can hold the code spec for creation of an EntityManagerFactory.

<u>To keep things simpler, let's not use a helper class.</u>

Instance Methods In DAO Classes

CityDAO.java [com.development.hibernate.city]

Edit the CityDAO.java as:

```
package com.development.hibernate.city;

import com.development.utils.BaseDAO;
import java.util.List;

public class CityDAO extends BaseDAO {
    public void save(City city) {
        try {
            beginTransaction();
            getSession().persist(city);
            commitTransaction();
        }
        catch (RuntimeException re) {
            re.printStackTrace();
            throw re;
        }
    }

    public List<City> findAll() {
        beginTransaction();
        List<City> list = getSession().createQuery("from City").getResultList();
        commitTransaction();
        return list;
    }

    public List<City> findByStateCode(Integer stateCode) {
        beginTransaction();
        List<City> list = getSession().createQuery("select c from City c where c.state.statecode = :stateCode")
                .setParameter("stateCode", stateCode)
                .getResultList();
        commitTransaction();
        return list;
    }
}
```

Replaced with save() method

Replaced with list() method

Replaced with list() method

Explanation:

Different ORM solutions use different terminologies. For example, the API in Hibernate is the Session.

As seen in the above code spec, the method names that are changed are almost equivalent to Hibernate. In fact, most of the methods of the Session have a counterpart in the EntityManager API.

In the above code spec,

- Hibernate Session's **save()** is replaced with JPA Entity Manager's **persist()**
- Hibernate Session's **list()** is replaced with JPA Entity Manager's **getResultList()**

The city object becomes persistent as soon persist() is invoked on it.

CountryDAO.java [com.development.hibernate.city]

Edit the CountryDAO.java as:

```
package com.development.hibernate.city;

import com.development.utils.BaseDAO;
import java.util.List;

public class CountryDAO extends BaseDAO {
    public void save(Country country) {
        try {
            beginTransaction();
            getSession().persist(country);
            commitTransaction();
        }
        catch (RuntimeException re) {
            re.printStackTrace();
            throw re;
        }
    }

    public List<Country> findAll() {
        beginTransaction();
        List<Country> list = getSession().createQuery("from Country").getResultList();
        commitTransaction();
        return list;
    }
}
```

Replaced with save() method

Replaced with list() method

StateDAO.java [com.development.hibernate.city]

Edit the StateDAO.java as:

```
package com.development.hibernate.city;

import com.development.utils.BaseDAO;
import java.util.List;

public class StateDAO extends BaseDAO {
    public void save(State state) {
        try {
            beginTransaction();
            getSession().persist(state);
            commitTransaction();
        }
        catch (RuntimeException re) {
            re.printStackTrace();
            throw re;
        }
    }

    public List<State> findAll() {
        beginTransaction();
        List<State> list = getSession().createQuery("from State").getResultList();
        commitTransaction();
        return list;
    }

    public List<State> findByCountryCode(Integer countryCode) {
        beginTransaction();
        List<State> list = getSession().createQuery("select s from State s where
        s.country.countrycode = :countryCode")
```

Replaced with save() method

Replaced with list() method

```
            .setParameter("countryCode", countryCode)
            .getResultList();
        commitTransaction();
        return list;
    }
}
```

Replaced with list() method

CustomerDAO.java [com.development.hibernate.customer]

Edit the CustomerDAO.java as:

```
package com.development.hibernate.customer;

import com.development.utils.BaseDAO;
import java.util.List;

public class CustomerDAO extends BaseDAO {
    public void save(Customer customer) {
        try {
            beginTransaction();
            getSession().persist(customer);
            commitTransaction();
        }
        catch (RuntimeException re) {
            re.printStackTrace();
            throw re;
        }
    }

    public void update(Customer customer) {
        try {
            beginTransaction();
            getSession().merge(customer);
            commitTransaction();
        }
        catch (RuntimeException re) {
```

Replaced with save() method

Replaced with update() method

```
            re.printStackTrace();
            throw re;
        }
    }

    public void delete(Customer customer) {
        try {
            beginTransaction();
            getSession().remove(customer);
            commitTransaction();
        }
        catch (RuntimeException re) {
            re.printStackTrace();
            throw re;
        }
    }

    public List<Customer> findAll() {
        beginTransaction();
        List<Customer> list = getSession().createQuery("select c from Customer c").getResultList();
        commitTransaction();
        return list;
    }

    public Customer findByCustomerCode(Integer customerCode) {
        beginTransaction();
        Customer customer = new Customer();
        customer = (Customer) getSession().find(Customer.class, customerCode);
        commitTransaction();
        return customer;
    }
}
```

Replaced with delete() method

Replaced with list() method

Replaced with load() method

EmailDAO.java [com.development.hibernate.customer]

Edit the EmailDAO.java as:

```
package com.development.hibernate.customer;

import com.development.utils.BaseDAO;

public class EmailDAO extends BaseDAO {
    public void deleteAll(int customerid) {
        try {
            beginTransaction();
            getSession().createQuery("DELETE FROM Email WHERE customerid = :customerid")
                    .setParameter("customerid", customerid)
                    .executeUpdate();
            commitTransaction();
        }
        catch (RuntimeException re) {
            re.printStackTrace();
            throw re;
        }
    }
}
```

Explanation:

This DAO class remains unchanged.

Adding Persistence Unit [persistence.xml]

A SessionFactory represents a particular logical data-store configuration in a Hibernate application.

The **EntityManagerFactory** in JPA is equivalent to the SessionFactory in Hibernate. The EntityManagerFactory can either use configuration files or programmatic configuration code spec in the application code very similar to SessionFactory.

In JPA, this configuration, together with a set of mapping metadata, is called a **persistence unit** [persistence.xml].

Create the persistence unit in a file called persistence.xml.

```
<?xml version="1.0" encoding="UTF-8"?>
<persistence version="1.0" xmlns="http://java.sun.com/xml/ns/persistence"
xmlns:xsi="http://www.w3.org/2001/XMLSchema-instance"
xsi:schemaLocation="http://java.sun.com/xml/ns/persistence
http://java.sun.com/xml/ns/persistence/persistence_1_0.xsd">
  <persistence-unit name="CustomerDatabasePU">
    <provider>org.hibernate.ejb.HibernatePersistence</provider>
    <properties>
      <property name="hibernate.ejb.cfgfile" value="/hibernate.cfg.xml"/>
    </properties>
  </persistence-unit>
</persistence>
```

This file will be placed under Configuration Files:

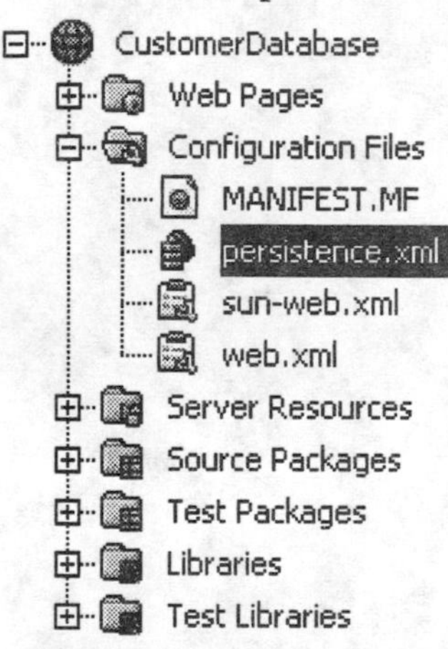

Explanation:

Since, the Hibernate configuration file called hibernate.cfg.xml already exists, the same file is referred.

```
<property name="hibernate.ejb.cfgfile" value="/hibernate.cfg.xml"/>
```

```
<persistence-unit name="CustomerDatabasePU"
```

CustomerDatabasePU is the persistence unit name which will be referred by the createEntityManagerFactory() method of the Persistence interface.

In this application, the BaseDAO class uses the persistence unit name:

```
public BaseDAO() {
    entityManagerFactory =
    Persistence.createEntityManagerFactory("CustomerDatabasePU");
    entityManager = entityManagerFactory.createEntityManager();
    trans = entityManager.getTransaction();
}
```

Modifying Hibernate Configuration File [hibernate.cfg.xml]

Now that this application uses Hibernate EntityManager, it is no longer required to list all annotated classes or XML mapping files in the Hibernate configuration file. These are automatically detected at runtime.

Hence, edit Hibernate configuration file:

```
<?xml version="1.0" encoding="UTF-8"?>
<!DOCTYPE hibernate-configuration PUBLIC "-//Hibernate/Hibernate Configuration DTD 3.0//EN"
"http://hibernate.sourceforge.net/hibernate-configuration-3.0.dtd">
<hibernate-configuration>
  <session-factory>
    <property name="hibernate.dialect">org.hibernate.dialect.MySQLDialect</property>
    <property name="hibernate.connection.driver_class">com.mysql.jdbc.Driver</property>
    <property name="hibernate.connection.url">jdbc:mysql://localhost:3306/CustomerDB</property>
    <property name="hibernate.connection.username">root</property>
    <property name="hibernate.connection.password">123456</property>
    <property name="hibernate.default_catalog">CustomerDB</property>
    <mapping resource="com/development/hibernate/city/State.hbm.xml"/>
    <mapping resource="com/development/hibernate/city/Country.hbm.xml"/>
    <mapping resource="com/development/hibernate/city/City.hbm.xml"/>
    <mapping resource="com/development/hibernate/customer/Customer.hbm.xml"/>
    <mapping resource="com/development/hibernate/customer/Email.hbm.xml"/>
  </session-factory>
</hibernate-configuration>
```

Remove this

Adding The Hibernate EntityManager Library Files

This application now uses JPA with Hibernate. Hence, appropriate library files have to be added to the project.

Downloading The Required Library Files

This application requires the following:

Hibernate EntityManager

The Hibernate EntityManger can be downloaded from http://www.hibernate.org → Download.

Copying Library Files To The Dedicated Directory

Copy the following library files to the lib directory of this application:

- From the **hibernate-entitymanager-3.4.0.GA** directory
  - hibernate-entitymanager.jar
- From the **hibernate-entitymanager-3.4.0.GA → lib** directory
  - ejb3-persistence.jar

HINT

Now add these libraries to the application using the NetBeans IDE. Refer to *Chapter 03: Writing The First Application* for the steps to add libraries using the NetBeans IDE.

This completes building the application.

Run the application to see it working.

The Book CDROM holds the complete application source code built using the NetBeans IDE for the following application:

- CustomerDatabase_Chap24

This can be directly used by making appropriate changes [username/password] to the configuration file.

SECTION VI: APPLICATION DEVELOPMENT WITH HIBERNATE

Customer Database Using Struts^2

Hibernate can be used in just about any kind of Java application. It may run inside a Servlet, JSP, JSF, a Swing client and so on. It can also be used along with Model-View-Controller [MVC] Web application frameworks such as Struts, Spring, Tapestry and so on.

This chapter uses Struts^2 to demonstrate building the **Customer Database** application [as defined in *Chapter 23: Customer Database Using JSP*] with Hibernate as the ORM tool.

This application will use:

- **JSP** as the delivery mechanism
- **Struts^2** as the web application framework

- **Hibernate** as the ORM tool
- **DAO** as the design pattern
- **MySQL** as the database
- **Ajax** wherever required

All the code spec will be built and deployed using the **NetBeans IDE**.

Database Tables

Entity Relationship Diagram

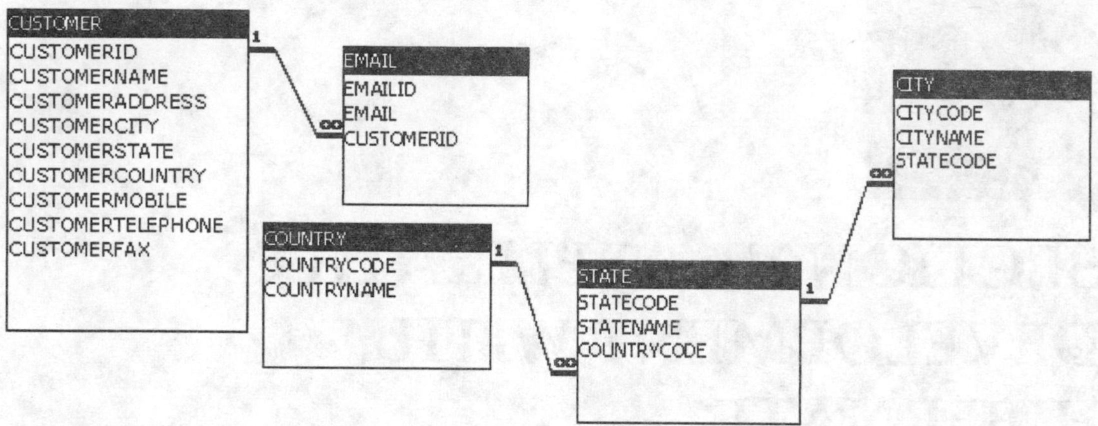

For table specifications refer to *Chapter 23: Customer Database Using JSP*.

The table creation code spec is available as an SQL script **[CustomerDBMySQL.sql]** in the Book's accompanying CDROM.

Prior proceeding, ensure that the following is ready:

- A database called **CustomerDB**
- The above defined tables within this database

Building The Application

Creating Web Application

Since NetBeans is the IDE of choice throughout this book. Use it to create a new Web Application Project called **CustomerDatabase**.

Run the NetBeans IDE and create a new **Web Application** project, as shown in diagram 25.1.1.

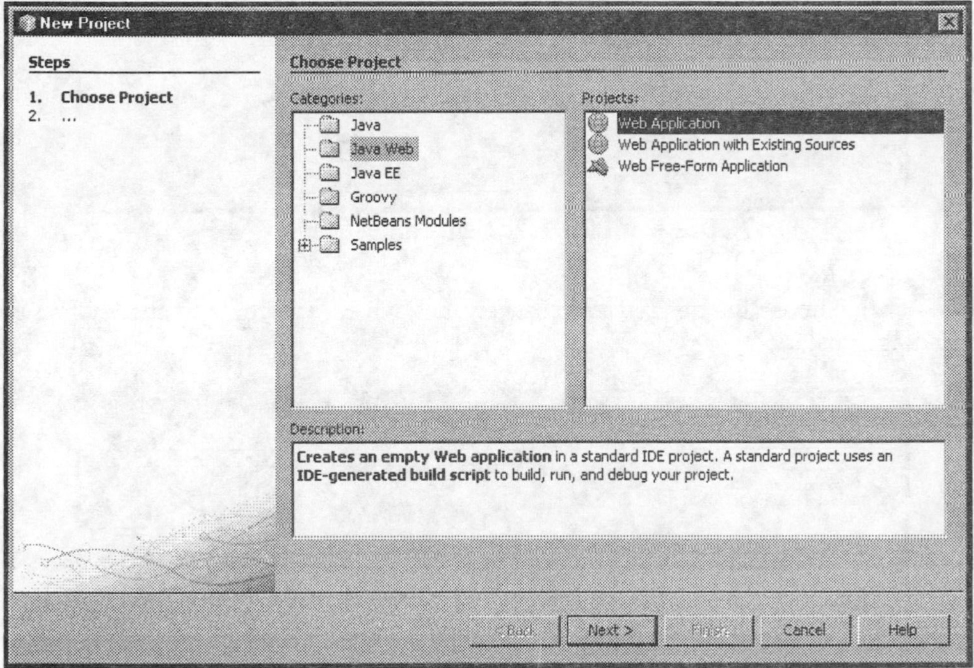

Diagram 25.1.1: New Project

Click Next >. Name this Web application as **CustomerDatabase** as shown in diagram 25.1.2.

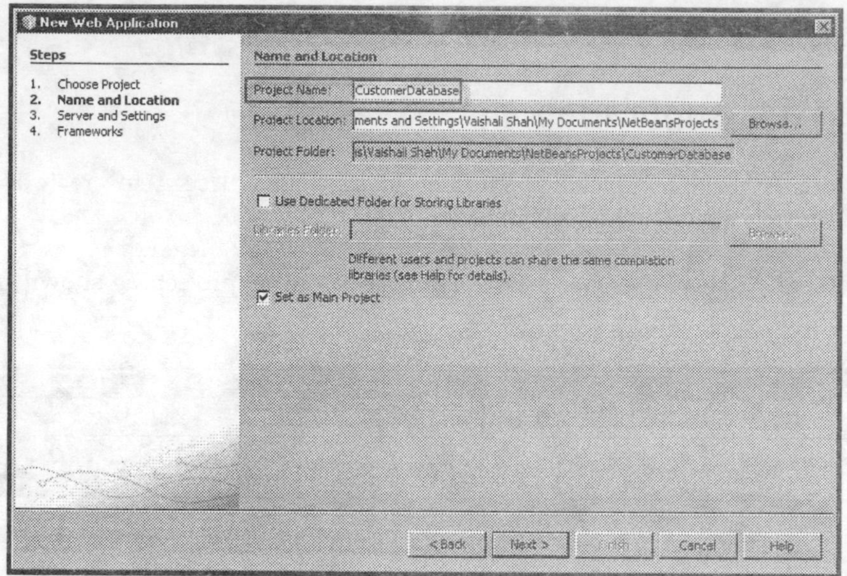

Diagram 25.1.2: Name and Location

Click Next >. Choose the desired Web server, the Java EE version and the context path as shown in diagram 25.1.3.

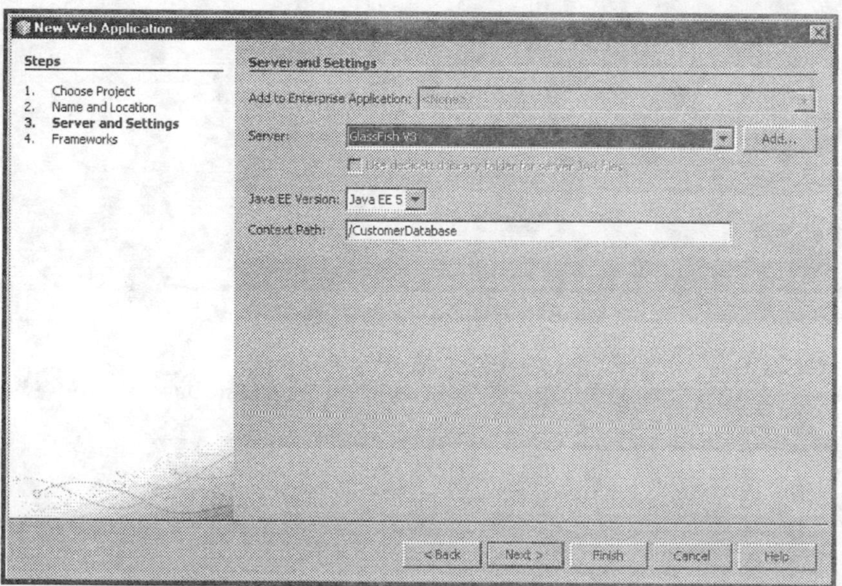

Diagram 25.1.3: Server and Settings

Click Next >. Do not choose a framework, in the Frameworks dialog box.

Click Finish.

The CustomerDatabase application is created in the NetBeans IDE as shown in diagram 25.1.4.

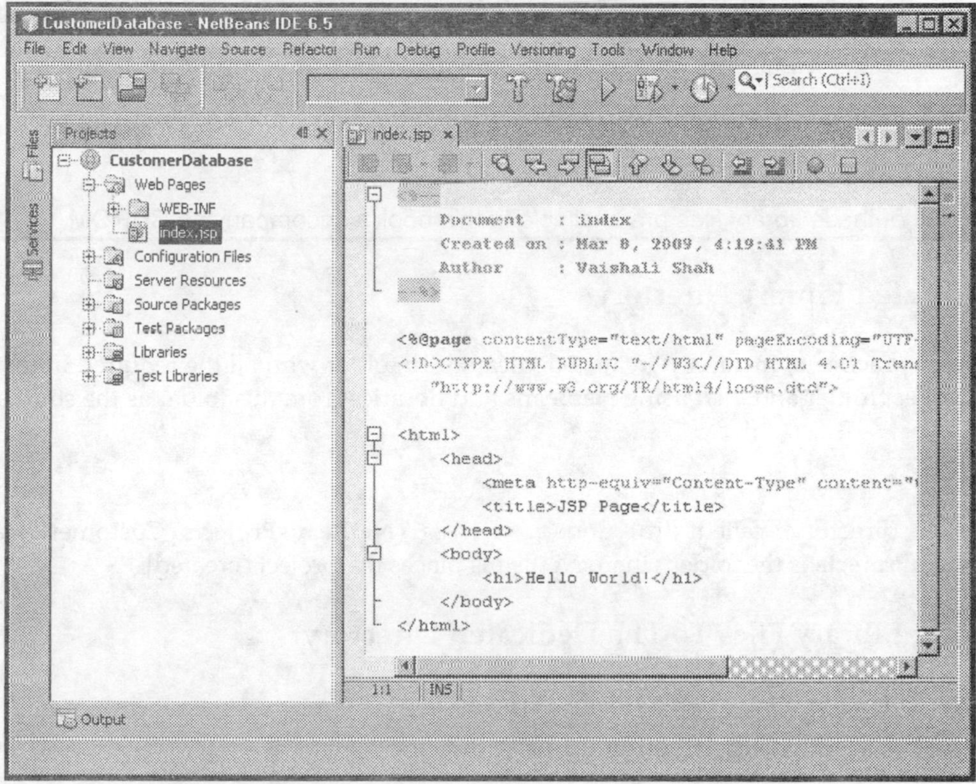

Diagram 25.1.4: CustomerDatabase in NetBeans IDE

Once the NetBeans IDE brings up the CustomerDatabase application, the next step is to add the required library files [JDBC driver, Hibernate, **Struts^2**, DisplayTag] to the CustomerDatabase application.

Adding The Library Files To The Project

This application uses Hibernate, Struts^2, a JDBC driver and Display Tag. Hence, appropriate library files have to be added to the project.

Downloading The Required Library Files

This application requires the following:

To download Hibernate, Display tag, iText, Beanutils, Lang and the Logging components, refer to the steps in *Chapter 23: Customer Database Using JSP*.

***Struts* 2**

The Struts 2.1.x framework. This can be downloaded from http://struts.apache.org → Download.

REMINDER

All of these library files are available in this book's accompanying CDROM.

A Dedicated Library Directory

It's a good practice to manually create a dedicated **lib** folder with all the required library files in the project folder and then using NetBeans add libraries from this folder as the source.

To do so,

Create a directory called **lib** under <Drive>:**NetBeansProjects**\CustomerDatabase. [**NetBeansProjects** is the folder where NetBeans places the projects created]

Copying Library Files To The Dedicated Directory

Copy the following library files to the lib directory:

- From the **hibernate-distribution-3.3.1.GA** directory
  - hibernate3.jar
- From the **hibernate-distribution-3.3.1.GA → lib → required** directory
  - antlr-2.7.6.jar
  - jta-1.1.jar
  - javassist-3.4.GA.jar
  - commons-collections-3.1.jar
  - dom4j-1.6.1.jar
- From the **hibernate-distribution-3.3.1.GA → lib → bytecode → cglib** directory
  - hibernate-cglib-repack-2.1_3.jar

- From the **hibernate-annotations-3.4.0.GA** directory
  - hibernate-annotations.jar
- From the **hibernate-annotations-3.4.0.GA → lib** directory
  - hibernate-commons-annotations.jar
  - slf4j-api.jar
  - slf4j-log4j12.jar
- From the **hibernate-annotations-3.4.0.GA → lib → test** directory
  - asm.jar
  - asm-attrs.jar
  - log4j.jar
- From the **struts-2.1.6 → lib** directory
  - commons-fileupload-1.2.1.jar
  - freemarker-2.3.13.jar
  - ognl-2.6.11.jar
  - struts2-core-2.1.6.jar
  - struts2-dojo-plugin-2.1.6.jar
  - struts2-pell-multipart-plugin-2.1.6.jar
  - xwork-2.1.2.jar
- From the **mysql-connector-java-5.1.7** directory [MySQL **JDBC Driver**]
  - mysql-connector-java-5.1.7-bin.jar
- From the **Display tags** directory **[explanation and donwload]**
  - displaytag-1.2.jar
  - displaytag-export-poi-1.2.jar
  - displaytag-portlet-1.2.jar
- For **PDF** export support with the **Display tags**
  - itext-1.4.7.jar
- From the **commons** directory [commons.apache.org]
  - commons-beanutils-1.7.0.jar
  - commons-lang-2.1.jar
  - commons-logging-1.0.4.jar

HINT

Now add these libraries to the application using the NetBeans IDE.

Refer to *Chapter 03: Writing The First Application* for the steps to add libraries using the NetBeans IDE.

The Hibernate Configuration

Since Hibernate is the ORM of choice for this application, it is necessary to have a configuration file that defines connection and the mapping resources.

Using NetBeans IDE, create an XML based configuration file named hibernate.cfg.xml. Refer to *Chapter 23: Customer Database Using JSP* for the code spec and the steps.

The Hibernate Utility Class [com.development.utils]

The standard and the most recommended practice is to have a helper class called **HibernateUtil** that manages the SessionFactory component for the entire application.

Create a Java class called **HibernateUtil** under the package com.development.utils. Refer to *Chapter 23: Customer Database Using JSP* for the code spec and the steps.

The Base Hibernate DAO Interface [com.development.utils]

Create a Java class called **IBaseHibernateDAO** under the package com.development.utils. Refer to *Chapter 23: Customer Database Using JSP* for the code spec and the steps.

The Base Hibernate DAO [com.development.utils]

Now that the interface is ready, the implementation class needs to be created.

Create a Java class called **BaseDAO** under the package com.development.utils. Refer to *Chapter 23: Customer Database Using JSP* for the code spec and the steps.

The Development Support [com.development.utils]

This application uses AJAX to retrieve States [for a country] and Cities [for a state], which requires an HttpServletResponse to obtain a PrintWriter. This PrintWriter will be used to return a list of states and cities.

To make available HttpServletResponse, an action class is required with appropriate getter and setter methods.

Create a Java class called **BaseDAO** under the package com.development.utils with the following code spec:

```
package com.development.utils;

import com.opensymphony.xwork2.ActionSupport;
import javax.servlet.http.HttpServletRequest;
import javax.servlet.http.HttpServletResponse;
import javax.servlet.http.HttpSession;
import org.apache.struts2.ServletActionContext;
import org.apache.struts2.interceptor.ServletRequestAware;
import org.apache.struts2.interceptor.ServletResponseAware;

public class DevelopmentSupport extends ActionSupport implements ServletRequestAware,
ServletResponseAware {
    private static final long serialVersionUID = 3515078654701117288L;
    private HttpServletRequest request;
    private HttpServletResponse response;

    public void setServletRequest(HttpServletRequest request) {
        this.request = request;
    }

    public void setServletResponse(HttpServletResponse response) {
        this.response = response;
    }

    public HttpServletRequest getRequest() {
        if (request == null) {
            request = ServletActionContext.getRequest();
        }
```

```
        return request;
    }

    public HttpServletResponse getResponse() {
        if (response == null) {
            response = ServletActionContext.getResponse();
        }
        return response;
    }

    public HttpSession getSession() {
        return getRequest().getSession();
    }
}
```

POJOs, Mapping Documents And DAOs

This application uses the following tables:

- City
- State
- Country
- Customer
    - Email

The customer data entry form holds drop down list boxes where the user can choose a country, state and a city to define the customer's address.

Appropriate POJO that represent these tables have to be created. For each POJO an XML based mapping document will be created.

All the code spec that allows performing database operations such as **C**reate, **R**ead, **U**pdate, and **D**elete will be placed in the DAO. POJOs and Mapping Document can be created manually by typing the code spec or by using a wizard [Hibernate Tools → Reverse Engineering] using the NetBeans IDE.

Create the appropriate POJOs, Mapping documents and the DAO classes as explained in *Chapter 23: Customer Database Using JSP*.

Action Classes

AjaxAction

This application uses Ajax to retrieve States [for a Country] and Cities [for a State]. The retrieval is done by an Action class called **AjaxAction**. This class holds the code spec that helps retrieve states and cities. Create **AjaxAction.java** under **com.development.struts.ajax**.

```
package com.development.struts.ajax;

import com.development.hibernate.city.City;
import com.development.hibernate.city.CityDAO;
import com.development.hibernate.city.State;
import com.development.hibernate.city.StateDAO;
import com.development.utils.DevelopmentSupport;
import com.opensymphony.xwork2.Action;
import java.io.PrintWriter;
import java.util.List;

public class AjaxAction extends DevelopmentSupport {
    private String outstr = "";
    private String searchValue;

    public String getOutstr() {
        return outstr;
    }
    public void setOutstr(String outstr) {
        this.outstr = outstr;
    }

    public String getSearchValue() {
        return searchValue;
    }
    public void setSearchValue(String searchValue) {
        this.searchValue = searchValue;
    }

```

```
public String getStateList() throws Exception {
    PrintWriter out = getResponse().getWriter();

    if (searchValue.length() > 0) {
        List<State> stateList = null;
        StateDAO stateDao = new StateDAO();

        try {
            stateList = stateDao.findByCountryCode(Integer.parseInt(searchValue));

            if (stateList != null && !stateList.isEmpty()) {
                for (State state : stateList) {
                    Integer val = state.getStatecode();
                    String str = state.getStatename();

                    if (outstr.length() == 0) {
                        outstr = val + "|" + str;
                    }
                    else {
                        outstr += "," + val + "|" + str;
                    }
                }
            }
        }
        catch (Exception e) {
            e.printStackTrace();
        }

        out.print(outstr);
        out.flush();
        out.close();
    }
    return Action.SUCCESS;
}

public String getCityList() throws Exception {
```

```
        PrintWriter out = getResponse().getWriter();

        if (searchValue.length() > 0) {
            List<City> cityList = null;
            CityDAO cityDao = new CityDAO();

            try {
                cityList = cityDao.findByStateCode(Integer.parseInt(searchValue));

                if (cityList != null && !cityList.isEmpty()) {
                    for (City city : cityList) {
                        Integer val = city.getCitycode();
                        String str = city.getCityname();

                        if (outstr.length() == 0) {
                            outstr = val + "|" + str;
                        }
                        else {
                            outstr += "," + val + "|" + str;
                        }
                    }
                }
            }
            catch (Exception e) {
                e.printStackTrace();
            }

            out.print(outstr);
            out.flush();
            out.close();
        }
        return Action.SUCCESS;
    }
}
```

Explanation:

This Action class:

- Receives the CountryCode as a request parameter via Ajax [searchValue]
- getStateList():
  - Passes the CountryCode to the StateDAO object's findByCountryCode()
    - findByCountryCode() returns a list of states for that country
  - Prints the list to the PrintWriter for Ajax to receive
- Receives the StateCode as a request parameter via Ajax [searchValue]
- getCityList():
  - Passes the StateCode to the CityDAO object's findByStateCode()
    - findByStateCode() returns a list of cities for that state
  - Prints the list to the PrintWriter for Ajax to receive

CustomerIndexAction

The Customer database data entry form when invoked requires the following initialization:

- Populating the Country drop down list box

Country: -- Please Select --
State:
City:
Contact Details
Mobile Number:
Telephone Number*:
Fax Number:

-- Please Select --
Australlia
Bahrain
Bangladesh
Belgium
Canada
Doha
Dubai
France
Germany
HongKong

- Populating the data grid

Customer Name	Address	Mobile
Sharanam Shah	Shivaji Park	222
Vaishali Shah	22222	2224

The retrieval is done by an Action class called **CustomerIndexAction**. This class holds the code spec that helps retrieve these. Create **CustomerIndexAction.java** under **com.development.struts.customer**.

```
package com.development.struts.customer;

import com.development.hibernate.city.City;
import com.development.hibernate.city.Country;
```

```
import com.development.hibernate.city.CountryDAO;
import com.development.hibernate.city.State;
import com.development.hibernate.customer.Customer;
import com.development.hibernate.customer.CustomerDAO;
import com.development.utils.DevelopmentSupport;
import java.util.ArrayList;
import java.util.List;

public class CustomerIndexAction extends DevelopmentSupport {
    private List<Country> countryList = new ArrayList<Country>();
    private List<State> stateList = new ArrayList<State>();
    private List<City> cityList = new ArrayList<City>();
    private List<Customer> customerList = new ArrayList<Customer>();

    public List<City> getCityList() {
        return cityList;
    }
    public void setCityList(List<City> cityList) {
        this.cityList = cityList;
    }

    public List<Country> getCountryList() {
        return countryList;
    }
    public void setCountryList(List<Country> countryList) {
        this.countryList = countryList;
    }

    public List<State> getStateList() {
        return stateList;
    }
```

```
    public void setStateList(List<State> stateList) {
        this.stateList = stateList;
    }

    public List<Customer> getCustomerList() {
        return customerList;
    }
    public void setCustomerList(List<Customer> customerList) {
        this.customerList = customerList;
    }

    @Override
    public String execute() throws Exception {
        CountryDAO countryDao = new CountryDAO();
        CustomerDAO customerDao = new CustomerDAO();
        countryList = countryDao.findAll();
        customerList = customerDao.findAll();
        return SUCCESS;
    }
}
```

Explanation:

This Action class is invoked when the Customer Database data entry form [JSP] appears. The **execute()** method uses the methods of the **CountryDAO** and **CustomerDAO** classes to retrieve the required data.

This data is made available the JSP using getter/setter methods.

CustomerAction

This action class is invoked by the Customer database data entry form to perform database operations when the user clicks Save, Edit, Delete or Clear.

Create **CustomerAction.java** under **com.development.struts.customer**.

```
package com.development.struts.customer;
```

```

import com.development.hibernate.city.*;
import com.development.hibernate.customer.*;
import com.development.utils.DevelopmentSupport;
import java.util.ArrayList;
import java.util.List;
import java.util.Set;

public class CustomerAction extends DevelopmentSupport {
    private Customer customer;
    private String emailone;
    private String emailtwo;
    private String emailthree;
    private String customerid;
    private String editFlag;
    private List<Customer> customerList = new ArrayList<Customer>();
    private List<Country> countryList = new ArrayList<Country>();
    private List<State> stateList = new ArrayList<State>();
    private List<City> cityList = new ArrayList<City>();
    private CountryDAO countryDao = new CountryDAO();
    private CustomerDAO customerDao = new CustomerDAO();
    private StateDAO stateDao = new StateDAO();
    private CityDAO cityDao = new CityDAO();
    private EmailDAO emailDao = new EmailDAO();

    @Override
    public String execute() throws Exception {
        customer.getEmails().add(new Email(customer, emailone));
        customer.getEmails().add(new Email(customer, emailtwo));
        customer.getEmails().add(new Email(customer, emailthree));

        if (editFlag != null && editFlag.equals("Y")) {
            emailDao.deleteAll(Integer.parseInt(customerid));
            customer.setCustomerid(Integer.parseInt(customerid));
            customerDao.update(customer);
        }
        else {
            customerDao.save(customer);
        }
        customer = new Customer();
```

```
        emailone = "";
        emailtwo = "";
        emailthree = "";
        countryList = countryDao.findAll();
        customerList = customerDao.findAll();
        return SUCCESS;
    }

    public String edit() {
        countryList = countryDao.findAll();
        customer = customerDao.findByCustomerCode(Integer.parseInt(getCustomerid()));
        Set<Email> emails = customer.getEmails();
        String[] mailArray = new String[3];
        int count = 0;

        if (!emails.isEmpty()) {
            for (Email mail : emails) {
                if (mail.getEmail() != null && !mail.getEmail().equals("")) {
                    mailArray[count] = mail.getEmail();
                }
                else {
                    mailArray[count] = "";
                }
                count++;
            }
        }
        emailone = mailArray[0];
        emailtwo = mailArray[1];
        emailthree = mailArray[2];
        stateList =
        stateDao.findByCountryCode(Integer.parseInt(customer.getCustomercountry()));
        cityList = cityDao.findByStateCode(Integer.parseInt(customer.getCustomerstate()));
        customerList = customerDao.findAll();
        return SUCCESS;
    }

    public String delete() {
        countryList = countryDao.findAll();
        Customer customerForDelete =
        customerDao.findByCustomerCode(Integer.parseInt(getCustomerid()));
```

```
        customerDao.delete(customerForDelete);
        customerList = customerDao.findAll();
        return SUCCESS;
    }

    public String clear() {
        customer = new Customer();
        emailone = "";
        emailtwo = "";
        emailthree = "";
        editFlag = "";
        customerid = "";
        countryList = countryDao.findAll();
        customerList = customerDao.findAll();
        return SUCCESS;
    }

    public Customer getCustomer() {
        return customer;
    }
    public void setCustomer(Customer customer) {
        this.customer = customer;
    }

    public String getEmailone() {
        return emailone;
    }
    public void setEmailone(String emailone) {
        this.emailone = emailone;
    }

    public String getEmailthree() {
        return emailthree;
    }
    public void setEmailthree(String emailthree) {
        this.emailthree = emailthree;
    }

    public String getEmailtwo() {
```

```
        return emailtwo;
    }
    public void setEmailtwo(String emailtwo) {
        this.emailtwo = emailtwo;
    }

    public String getCustomerid() {
        return customerid;
    }
    public void setCustomerid(String customerid) {
        this.customerid = customerid;
    }

    public List<Customer> getCustomerList() {
        return customerList;
    }
    public void setCustomerList(List<Customer> customerList) {
        this.customerList = customerList;
    }

    public List<City> getCityList() {
        return cityList;
    }
    public void setCityList(List<City> cityList) {
        this.cityList = cityList;
    }

    public List<Country> getCountryList() {
        return countryList;
    }
    public void setCountryList(List<Country> countryList) {
        this.countryList = countryList;
    }

    public List<State> getStateList() {
        return stateList;
    }
    public void setStateList(List<State> stateList) {
        this.stateList = stateList;
```

```
    }

    public String getEditFlag() {
        return editFlag;
    }
    public void setEditFlag(String editFlag) {
        this.editFlag = editFlag;
    }
}
```

Explanation:

This Action class is invoked when the user clicks Save, Edit, Delete or Clear.

execute()

Save when clicked invokes the **execute()** method. This method based on the value available in the **editFlag**, determines whether to **update** or **insert**.

```
if (editFlag != null && editFlag.equals("Y")) {
```

If the mode is update:

All the existing emails are deleted using:

```
emailDao.deleteAll(Integer.parseInt(customerid));
```

The existing customer identity is set:

```
customer.setCustomerid(Integer.parseInt(customerid));
```

The customer object is updated using:

```
customerDao.update(customer);
```

If the mode is insert:

The customer object is saved using:

```
customerDao.save(customer);
```

In either case, the save operation happens for the associated objects [Email] as well because of the cascade mode.

Finally, the customer object is re-initialized and the **countryList** and **customerList** List objects are re-populated to serve fresh data to the user.

edit()

Edit when clicked invokes the edit() method. This method populates the customer object with the appropriate customer's data based on the customer id.

```
customer = customerDao.findByCustomerCode(Integer.parseInt(getCustomerid()));
```

Multiple Emails of that customer [if any] are retrieved using:

```
Set<Email> emails = customer.getEmails();
```

Country, State and City drop down List objects are populated based on the customer's country, state and city.

Finally, the **customerList** object is re-populated to serve fresh data in the data grid.

delete()

Delete when clicked invokes the delete() method. This method populates the customer object with the appropriate customer's data based on the customer id.

```
Customer customerForDelete =
customerDao.findByCustomerCode(Integer.parseInt(getCustomerid()));
```

Invokes the DAO object's method to delete that object.

```
customerDao.delete(customerForDelete);
```

The delete operation happens for the associated objects [Email] as well because of the cascade mode.

JSP

Customer.jsp [jsp/customer]

Now that all the required functionality is in place, let's build the view.

The JSP:

- Holds a data entry form
    - To accept fresh customer data
    - To edit existing customer's data
- Holds a data grid

- o To view existing customers
- o To initiate
    - Edit
    - Delete

- Holds a footer [jsp/footer.jsp]

Technically, this JSP will allow:

- Insert
- Update
- Delete
- View

All these actions are submitted to the appropriate action class for processing.

These actions are bifurcated as:

- Application Initialization & View Operation [handled by CustomerIndexAction.java → **execute()**]
- Save Operation [handled by CustomerAction.java → **execute()**]
- Edit Operation [handled by CustomerAction.java → **edit()**]
- Delete Operation [handled by CustomerAction.java → **delete()**]

Once the action is determined, the DAO object's methods are invoked to perform the appropriate database operation.

Create a JSP called **Customer** under the directory **jsp/customer** with the following code spec:

```
<%@ page contentType="text/html; charset=UTF-8"%>
<%@ taglib prefix="s" uri="/struts-tags"%>
<%@ taglib uri="http://displaytag.sf.net" prefix="display"%>
<html>
   <head>
      <title>Customer Database</title>
      <script language="JavaScript" type="text/JavaScript"
      src="../javaScript/ajax/jquery2.js"></script>
      <script language="JavaScript" type="text/JavaScript"
      src="../javaScript/customer/customer.js"></script>
      <link href="../css/stylesheet.css" type="text/css" rel="stylesheet">
   </head>
   <body>
```

```
<div id="header"></div>
<s:form action="SaveCustomer" validate="true">
    <s:hidden name="editFlag" />
    <s:hidden name="customerid" />
    <table width="100%" border="0" align="center" cellpadding="0" cellspacing="0">
        <tr>
            <td>
                <table border="0" cellpadding="0" cellspacing="0" width="100%">
                    <tr>
                        <td valign="top" align="left" class="spanHeader">
                            <span>Customer Database</span>
                        </td>
                        <td class="treb13blacknormal" valign="top" align="right">
                            It is mandatory to enter information in all information
                            <br>capture boxes which have a <span
                            class="mandatory">*</span> adjacent
                        </td>
                    </tr>
                </table>
            </td>
        </tr>
        <tr align="left" valign="top">
            <td height="20" style="background:url('../images/hr.jpg')
            repeat-x;"> </td>
        </tr>
        <tr align="left" valign="top">
            <td>
                <table width="90%" border="0" align="center" cellpadding="0"
                cellspacing="0">
                    <tr>
                        <td>
                            <table width="100%" border="0" cellpadding="0" cellspacing="0">
                                <tr>
                                    <td class="Arial13BrownB">
                                        <br />Name<br /><br />
                                    </td>
                                </tr>
                                <s:textfield required="true" requiredposition="right"
                                label="Customer Name" name="customer.customername"
                                title="Enter the customer name" maxLength="25" size="55"/>
```

To determine Insert or Update

For Update and Delete

```
<tr>
    <td class="Arial13BrownB">
        <br />Mailing Address<br /><br />
    </td>
</tr>
<s:textfield label="Address" name="customer.customeraddress"
title="Enter the street address" maxLength="50" size="55"/>
<s:select label="Country" name="customer.customercountry"
headerKey="" headerValue="-- Please Select --"
list="countryList" listKey="countrycode" listValue="countryname"
onchange="getStateList()"/>
<s:select label="State" name="customer.customerstate"
headerKey="" headerValue="-- Please Select --" list="stateList"
listKey="statecode" listValue="statename"
onchange="getCityList()"/>
<s:select label="City" name="customer.customercity"
headerKey="" headerValue="-- Please Select --" list="cityList"
listKey="citycode" listValue="cityname" />
<tr>
    <td class="Arial13BrownB">
        <br />Contact Details<br /><br />
    </td>
</tr>
<s:textfield label="Mobile Number"
name="customer.customermobile" title="Enter the mobile
number" />
<s:textfield required="true" requiredposition="right"
label="Telephone Number"
name="customer.customertelephone" title="Enter the
telephone number" />
<s:textfield label="Fax Number" name="customer.customerfax"
title="Enter the fax number" />
<tr>
    <td class="Arial13BrownB">
        <br />Email<br /><br />
    </td>
</tr>
<s:textfield required="true" requiredposition="right"
label="First Email Address" name="emailone" title="Enter the
first email address" />
```

```
                        <s:textfield label="Second Email Address" name="emailtwo"
                        title="Enter the second email address" />
                        <s:textfield label="Third Email Address" name="emailthree"
                        title="Enter the third email address" />
                    </table>
                </td>
            </tr>
            <tr>
                <td>
                    <br /><br />
                    <s:submit theme="simple"
                    cssStyle="background:url(../images/submit_bg.gif) no-repeat
                    scroll 37px 0px;" cssClass="buttonText" name="btnSubmit"
                    value="Save" />
                    <s:submit theme="simple"
                    cssStyle="background:url(../images/submit_bg.gif) no-repeat
                    scroll 37px 0px;" cssClass="buttonText" name="btnReset"
                    value="Clear" onclick="javascript:clearCustomerFields();" />
                </td>
            </tr>
        </table>
    </td>
</tr>
<tr align="left" valign="top">
    <td height="20" style="background:url('../images/hr.jpg')
    repeat-x;"> </td>
</tr>
</table>
<table width="100%" border="0" cellspacing="0" cellpadding="0">
    <display:table name="customerList" pagesize="15"
            excludedParams="*" export="true" cellpadding="0"
            cellspacing="0"
            requestURI="">
        <display:column property="customername" title="Customer Name"
        maxLength="35" headerClass="gridheader" class="griddata" style="width:30%"
        sortable="true"/>
        <display:column property="customeraddress" title="Address" maxLength="35"
        headerClass="gridheader" class="griddata" style="width:50%"/>
```

```
                <display:column property="customermobile" title="Mobile"
                headerClass="gridheader" class="griddata" style="width:15%"/>
                <display:column paramId="customerid" paramProperty="customerid"
                href="/CustomerDatabase/customer/Edit.action?editFlag=Y"
                headerClass="gridheader" class="griddata" media="html">
                    <img align="right" src="../images/edit.jpg" border="0" alt="Edit"
                    style="cursor:pointer;"/>
                </display:column>
                <display:column paramId="customerid" paramProperty="customerid"
                href="/CustomerDatabase/customer/Delete.action" headerClass="gridheader"
                class="griddata" media="html">
                    <img align="left" src="../images/TrashIcon.png" border="0" alt="Delete"
                    style="cursor:pointer;"/>
                </display:column>
            </display:table>
        </table>
    </s:form>
    <s:include value="/jsp/footer.jsp" />
  </body>
</html>
```

footer.jsp [jsp/]

Create a JSP called **footer** under the directory **jsp** with the following code spec:

```
<%@page contentType="text/html" pageEncoding="UTF-8"%>
<%@ taglib prefix="s" uri="/struts-tags" %>
<table align="center" width="100%" border="0" cellspacing="0" cellpadding="0">
    <tr height="50px">
        <td align="center"> </td>
    </tr>
    <tr height="50px" id="footer">
        <td align="center">
            <strong>Copyright © 2009, <a
            href="http://www.sharanamshah.com">Sharanam</a> And <a
            href="http://www.vaishalishahonline.com">Vaishali</a> Shah</strong>
        </td>
    </tr>
</table>
```

This file is included in the Customer.jsp.

```
<s:include value="/jsp/footer.jsp" />
```

ajax.jsp [jsp/ajax]

Create a JSP called **ajax** under the directory **jsp/ajax** with no code spec. This is a blank file required to emulate a result type when returning state and city list using Ajax.

JavaScript

customer [javaScript\customer]

This script holds the following functions:

- clearCustomerFields()
- getStateList()
- getCityList()

These functions are invoked by Customer.jsp to:

- Clear form fields when the user clicks **Clear**
- Populate states when the user chooses a Country
- Populate cities when the user chooses a State

```
<script language="JavaScript" type="text/JavaScript"
src="../javaScript/customer/customer.js"></script>
```

Create a JavaScript file called customer under the directory **javaScript\customer** with the following code spec:

```
function clearCustomerFields(){
   document.forms[0].action = "/CustomerDatabase/customer/Clear.action";
   document.forms[0].submit();
   return false;
}

function getStateList() {
   var searchValue =
   document.getElementById("SaveCustomer_customer_customercountry").value;

   if (searchValue != "") {
```

```
        var msg = $.ajax({
            url:"/CustomerDatabase/ajax/getStateList.action?searchValue=" + searchValue,
            async:false
        }).responseText;
        var listText = unescape(msg);
        var TypeArray = new Array();
        var TypeArrayInfo = new Array();
        TypeArray = listText.split(",");
        document.getElementById("SaveCustomer_customer_customerstate").options.length = 0;
        document.getElementById("SaveCustomer_customer_customerstate").options.add(new
        Option("-- Please Select --", ""));
        for (i = 0; i < TypeArray.length; i++) {
            TypeArrayInfo = TypeArray[i].split("|");
            document.getElementById("SaveCustomer_customer_customerstate").options.add(new
            Option(TypeArrayInfo[1], TypeArrayInfo[0]));
        }
    }
    else{
        document.getElementById("SaveCustomer_customer_customerstate").options.length = 0;
        document.getElementById("SaveCustomer_customer_customerstate").options.add(new
        Option("-- Please Select --", ""));
        document.getElementById("SaveCustomer_customer_customercity").options.length = 0;
        document.getElementById("SaveCustomer_customer_customercity").options.add(new
        Option("-- Please Select --", ""));
    }
}
function getCityList() {
    var searchValue = document.getElementById("SaveCustomer_customer_customerstate").value;
    if (searchValue != "") {
        var msg = $.ajax({
            url:"/CustomerDatabase/ajax/getCityList.action?searchValue=" + searchValue,
            async:false
        }).responseText;
        var listText = unescape(msg);
        var TypeArray = new Array();
        var TypeArrayInfo = new Array();
        TypeArray = listText.split(",");
        document.getElementById("SaveCustomer_customer_customercity").options.length = 0;
```

```
        document.getElementById("SaveCustomer_customer_customercity").options.add(new Option("-- Please Select --", ""));

        for (i = 0; i < TypeArray.length; i++) {
            TypeArrayInfo = TypeArray[i].split("|");
            document.getElementById("SaveCustomer_customer_customercity").options.add(new Option(TypeArrayInfo[1], TypeArrayInfo[0]));
        }
    }
    else{
        document.getElementById("SaveCustomer_customer_customercity").options.length = 0;
        document.getElementById("SaveCustomer_customer_customercity").options.add(new Option("-- Please Select --", ""));
    }
}
```

jquery2 [javaScript\ajax]

jQuery is a lightweight JavaScript library that emphasizes interaction between JavaScript and HTML. It is great library for developing Ajax based application.

This file can be downloaded from:
http://docs.jquery.com/Downloading_jQuery#Current_Release.

Download it and place it under **javaScript\ajax**.

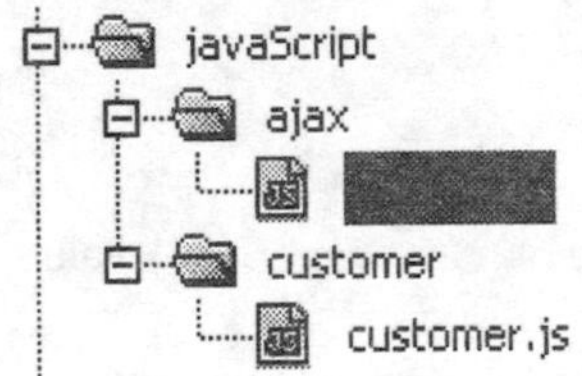

CSS

The application uses a CSS file stylesheet.css to style the JSP.

Customer.jsp uses it.

```
<link href="../css/stylesheet.css" type="text/css" rel="stylesheet">
```

This file is available on this book's accompanying CDROM. Place it under css.

Images

The application uses a few images to style the JSP. Customer.jsp uses it. These files are available on this book's accompanying CDROM.

Copy these files and place then under **images**.

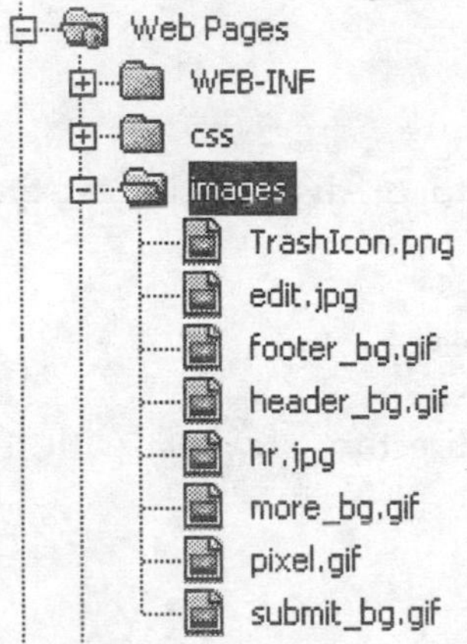

Index Page

This application uses an index.html file to invoke the application. Create this file under **/**, if it is not available.

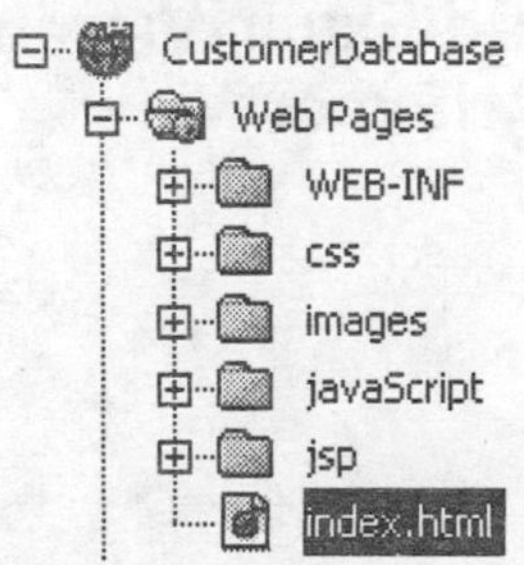

Add the following code spec in this file:

```
<!DOCTYPE HTML PUBLIC "-//W3C//DTD HTML 4.0 Transitional//EN">
<html>
<head>
   <meta http-equiv="Refresh" content="0;URL=customer/index.action">
</head>
<body>
   <p>Loading ...</p>
</body>
</html>
```

Display Tag Properties

Since this application uses Display Tag to produce a data grid to display the existing customers, a few properties need to be set.

This can be done using a properties file called **displaytag.properties.**

Create a properties file called **displaytag.properties** under the directory **src\java** with the following code spec:

```
export.types=csv excel xml pdf rtf
export.excel=true
export.csv=true
export.xml=true
export.pdf=true
export.rtf=true
export.pdf.class=org.displaytag.export.DefaultPdfExportView
export.rtf.class=org.displaytag.export.DefaultRtfExportView
export.excel.filename=customer.xls
export.pdf.filename=customer.pdf
export.xml.filename=customer.xml
export.csv.filename=customer.csv
export.rtf.filename=customer.rtf
```

Struts^2 XML Configuration Files

Now that the JSP and the Actions classes are in place, let's bind the two together using the struts.xml file.

Create **struts.xml** file under **/**

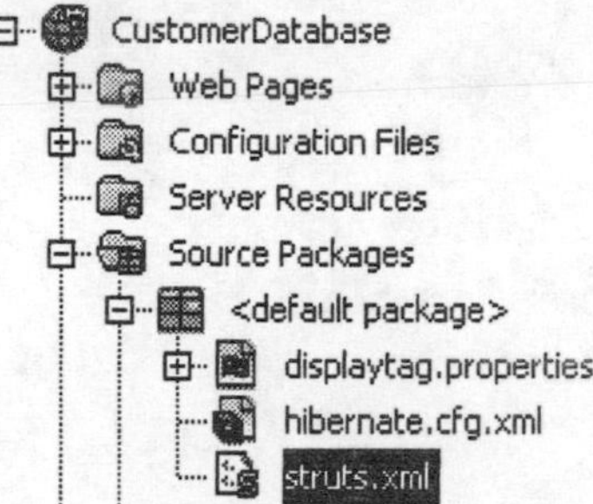

Add the following code spec:

```
<!DOCTYPE struts PUBLIC
"-//Apache Software Foundation//DTD Struts Configuration 2.0//EN"
"http://struts.apache.org/dtds/struts-2.0.dtd">
<struts>
    <include file="/com/development/struts/customer/customer.xml"/>
    <include file="/com/development/struts/ajax/ajax.xml"/>
</struts>
```

Create **customer.xml** file under the **com.development.struts.customer** package

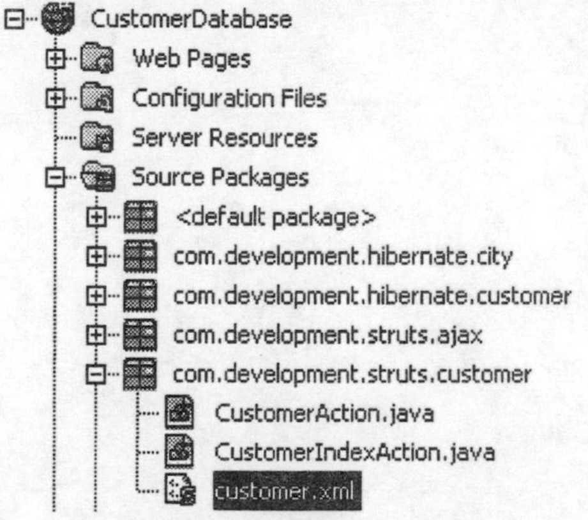

Add the following code spec:

```
<?xml version="1.0" encoding="UTF-8" ?>
<!DOCTYPE struts PUBLIC
      "-//Apache Software Foundation//DTD Struts Configuration 2.0//EN"
      "http://struts.apache.org/dtds/struts-2.0.dtd">
<struts>
   <package name="customer" namespace="/customer" extends="struts-default">
      <action name="Index"
      class="com.development.struts.customer.CustomerIndexAction">
         <result name="success">/jsp/customer/Customer.jsp</result>
      </action>

      <action name="SaveCustomer"
      class="com.development.struts.customer.CustomerAction">
         <result>/jsp/customer/Customer.jsp</result>
      </action>

      <action name="Edit" method="edit"
      class="com.development.struts.customer.CustomerAction">
         <result>/jsp/customer/Customer.jsp</result>
      </action>

      <action name="Delete" method="delete"
      class="com.development.struts.customer.CustomerAction">
         <result>/jsp/customer/Customer.jsp</result>
      </action>

      <action name="Clear" method="clear"
      class="com.development.struts.customer.CustomerAction">
         <result>/jsp/customer/Customer.jsp</result>
      </action>
   </package>
</struts>
```

Create **ajax.xml** file under the **com.development.struts.ajax** package

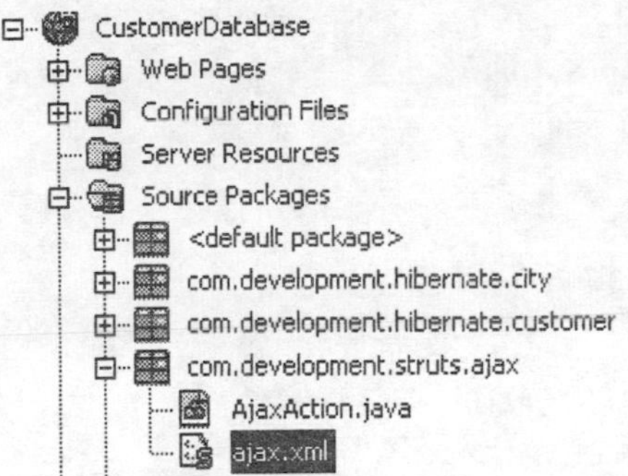

Add the following code spec:

```
<?xml version="1.0" encoding="UTF-8" ?>
<!DOCTYPE struts PUBLIC
        "-//Apache Software Foundation//DTD Struts Configuration 2.0//EN"
        "http://struts.apache.org/dtds/struts-2.0.dtd">

<struts>
    <package name="ajax" namespace="/ajax" extends="struts-default">
        <action name="getStateList" method="getStateList"
        class="com.development.struts.ajax.AjaxAction">
            <result name="success">/jsp/ajax/Ajax.jsp</result>
        </action>

        <action name="getCityList" method="getCityList"
        class="com.development.struts.ajax.AjaxAction">
            <result name="success">/jsp/ajax/Ajax.jsp</result>
        </action>
    </package>
</struts>
```

Editing Web.XML

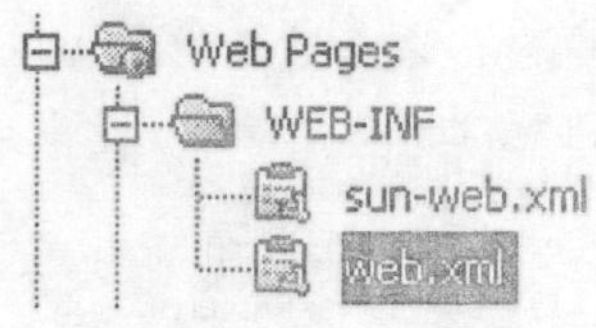

This application uses Struts^2 and Display Tag library which requires creating a few filters mappings for Struts^2 and Display Tag.

Edit the web.xml file available under WEB-INF with the following code spec:

```
<?xml version="1.0" encoding="UTF-8"?>
<web-app version="2.5" xmlns="http://java.sun.com/xml/ns/javaee"
xmlns:xsi="http://www.w3.org/2001/XMLSchema-instance"
xsi:schemaLocation="http://java.sun.com/xml/ns/javaee
http://java.sun.com/xml/ns/javaee/web-app_2_5.xsd">
    <filter>
        <filter-name>struts2</filter-name>
        <filter-class>org.apache.struts2.dispatcher.FilterDispatcher</filter-class>
    </filter>
    <filter>
        <filter-name>ResponseOverrideFilter</filter-name>
        <filter-class>org.displaytag.filter.ResponseOverrideFilter</filter-class>
    </filter>
    <filter-mapping>
        <filter-name>ResponseOverrideFilter</filter-name>
        <url-pattern>*.action</url-pattern>
    </filter-mapping>
    <filter-mapping>
        <filter-name>ResponseOverrideFilter</filter-name>
        <url-pattern>*.jsp</url-pattern>
    </filter-mapping>
    <filter-mapping>
        <filter-name>struts2</filter-name>
        <url-pattern>/*</url-pattern>
    </filter-mapping>
    <session-config>
```

For Struts 2

For Display Tag

For Struts 2

```
        <session-timeout>
            30
        </session-timeout>
    </session-config>
    <welcome-file-list>
        <welcome-file>index.html</welcome-file>
    </welcome-file-list>
</web-app>
```

The Index Page that invokes Customer Database form

This completes building the application using the NetBeans IDE.

Running The Application

Run the application. To do so, right click the application and choose **Clean and Build**.

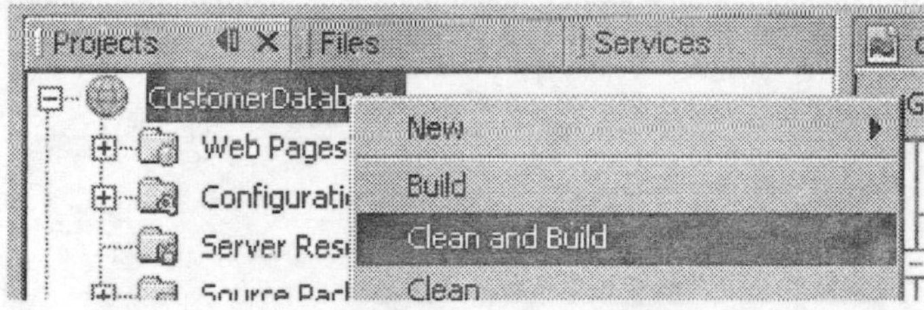

Once done, Run the application.

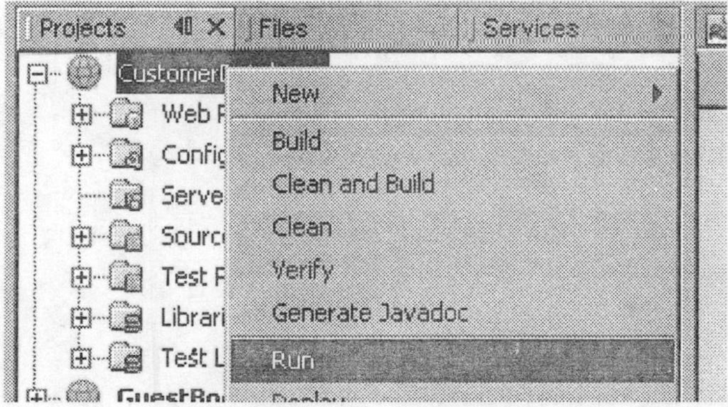

This brings up the application in the default web browser as shown in diagram 25.2.

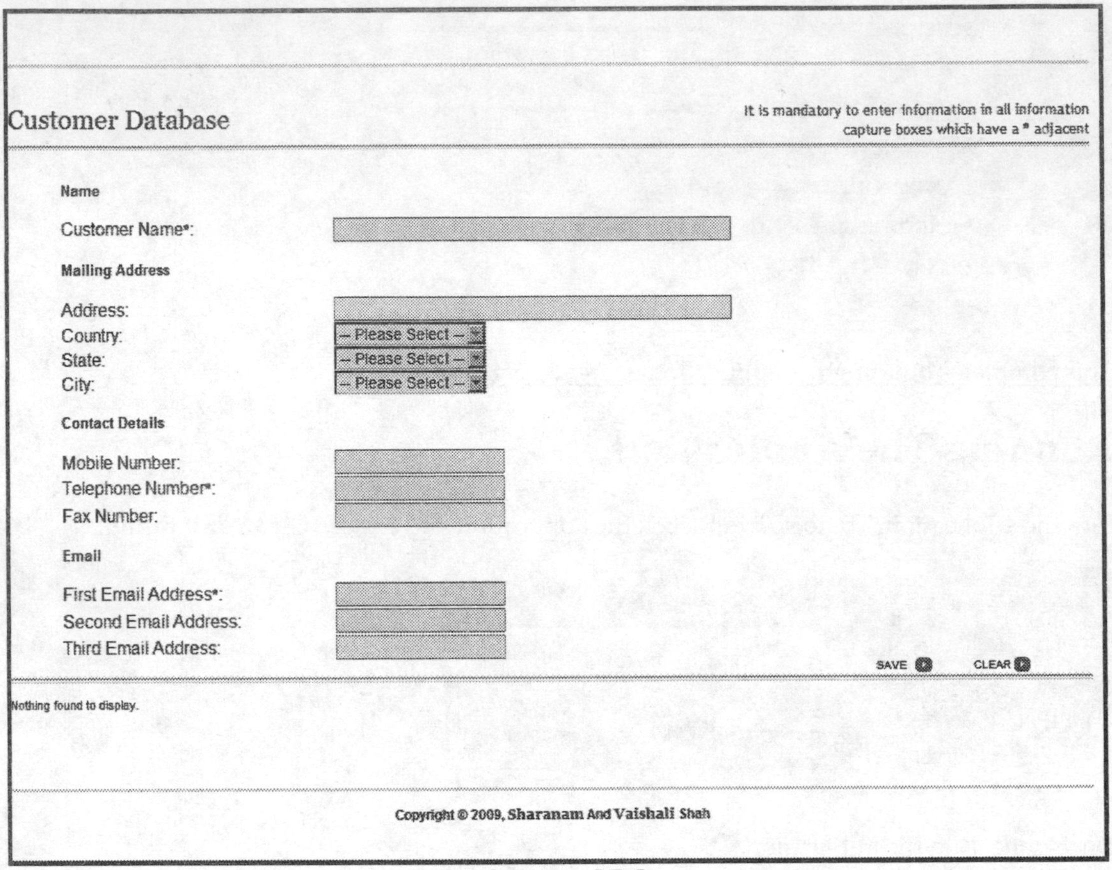

Customer Database

It is mandatory to enter information in all information capture boxes which have a * adjacent

Name

Customer Name*:

Mailing Address

Address:
Country: -- Please Select --
State: -- Please Select --
City: -- Please Select --

Contact Details

Mobile Number:
Telephone Number*:
Fax Number:

Email

First Email Address*:
Second Email Address:
Third Email Address:

SAVE CLEAR

Nothing found to display.

Copyright © 2009, Sharanam And Vaishali Shah

Diagram 25.2

Process Flow

Diagrammatically this process can be represented as show in diagram 25.3.1 and 25.3.2.

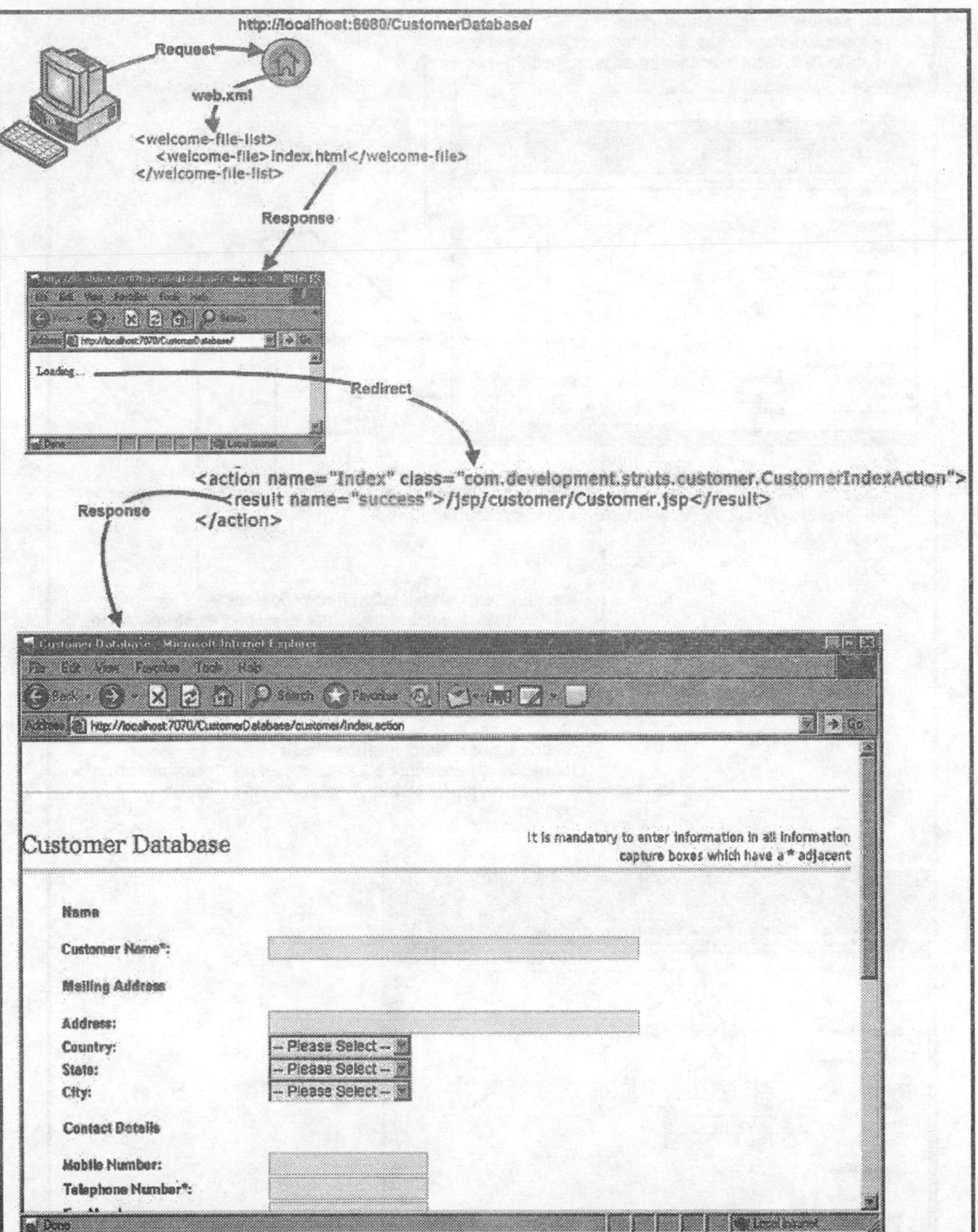

Diagram 25.3.1: Customer Database Invocation

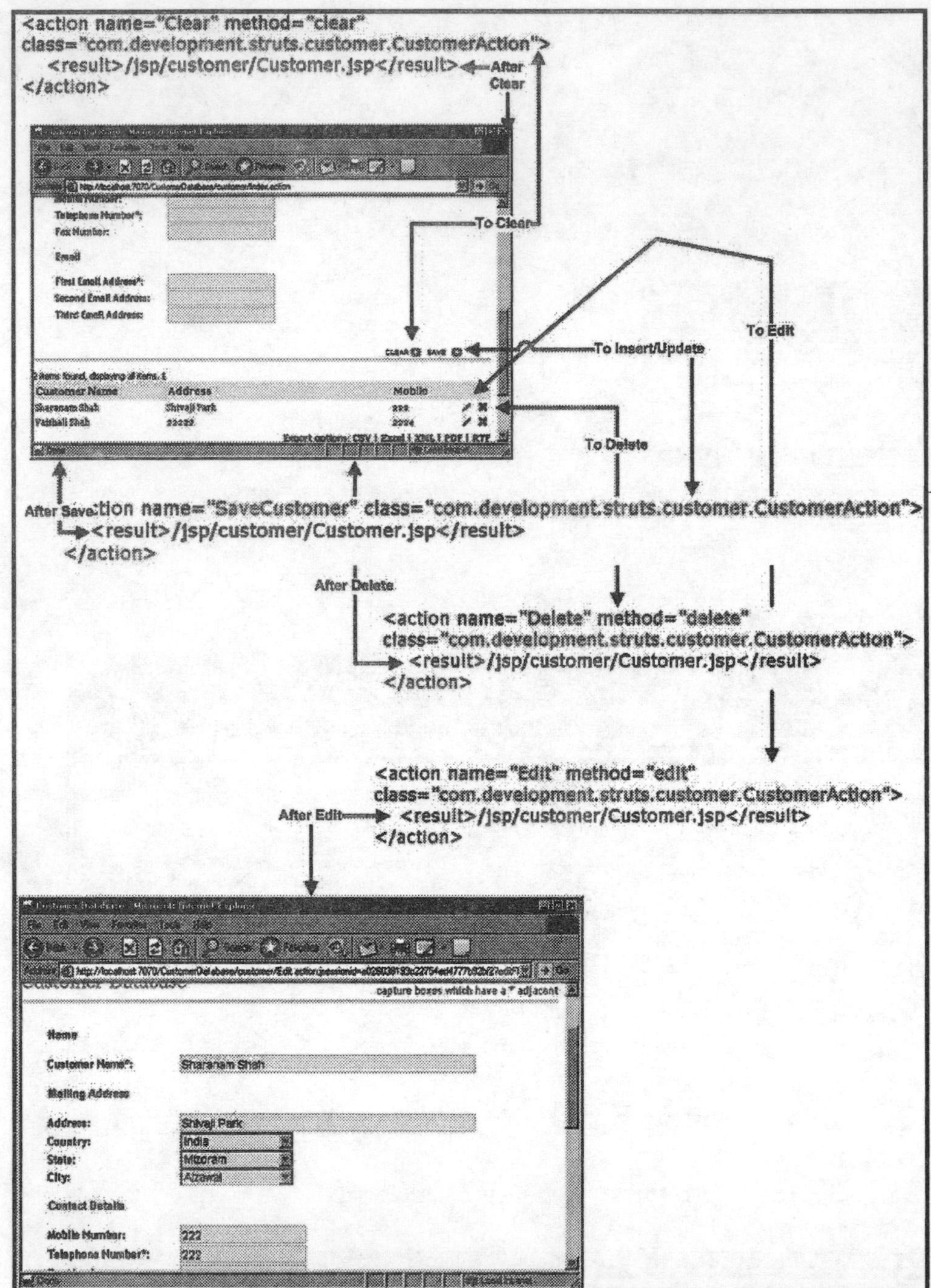

Diagram 25.3.2: Database Operations

The Book CDROM holds the complete application source code built using the NetBeans IDE for the following application:

- CustomerDatabase_Chap25

This can be directly used by making appropriate changes [username/password] to the configuration file.

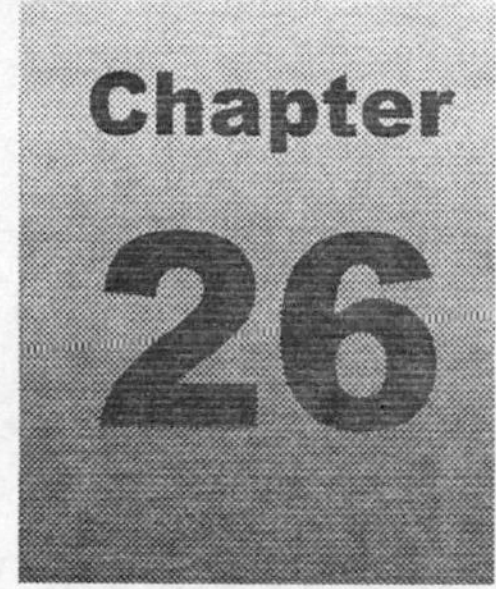

SECTION VI: APPLICATION DEVELOPMENT WITH HIBERNATE

Switching The Database [MySQL To Oracle]

Hibernate's portability across the relational databases is simply amazing.

It is literally a configuration change. The only change that is required is the configuration file property values.

All that is required is a Hibernate Dialect and a database connection driver to allow such change.

This portability is very useful especially in companies where deployment take place on a wide range of databases. Usually the development team is not even aware about which database the DBA manager would allocate depending on the license availability, for example, Oracle, Sybase or DB2.

The development team can simply begin and undergo the development phase using an open source database such as MySQL and then deploy the same on another database.

In this book, the Customer Database that is developed in *Chapter 23: Customer Database Using JSP* uses MySQL as the data store.

Let's use Oracle Database 10g as the data store. Since Hibernate is used as the Object Mapping Framework, it's quite simple to switch the project to begin using Oracle Database 10g as the data store.

The following is what will be needed to switch from MySQL to Oracle:

Oracle Database 10g

1. Installing Oracle Database 10g
2. Creating a User / Schema with appropriate privileges
3. Creating an identical table structure

Application

1. Adding Oracle's JDBC driver [ojdbc14.jar] to the project's library files
2. Modifying the Hibernate configuration file [hibernate.cfg.xml] to begin using Oracle Database 10g as the database
3. Modifying the Hibernate Mapping Documents to set the generator strategy of the identity columns [CUSTOMERID, EMAILID, CITYCODE, STATECODE, COUNTRYCODE]

That's it. Let's begin.

Installing Oracle Database 10g

The eXpress Edition of the Oracle Database 10g is available on this Book's accompany CDROM [<CDROM Drive>:/Setup Files/00_Oracle].

Simply double click the setup file called OracleXEUniv.exe to run through the installation wizard.

Creating User / Schema With Appropriate Privileges

Login to the Oracle Database using its web interface. This is available as a menu option as shown in diagram 26.1.1.

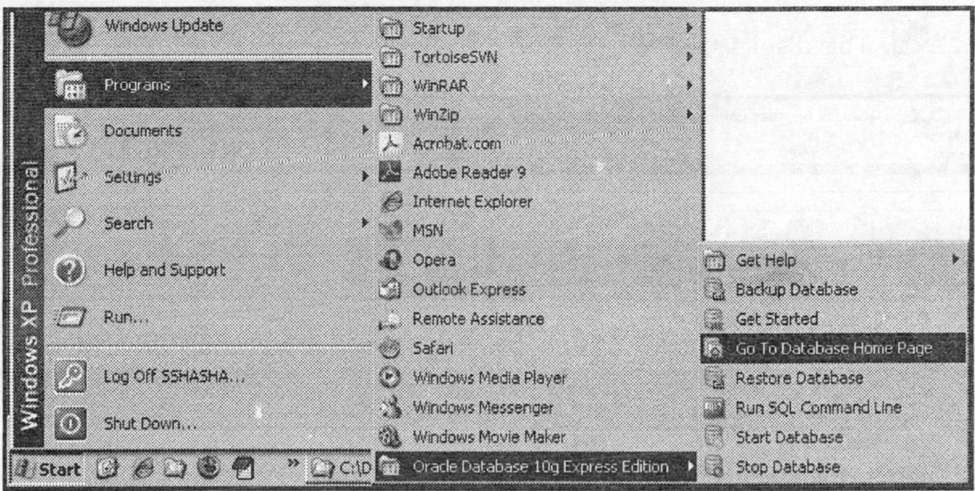

Diagram 26.1.1

This brings up the login form as shown in diagram 26.1.2. Login to Oracle using System as the username and the appropriate password [the one that was chosen whilst installing Oracle Database 10g XE].

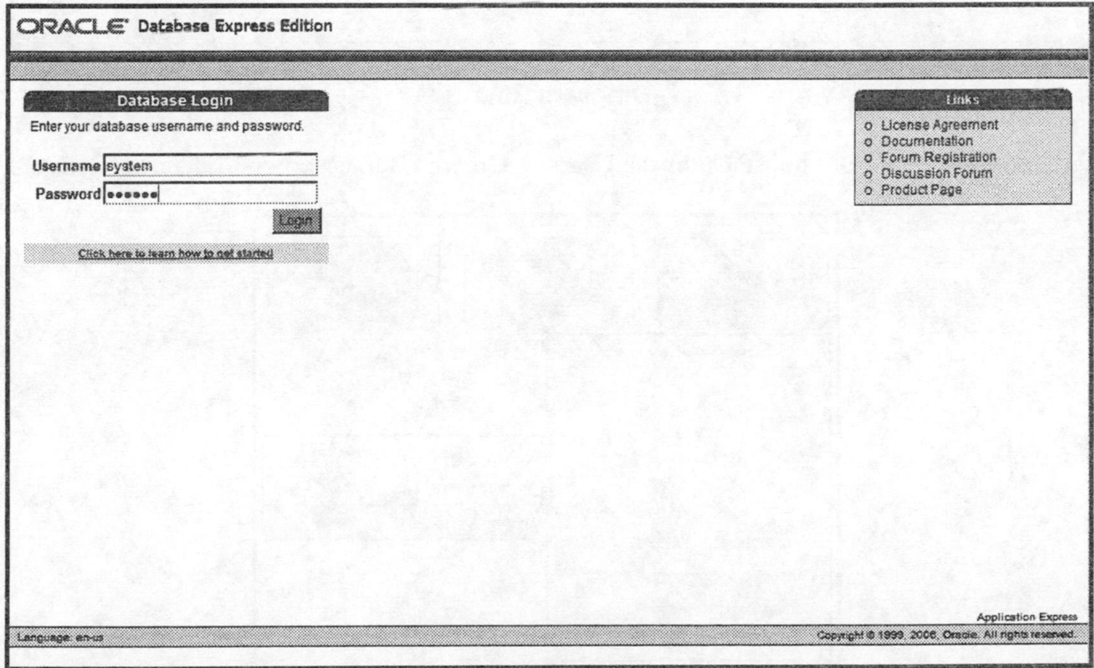

Diagram 26.1.2

Click Login. This displays the homepage as shown in diagram 26.1.3.

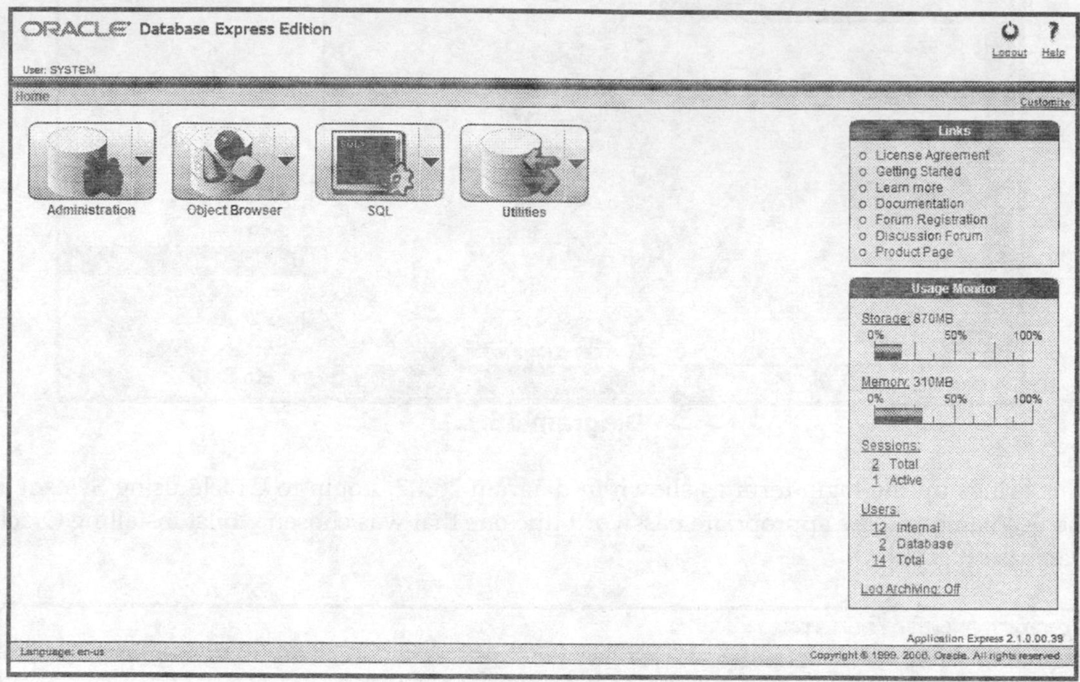

Diagram 26.1.3

Under **Administration**, choose **Database Users → Create User** as shown in diagram 26.1.4.

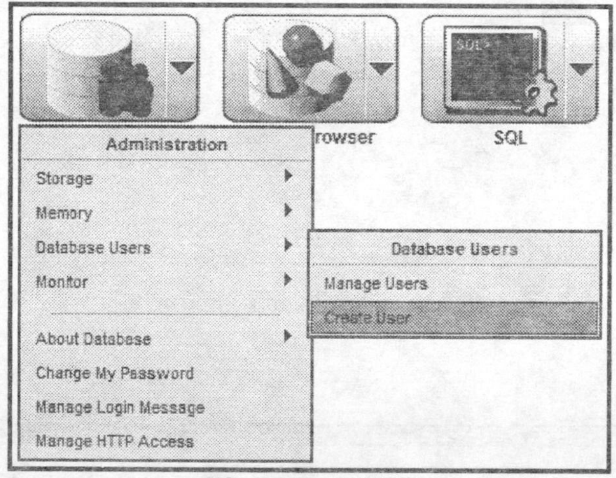

Diagram 26.1.4

This displays the **Create Database User** data entry form. Key in the details as shown in diagram 26.1.5.

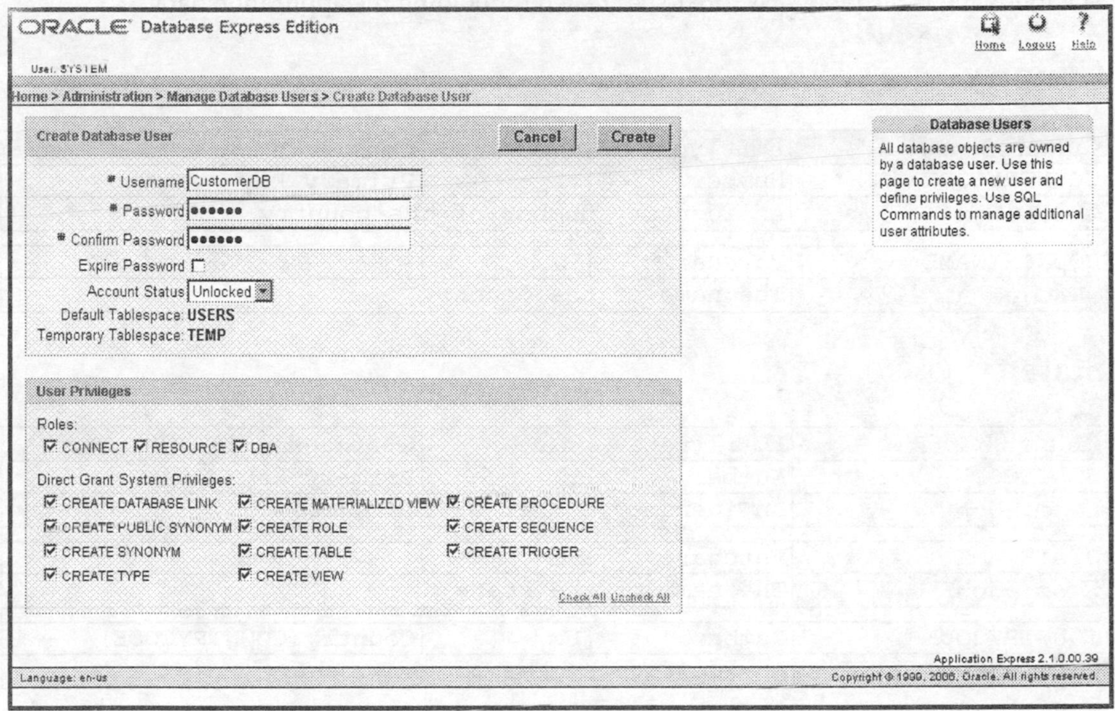

Diagram 26.1.5

The following are the details chosen for this user.

- **Username:** CustomerDB
- **Account Status:** Unlocked
- **Roles:** CONNECT, RESOURCE, DBA
- **Privileges:** CREATE DATABASE LINK, CREATE MATERIALIZED VIEW, CREATE PROCEDURE, CREATE PUBLIC SYNONYM, CREATE ROLE, CREATE SEQUENCE, CREATE SYNONYM, CREATE TABLE, CREATE TRIGGER, CREATE TYPE, CREATE VIEW

Click [Create] to create this user. This creates the user **CustomerDB**. Logout from there and close that window.

Creating Identical Table Structure

The following is the table structure to be created for holding the application data.

Country

Column Name	Data Type	Size	Constraints
COUNTRYCODE	Number	11	Primary key
Description	An identity number of the country		
COUNTRYNAME	Varchar2	50	- -
Description	The name of the country		

State

Column Name	Data Type	Size	Constraints
STATECODE	Number	10	Primary key
Description	An identity number of the state		
STATENAME	Varchar2	50	- -
Description	The name of the state		
COUNTRYCODE	Number	11	Country(COUNTRYCODE)
Description	An identity number of the country		

City

Column Name	Data Type	Size	Constraints
CITYCODE	Number	11	Primary key
Description	An identity number of the city		
CITYNAME	Varchar2	50	- -
Description	The name of the state		
STATECODE	Number	11	State(STATECODE)
Description	An identity number of the state		

Customers

Column Name	Data Type	Size	Constraints
CUSTOMERID	Number	11	Primary key
Description	An identity number of the customer		

Column Name	Data Type	Size	Constraints
CUSTOMERNAME	Varchar2	50	- -
Description	The name of the customer		
CUSTOMERADDRESS	Varchar2	150	- -
Description	The street address where the customer resides		
CUSTOMERCITY	Varchar2	25	- -
Description	The name of the city where the customer resides		
CUSTOMERSTATE	Varchar2	25	- -
Description	The name of the state where the customer resides		
CUSTOMERCOUNTRY	Varchar2	25	- -
Description	The name of the country where the customer resides		
CUSTOMERMOBILE	Varchar2	10	- -
Description	The mobile number of the customer		
CUSTOMERTELEPHONE	Varchar2	15	- -
Description	The telephone number of the customer		
CUSTOMERFAX	Varchar2	15	- -
Description	The fax number of the customer		

City

Column Name	Data Type	Size	Constraints
EMAILID	Number	11	Primary key
Description	An identity number of the email address		
EMAIL	Varchar2	75	- -
Description	The email address of the customer		
CUSTOMERID	Number	11	Customer(CUSTOMERID)
Description	An identity number of the customer		

Importing Oracle Dump File

To create this structure, use the Oracle dump file provided in this book's CDROM [<CDROM Drive>:/Project/Database Dump Files/Oracle]. This file is named as **CustomerDBOracle.dat**.

Locate this file from the CDROM and copy it in a folder of choice.

Invoke the system command prompt and key in the following command as shown in diagram 26.2.1:

```
<System Prompt> imp
```

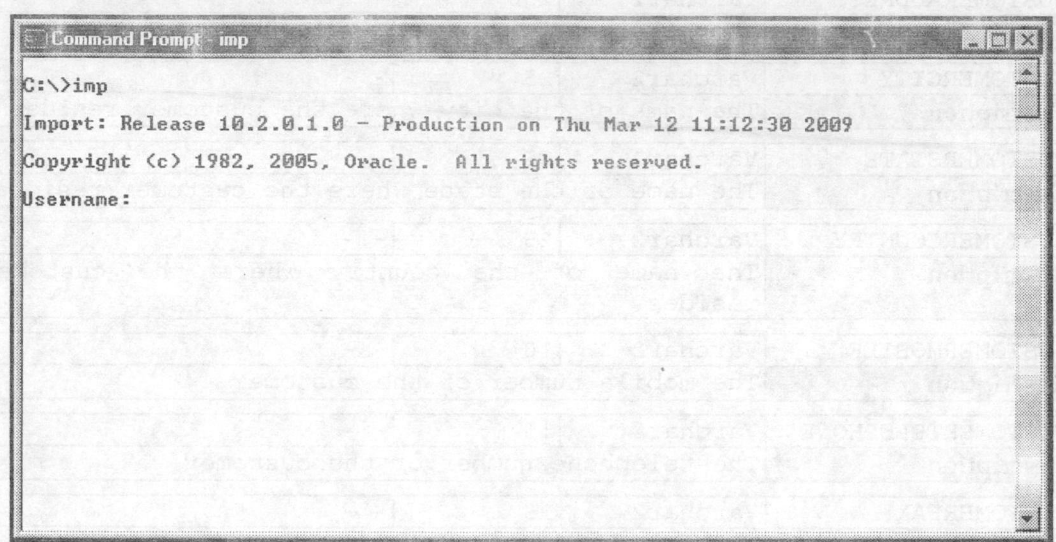

Diagram 26.2.1

Key in the username as **CustomerDB** [create earlier] and its associated password as shown in diagram 26.2.2.

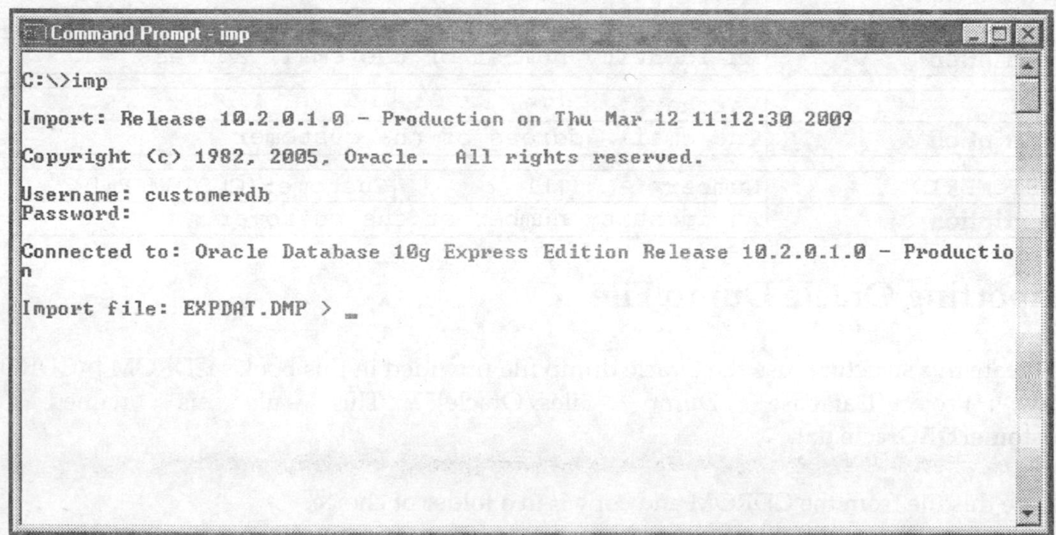

Diagram 26.2.2

Key in the path to the dump file [copied earlier] as shown in diagram 26.2.3.

```
Command Prompt - imp

C:\>imp

Import: Release 10.2.0.1.0 - Production on Thu Mar 12 11:12:30 2009

Copyright (c) 1982, 2005, Oracle.  All rights reserved.

Username: customerdb
Password:

Connected to: Oracle Database 10g Express Edition Release 10.2.0.1.0 - Productio
n

Import file: EXPDAT.DMP > c:\CustomerDBOracle.dat_
```

Diagram 26.2.3

Press **Enter**.

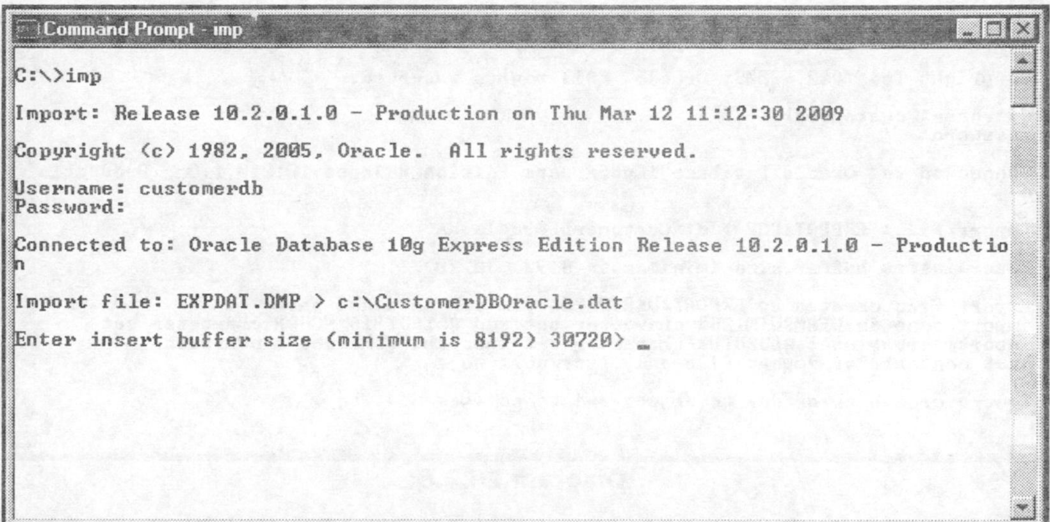

Diagram 26.2.4

Keep the default value and press **Enter**.

```
Command Prompt - imp

C:\>imp

Import: Release 10.2.0.1.0 - Production on Thu Mar 12 11:12:30 2009

Copyright (c) 1982, 2005, Oracle.  All rights reserved.

Username: customerdb
Password:

Connected to: Oracle Database 10g Express Edition Release 10.2.0.1.0 - Productio
n

Import file: EXPDAT.DMP > c:\CustomerDBOracle.dat

Enter insert buffer size (minimum is 8192) 30720>

Export file created by EXPORT:V10.02.01 via conventional path
import done in WE8MSWIN1252 character set and AL16UTF16 NCHAR character set
import server uses AL32UTF8 character set (possible charset conversion)
List contents of import file only (yes/no): no >
```

Diagram 26.2.5

Keep the default value and press **Enter**.

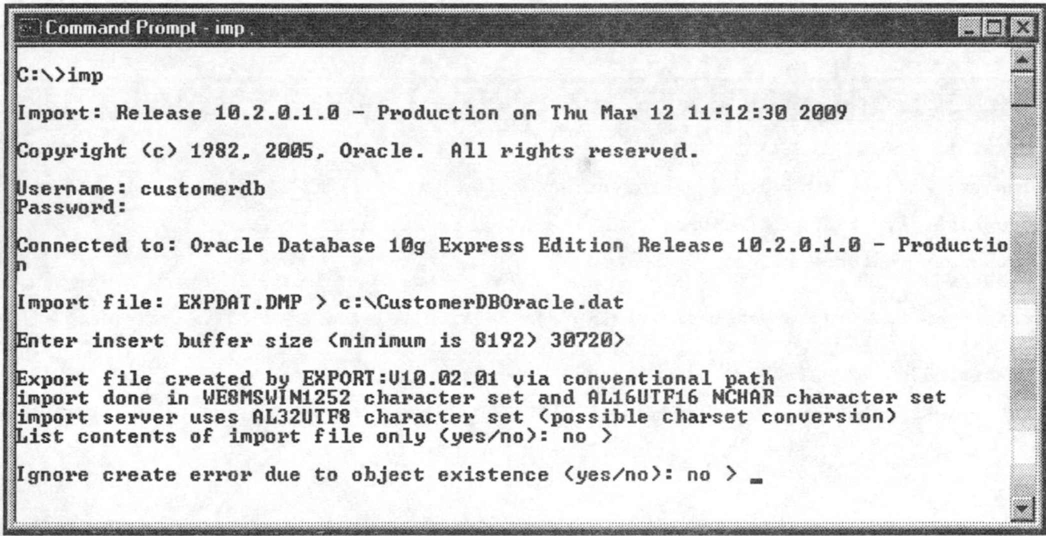

Diagram 26.2.6

Keep the default value and press **Enter**.

```
Command Prompt - imp

C:\>imp

Import: Release 10.2.0.1.0 - Production on Thu Mar 12 11:12:30 2009

Copyright (c) 1982, 2005, Oracle.  All rights reserved.

Username: customerdb
Password:

Connected to: Oracle Database 10g Express Edition Release 10.2.0.1.0 - Productio
n

Import file: EXPDAT.DMP > c:\CustomerDBOracle.dat

Enter insert buffer size (minimum is 8192) 30720>

Export file created by EXPORT:V10.02.01 via conventional path
import done in WE8MSWIN1252 character set and AL16UTF16 NCHAR character set
import server uses AL32UTF8 character set (possible charset conversion)
List contents of import file only (yes/no): no >

Ignore create error due to object existence (yes/no): no >

Import grants (yes/no): yes > _
```

Diagram 26.2.7

Keep the default value and press **Enter**.

```
Command Prompt - imp

Import: Release 10.2.0.1.0 - Production on Thu Mar 12 11:12:30 2009

Copyright (c) 1982, 2005, Oracle.  All rights reserved.

Username: customerdb
Password:

Connected to: Oracle Database 10g Express Edition Release 10.2.0.1.0 - Productio
n

Import file: EXPDAT.DMP > c:\CustomerDBOracle.dat

Enter insert buffer size (minimum is 8192) 30720>

Export file created by EXPORT:V10.02.01 via conventional path
import done in WE8MSWIN1252 character set and AL16UTF16 NCHAR character set
import server uses AL32UTF8 character set (possible charset conversion)
List contents of import file only (yes/no): no >

Ignore create error due to object existence (yes/no): no >

Import grants (yes/no): yes >

Import table data (yes/no): yes > _
```

Diagram 26.2.8

Keep the default value and press **Enter**.

```
Command Prompt - imp

Copyright (c) 1982, 2005, Oracle.  All rights reserved.

Username: customerdb
Password:

Connected to: Oracle Database 10g Express Edition Release 10.2.0.1.0 - Productio
n

Import file: EXPDAT.DMP > c:\CustomerDBOracle.dat

Enter insert buffer size (minimum is 8192) 30720>

Export file created by EXPORT:V10.02.01 via conventional path
import done in WE8MSWIN1252 character set and AL16UTF16 NCHAR character set
import server uses AL32UTF8 character set (possible charset conversion)
List contents of import file only (yes/no): no >

Ignore create error due to object existence (yes/no): no >

Import grants (yes/no): yes >

Import table data (yes/no): yes >

Import entire export file (yes/no): no > yes_
```

Diagram 26.2.9

Here, key in yes and press **Enter**. This begins and completes the import process as shown in diagram 26.2.10.

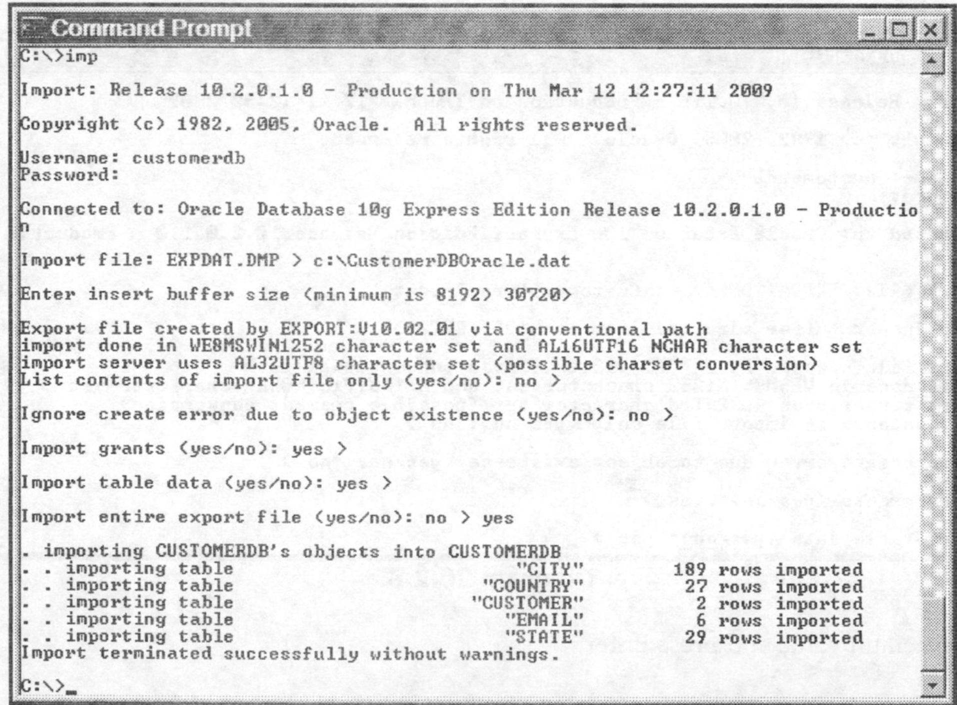

```
Command Prompt
C:\>imp

Import: Release 10.2.0.1.0 - Production on Thu Mar 12 12:27:11 2009

Copyright (c) 1982, 2005, Oracle.  All rights reserved.

Username: customerdb
Password:

Connected to: Oracle Database 10g Express Edition Release 10.2.0.1.0 - Productio
n

Import file: EXPDAT.DMP > c:\CustomerDBOracle.dat

Enter insert buffer size (minimum is 8192) 30720>

Export file created by EXPORT:V10.02.01 via conventional path
import done in WE8MSWIN1252 character set and AL16UTF16 NCHAR character set
import server uses AL32UTF8 character set (possible charset conversion)
List contents of import file only (yes/no): no >

Ignore create error due to object existence (yes/no): no >

Import grants (yes/no): yes >

Import table data (yes/no): yes >

Import entire export file (yes/no): no > yes

. importing CUSTOMERDB's objects into CUSTOMERDB
. . importing table                         "CITY"        189 rows imported
. . importing table                      "COUNTRY"         27 rows imported
. . importing table                     "CUSTOMER"          2 rows imported
. . importing table                        "EMAIL"          6 rows imported
. . importing table                        "STATE"         29 rows imported
Import terminated successfully without warnings.

C:\>_
```

Diagram 26.2.10

This creates all the required tables along with some sample data for development purpose.

Adding Oracle's JDBC driver [ojdbc14.jar]

Now that the database with the appropriate user and tables is available, the project can be configured to begin talking to the Oracle Database.

To achieve this, open the project [CustomerDatabase] using the **NetBeans IDE** as shown in diagram 26.3.1.

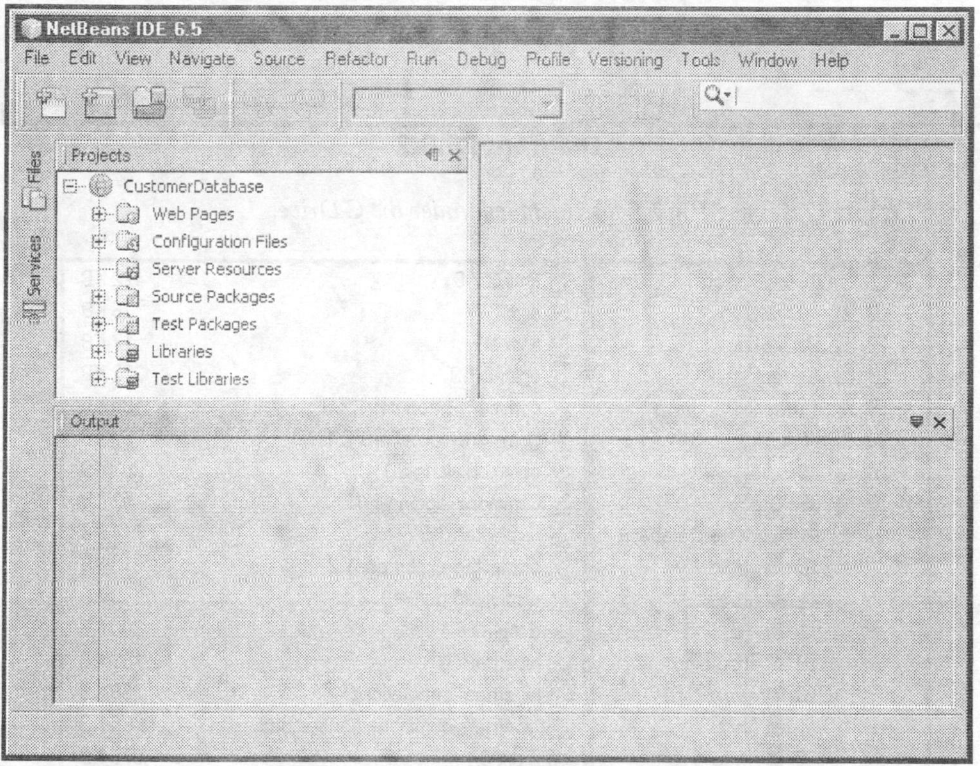

Diagram 26.3.1

Copy the library file called **ojdbc14.jar** from the Oracle database 10g's installed location as shown in diagram 26.3.2 to the project's dedicated lib folder as shown in diagram 26.3.3.

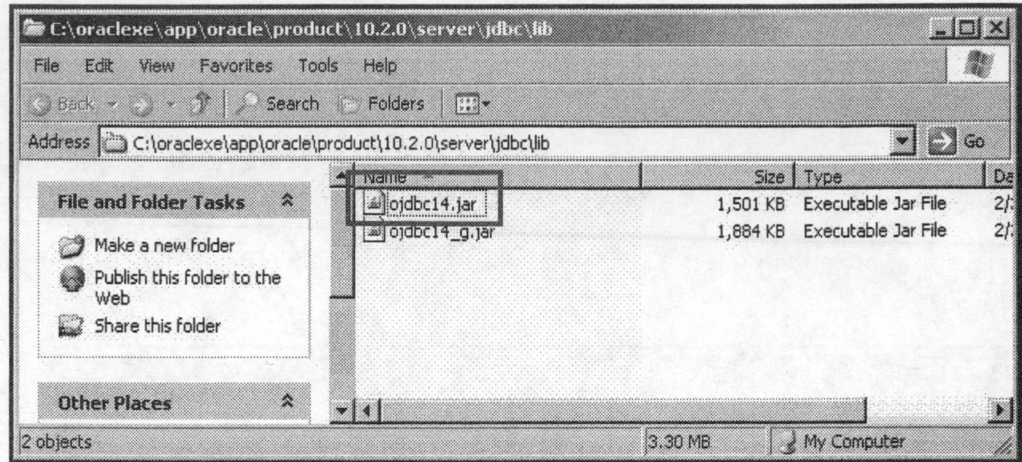

Diagram 26.3.2

In this case, **Oracle Database 10g XE** *was installed under the C Drive.*

Diagram 26.3.3

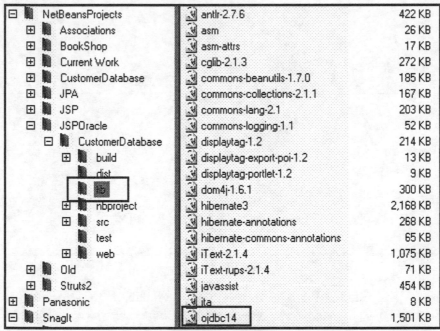

Using NetBeans add this jar file to the project's **Libraries** section as shown in diagram 26.3.4.

Diagram 26.3.4

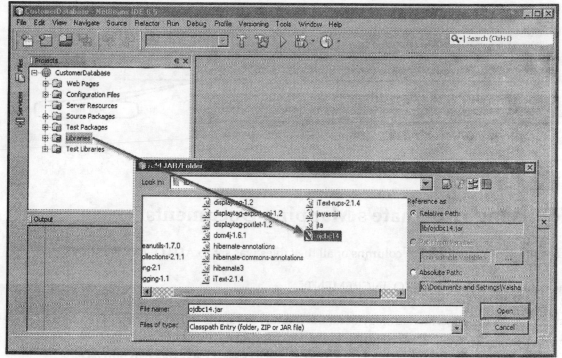

This library file allows talking to Oracle Database on demand.

Modifying Hibernate's Configuration File [hibernate.cfg.xml]

Open the Hibernate's configuration file called hibernate.cfg.xml and add the following code spec to connect to Oracle Database 10g.

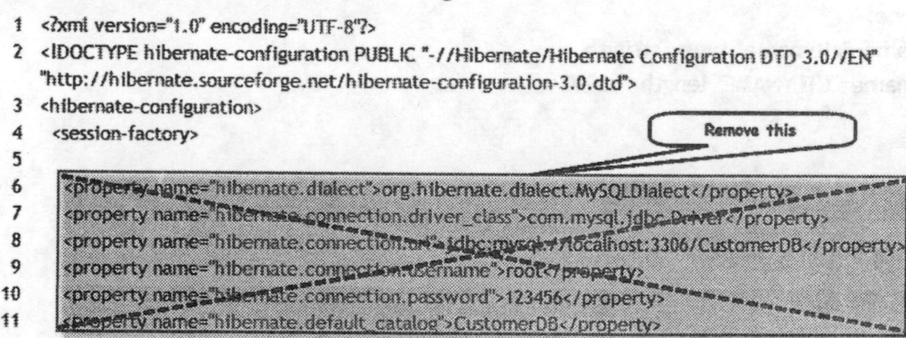

```
<?xml version="1.0" encoding="UTF-8"?>
<!DOCTYPE hibernate-configuration PUBLIC "-//Hibernate/Hibernate Configuration DTD 3.0//EN"
"http://hibernate.sourceforge.net/hibernate-configuration-3.0.dtd">
<hibernate-configuration>
  <session-factory>

    <property name="hibernate.dialect">org.hibernate.dialect.MySQLDialect</property>
    <property name="hibernate.connection.driver_class">com.mysql.jdbc.Driver</property>
    <property name="hibernate.connection.url">jdbc:mysql://localhost:3306/CustomerDB</property>
    <property name="hibernate.connection.username">root</property>
    <property name="hibernate.connection.password">123456</property>
    <property name="hibernate.default_catalog">CustomerDB</property>
```

```
<property name="hibernate.dialect">org.hibernate.dialect.OracleDialect</property>
<property name="hibernate.connection.driver_class">oracle.jdbc.OracleDriver</property>
<property name="hibernate.connection.url">jdbc:oracle:thin:@//localhost:1521/XE</property>
<property name="hibernate.connection.username">CustomerDB</property>
<property name="hibernate.connection.password">123456</property>

  <mapping resource="com/development/hibernate/city/State.hbm.xml"/>
  <mapping resource="com/development/hibernate/city/Country.hbm.xml"/>
  <mapping resource="com/development/hibernate/city/City.hbm.xml"/>
  <mapping resource="com/development/hibernate/customer/Customer.hbm.xml"/>
  <mapping resource="com/development/hibernate/customer/Email.hbm.xml"/>
 </session-factory>
</hibernate-configuration>
```

Add this

Modifying Hibernate's Mapping Documents

In case of MySQL the identity columns of all the tables was set to **AUTO_INCREMENT**.

Oracle **does not support** AUTO_INCREMENT.

Hence, change the generator strategy of all the Identity columns to **INCREMENT**.

```
<?xml version="1.0"?>
<!DOCTYPE hibernate-mapping PUBLIC "-//Hibernate/Hibernate Mapping DTD 3.0//EN"
"http://hibernate.sourceforge.net/hibernate-mapping-3.0.dtd">
<hibernate-mapping>
  <class name="com.development.hibernate.city.City" table="city">
    <id name="citycode" type="java.lang.Integer">
      <column name="CITYCODE" />
      <generator class="increment" />
    </id>
    <many-to-one name="state" class="com.development.hibernate.city.State" fetch="select">
      <column name="STATECODE" />
    </many-to-one>
    <property name="cityname" type="string">
      <column name="CITYNAME" length="50" />
    </property>
  </class>
</hibernate-mapping>
```

Replaced with identity

Do this for all the Mapping Documents:

- City.hbm.xml
- Country.hbm.xml

- State.hbm.xml
- Customer.hbm.xml
- Email.hbm.xml

This change informs Hibernate that it has to generate the identity values using the increment strategy.

That's it. Compile and run the project.

In the very same manner, this hibernate based project can be switched to any other database of choice provided a ***Hibernate Dialect*** *and the* ***Database Connection Driver*** *is available.*

The Book CDROM holds the complete application source code built using the NetBeans IDE for the following application:

- CustomerDatabase_Chap26

This can be directly used by making appropriate changes [username/password] to the configuration file.

SECTION VII: APPENDIX

Installing The NetBeans IDE

Before getting started with Hibernate development, the development environment needs to be set up first. There are several ways in which a complete development environment for Java EE with Struts2 can be setup.

To develop a Web application using the Hibernate library, the following is what is required:

- Java Development Kit
- A Web Server
- Hibernate libraries or the Hibernate plugins for Netbeans

To make the setting up of the development environment easy, this book uses an IDE called NetBeans.

What Is NetBeans?

NetBeans refers to both a platform for the development of Java applications and an IDE developed using the NetBeans Platform.

The NetBeans IDE is open source and is written in the Java programming language. It provides the services common to creating desktop applications such as window and menu management, settings storage and fully supports JDK 6.0 features.

The NetBeans platform and IDE are free for commercial and noncommercial use and they are supported by Sun Microsystems.

The two base products are NetBeans IDE and NetBeans Platform. Both products are free for commercial and non-commercial use. The source code to both is available to anyone to reuse as they see fit within the terms of use.

The NetBeans Development Platform

The NetBeans development platform comes bundled with the following based on the download option that is chosen:

- **Technologies**
  - Java SE
  - Java Web and EE
- **Web Servers**
  - GlassFish V2 UR2
  - GlassFish v3 Prelude
  - Apache Tomcat 6.0.18

Installation Of NetBeans IDE

Prior installing the IDE, the **Java SE Development Kit** [JDK] 5 Update 16 [version 1.5.0_16] or newer [including JDK 6 Update 7] **must be installed** on the system.

If this is not available on the machine, NetBeans cannot be installed.

Installing Java Development Kit

Visit **http://java.sun.com/javase/downloads/index.jsp** to download the latest version of the Java SE Development Kit. At the time of writing this book, the latest version was JDK 6 Update 11 [Available in the Book CDROM].

Download the latest version and install it.

HINT

Sometimes java.sun.com may provide a link to a **bundled version** of the JDK and NetBeans, which, if available, can be used to install both at the same time.

Otherwise install the JDK and then download and install NetBeans, which can be downloaded from www.netbeans.org.

This book uses an independent JDK with a bundled download of NetBeans.

To ensure that Java is already installed or to determine the Java version, issue the following command at the command prompt:

```
<System Prompt>java -version
```

Output:

```
java version "1.6.0_11"
Java(TM) SE Runtime Environment (build 1.6.0_11-b03)
Java HotSpot(TM) Client VM (build 11.0-b16, mixed mode, sharing)
```

If running this command does not show an appropriate output, **JDK needs to be installed** on the machine prior installing Struts[2] framework.

Download NetBeans

Download and install the latest version of NetBeans IDE from http://www.netbeans.org/downloads/ as shown in diagram A.1.

On the NetBeans IDE 6.5 Download page, one of several installers can be downloaded, each of which contains the base IDE and additional tools.

Kinds Of Installers

NetBeans offers the following kind of installers:

Java SE

Provides all standard features for Java SE development. Support for NetBeans Plugin Development is also included.

Java

Provides tools for developing Java SE, Java EE and Java ME applications. This download option also includes the GlassFish V2 UR2 application server, the GlassFish v3 Prelude application server and Apache Tomcat software.

Ruby

Provides tools for Ruby development and supports Rails and JRuby. Also contains the GlassFish v3 Prelude application server.

C/C++

Supports development in the C/C++ language.

PHP

Provides tools for PHP development. The PHP download option is available in Early Access.

All

This is a **full download option** for NetBeans IDE 6.5. It contains all the runtimes and packs available for the IDE. Includes tools for Service Oriented Architecture development.

At the time of writing this book the latest version that was available is **NetBeans IDE 6.5** and the kind of download that was chosen is **All** [Available in the Book CDROM].

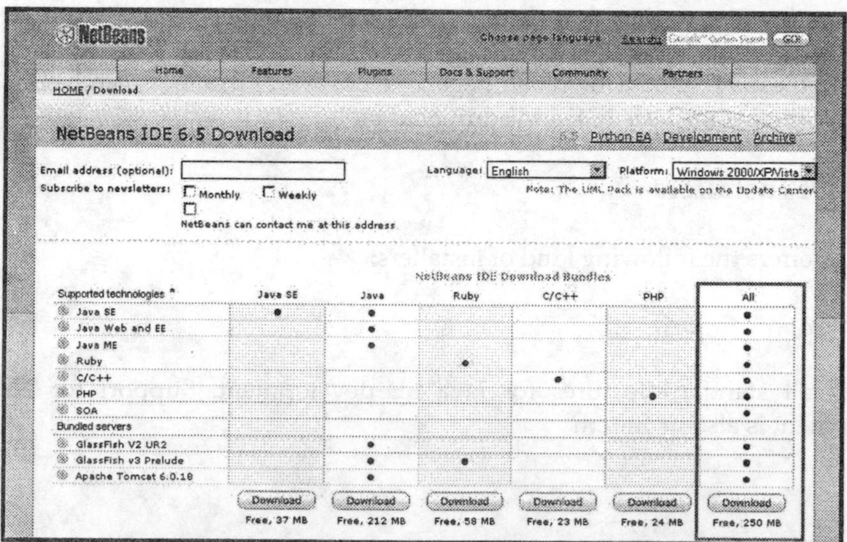

Diagram A.1: Download link for NetBeans IDE 6.5

In the upper right area of the page, select the platform from the drop down list box, click the **Download** button for the desired download option and save the setup file to the machine.

After the download completes, run the setup file.

Installation Of NetBeans IDE On Windows

To install NetBeans on a **Windows** based operating system simply initiate the installer by double clicking the setup file named **netbeans-6.5-ml-windows.exe**.

REMINDER

If the complete NetBeans installer i.e. **All** is downloaded, choose exactly what tools and runtimes to install. Click **Customize** at the Welcome page and select the desired features.

HINT

Apache Tomcat 6.0.18 is included in the **Java** and **All** download options but it is not installed by default from either of these options. To install Apache Tomcat from the **Java** or **All** download, launch the installer and select **Apache Tomcat 6.0.18** in the **Customize** Installation dialog box.

After the setup file is executed, the screen as shown in diagram A.2.1 appears.

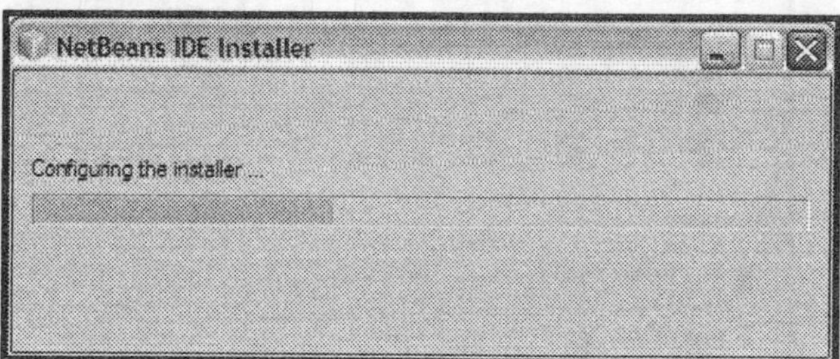

Diagram A.2.1: Netbeans IDE Installer

Just after the **configuration** is complete, the **Welcome page** of the installation wizard appears as shown in diagram A.2.2. Click **Customize** to select the tools and runtimes to be installed.

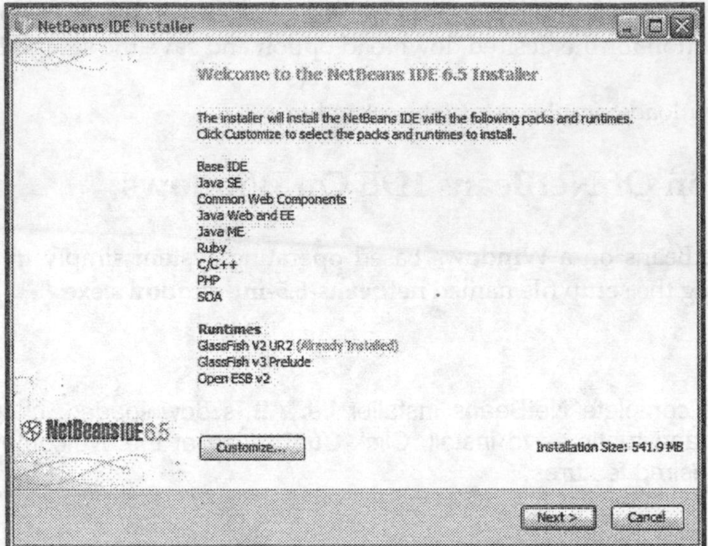

Diagram A.2.2: Welcome screen

The **Customize Installation** dialog box appears as shown in diagram A.2.3.

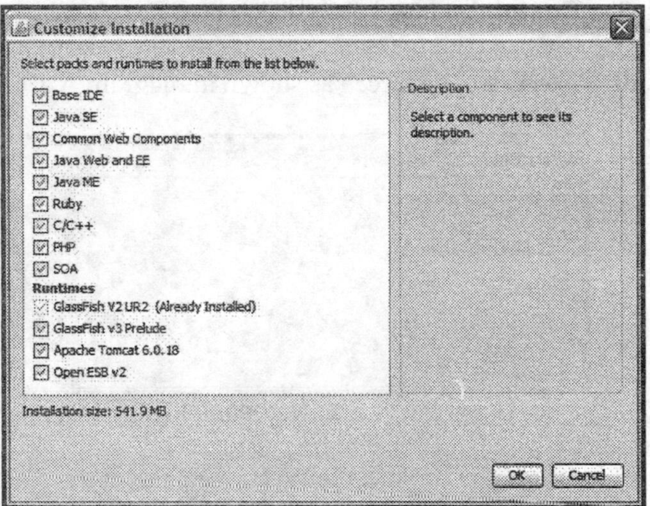

Diagram A.2.3: Customize installation

Select the desired packs and runtimes to install from the list. Click **OK**. The **Welcome page** of the installation wizard again appears.

Click Next >. This shows the **License agreement** screen as shown in diagram A.2.4, review the license agreement.

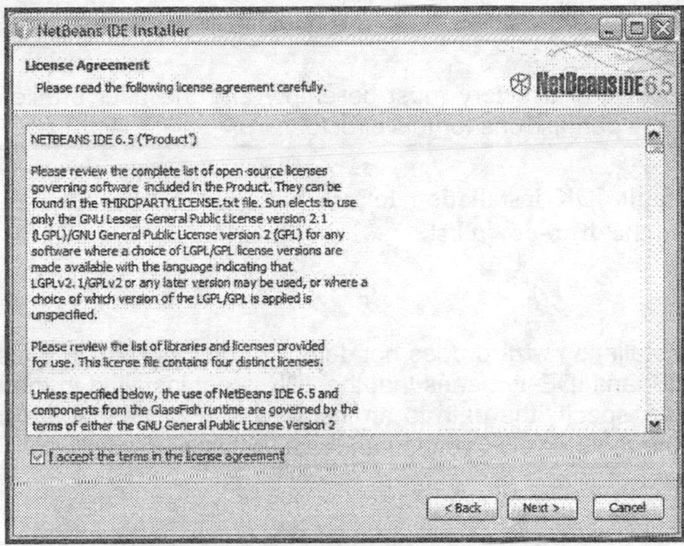

Diagram A.2.4: License Agreement screen

Select the acceptance checkbox and click Next >. This shows the **Installation** screen as shown in diagram A.2.5.

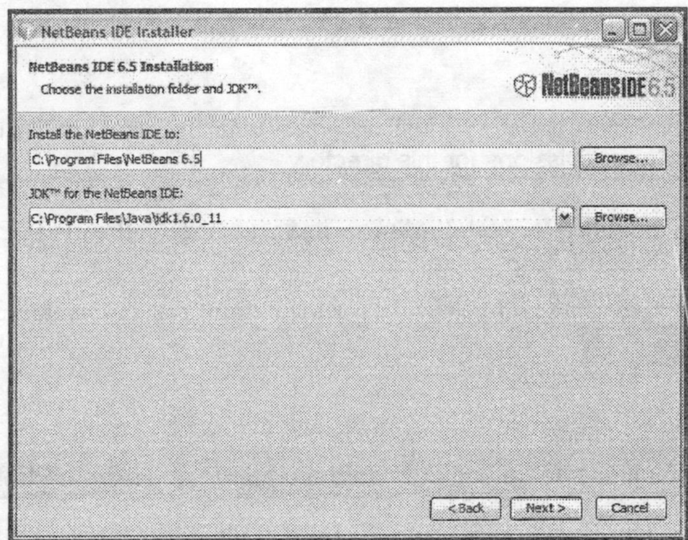

Diagram A.2.5: Installation screen

At the NetBeans IDE installation screen, do the following:

Accept the **default installation directory** for the **NetBeans IDE** or specify another directory.

REMINDER

The installation directory must be empty and the user profile in use must have **read/write** permissions for this directory.

Accept the default JDK installation to use with the NetBeans IDE or select a different installation from the drop-down list.

WARNING

If the installation wizard does not detect a compatible JDK installation to use with the NetBeans IDE, it means that the JDK is not installed in the default location. In this case, specify the path to an installed JDK or cancel the current installation, install the required JDK version and restart this installation.

Click 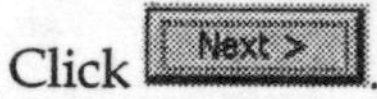

.

In case the GlassFish V2 UR2 application server installation page appears as shown in diagam A.2.6, then do the following:

1. Accept the **default installation directory** for the server or specify another installation directory

REMINDER

The installation directory must be empty and the user profile in use must have **read/write** permissions for this directory.

2. Accept the default **JDK installation** to use with the NetBeans IDE or select a different installation from the drop-down list
3. Change the username and password for the default server domain or accept the defaults and click Next >

HINT

The default username and password are **admin** and **adminadmin.**

4. Verify the default port values [**HTTP, HTTPS** and **Admin**] for the server or change them, if desired

5. Click Next >

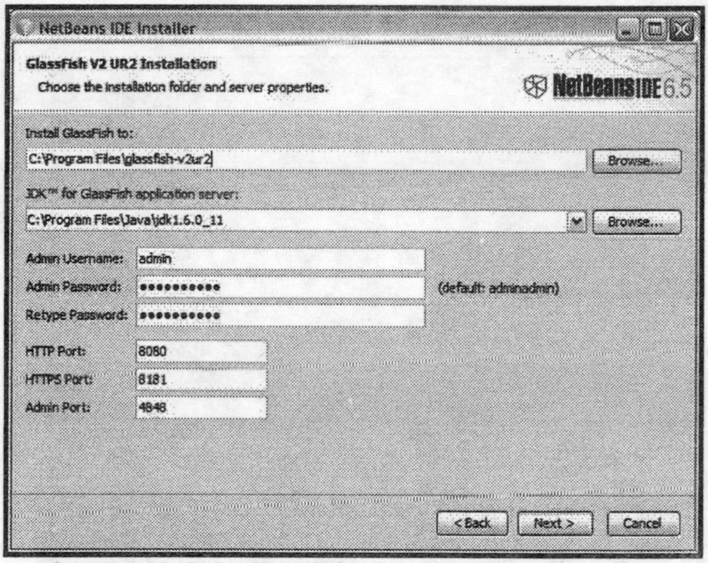

Diagram A.2.6: GlassFish V2 UR2 Web server screen

If the GlassFish application server was chosen the **installation page for the GlassFish v3 Prelude application server** appears as shown in diagram A.2.7. Accept the **default installation directory** for the server or specify another installation directory. Click Next >.

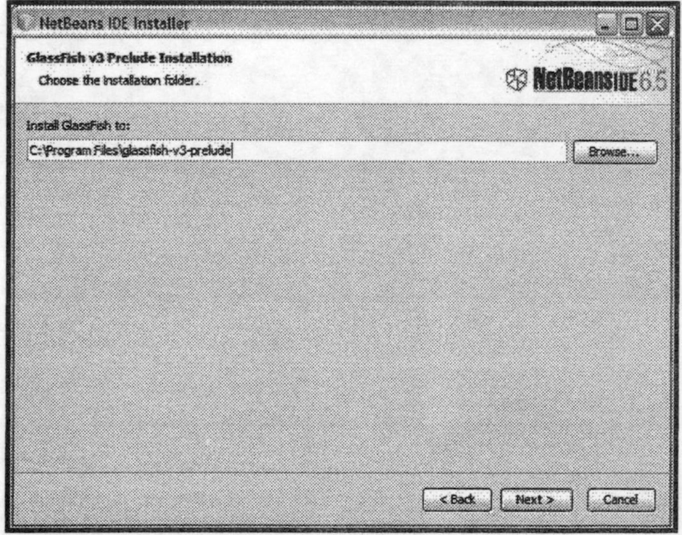

Diagram A.2.7: GlassFish v3 Prelude Web server screen

If Apache Tomcat server was chosen then the **installation page for the Apache Tomcat Server** appears as shown in diagram A.2.8.

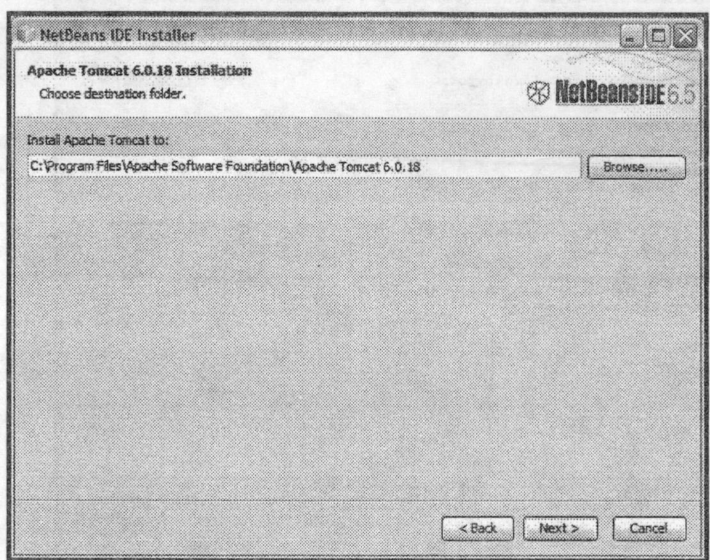

Diagram A.2.8: Tomcat web server screen

Here, accept the **default installation directory** or specify another installation location, if desired.

Click [Next >]. This brings up the **Summary** screen as shown in diagram A.2.9.

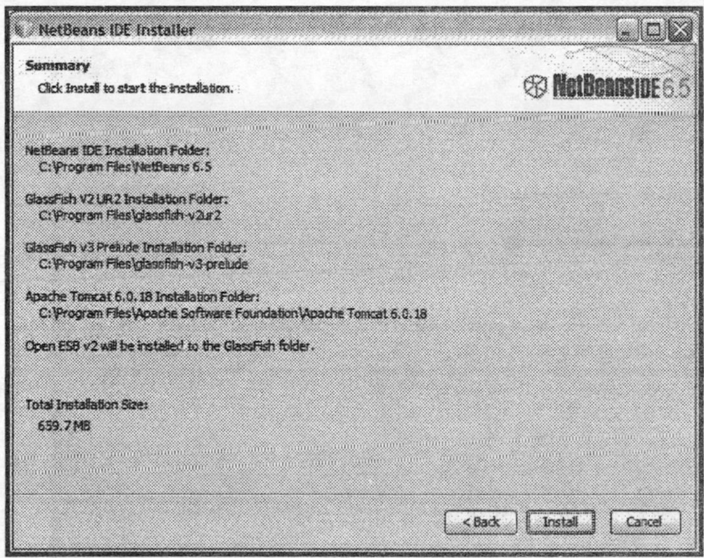

Diagram A.2.9: Tomcat Web server screen

Here, verify the components and the installation paths and ensure that adequate hard disk space is available on the system.

Click Install to begin the installation as shown in diagram A.2.10.

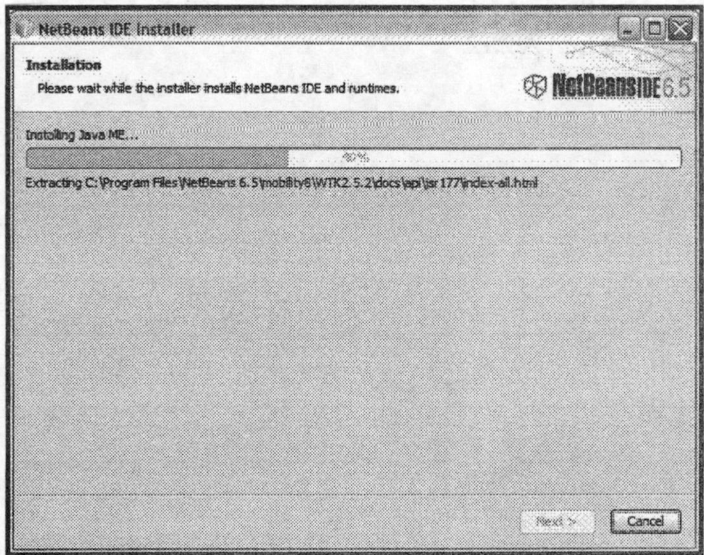

Diagram A.2.10: Installation Progress

After the installation completes, the installer displays the **registration screen** as shown in diagram A.2.11.

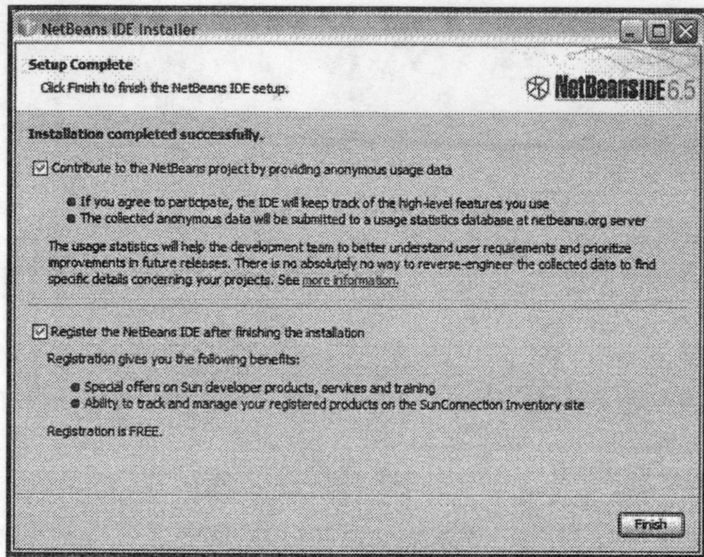

Diagram A.2.11: Installation Progress

Click the **Register** checkbox [if desired]. Click **Finish** to exit the installation wizard.

If the Register checkbox was chosen in the previous step, the **Registration** page appears in a web browser as shown in diagram A.2.12.

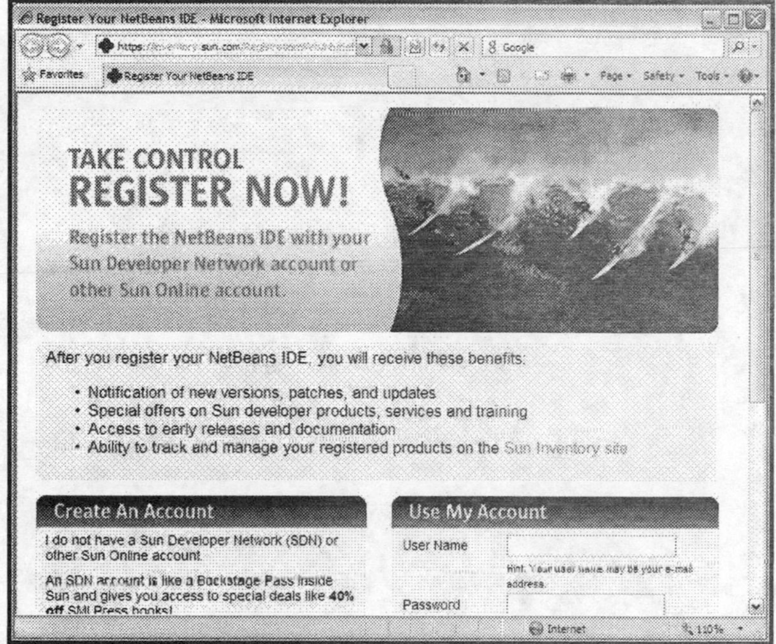

Diagram A.2.12: Registration page

This chapter helped build the development environment. After the development environment is built, to begin developing Hibernate applications, the minimum that is required is the base libraries of the Hibernate library.

These libraries have to be downloaded and plugged in to bring in the Hibernate support.

Index

G

H

L

M

N

O

P

Q

R

S

T

X

ISBN	Title	Author	Year	Price

Shroff Reprints & Original Titles

The X Team Series
(An Imprint of Shroff Publishers)

Computers

ISBN	Title	Author	Year	Price
9788184041569	Ajax for Beginners **(B/CD)**, 452 Pages	Bayross	2006	375.00
9788184041972	Application Development with Oracle & PHP on Linux for Beginners, 2/ed **(B/CD)**, 940 Pages	Bayross	2007	650.00
9789350233733	**Blogging for Beginners, 268 Pages**	**Harwani**	**2011**	**350.00**
9788184046397	C for Beginners, 532 Pages	Mothe	2009	375.00
9789350233900	**C Interviews Q&A, 119 Pages**	**Thorat**	**2011**	**150.00**
9788184046564	C++ for Beginners, 403 Pages	Harwani	2009	375.00
9789350231012	Core Java for Beginners, (B/CD), 892 Pages	Shah	2010	500.00
9788184046694	Database Concepts and Systems for Students, 3/ed, 428 Pgs	Bayross	2009	325.00
9788184048780	HTML for Beginners, 2/ed, 416 Pages	Aibara	2010	500.00
9788184047059	Hibernate 3 for Beginners - Covers Java Persistence API (B/CD), 680 Pages	Shah	2009	500.00
9788184045697	Java EE 5 for Beginners, 2/ed **(B/CD)**, 1,192 Pages	Bayross	2008	575.00
9788184049398	Java EE 6 for Beginners, (B/CD), 1092 Pages	Shah	2009	825.00
9788184049411	Java EE 6 Server Programming for Professionals (B/DVD), 1,328 Pages (H/B)	Shah	2010	750.00
9788184048063	Java EE Project using EJB 3, JPA and Struts 2 for Beginners, (B/CD), 1,258 Pages	Shah	2009	1,025.00
9788184043174	Java for Beginners **(B/CD)**, Covers Java SE 6 JDK, 600 Pages	Chavan	2007	450.00
9788184045932	Java for Professionals: A Practical Approach to Java Programming (Covers Java SE 6), 790 Pages	Harwani	2008	525.00
9788184046670	Java for Students, 690 Pages	Pherwani	2009	475.00
9789350233719	**Java for Students, 2/ed, 850 Pages**	**Pherwani**	**2011**	**600.00**
9788184047097	Java Persistence API in EJB 3 for Professionals, (B/CD) 756 Pgs	Shah	2009	550.00
9788184045925	JavaServer Pages Project for Beginners, **(B/CD)**, 746 Pages	Shah	2008	550.00
9788184045598	Java Server Programming for Professionals, Revised & Enlarged 2/ed (Covers Java EE 5) (B/CD), 1,612 Pages	Bayross	2008	700.00
9788184043594	Java Server Pages for Beginners **(B/CD)**, 872 Pages	Bayross	2007	500.00
9788184048438	Lamp Programming for Professionals, (B/CD), 1,284	Shah	2009	1,275.00
9788184040142	MySQL 5 for Professionals **(B/CD)**, 770 Pages	Bayross	2005	550.00
9788184045260	Oracle for Professionals **(B/CD)**, 1,420 Pgs	Shah	2008	750.00
9788184043228	PC Hardware for Beginners, 308 Pages	Sangia	2007	225.00
9788184040753	PHP 5.1 for Beginners **(B/CD)**, 1,284 Pages	Bayross	2006	650.00

ISBN	Title	Author	Year	Price
9788184048445	PHP Project for Beginners, (B/CD), 1,200 Pages	Shah	2010	600.00
9788184047073	Practical ASP.NET 3.5 Projects for Beginners, (B/CD), 550 Pgs	Harwani	2009	450.00
9788184048070	Practical EJB Project for Beginners, 312 Pages	Harwani	2009	325.00
9788184043426	Practical Java Project for Beginners **(B/CD)**, 164 Pages	Harwani	2007	150.00
9788184043419	Practical Web Services for Beginners, 168 Pages	Harwani	2007	150.00
9789350234907	**Programming with PI/SQL for Beginners, 236 Pages**	**Patil**	**2011**	**300.00**
9788184049725	QuickTest Professional (QTP) Version 10, 116 Pages	Mallepally	2010	125.00
9789350231241	QTP for Professionals, 480 Pages	Reddy	2010	450.00
9788184048100	SAP SD for Beginners, 324 Pages	Samad	2009	450.00
9789350233894	**SAP SD for Beginners 2/ed, 260 Pages**	**Samad**	**2011**	**350.00**
9788184047448	Struts 2 for Beginners, 2/ed, (B/CD), 566 Pages	Shah	2009	450.00
9788184046960	Struts 2 with Hibernate 3 Project for Beginners, (B/CD), 1,042 Pages	Shah	2009	675.00
9788184041071	Visual Basic 2005 for Beginners **(B/CD)**, 1,172 Pages	Bayross	2006	150.00

Other Computer Titles

ISBN	Title	Author	Year	Price
9789350230237	A Primer on Software Quality Models & Project Management, 640 Pages	Mehta	2010	600.00
9788184048827	Art of Creative Destruction: Illustarted Software Testing, Test Automation & Agile Testing, 2/ed, 348 Pages	Puranik	2010	425.00
9788173660030	AS/400 Architecture & Applications, 332 Pages	Lawrence	1993	250.00
9788173660047	AS/400: A Practical Guide to Programming & Operations, 284 Pgs	Zeilenga	1993	225.00
9789350232859	**Beginning Web Development for Smartphones Developing Web Applications with PHP, MySQL and jQTouch, 252 Pages**	**Harwani**	**2011**	**300.00**
9789350231029	**C# 4.0 Programming Made Easy, 624 Pages**	**Kadam**	**2011**	**425.00**
9789350230244	Computer Architecture and Maintenance, 320 Pages	Kadam	2010	250.00
9788173660016	CICS: A How-To for Cobol Programmers, 428 Pages	Kirk	1993	300.00
9788184048957	FAQ's in MFC and MFC Solutions, Vol I (B/CD) 510 Pages	P. G. Naik	2010	425.00
9788173666810	First Encounter with Java Including BlueJ, 386 Pages	Bhutta	2006	225.00
9789350230275	Instant Oracle, 100 Pages	Shah	2010	75.00
9788173664632	Introducing MySQL, 96 Pages	Oak	2005	50.00
9789350230251	Management Information System (MIS), 176 Pages	Kadam	2010	200.00
9789350231258	**Maximum Oracle with Oracle Best Practices, 772 Pages**	**Puranik**	**2011**	**675.00**
9789350233986	**Mobile Computing, 1,059 Pages [Forthcoming]**	**Shende**	**2011**	**TBA**
9788173660023	MVS / VSAM for the Application Programmer, 504 Pages	Brown	1993	325.00
9788184047899	Operating Systems, 2/ed, 408 Pages	Sumitradevi	2009	500.00
9789350234242	**Oracle Financials 11i: A Practical Guide for the Beginners, 392 Pages**	**Peri**	**2011**	**725.00**
9788173668012	Software Defect Prevention Concepts and Implementation, 180 Pages **(H/B)**	Kane & Bajaj	2003	300.00
9788173668814	Strategic Bidding: A Successful Approach, 192 Pgs	Garg	2004	250.00
9788173660078	TCP/IP Companion: A Guide For The Common User, 284 Pages	Arick	1993	225.00
9789350231005	Testing in 30^+ Open Source Tools (B/CD), 1,080 Pages	Shende	2010	900.00
9788173660429	Vijay Mukhi's ERP Odyssey: Implementing. PeopleSoft Financials 7.0/7.5, 528 Pages	Mukhi	1999	350.00

ISBN	Title	Author	Year	Price

Business, Management & Finance

ISBN	Title	Author	Year	Price
9788184046977	An Introduction to Foreign Exchange & Financial Risk Management, **(B/CD)**, 348 Pages	Lakshman	2009	400.00
9789350230268	Bootstrapping A Software Company, 348 Pages	Yadav	2010	425.00
9788184044287	Breaking the Black Box, **(B/CD)**, 276 Pages	Pring	2008	500.00
9788184044249	Break Your Negative Attitude, 114 Pages	Dr. Mishra	2007	125.00
9789350230220	Complete Guide to Technical Analysis: An Indian Perspective, 612 Pages	Pring	2010	650.00
9788184040425	Developing Analytical Skills: Case Studies in Management, 636 Pages	Dr. Natarajan	2008	500.00
9788173660993	Doing Business with the French, 150 Pages	Jhangiani	1999	150.00
9788184044959	Enabling Event-ful Experiences, 250 Pages	Balachandran	2008	200.00
9788184044744	Ethics, Indian Ethos and Management, 252 Pages	Balachandran	2008	175.00
9789350231227	Financial Decision Modeling Operations Research & Business Statistics (Group II, Paper 5 C.A. Final), 696 Pages	Sridhar	2010	350.00
9789350230794	Financial Management: Problems & Solutions, 4/ed, 1,228 Pgs	Sridhar	2010	750.00
9789350232965	**Futures & Options: Equities & Commodities, 4/ed, 392 Pgs**	**Sridhar**	**2011**	**475.00**
9789350233917	**Globally Distributed Work, 280 Pages**	**Mehta**	**2011**	**425.00**
9789350233887	**Hospitality Management, 304 pages**	**Shirke**	**2011**	**525.00**
9788184040432	How to Eat The Elephant? The CEO's Guide To An Enterprise System Implementation, 104 Pages	Tulsyan	2007	325.00
9789350230459	How to Learn Management from your wife (PB), 96 Pages	Rangnekar	2010	125.00
9789350233108	How to Learn Management from your wife (HB), 96 Pages	Rangnekar	2010	275.00
9788184044447	How to Select Stocks Using Technical Analysis, **(B/CD)**, 338 Pages	Pring	2008	500.00
9788184044164	Logistics in International Business, 2/ed, 428 Pages	Aserkar	2007	450.00
9788184047547	Magic and Logic of Elliott Waves, The, 204 Pages	Kale	2009	500.00
9788184048568	Management Accounting & Financial Analysis for C.A.Final (June 2009), 9/ed, 540 Pages	Sridhar	2009	400.00
9789350235126	**Management of Services, 348 Pages**	**Jain**	**2011**	**450.00**
9788184044454	Momentum Explained, Volume I **(B/CD)**, 366 Pages	Pring	2008	600.00
9788184044461	Momentum Explained, Volume II **(B/CD)**, 338 Pages	Pring	2008	550.00
9788184047066	Purchasing and Inventory Management, 338 Pages	Menon	2009	475.00
9789350233870	**Quantitative Techniques for Project Management, 256 Pages**	**Velayoudam**	**2011**	**600.00**
9788173666797	Rules of Origin in International Trade, 238 Pages	Dr. Sathpathy	2005	300.00
9789350233580	**Services Marketing, 448 Pages**	**Balachandran**	**2011**	**450.00**
9789350233115	**Soft Skills In Management, 148 Pages**	**Rangnekar**	**2011**	**125.00**
9789350235560	**Strategic Financial Management for C.A. Final, 7/ed 928 Pgs**	**Sridhar**	**2011**	**650.00**
9788173668814	Strategic Bidding: A Successful Approach (for IT / Consultancy), 192 Pages	Garg	2004	250.00
9788184043211	Time Your Trades With Technical Analysis **(B/CD)**, 348 Pages	Pradhan	2007	600.00

ISBN	Title	Author	Year	Price
Catering & Hotel Management				
9788173668739	Careers in Hospitality - Hotel Management Entrance Exam Guide, 332 Pages	Rego	2004	200.00
9789350233887	**Hospitality Management, 303 Pages**	**Shirke**	**2011**	**525.00**
9789350230817	**Marvels of Indian Snacks, 264 Pages**	**Shankaran**	**2011**	**350.00**
9788184044751	Marvels of South Indian Cuisine, 220 Pages	Shankaran	2008	250.00
9788184046687	Marvels of North Indian Cuisine, 196 Pages	Shankaran	2009	325.00
Civil Engineering				
9789350233252	**Concrete for High Performance Sustainable Infrastructure, 312 Pages**	**Newlands**	**2011**	**750.00**
9789350233245	**New Developments in Concrete Construction, 296 Pages**	**Dhir**	**2011**	**750.00**
9788173663772	Principles of Environmental Science Engineering and Maintenance, 288 Pages	Dr. Thirumurthy	2004	175.00
9788184048056	Raina's Concrete Bridge Practice: Construction, Maintenance and Rehabiliation 2/ed, 452 Pages (H/B) [14 Full Color Inserts]	Dr. Raina	2010	625.00
9788184048049	Raina's Concrete Bridge: Inspection, Repair, Strengthening, Testing, Load Capacity Evaluation 2/ed, 800 Pages (H/B) [32 Full Color Inserts]	Dr. Raina	2010	1,200.00
9788184047530	Raina's Concrete for Construction: Facts & Practice, 400 Pgs **(H/B)**	Dr. Raina	2009	650.00
9788184047875	Raina's Construction & Contract Management, 2/ed Inside Story, 585 Pages **(H/B)**	Dr. Raina	2009	750.00
9788184043785	Raina's Concrete Bridge Practice, 3/ed : Analysis, Design & Economics, 856 Pages	Dr. Raina	2007	1,000.00
9788184046618	Raina's Field Manual for Highway and Bridge Engineers, 3/ed,1,404 Pages	Dr. Raina	2009	1,800.00
9789350231418	**Raina's Handbook for Concrete Bridges, 1500 Pages (H/B) [Forthcoming]**	**Dr. Raina**	**2011**	**TBA**
9788184040135	The World of Bridges, 300 Pages **(H/B)** [4 color]	Dr. Raina	2006	500.00
9789350231180	Using Primavera 6: Planning, Executing, Monitoring and Controlling Projects, 228 Pages	Al-Saridi	2010	275.00
Communication				
9789350231265	**Knowing Your Word's Worth: A Practical Guide to Communicating Effectively in English, 180 Pages**	**Shirodkar**	**2011**	**175.00**
Dental / Health / Medical				
9788173669798	The Balancing Act "A Win Over Obesity", 296 Pages	Dr. Gadkari	2005	225.00
9788184049480	The Balancing Act "Know Your Heart", 368 Pages	Dr. Gadkari	2010	250.00
9788173668975	Splinting Management of MOBILE & Migrating Teeth, 104 Pgs	Dr. Kakar	2004	150.00
Economics				
9788184043266	Analysing Macroeconomics: A Toolkit for Managers, Executives & Students **(H/B)**, 156 Pages	Rakesh Singh	2007	500.00

ISBN	Title	Author	Year	Price
9788184044171	Analysing Macroeconomics: A Toolkit for Managers, Executives & Students **(P/B)**, 156 Pages	Rakesh Singh	2007	250.00

Electrical Engineering

ISBN	Title	Author	Year	Price
9788184043235	Basic Electrical Circuits, 2/ed, 368 Pages	Dr. Salam	2007	250.00

Electronics & Communication

ISBN	Title	Author	Year	Price
9788173669002	Electronic Components and Materials, 3/ed, 404 Pages	Joshi	2004	175.00

Environmental Engineering

ISBN	Title	Author	Year	Price
9788173663772	Principles of Environmental Science Engineering and Maintenance, 288 Pgs	Dr. Thirumurthy	2004	175.00

Event Management

ISBN	Title	Author	Year	Price
9788184044959	Enabling Event-ful Experiences, 250 Pages	Balachandran	2008	250.00

General Titles

ISBN	Title	Author	Year	Price
9788184045642	Hello Police Station (Marathi), 118 Pages	Shinde	2008	100.00
9789350231760	Mom Don't Spoil Me, 140 Pages	Dr. Mishra	2010	150.00

HRD

ISBN	Title	Author	Year	Price
9788184047080	Departmental Enquiries: Concept, Procedure & Practice, 534 Pages	Goel	2009	475.00
9788184046229	How To Improve Trainer Effectiveness, 170 Pages	Balachandran	2008	200.00

Law

ISBN	Title	Author	Year	Price
9789350230800	A Handbook on the Maintenance & Welfare of Parents and Senior Citizens Act, 2007.	Gracias	2010	150.00
9788173664151	Customs Valuation in India 3/ed, 262 Pages	Satapathy	2002	375.00
9788184042481	Laws Of Carriage Of Goods By Sea & Multimodal Transport In India, 92 Pages	Hariharan	2007	60.00
9788173661426	Law of Sale of Goods & Partnership, 228 Pages	Chandiramani	2000	150.00
9789350231289	**Social Security, Insurance & The Law, 460 Pgs**	**Gopalakrishna**	**2011**	**600.00**

Marine

ISBN	Title	Author	Year	Price
9788184043242	Containerisation, Multimodal Transport and Infrastructure Development in India, 5/ed, 852 Pages	Hariharan	2007	650.00
9788173660375	M.S. (STCW) Rules, 1998 incl. Training & Assessment Programme - 1,216 Pages	DG Shipping	1998	225.00
9788173661419	Maritime Education, Training & Assessment Manual (TAP) - Vol II, 474 Pages	DG Shipping	1999	400.00
9788184043136	Marine Control Technology, 336 Pages	Majumder	2007	400.00
9788173669279	Marine Diesel Engines, 428 Pages	Aranha	2004	250.00
9788184048544	Marine Electrical Technology, 5/ed, 1,250 Pages	Fernandes	2010	750.00

ISBN	Title	Author	Year	Price
9788173660801	Marine Internal Combustion Engines, 272 Pages	Kane	2003	150.00
9788173660146	Safety Management Systems - An Underconstruction Activity, 98 Pages	Capt. Singhal	1998	95.00
9788173665516	A Textbook on Container & Multimodal Transport Management, 522 Pgs	Dr. Hariharan	2002	500.00

Motivation

ISBN	Title	Author	Year	Price
9788184044249	Break Your Negative Attitude, 114 Pages	Dr. Mishra	2007	125.00
9788184044768	Hard-Knocks Communication: Thirty Six Timeless Rules for Success **(H/B)**, 222 Pages	Subramanian	2008	250.00
9788173665271	Heads You Win, Tails You Win, 2/ed, 200 Pages	Dr.Mishra	2005	200.00
9789350230206	Nothing Is Absolute, 274 Pages	Balachandran	2010	300.00

Parenting

ISBN	Title	Author	Year	Price
9789350231760	Mom Don't Spoil Me, 140 Pages	Dr. Mishra	2010	150.00

Patent

ISBN	Title	Author	Year	Price
9788184047882	Breeding Innovation and Intellectual Capital, 2/ed 196 Pgs	Dr.Batra	2009	600.00

Physics

ISBN	Title	Author	Year	Price
9788184043259	Gravitation Demythicised: An Introduction to Einstein's General Relativity and Cosmology for Common Man, 258 Pages	Shenoy	2007	250.00
9788184047929	Study Aid Theoretical Physics - Volume I: Relativistic Theory and Electrodynamics, 418 Pgs	Prof Fai	2010	300.00
9788184047912	Theoretical Physics - Volume I: Relativistic Theory and Electrodynamics, 490 Pages	Prof Fai	2010	400.00

Project Management

ISBN	Title	Author	Year	Price
9789350230237	A Primer on Software Quality Models & Project Management, 640 Pages	Mehta	2010	600.00
9788184048568	Management Accounting & Financial Analysis for C.A.Final 9/ed, 540 Pages	Sridhar	2009	400.00

Self-Help

ISBN	Title	Author	Year	Price
9788184047905	Enhancing Soft Skills, 346 Pages	Biswas	2009	375.00

- **All Prices are in Indian Rupees**
- **Titles Released after January 2011 are marked in Bold.**